The Border of Lights Reader

BEARING WITNESS TO GENOCIDE IN THE DOMINICAN REPUBLIC

Edited by

Megan Jeanette Myers

Edward Paulino

Amherst College Press
Amherst, Massachusetts

DOI: https://doi.org/10.3998/mpub.12278109
ISBN 978-1-943208-26-5 (paper)
ISBN 978-1-943208-27-2 (OA)

Featured in the Foreword: Rita Dove, "Parsley" from *Museum* (Pittsburgh: Carnegie Mellon University Press, 1983). Copyright © 1983 by Rita Dove. Reprinted with the permission of the author.

Source: *Museum* (Carnegie Mellon University Press, 1983)
From: https://www.poetryfoundation.org/poems/43355/parsley

Cover design by Derek Thornton / Notch Design

The proposal and complete manuscript of this work was subjected to a partly closed ("single blind") review process. For more information, visit https://acpress.amherst.edu/peerreview/.

Published in the United States of America by
Amherst College Press
Manufactured in the United States of America

Contents

Section II: Artistic Endeavors

Section III: Interviews

Section IV: Voice Notes from *la frontera*   315

FOREWORD

Parsley[*]

Rita Dove

1. The Cane Fields

There is a parrot imitating spring
in the palace, its feathers parsley green.
Out of the swamp the cane appears

to haunt us, and we cut it down. El General
searches for a word; he is all the world
there is. Like a parrot imitating spring,

we lie down screaming as rain punches through
and we come up green. We cannot speak an R—
out of the swamp, the cane appears

and then the mountain we call in whispers *Katalina*.
The children gnaw their teeth to arrowheads.
There is a parrot imitating spring.

El General has found his word: *perejil*.
Who says it, lives. He laughs, teeth shining
out of the swamp. The cane appears

---

*On October 2, 1937, Rafael Trujillo (1891-1961), dictator of the Dominican Republic, ordered 20,000
blacks killed because they could not pronounce the letter "r" in *perejil*, the Spanish word for parsley.

in our dreams, lashed by wind and streaming.
And we lie down. For every drop of blood
there is a parrot imitating spring.
Out of the swamp the cane appears.

2. *The Palace*

The word the general's chosen is parsley.
It is fall, when thoughts turn
to love and death; the general thinks
of his mother, how she died in the fall
and he planted her walking cane at the grave
and it flowered, each spring stolidly forming
four-star blossoms. The general

pulls on his boots, he stomps to
her room in the palace, the one without
curtains, the one with a parrot
in a brass ring. As he paces he wonders
Who can I kill today. And for a moment
the little knot of screams
is still. The parrot, who has traveled

all the way from Australia in an ivory
cage, is, coy as a widow, practising
spring. Ever since the morning
his mother collapsed in the kitchen
while baking skull-shaped candies
for the Day of the Dead, the general
has hated sweets. He orders pastries
brought up for the bird; they arrive

dusted with sugar on a bed of lace.
The knot in his throat starts to twitch;
he sees his boots the first day in battle
splashed with mud and urine
as a soldier falls at his feet amazed—
how stupid he looked!— at the sound
of artillery. *I never thought it would sing*
the soldier said, and died. Now

the general sees the fields of sugar
cane, lashed by rain and streaming.

He sees his mother's smile, the teeth
gnawed to arrowheads. He hears
the Haitians sing without R's
as they swing the great machetes:
Katalina, they sing, *Katalina*,

mi madle, mi amol en muelte. God knows
his mother was no stupid woman; she
could roll an R like a queen. Even
a parrot can roll an R! In the bare room
the bright feathers arch in a parody
of greenery, as the last pale crumbs
disappear under the blackened tongue. Someone

calls out his name in a voice
so like his mother's, a startled tear
splashes the tip of his right boot.
My mother, my love in death.
The general remembers the tiny green sprigs
men of his village wore in their capes
to honor the birth of a son. He will
order many, this time, to be killed

for a single, beautiful word.

INTRODUCTION

Bearing Witness on and Beyond the Border

Megan Jeanette Myers and Edward Paulino

> Here at the border of massacre
> we create a new border
> of hope;
> here in the killing fields
> we sow the seeds of the future
> and await
> the flowering of peace . . .
>
> "THERE ARE TWO COUNTRIES," JULIA ALVAREZ

The mural depicted in Figure 1, painted near the Dominican-Haitian border in October of 2017 and funded by the Border of Lights (BOL) collective, stretches across the cement wall of a busy street corner in Dajabón, Dominican Republic. On one street passersby see the word "Kiskeya," the Dominican Republic's indigenous name, and upon turning the corner they encounter the impossible-to-miss blue face of an indigenous woman with a shell of the island's outline held close to one ear. To the right of the face, the words "Amor," "Arte," "Respeto," and "Frontera de Luces" (the name in Spanish for Border of Lights) confront pedestrians and drivers. Accompanying these words are symbols: the dove and flowers represent peace and the "ø + ACRE" is a clever logogram and an unmistakable tribute to the 1937 Massacre of Haitians and Dominicans of Haitian descent: "NO MÁS+ACRE" (no massacre).

The 1937 Haitian Massacre was ordered by the Dominican dictator Rafael Leónidas Trujillo who was in power in the Dominican Republic from 1930-1961. While the extant scholarship references no definitive explanation from the Dominican state detailing the reasons behind this mass murder, it is a clear example of anti-Blackness. An estimated 15,000 Haitian men, women, and children—including their Dominican-born descendants—were brutally murdered by the Dominican army and conscripted civilians. According to scholars, the bulk of this genocidal event occurred throughout the border region over the course of several weeks starting in late September and ending around late October.[1]

Figure 1: Border of Lights/Azueï mural in October 2017.

Ethnic black Haitians and Dominicans of Haitian descent were rounded up, taken to secluded areas, and murdered. The weapon of choice was the machete, to avoid subsequent international recriminations that could claim the killings as organized and premeditated. The individuals (military and conscripted civilians) who carried out the killings buried or burned most of the bodies, discarding the remains. Neither Trujillo nor anyone in his government was tried in court for this crime against humanity. Moreover, in an effort to head off subsequent claims and lawsuits, the Dominican government signed a settlement in the form of a League of Nations treaty absolving it from future prosecutions. The settlement also allowed Trujillo and his government and military officials to avoid sentencing in future domestic and international tribunals.[2] The Dominican government did ultimately pay the Haitian government $525,000 in "reparations" or "blood money" for the survivors. Unfortunately, survivors never received any of such funds.[3]

In the last act of the one-man show "Eddie's Perejil," written and performed by Edward Paulino and directed by Samantha Galarza, the protagonist states that the 1937 Massacre is the largest lynching of Black people in the Americas in the twentieth century. The statement aims to do two things: to acknowledge an often-ignored case of anti-Black violence and to connect the systemic nature of such anti-Black violence in the Dominican Republic to hemispheric examples. The word "lynching" is a uniquely American term for a particular type of racialized murder: the hanging from a tree of African Americans in the United States. As it is used in Paulino's play and herein, "lynching" describes the intentional and racialized murder of Black Haitian and Black Dominican border residents in an attempt to underscore, include, and connect the 1937 Massacre with the wider hemispheric anti-Black state projects occurring during this same time period. In his book *Dividing Hispaniola*, Paulino cites official American documents describing lynching as one of the crimes committed by the white American soldiers during the US occupations of both Haiti (1915-1934) and the Dominican Republic (1916-1924).

While there have been many cases in the Western hemisphere throughout the twentieth century of massacres (racial terror) against Black communities—such as the lynching of 4,743 African Americans over many decades (1882-1968) and the 1912 massacre of an estimated 5,000 Afro-Cubans in the span of several months—the 1937 Haitian Massacre exceeds these examples with regard to the estimated number of deaths and the more time-intensive killing.

As a native-born New Yorker of Dominican immigrant parents, Paulino employs the term "lynching" as he came to learn it in history books: Black men and women being hanged from a tree, which is universally understood as a term to describe racialized anti-Black violence in the United States.[4] Thus, he uses the term to describe the 1937 Massacre, but not as a provocation or to devalue the particular racialized violence and history of lynching in the United States. Instead, the use of the term herein reflects recent collective reactions on a global scale that include responses to the murder of George Floyd (a murder in a long line of Black murders by law enforcement in the United States) and the Black Lives Matter Movement. Many societies in the Americas, too—from Brazil to the Dominican Republic—are also grappling with the history of state violence and its impact on Black communities.[5] These movements challenge white supremacy by questioning traditional narratives of what and who gets to define a nation and who disproportionately has or lacks the benefits of citizenship and can deploy notions of liberty. By using the term lynching, the goal is to intentionally connect the 1937 Haitian Massacre with other cases of anti-Black violence including, but not limited to, the 1921 Tulsa Massacre and the 1917 East St. Louis Race Riot in the United States, the aforementioned massacre of Afro-Cubans in 1912, and the 1897 Canudos Massacre in Brazil where Black people were mobilized by a charismatic preacher, Antonio Conselheiro, who came to be viewed as a threat to the state.[6] With reference to Cuba in particular, in the late 1930s Cuban authorities targeted Haitian workers and transported them to "concentration camps" in Santiago, Cuba before shipping them back to Haiti—deporting nearly 38,000 (McLeod 599). In all of these cases—occurring throughout the Americas—the common denominator again for mass murder was Black annihilation, either of the body or the community.

The usage of the term lynching in a way that aims to connect the large-scale anti-Haitian violence with hemispheric violence against Black communities provides an alternative to scholars of violence who instead elect to differentiate between acts of collective violence with collective liability and acts of collective violence with individual liability. Collective liability here refers to acts in which perpetrators target victims on a large-scale for simply belonging to a group whereas individual liability traditionally targets only individuals accused of a particular offense. Oftentimes, massacres and riots fall into the collective category whereas lynching falls into the latter. Roberta Senechal de la Roche determines that "collective violence is personal injury by a group" (97) and she includes lynching in her classification of various forms of unilateral *collective violence*. She concludes that acts of collective violence are defined by two dimensions: "breadth of liability and degree of organization" (102). Senechal de la Roche clarifies that these two dimensions also define both rioting and terrorism.

In addition to the history of the 1937 Haitian Massacre—an act of collective violence—the last few years in the Dominican Republic have led to increases in xenophobia and anti-Haitianism at the level of policy, largely reflected in the 2013 ruling (TC-0168-13 or *la sentencia*). Further, homicidal crimes such as the 2015 traditional lynching of a Haitian fruit vendor named Tulile in the city of Santiago and, later, in 2019 the hanging from a tree of Eddy Pie, a young man of Haitian descent, in the northern coastal town of Puerto Plata. Both of these crimes—Black men hung from a tree—remain unsolved.[7] Local activist organizations in the Dominican Republic—including, but not limited to, Rerconoci. do, MUDHA, and OBMICA (El Centro para la Observación Migratoria y el Desarrollo Social en el Caribe)—have long documented the impact of anti-Haitian/anti-Black policies on the community of Dominicans of Haitian descent often described as stateless, documenting countless stories of how this systemic legal and social exclusion has negatively impacted their lives and future potential.[8] Reconoci.do, for example, recently published a collection of testimonies titled *Nos cambió la vida* that highlights the experiences of youth of Haitian descent in the Dominican Republic.

Scholars have noted that the term "lynching" has been used to describe murders around the world.[9] But using this term—as it is used in the United States—serves as a way to argue that despite its unprecedented casualty rate in terms of anti-Black violence, the 1937 Massacre was not unique. By examining the 1937 Massacre and its antecedents and consequences through a "hemispheric perspective," we see clearly that there is a vast network of cases and patterns that transcend borders in which Black communities throughout the Americas have been systematically targeted by their respective states. Therefore, a discussion of lynching can be a short-hand way to call attention to hemispheric anti-Black violence while bearing witness to the genocidal 1937 Massacre.[10]

The Border of Lights Reader, then, strives to bear witness to the 1937 Massacre by not just connecting it as an example of another hemispheric case of anti-Black violence, but also by arguing for this anti-Black violence to be defined specifically as genocidal. In this way, the Reader seeks to expand the mainstream definition of genocide that is used to classify the many, often silenced, cases of anti-Black mass violence in the Americas over time and space. *The Border of Lights Reader* intensifies a cross-hemispheric dialogue with goals to incorporate the 1937 Massacre—and by extension other forgotten and ignored hemispheric cases of anti-Black violence—as part of the continuum of genocide history in the twentieth century (a history that, of course, began long before the seventeenth century in the Americas).

The 1619 Project, an ongoing initiative from *The New York Times Magazine*, seeks to reframe US history and center the consequences of slavery within a national narrative.[11] These discussions in the US provide linkages to similar discussions in other contexts. As the CUNY Dominican Studies Institute's path-breaking study states: "Black people began to arrive in La Española with the first transatlantic expedition led by Christopher Columbus in 1492 and continued to do so throughout the sixteenth century, either as free individuals, as servants, or, mostly, as enslaved laborers; either under legal permits issued by the Spanish monarchy or smuggled in as contraband in legally dispatched ships or in un-authorized, non-licensed vessels of pirates or corsairs, usually from countries hostile to Spain at any given time during the century" ("First Blacks"). Alternatively, this hemispheric perspective can also be understood by means of another metaphor: the pannier. As Silvio Torres-Saillant has written, it is the Caribbean, specifically the country that would become the Dominican Republic on the island of Hispaniola—not Virginia, not the United States—that is in fact the "cradle of blackness in the Americas" (126).

In genocide scholarship, scholars have noted the (mis)use of the term genocide. Some argue for a more restrictive or traditionalist definition while others suggest the term can be used more widely. Michael Ignatieff, for example, shared with the BBC that "Those who should use the word genocide never let it slip their mouths. Those who unfortunately do use it, banalise it into a validation of every kind of victimhood."[12] Ignatieff, then, represents the traditionalist wing of the debate regarding the definition of genocide. He further argues in the same article that Atlantic slavery does not fall under the definition of genocide because "whatever it was," slavery was defined as an exploitative system instead of a system aiming "to exterminate the living."

But scholars such as Adam Jones disagree and note that such "arguments are mostly sophistry, serving to deflect responsibility for one of history's greatest crimes" (52). Approaching transatlantic slavery as a form of genocide is important for the Reader's premise because it frames the violent legacies of anti-black policies of mass murder in the twentieth and twenty-first centuries as genocidal events. It thus positions slavery as a foundational historical moment, with genocidal origins, and with the power to inform anti-Black policies.[13] Jones suggests that "regardless of strategy" there is a consensus among scholars regarding the definition of genocide: "'committed with intent to destroy' (UN Convention), is 'structural and systematic' (Horowitz), 'deliberate [and] organized' (Wallimaan and Dobkowski), and 'a series of purposeful actions'" (Fein; see also Thompson and Quets) (31-32). Building on Jones' and other scholars' understandings of genocide, the 1937 Massacre satisfies both the scholarly and legal UN criteria that defines genocide. The 1937 Haitian Massacre aligns with Article II of the 1948 United Nations' "Convention on the Prevention and Punishment of the Crime of Genocide" using the term coined by the lawyer Raphael Lemkin. The Article states:

> ... genocide means any of the following acts committed with intent to destroy, in whole or in part, a national, ethnical, racial or religious group, as such: (a) Killing members of the group; (b) Causing serious bodily or mental harm to members of the group; (c) Deliberately inflicting on the group conditions of life calculated to bring about its physical destruction in whole or in part; (d) Imposing measures intended to prevent births within the group; (e) Forcibly transferring children of the group to another group. ("Genocide").

The lack of public acknowledgement by the Dominican government in regard to the 1937 Massacre and the absence of any tangible memorialization of this crime against humanity in the twentieth century constitute two of the primary factors leading to the creation of Border of Lights in 2012. Border of Lights, a volunteer collective, returns each October to the Dominican-Haitian border towns of Dajabón, Dominican Republic and Ouanaminthe, Haiti to fulfill three objectives: 1) commemorate the 1937 Massacre by remembering the victims; 2) acknowledge and celebrate historic cross-border solidarity and collaboration between both countries often ignored by the Dominican government and academic scholarship; and 3) fortify the connections between the 1937 Massacre and vestiges of contemporary anti-Haitianism in Dominican society and politics today. The fact that descendants of the massacre's victims and over 200,000 Dominicans of Haitian descent—sometimes referred to as "Dominican Dreamers"—are today forced to confront the discriminatory policies of the 2013 Dominican Supreme Court ruling (TC 0168-13) is a palpable example of twenty-first century anti-Haitianism. Border of Lights's volunteers and organizers, in collaboration with community partners in Dajabón and Ouanaminthe, ask: *How do Dominicans and Dominicans of the diaspora bear witness to a genocidal event that occurred more than 80 years ago? How can we remember and pay homage to an event in which most of the survivors have died and most, if not all, the forensic evidence or human remains was either incinerated, buried, or never recovered?*

In many ways, *The Border of Lights Reader* responds to and challenges the underlying pulse of the questions posed above, all related to the collective's guiding motive of bearing witness. As coeditors, our hope is that this project functions as a multimodal and multivocal space for activists, artists, scholars, and others connected in diverse ways to the BOL movement. Moreover, *The Border of Lights Reader* allocates space for these individuals and groups to bear witness via-à-vis a permanent and widely accessible format. The Reader then becomes a type of memorial.

We elected to start this introduction with a photograph of a mural painted during Border of Lights in 2017 to function as a signpost for the border art, memorials, and other community responses that have resulted since the onset of Border of Lights in 2012; many of these examples of art and memorials are represented in the photographs following the introduction. This particular mural's short history, however, also serves to nuance and challenge the traditional, dominant understanding of Dominicans positioning Haitians as the racial and ethnic Other.

This 2017 mural—painted by Dominican and Haitian artists from the non-profit, trans-border, and bi-national art collective, Azueï, (that joined BOL for the first time in 2017 and again in 2019)—reflects the historic collaboration that BOL espouses. The mural, however, no longer looks as pristine and freshly painted as it does in the previous photo. A few short months after the installation of the mural, unknown individuals vandalized the artwork by pouring buckets of hot black oil on the wall. Like in many countries around the world, this vandalism reflects rising and dangerous racism and xenophobia. In the case of the Dominican Republic, such anti-Black and anti-Haitian views crystallized during the Trujillo dictatorship, have seen an intense resurgence in recent decades.[14] The response of local community members to the defacement of this mural in December of 2017, a fixture of community-based collaborative and commemorative art, represents the historic cross-border collaboration and solidarity that this Reader aims to highlight. Community members removed the oil in an effort to restore the mural to its original state. In the last two years since the initial vandalism and act of restoration, new elements appear altered; the images below show the mural in 2019. Black paint covers the "NO MÁS" of "NO MÁS+ACRE" as well as the united outline of Hispaniola inside the conch shell.[15] We also acknowledge the historic contradiction in the Dominican Republic in which solidarity with Haitians—alongside enmity—has always existed.

Figures 2 and 3: Border of Lights/Azueï mural in October 2019.

The aim of BOL, and by extension the aim of *The Border of Lights Reader*, is to provide an alternative to the traditional, dominant narrative that sets Dominicans and Haitians in opposition to one another as eternal adversaries, a chronicle that ignores a cross-border and collaborative history. BOL gained momentum and entered into initial planning stages following the December 2011 untimely death of the late human rights activist Sonia Pierre. The winner of the 2006 Robert F. Kennedy Human Rights Award, Pierre was a tireless defender of human rights. She challenged the Dominican state to grant citizenship to those like herself who were born and raised in the Dominican Republic by undocumented Haitian parents and grandparents. She was then, and remains today, a symbol for the stateless

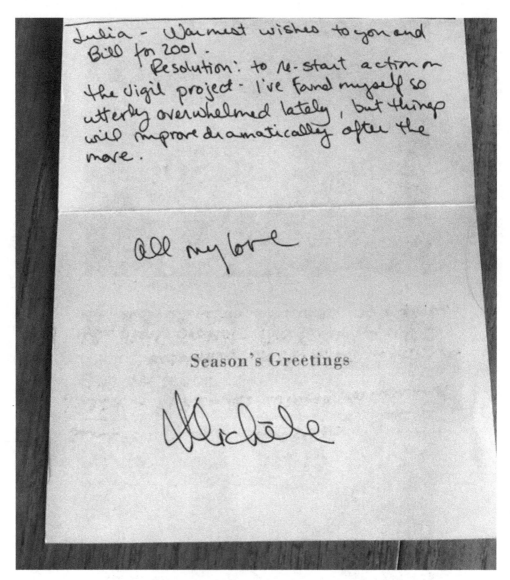

Figure 4: Written correspondence between Michele Wucker and Julia Alvarez in 2001 addressing a New Year resolution "to re-start action on the vigil project."

in her home country of the Dominican Republic. Heartbroken by his dear friend's passing, Edward Paulino, with the prompting of Professor Silvio Torres-Saillant, reached out to Dominican American writer and activist Julia Alvarez. In this initial virtual meeting, Alvarez shared her idea with Paulino to bring "light" to the Haitian-Dominican border. Michele Wucker's *Why the Cocks Fight* (1999) inspired Alvarez to begin brainstorming alongside Wucker ways to shift the meta-adversarial Dominican-Haitian border narrative by underscoring its rich (but often silenced) collaborative history (in the nineties this narrative was informed largely by the increasingly anti-immigrant governmental policies targeting Haitians and their children). When these conversations first began in the late 1990s, however, both Alvarez and Wucker were busy with other projects. The "light" idea re-emerged in early 2011 following Pierre's death when Paulino reached out to Alvarez. Around this same time, Alvarez began sharing her vision of bringing light to the border with other founding members of BOL, like Cynthia Carrión, whom she met on her book tour in 2011.

Alongside Alvarez, Wucker, Paulino, and Carrión founding members of BOL included Megan Myers, Rana Dotson, DeAndra Beard, Sady Díaz, Scherezade García, Erika Martínez, Nehanda Loiseau Julot, and Lesly Manigat, M.D.. As mentioned, the group emerged in the US diaspora partially through Alvarez's book tour, on which she met some of the co-founders—not only Carrión, but also Sady Díaz—and encouraged them to help see the plan to fruition. By the Spring of 2012, a committed group of BOL organizers began to meet via the Wiggio conference call platform every Wednesday night at 10pm. From the beginning, the group battled existential questions, albeit on a smaller scale, that have plagued the reconstruction of post-atrocity and/or post-dictatorial societies concerning how an individual or a community can and should bear witness. Statues? Art? Street mobilizations? Exhibitions? Designing a K-12 curriculum?

The group quickly discovered that "bearing witness" required a significant degree of financial investment. As a response to the need for funding, Border of Lights launched its first crowdsourcing campaign on Kickstarter in August of 2012; the platform allowed the collective to both geographically expand the reach of fundraising efforts and to begin to broadcast the mission and message of BOL to a wider audience. Harnessing the power of the internet has been crucial for BOL, allowing the organization to bear witness in an accessible, inexpensive, and global manner. Over the last eight years, BOL successfully raised an estimated US $30,000. Beyond the geographic reach of fundraising, from the onset BOL organizers understood the imperative role of Hispaniola-based community partners. Given the fact that most, (but not all), of the founding members of BOL lived outside the Dominican Republic and Haiti—many forming part of the Dominican diaspora—organizations like Solidaridad Fronteriza (re-named Centro Montalvo in 2016), Consejo Municipal de Dajabón (CMD), the Hermanas Juanistas in Ouanaminthe, the DREAM Project and Catherine DeLaura, the Mariposa Foundation, Yspaniola, Reconoci.do, MUDHA (Movimiento de Mujeres Dominico-Haitiana), MOSCTHA, Oxfam, Plateforme Genre du Nord-est (PGNE), El Museo Memorial de la Resistencia Dominicana in Santo Domingo, and more recently Azueï and AJWS (American Jewish World Services), have all been instrumental in bearing witness to the victims of 1937. Equally important, the physical presence of these Hispaniola-based organizations reflect and model tangible, on-the-ground, contemporary, and historic cross-border collaboration. BOL's bi-national projects have resulted in peaceful and sustained mutual cooperation without violence or antagonism, a non-violent movement to remember a forgotten violent past during a time in which the Haitian community and Dominicans of Haitian descent are targeted both legally and socially by draconian policies while also providing the Dominican Republic with an indispensable source of cheap labor. We also want to highlight the many behind-the-scenes supporters of Border of Lights from the collective's onset in 2011. Junot Díaz and Edwidge Danticat were two of BOL's earliest supporters and they have both donated

Figure 5: Young Dajabón community members participate in the first inaugural candlelit vigil. BOL 2012. (Photo: Tony Savino.)

dozens of signed books to BOL fundraisers over the years. Julian Dotson, president of the D.C. Urban Debate League, created the BOL logo that is still used today. Miguel Elias Díaz worked pro-bono on the original configuration of the BOL webpage and has contributed to numerous updates of the page over the years. We are grateful to these individuals, and many others, for generously lending their talents and skills to contribute positively to BOL over the past decade.

During the first weekend of October in 2012, after countless conference calls, visits with community partners—both virtual and face-to-face—and the culmination of a successful fundraising campaign, the first October convergence of its kind at the border to bear witness to 1937 took place. The general organization of this inaugural BOL event, outlined to follow, has remained intact for subsequent meetings. The BOL weekend begins on a Friday, but organizers and volunteers traditionally begin arriving in the border town of Dajabón, three hours northwest of Santiago, as early as Wednesday. In 2012, the official and scheduled events began on Friday morning, October 5, with cultural and educational activities for local youth on both sides of the border. Meanwhile, in the main plazas of Dajabón and Ouanaminthe, an interactive art exhibition created by the Dominican American artist Scherezade García began on Friday afternoon and continued until Saturday night. Also, on Friday, BOL sponsored a lecture at the Technological University of Santiago's campus in Dajabón (Universidad Tecnológica de Santiago or UTESA) that brought together important voices from both sides of the border and centered on bi-national topics including identity, environmental concerns, and the bi-national market in Dajabón. Every BOL weekend since 2012 has included two Jesuit-led masses on Friday evening—one on each side of the border—led and organized by local authorities. As parishioners exit the church, they are each given a flower and a candle. Those exiting the mass in Dajabón, and also in Ouanaminthe, form a processional march to the border and the banks of the Massacre River. Following the approximately ten-minute walk to the border, those in attendance recite poetry, and yell greetings across the river to counterparts arriving on the opposite side of the Massacre River. For many, this moment represents the most symbolic and emotional part of the weekend. For the first time in 2012, and for the last seven years, BOL and the local border communities have mobilized to remember the estimated 15,000 Black men, women, and children murdered in October 1937, paying tribute to the innocent lives lost. The ceremony is somber and the hundreds of marchers leave their lighted candles along the border fence as a memorial to the dead. The following day, Saturday, typically consists of a variety of youth-centered workshops. From 2015 to 2018, BOL hosted a *partido de la amistad* (a game of friendship) where local soccer teams from both Dajabón and Ouanaminthe met for a friendly, relaxed soccer game followed by a free lunch for all involved.

For people who cannot travel to the Dominican Republic for the BOL events, beginning in 2013 BOL has organized a virtual vigil that includes a Q&A wherein BOL volunteers and members of the local and international community respond to questions about the Dominican Republic, Haiti, and the 1937 Massacre on Facebook, Instagram, and Twitter. Technology and social media platforms have allowed BOL to reach a global audience; these virtual conversations became in and of themselves acts of bearing witness especially when tens of hundreds of people from around the world participate in the virtual vigil by contributing selfies posing with a candle, offering their own show of solidarity.

While the virtual vigil traditionally takes place on Saturday night, in 2013, 2014, 2016, 2017, and 2018 BOL organized a meeting and workshop for Hispaniola-based activists—many of whom are Dominicans of Haitian descent—in Santiago with the goal of bringing together BOL's various community partners as well as leaders from other nonprofits and organizations. These meetings have provided a space to strategize best practices concerning how to adequately support the ongoing struggle with regard to the situation of statelessness and discerning paths to securing equal citizenship for Dominicans of Haitian descent.

Beyond hosting spaces for inter-community and bi-national dialogue, BOL has also consistently valued the emergent needs of its local partners. In 2017, for example, BOL supported local communities by donating materials to border organizations and individuals affected by the aftermath of Hurricane Maria. Earlier, in 2012, BOL made fiscal donations to MUDHA and Reconoci.do, earmarking the funds for the organizations' work with legal counselors to obtain temporary or permanent residency for Dominicans of Haitian descent. We are conscious of the fact that one critique BOL has confronted in the past portrays the collective as outsiders primarily composed of Dominican Americans. Catherine Bourgeois, for example, claims in *Masacre de 1937*, with respect to Border of Lights events, that "Las conmemoraciones también constituyen un momento donde se discuten las representaciones sobre los 'otros'. Sin embargo, aún queda por evaluar el impacto local de las conmemoraciones, pues la población fronteriza participa relativamente poco de las mismas donde tiene escasa posibilidad de tomar la palabra" (76). The aforementioned efforts that center on inter-community and bi-national dialogue, and the fact that the original motivation for BOL emphasized *local* border residents organically bearing witness to the 1937 Massacre, emphasizes the importance of local partners and border residents. Since the first BOL weekend, our community partners have taken on increasing responsibility for the events and, thus, have expanded BOL through their own initiatives. One example of BOL programming originating on-island and on-border is the 2019 mural and inauguration ceremony in Dosmond, Haiti, further explained in the following paragraph, this event exemplifies how BOL assists local counterparts and positions them as the protagonists and the most valued voices of BOL.

The efforts to support Hispaniola-based community partners with funds for programming and initiatives, supplies, or travel stipends for conferences and community meetings reflects the collective's recognition that BOL represents just three days of programming. On the other 362 days of the year, residents of the Northern border towns of Dajabón and Ouanaminthe and our hardworking community partners needed to decide that commemorating the lives lost in the 1937 Massacre was important to *them* and to their communities; they decided it was. On the 80th anniversary of the 1937 Massacre in 2017, (the sixth Border of Lights meeting), the BOL team supported community members from Dajabón and Ouanaminthe to erect the first and only physical memorial to the massacre in the Dominican Republic: a plaque that sits permanently below a mural painted by local artists during the 2012 Border of Lights on the wall of the Dajabón community's church parish (Nuestra Señora del Rosario). Mario Serrano Marte was instrumental in making this memorial a reality. More recently, on October 3, 2019, the community of Dosmond, Haiti inaugurated the first physical memorial to victims of the 1937 Massacre on the Western side of the island. The day-long event began with a mass in the Catholic Church in Dosmond, a community about 20 minutes from Ouanaminthe. Following the mass, the community group Association des Colons Dosmond (ACD)—composed of three generations of descendants of victims of the massacre—led approximately 200 people in a peace march to the site of the memorial for an inauguration ceremony. Following the ceremony, and while the painting of a mural by Dominican and Haitian artists continued at the site of the memorial, a community panel, musical theatre production by Komedi Mikal PGNE (Grupo Cultural de la PGNE), and lunch rounded out the scheduled events. Given the importance of the physical memorials in both Dosmond and Dajabón, the virtual gallery directly at the end of this introduction contains images of both memorials and inauguration ceremonies as well as other representative moments from Border of Lights events (2012-2019).

In particular, these physical memorials model the primary and most outward-facing motive of BOL: bearing witness to the victims of the 1937 Haitian Massacre. These tangible memorials prove that their lives mattered and matter; black lives matter. As we share earlier in the introduction, the foundation of BOL centers on not just one, but three core ideas that function like a three-legged stool. Each leg represents an essential idea to the volunteer collective that is collaborative in nature and reflective of Border of Lights' *raison d'etre*. Alongside the objective of bearing witness is acknowledging and celebrating the historic cross-border collaboration between Dominicans and Haitians and, lastly, calling attention to and supporting the struggle for citizenship rights on behalf of Dominicans of Haitian descent. *The Border of Lights Reader* seeks to combine these three core motives in one coherent and accessible source. At the most basic level, this anthology encapsulates many of the issues that are challenging nations around the world, including the United States: How do societies commemorate the past? Who decides what historical events are worthy of attention? How do individuals in the face of a tumultuous past and present create spaces of common, historic, and extant solidarity? With respect to memorialization, can and should diasporic communities play an influential role in remembering historic atrocities in their ancestral home country? Further, should this engagement with the past also be commensurate with diasporic groups in the countries in which they were born and raised?

Lastly, how do we speak truth to power by questioning and challenging the legacies of exclusion in present-day discriminatory policies that decide who should or should not be considered citizens? *The Border of Lights Reader* engages squarely with these issues, functioning as a case study for these large-scale, universal questions regarding historical memory and revisionism that a litany of countries around the world are grappling with today such as the exhumation and relocation of Francisco Franco's remains in Spain, the official refusal to recognize government responsibility with respect to Korean comfort women in Japan, the failure to acknowledge government complicity in the anti-communist mass murders in Indonesia, and the debates surrounding whether or not to offer African Americans reparations in the United States. All of these examples reflect the profound and complicated legacies and challenges confronting governments assessing how to appropriately acknowledge and bear witness to past crimes.[16]

Our hope is that *The Border of Lights Reader*, while serving as a "living memorial" of sorts online, becomes a pedagogical resource within the wider international conversation of how transnational communities and their respective diasporas deal with their past in an increasingly complicated globalized world. The Reader will also provide a lens through which to consider contemporary issues such as immigration and statelessness. Today, for example, long-term Dominican residents living in the United States are deported from the United States to the Dominican Republic, and Haitians deported back to Haiti, and in the Dominican Republic long-term residents who are Haitians and Dominicans of Haitian descent—critical to the Dominican labor force but stigmatized for their ethnicity and race/color—are also deported to Haiti.

This Reader builds on previous anthologies focused on the Dominican Republic and/or Haiti such as *Transnational Hispaniola, The Dominican Republic Reader, The Haiti Reader, Masacre de 1937: 80 años después, and Libète: A Haiti Anthology,* but it is also different from these other volumes addressing Dominican-Haitian issues for two main reasons. First, with the exception of *Masacre de 1937,* these earlier anthologies concerning Hispaniola follow a traditional print format. *The Border of Lights Reader* instead is an open-access resource that lives online. This virtual format allows for the Reader to fall into the hands of a global public, one that both includes and extends beyond its diverse group of contributors. The goal is that anyone, especially Haitian and Dominican students on both sides of the border, are able to access the contents of this Reader free of charge. One of our aims in discussing the ideal format for this project centered on moving away from a hierarchical organization, in particular one that is published in one language, but not another. We encouraged contributors to submit in their language of choice. Our hope is that readers will appreciate our attempt to be as inclusive as possible in curating this volume. Given the wide geographic readership of digital and open access books, we decided to include voices in various languages. A monolingual English speaker will not access the volume, only to realize they can only understand, without translation, a portion of the contributions. Instead, there is something here for diverse groups of linguistic communities and given that there is no cost involved in procuring the volume, readers can freely access contributions in whichever languages—be it just one or all four (including English, French, Kreyòl, and Spanish)—they choose. Relatedly, the contributor biographies included at the end of the anthology are each published in Spanish, English, and Kreyòl.[17] Although two academics comprise the coeditors of *The Border of Lights Reader*, the diverse compilation of texts, photography, and art prioritizes voices often silenced and brings together a vast array of activist essays, testimonies, and scholarly articles that are not often grouped together. This unique compilation of contributions—spanning well beyond the academic realm and expanding beyond solely text-based submissions—is the second factor that distinguishes this diverse anthology from others. For example, activist, Black, female, and de-nationalized voices on the ground in the Dominican Republic and Haiti have a prominent place within the pages of *The Border of Lights Reader*.

By design, *The Border of Lights Reader* is multimodal. The anthology's organization constitutes an exercise in multi-perspectivism. From the onset of the project, we grounded our primary goal in a conscious effort to underscore what it means for different communities and individuals of diverse genders, nationalities, races, ethnicities, and geographies, to bear witness to history, specifically as related to the 1937 Massacre. While prioritizing the act of giving voice to those traditionally silenced and left out of our historical annals and literary canons, we also pointedly elected to interweave the diverse voices that this Reader attempts to bring together; the perspective of a US scholar follows that of a Haitian Dominican activist, the poem of a Dominican American woman precedes photographs of a mural by a group of Haitians from the border town Ouanaminthe, and so on. For this reason, we have consciously elected to intermix these varying models of contributions to the Reader; while there are four general sections of the volume—outlined in the following paragraphs—each of these sections moves fluidly between works by Dominicans and Haitians of the diaspora and those living on the island, between scholarly texts and short-form activist essays, and between monologues and poetry, photographs and paintings. Publishing a volume in which non-academic Dominicans and Haitians and their respective diasporas on the island of Hispaniola and beyond are engaged in the silences of the past in constructing creative, constructive, and pedagogical spaces that are made accessible to an international community, is unprecedented. At the same time, we recognize the predominant dominicanist perspective of this anthology, and we acknowledge that the project primarily explores how and why the Dominican and Dominican diasporic communities have a unique responsibility to bear witness to the 1937 Massacre and its aftermath. *The Border of Lights Reader* does, however, expand beyond an insular dominicanist perspective to also explore the opportunities to foster historic solidarity *between* Dominican and Haitian communities.

The first general section of the Reader, entitled "Bearing Witness: Activist and Academic Essays," includes both micro-essays from Dominican, Haitian, and Dominican-Haitian activists as well as longer essays from scholars conducting research in the interdisciplinary fields of Haitian and Dominican studies. These voices include, but are not limited to, Rosa Iris Diendomi Álvarez of Reconoci.do, historians Lauren Derby and Richard Turits, Haitian-Dominican reporter and writer Deisy Toussaint, and Jhonny Rivas.[18] Rivas was arrested in 2013, just months before *la sentencia*, in Monte Cristi, Dominican Republic on unverified charges of murder. His case exemplifies the common civil and human rights violations against Haitians and their descendants in the Dominican Republic. This text-based section includes both a transcription of Rivas's speech on a community panel in Dajabón during Border of Lights in 2018, (transcribed by John Presimé), as well as an essay written by Chiqui Vicioso, who attended Border of Lights in 2012, about Rivas's unjust incarceration. Julia Alvarez and Bill Eichner also share their thoughts about visiting Rivas in prison in the interview section; this is just one example of how the various sections of this project are fluid and intersectional. "Bearing Witness: Activist and Academic Essays" also includes the narratives of several co-founders of the Border of Lights collective: Cynthia Carrión, DeAndra Beard, and Rana Dotson.

The perspectives of these diaspora-based organizers and activists bridges the Hispaniola-based activist texts and the US-based academic essays that represent the foundation of this first section. This section also includes an article by Maria Cristina Fumagalli and Bridget Wooding entitled "Memorialization, solidarity, ethnically mixed couples, and the mystery of hope: mainstreaming Border of Lights." This piece is just one of the many essays that exemplify the interdisciplinarity of the scholarly contributions. Fumagalli also wrote the foreword to the first English translation of *El Masacre se pasa a pie* by Freddy Prestol Castillo. *You Can Cross the Massacre on Foot*, translated by Margaret Randall and published by Duke University Press in 2019, brings Prestol Castillo's controversial bestseller chronicling the massacre to an English-speaking audience. Also, of note, two short essays in this section reference documentary films released in the last decade that address Haitian and Dominican relations. *Muerte por mil cortes/Death by a Thousand Cuts*, referenced in Jake Kheel's essay, was screened at Border of Lights in 2016 and *Hasta la Raíz*, directed by Juan Carlos González Díaz, who also contributed an essay to this anthology, protagonizes two women engaged with Border of Lights in different ways: Deisy Toussaint and Ana María Belique. These two documentaries are in conversation with even more recent films including *Stateless* (2019), directed by Michèle Stephenson, and *Massacre River: The Woman Without a Country* (2019), directed by Suzan Beraza. *Stateless* primarily follows the struggles of young attorney Rosa Iris, a contributor to *The Border of Lights Reader* and BOL collaborator mentioned previously. While the majority of the contributions to this section are unpublished prior to the Reader, Sophie Maríñez's piece on the twentieth-century Haitian-Dominican poet Jacques Viau Renaud is a reprint, as is Nehanda Loiseau Julot's and Edward Paulino's and Scherezade García's *Afro-Hispanic Review* articles. We elected to include them in this volume—with permission—in an effort to address not only the contemporary reality of the Haitian-Dominican frontier, but also border residents and border realities of centuries past and also in an effort to archive previous publications related directly to the Border of Lights movement.

The second section of the Reader, titled "Artistic Endeavors," also succeeds in intertwining diverse approaches to the 1937 Massacre and Dominican-Haitian relations. Both textual and visual, this section encompasses photographs of murals and interactive art exhibits from eight years of Border of Lights events (2012-2019) and other artistic portrayals of Dominican-Haitian relations; the work in this section includes, among other contributions, the artwork of Dominican American Scherezade García, photographs of Polibio Díaz, and a poem, reproduced here in English and Spanish, by Rhina Espaillat. "Artistic Endeavors" positions art and narrative produced from the space of the Dominican and Haitian diaspora as an anchor in the sense that such aesthetic representations of the massacre and the shared history of Hispaniola serve as a unique way for non-islanders to engage with the past. Scherezade García's images, for example, are accompanied by an article published in a special issue of the *Afro-Hispanic Review* in 2013 that focused on Transnational Hispaniola. The piece, written jointly by García and Paulino, addresses the interactive art exhibit and García's postcard project.[19] The contributions to this section are diverse and also include monologues by Magaly Colimon and Rebecca Osborne. Osborne's piece was written for the Border of Lights monologue night in 2012 in New York City to raise money for the inaugural BOL events. Following Osborne's monologue is an article written by Loiseau Julot who organized the 2012 monologue night and a similar event at Duke University in 2016.[20] Laura Ramos, Daniel Ramos, and Ilses Toribio, three Dajabón-based artists who share and sell their work annually at the October *Feria del arte* in Dajabón, also have artwork included herein, as do numerous others including Haitian photojournalist Pierre Michel Jean, who shares his responses to questions about Border of Lights and his recent documentary project *L'oubli pour mensonge*.

The penultimate section of *The Border of Lights Reader* showcases three interviews with individuals linked in unique ways to the Border of Lights movement. The first is with Dominican American Julia Alvarez, a writer, activist, and the "madrina" of BOL, and Bill Eicher, "padrino" of BOL. There is also an interview with Haitian American author and activist Edwidge Danticat, a supporter of BOL from the beginning and an important voice for the US Haitian diaspora. The final interview is with Jesuit Priest and long-term border resident Padre Regino Martínez Bretón, a tireless advocate for human rights in the Northern border region. These three interviews, one in Spanish and two in English, speak to the very beginning of Border of Lights and highlight how four different individuals' approach and make possible the action of bringing "light" to the Haitian-Dominican border.

The Reader culminates with a final, unorthodox section titled "Voice Notes from *la frontera*." This compiles voice notes, primarily recorded in Dajabón, with residents of the Dominican border community. While many of the recordings included are brief interviews with individuals responding to a specific prompt, the section begins with a recording from a radio show centered on Border of Lights events in 2019 with Dajabón's Radio Marién. The other voices readers can find in this section range from Doña Carmen Rodríguez, owner of Hotel Raydan and Farmacia Raydan in Dajabón; Polibío Díaz; Nancy Betances, Dajabón border resident and community leader; Ilses Toribio; and Carlos Alomia Kollegger, a Peruvian Jesuit who directed Human Rights initiatives at Centro Montalvo in Dajabón until May 2020.

The structure of *The Border of Lights Reader* seeks to provide an equal platform for voices from both on and off Hispaniola while also aiming to de-prioritize a US-based academic lens. The organization of this anthology speaks to the bilateral relations between the Dominican Republic and Haiti, a two-sided relationship that by nature does not prioritize one over the other. For this reason, we also elected to publish contributions in the language(s) we received them. As previously noted, there are submissions in English, Spanish, Kreyòl, and French. While the Reader attempts to position diverse voices—in terms of format, language, and topic—alongside one another, the "Trilingual Contributor Biographies" section at the end of the Reader provides short introductions to each contributor thus helping to plot the interconnectedness of this multi-vocal work.

By engaging with this Reader, you too, are actively bearing witness. *The Border of Lights Reader* is inherently interdisciplinary and activist centered. Each carefully curated contribution to this diverse anthology engages with the past while also looking toward the future. We ask and hope that you will keep this in mind as you explore the contents to follow. We encourage you, readers, to bear witness to the past and remember and honor the victims of the 1937 Haitian Massacre, but also to position yourself and your voice in the present.

Join the Border of Lights online community: Website: www.borderoflights.org, Twitter: @ border_oflights, and Facebook: https://www.facebook.com/BorderofLights/ [21]

Notes

1. There is significant historiography on the 1937 Massacre. However, the number of books based on primary sources is surprisingly low. See Turits, Price Mars, Castor, Vega, and Paulino.

2. This agreement also "liquidates and terminates definitively by means of a settlement all claims whatsoever on the part of the Haitian Government or persons of Haitian nationality against the Dominican Government or against persons of Dominican nationality" (Paulino 109n108). Paulino draws from the *League of Nations Treaty Series*, "Dominican Republic and Haiti, Agreement regarding Frontier Questions and the Settlement of All Disputes Resulting from the Events Which Have Occurred During the Last Months of the Year 1937 near the Frontier Between the Two Countries." The treaty was signed in Washington D.C on January 31, 1938.

3. For more information on the indemnity payment see Turits's "A World Destroyed, A Nation Imposed: the 1937 Haitian Massacre in the Dominican Republic."

4. For a history of lynching in the United States see Michael J. Pfeifer's *Rough Justice: Lynching and American Society, 1874-1947*.

5. See "A teen's killing stirs Black Lives Matter protests in Brazil," https://www.latimes.com/ world-nation/story/2020-06-17/a-teens-killing-stirs-black-lives-matter-protests-in-brazil)

6. For information on the Canudos Rebellion or Massacre see both Euclides Da Cunha's *Rebellion in the Backlands (Os Sertoes)* and George Reid Andrews's *The Afro-Argentines Buenos Aires, 1800-1900* in which he writes that "The historical case of the Afro-Argentines might be of little more than passing interest were it not that similar disappearances of black people from the pages of their countries' histories have occurred in virtually every Spanish American republic" (6). Similarly, see Lorgia García-Peña's *The Borders of Dominicanidad* for her analysis of the pre-1937 millenarian movement (Liborismo) in the Dominican-Haitian border led by an Afro-Dominican religious leader Olivorio Mateo (Papá Liborio), a movement violently suppressed by the state military then-occupied by the United States. Finally, for an

in-depth exploration of Brazil post-abolition with regard to the importance of race, see Thomas Skid-more's "Fact and Myth: Discovering a Racial Problem in Brazil."

7. For more on the TC-0168-13 ruling see "The Dominican Republic and Haiti: Shame": https://www.americasquarterly.org/fulltextarticle/the-dominican-republic-and-haiti-shame/.

For the two cases of lynching see: https://www.theguardian.com/world/2015/feb/12/dominican-republic-lynching-haiti-fears-human-rights and http://www.puertoplatadigital.com/verNoticia.aspx?Id=31205).

8. See Reconoci.do and MUDHA websites: https://www.reconoci.do/ and http://mudhaong.org/.

9. See Pfeifer's *Global Lynching and Collective Violence Vol. 1: Asia, Africa, and the Middle East*, ed.

10. We use the term "hemispheric perspective" to describe an expanded and inclusive rethinking in connecting and understanding anti-Black state violence throughout the Americas.

11. See more on the 1619 Project here: https://www.nytimes.com/interactive/2019/08/14/magazine/1619-america-slavery.html.

12. See https://www.bbc.com/news/world-11108059

13. This foundational moment of transatlantic slavery should be placed in conversation with the hemisphere's first genocide: the genocide of the indigenous peoples of the Americas. As Jones writes: "The European holocaust against indigenous peoples in the Americas was arguably the most extensive and destructive genocide of all time" (70).

14. See Lauren H. Derby's *The Dictator's Seduction: Politics and the Popular Imagination in the Era of Trujillo* (2009), Ernesto Sagás's *Race and Politics in the Dominican Republic* (2000), April J. Mayes's *The Mulatto Republic: Class, Race, and Dominican Identity* (2015), and Silvio Torres-Sailliant's *The Tribulations of Blackness: Stages in Dominican Racial Identity* (1998) for more information on anti-Haitianism during the Trujillato.

15. This act of vandalism in 2017 was, in part, caught on camera and posted on Facebook. The video can be accessed here: https://www.facebook.com/santiago.riveron.1/videos/1506555739457673/

16. For more information on these contemporary examples see the following links: "Franco's remains are exhumed and Buried After Bitter Battle," https://www.nytimes.com/2019/10/24/world/europe/francoexhumed.html?searchResultPosition=1; *Shusenjo: The Main Battleground of the Comfort Women Issue*, https://www.shusenjo.com/; "The Cold Legacy: Indonesia," https://www.bbc.co.uk/sounds/play/w3cszz6d; and "Talk of Reparations for Slavery moves to State Capitols," https://www.pewtrusts.org/en/research-and-analysis/blogs/stateline/2019/10/03/talk-of-reparations-for-slavery-moves-to-state-capitols.

17. We are extremely grateful to our Cabarete-based friend John Presimé for assisting with the translations into Kreyòl for the contributor biographies.

18. Jhonny Rivas appears spelled in various publications as Jhonny, Johnny, and Jonny.

19. This article was originally published in the *Afro-Hispanic Review* 32.2 (2013). Megan Jeanette Myers, then Assistant Editor of the *Afro-Hispanic Review*, curated the special issue focused on Hispaniola.

20. This article was originally published in the *Afro-Hispanic Review* 35.2 (2016).

21. All photos property of Border of Lights unless otherwise noted.

Works Cited

Alvarez, Julia. "There are Two Countries." *The Afro-Hispanic Review* vol. 32, no. 2, 2013, pp. 145-48.

Bourgeois, Catherine. "'Nadie puede contar lo que pasó': Memorias de la Masacre de 1937 en República Dominicana. In *Masacre de 1937: 80 años después: Reconstruyendo la memoria*. Ed. Matías Bosch Carcuro et al., CLACSO, 2018, pp. 47–81.

Castor, Suzy. *Le massacre de 1937 et les relations haïtiano-dominicaines.* CRESFED, 1988.

---. *Migraciones y relaciones internacionales: el caso haitiano-dominicano.* Facultad de Ciencias Políticas y Sociales, Universidad Nacional Autónoma de México, Centro de Estudios Latinoamericanos, 1983.

Da Cunha, Euclides. *Rebellion in the Backlands (Os Sertoes).* U of Chicago P, 1957.

Derby, Lauren H. *The Dictator's Seduction: Politics and the Popular Imagination in the Era of Trujillo.* Duke UP, 2009.

"Dominican Republic and Haiti, Agreement regarding Frontier Questions and the Settlement of All Disputes Resulting from the Events Which Have Occurred During the Last Months of the Year 1937 near the Frontier Between the Two Countries." *League of Nations Treaty Series. Treaties and International Engagements Registered with the Secretariat of the League of Nations.* Vol. 1987, nos. 4328–349, 1938, p. 176.

"First Blacks in the Americas: The African Presence in the Dominican Republic." CUNY Dominican Studies Institute, http://firstblacks.org/en/summaries/arrival-06-introduction/.

"Genocide." United Nations Office on Genocide Prevention and the Responsibility to Protect, https://www.un.org/en/genocideprevention/genocide.shtml.

Helg, Aline. *Our Rightful Share: The Afro-Cuban Struggle for Equality, 1886-1912.* The U of North Carolina P, 1995.

Jones, Adam. *Genocide: A Comprehensive Introduction,* 3rd Edition, Routledge, 2017.

Mayes, April J. *The Mulatto Republic: Class, Race, and Dominican Identity.* UP of Florida, 2015.

McLeod, Marc C. "Undesirable Aliens: Race, Ethnicity, and Nationalism in the Comparison of Haitian and British West Indian Immigrant Workers in Cuba, 1912-1939. *Journal of Social History,* vol. 31, no. 3, 1998, 599-623.

Paulino, Edward. *Dividing Hispaniola: The Dominican Republic's Border Campaign against Haiti, 1930-1961.* U of Pittsburgh P, 2016.

Pfeifer, Michael. *Rough Justice: Lynching and American society, 1974-1947.* University of Illinois Press, 2006.

---, Editor. *Global Lynching and Collective Violence Vol. 1: Asia, Africa, and the Middle East.* The U of Illinois P, 2017.

Price Mars, Jean. *La república de Haití y la República Dominicana. Diversos aspectos de un problema histórico, geográfico, y etnológico, vol. 1.* Industrias Gráficas España, 1953.

Reid Andrews, George. *The Afro-Argentines Buenos Aires, 1800-1900.* U of Wisconsin P, 1980.

Sagás, Ernesto. *Race and Politics in the Dominican Republic.* UP of Florida, 2000.

Senechal de la Roche, Roberta. "Collective Violence as Social Control." *Sociological Forum,* vol. 11, no. 1, 1996, pp. 97-128.

Skidmore, Thomas. "Fact and Myth: Discovering a Racial Problem in Brazil." *Kellogg Institute,* working paper, https://kellogg.nd.edu/sites/default/files/old_files/documents/173_0.pdf.

Torres-Sailliant, Silvio. *The Tribulations of Blackness: Stages in Dominican Racial Identity. Latin American Perspectives,* vol. 25, no. 3, 1998, pp. 126-46.

Turits, Richard Lee. *Foundations of Despotism: Peasants, the Trujillo Regime, and Modernity in Dominican History.* Stanford UP, 2003.

Turits, Richard Lee. "A World Destroyed, A Nation Imposed: the 1937 Haitian Massacre in the Dominican Republic," *HAHR,* vol. 82, no. 3, Aug. 2002, pp. 589-635

Vega, Bernardo. *Trujillo y Haití. Vol. 1.* Santo Domingo: Fundación Cultural Dominicana, 1988.

---. *Trujillo y Haití. Vol. 2.* Santo Domingo: Fundación Cultural Dominicana, 1995.

VIRTUAL GALLERY

Figure 6: Following the walk to the border in Dajabón, participants stop at the fence and position their candles. BOL 2012. (Photo: Tony Savino.)

Figure 7: Park and river clean-up in Ouanaminthe, Haiti. BOL 2012. (Photo: Tony Savino).

Figure 8: Students oversee the park clean-up in Ouanaminthe. BOL 2012.

Figure 9: Participant holds up one of Scherezade García's postcards in the Central Park in Dajabón. BOL 2013.

Figure 10: BOL organizers after the candlelit vigil. BOL 2013.

Figure 11: Candles left on top of the fence along the Massacre River in Dajabón. BOL 2013.

Figure 12: Mariposa volunteer coordinates *dinámicas* in the Central Park in Dajabón. BOL 2014.

Figure 13: Students pose with recycled art project. BOL 2014.

Figure 14: Candlelit vigil. BOL 2014.

Figure 15: Community leaders meeting at Centro Bellarmino in Santiago. BOL 2014.

Figure 16: Panelists at community conversation table at UTESA in Dajabón. BOL 2015.

Figure 17: BOL volunteers hold up donations for the Children's Home in Ouanaminthe at the border. BOL 2015.

Figure 18: A young participant holds up her lit candle in the middle of the circle after Padre Mario Serrano spoke. BOL 2016.

Figure 19: The fences that divide us. BOL 2016.

Figure 20: Students from the Mariposa Foundation leave the church and begin the march to the border. BOL 2016.

Figure 21: Meeting of community partners in Santiago, Dominican Republic. BOL 2016.

Figure 22: Readings at the border. BOL 2016.

Figure 23: Partido de Amistad in Dajabón, Dominican Republic. BOL 2016.

Figure 24: Haiti processional at the border, through the fence. BOL 2017.

Figure 25: Grupo Azueï and their completed mural. BOL 2017.

Figure 26: The new plaque under the mural, painted by Daniel Ramos, in 2012. BOL 2017.

Figure 27: Students at the Mariposa Foundation hold hands in solidarity along the beach in Cabarete to honor the victims of the 1937 Massacre. October 2017. (Photo (taken by drone): The Mariposa Foundation, courtesy of Patricia Thorndike Suriel.)

Figure 28: The first reading of the memorial plaque in Dajabón. BOL 2017.

Figure 29: DREAM leads workshops at El Hogar in Dajabón. BOL 2018.

Figure 30: Centro Montalvo staff, Jhonny Rivas, John Presimé, and Megan Myers following panel with Suzy Castor, author of *Le masacre de 1937*, at Hotel Orix in Ouanaminthe. BOL 2018.

Figure 31: Lanterns released into the night sky after the processional. BOL 2018.

Figure 32: Padre Regino Martínez speaks to inmates at the Dajabón prison about border solidarity. BOL 2018.

Figure 33: Lunch with community partners. BOL 2018.

Figure 34: Theatre group, Oxfam Group, presents a re-enactment of the Massacre. BOL 2018. (Photo: Presuma Bulgary.)

Figure 35: Bi-national art panel at Nuestra Señora del Rosario. BOL 2018.

Figure 36: Community panel at UTESA in Dajabón with Matías Bosch, Quisqueya Lora, and Jésula Blanc. BOL 2019. (Photo: Radio Marién.)

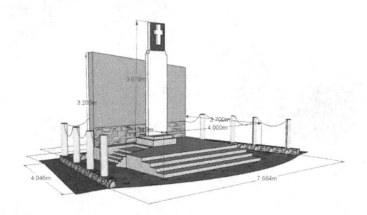

Figure 37: Architectural plans for Dosmond, Haiti memorial. BOL 2019.

Figure 38: Candlelit vigil at the border in Ouanaminthe, Haiti. BOL 2019. (Photo: Presuma Bulgary.)

Figure 39: Azueï muralists in Dosmond, Haiti. BOL 2019. (Photo: Azueï, Marisol Peláez y Omar Pepa Tavarez.)

Figure 40: Azueï muralists and Cap-Haïtien artists working together on memorial in Dosmond. BOL 2019. (Photo: Azueï, Marisol Peláez y Omar Pepa Tavarez.)

SECTION I

BEARING WITNESS

ACTIVIST AND ACADEMIC ESSAYS

Haitian-Dominican History and the 1937 Haitian Massacre

Richard Turits and Lauren Derby

> Out of the swamp the cane appears
> to haunt us, and we cut it down . . .
> The general sees the fields of sugar
> cane, lashed by rain and streaming.
> . . . He hears
> the Haitians sing without R's
> as they swing the great machetes:
> *Katalina,* they sing, *Katalina,*
> . . . He will
> order many, this time, to be killed . . .
>
> —RITA DOVE, "PARSLEY," 1983[1]

In the mid-1980s, poet Rita Dove was not alone in representing the Haitian Massacre as of a piece with another horror, that of the exploitation, intolerable living conditions, and denial of rights of Haitian and Haitian-descended cane cutters on Dominican sugar plantations. This is not surprising, given that these phenomena are intertwined parts of a long history of violent and brutal Dominican anti-Haitianism. Yet, through years of research on Haitian-Dominican relations, including oral histories and archival work conducted in the 1980s, we found that this analysis views the massacre through too presentist a lens, one that mistakenly fuses distinct histories of anti-Haitian horror that were the product of dissimilar forces and motivations. In this essay, we summarize findings from our larger work on these questions and discuss related insights from exciting new research by other scholars on Haitian-Dominican relations since the Haitian Revolution.

Contrary to the image offered in Rita Dove's powerful poem "Parsley," some 15,000 victims of the massacre ordered by the Dominican dictator, Rafael Trujillo, were not the country's cane cutters. Nor were they migrant laborers of any sort. There were no plantations in the relatively large northern provinces that bordered Haiti (a region known in the Dominican Republic as "the frontier") where the military killed thousands by machete during the first week of October 1937. Similarly, Dominican troops did not attack sugar plantation workers several months later during a massive eviction and the murder of hundreds of ethnic Haitians in the southern frontier zones of the Dominican Republic. Most people of Haitian descent in the northern frontier areas of the country were small farmers, and, according to elderly people from the area whom we interviewed, the majority hailed from families that had lived in the region for generations. Those of Haitian descent living in the towns rather than more rural areas were typically money lenders, teachers, shoemakers, and other artisans—not plantation laborers. At the time, there were no restrictions in either law or practice on Haitian immigration to the Dominican Republic other than an annual fee imposed on migrants that was neither insignificant nor prohibitive.[2] Not only, then, were most people of Haitian descent living in the Dominican Republic Dominican citizens because they had been born in the country. In addition, their parents or earlier ancestors had come to the Dominican Republic legally, contrary to later assertions by anti-Haitian Dominican nationalists and recently the Dominican Supreme Court. Many also lived on land whose sovereignty was contested due to the lack of a ratified border treaty until 1936.[3]

Perhaps most contrary to common assumptions was that in the Dominican Republic's northern frontier provinces, where Haitians and Dominicans of Haitian descent made up a large part of the population,[4] Haitian-Dominican integration and cooperation, not differentiation and conflict, prevailed. In the pre-massacre years, not only was the physical boundary between Haiti and the Dominican Republic highly porous—in certain senses a political fiction given that people crossed freely between the two countries on a daily basis—but the distinction between "Haitians" and "Dominicans" in terms of culture, kinship, religion, and language was itself far from clear in the frontier. In researching the region where the 1937 massacre took place, we discovered a highly integrated, bicultural, transnational world, where cultural hybridity went together with a high degree of socioeconomic and demographic equality among Haitians and Dominicans. Most of the region's population, both Haitian and Dominican, lived independently through small-scale farming and by hunting and raising animals on collectively-used lands with ample woods available for all to clear and cultivate (as was the case still in much of the Dominican countryside in 1930).[5] Those of Haitian descent were probably on average more oriented around growing crops for the market and less around hunting and raising stock on the open range than those of solely Dominican descent. But this was not a socially significant difference. How then could this region have become the site of the most horrific form of differentiation imaginable, that of genocide? This question haunted many Haitian refugees who fled the Massacre and with whom we spoke in the 1980s. These refugees often expressed utter perplexity at what could have caused Trujillo to order this genocidal slaughter and destruction of the frontier community they had helped to build in the Dominican Republic. This question came to shape our research and analysis, as we dug simultaneously into the history of the pre-1937 Haitian-Dominican frontier world and into the horrors of the massacre itself.

It was not only the Massacre that made the pre-1937 community of Haitians and Dominicans in the Dominican Republic's frontier provinces so unexpected. It was also the long history of unabashed anti-Haitianism among urban elite Dominicans and Dominican intellectuals (since Dominican independence in the 1840s, at least).[6] Yet we discovered that, in general, a giant gulf existed between elite urban Dominican worlds and popular rural society and between the national state and the countryside. Until the U.S. Occupation (1916-1924), the Dominican government had little reach into the vast rural interior and its highly dispersed population, and the state exercised particularly little control in the frontier regions bordering with Haiti. These regions had long been in many senses a stateless space, with a border across which people and goods flowed freely—despite continuous government efforts to regulate, tax, and monitor them.[7] This went hand in hand with intellectuals and other elite Dominicans' inability to impose ideas of a Dominican nation that excluded people of Haitian descent. There were status distinctions certainly in the northern frontier provinces of the Dominican Republic, as in all societies. Distinct Dominican and Haitian identities persisted, even among second and third-generation immigrants, and exoticist and negative stereotypes of Haitians circulated in this remote region.[8] Throughout the country, too, in this mostly Afro-descended and "mixed" nation, a prejudicial preoccupation with micro-distinctions of skin tone and other features prevailed, a colorist preoccupation analogous to that in many other twentieth-century Caribbean and Latin American nations. This mode of racism cast its shadow over both Haitians and Dominicans, the latter a population that had been overwhelmingly of African descent since the formation of the early sixteenth-century slave plantation economy in Spanish Santo Domingo.[9] Other forms of racism in the frontier provinces were, it seems, targeted specifically at people of Haitian descent, surely recent migrants above all. Historian Sabine Cadeau's dissertation, for instance, provides an important portrait of prejudicial treatment that Haitian migrants experienced in the frontier at the hands of local Dominican authorities.[10]

Nonetheless, what remains most striking is the high level of community and integration among Haitians and Dominicans in the pre-Massacre Dominican frontier. It seems, too, that this was not simply a product of the constant back-and-forth flow of people across the border and the many families, businesses, and lives that spanned its two sides. This entanglement also emerged out of shared historical experiences. Both Haitians and Dominicans were descendants mostly of enslaved Africans who seized their own freedom against the wishes and power of their owners. The enslaved people in the French colony of Saint Domingue overthrew the entire slave system through revolution in the 1790s, while the majority of those enslaved in the Spanish colony of Santo Domingo managed to escape to at least de facto freedom through individual flight by the late 1600s. And in the nineteenth century, both Haitians and Dominicans successfully battled for independence against colonial rulers long before other nations in the Caribbean. After independence, they were both governed mostly—or entirely in Haiti's case—by presidents of African descent. (In the Dominican Republic, this was the case only in the nineteenth century.) And perhaps, above all, in a region long dominated by plantations, both Haitians and Dominicans succeeded in resisting state and elite efforts to develop large-scale agriculture and to turn the majority of the population into wage laborers. Remarkably, in the nineteenth and early twentieth centuries, most people across the island remained independent farmers and hunters with free access to land.[11]

In fact, it was largely this peasant autonomy that drove the U.S. government to invade and occupy simultaneously the two sides of the island for many years, from 1915 to 1934 in Haiti and from 1916 to 1924 in the Dominican Republic. Through occupation, the U.S. government sought, and insisted on, establishing new central states that were both willing and able to act in ways that suited U.S. strategic and business interests. Past Haitian and Dominican leaders had attempted in vain to respond to the wishes and preoccupations of the U.S. government and U.S.-owned corporations on the island, concerns that Haitian and Dominican leaders shared for the most part. But they had largely been unable to do so. The police and military could not protect sugar plantations from banditry and extortion. Nor, U.S. leaders argued, could they be counted on to stop possible future European—in particular, then, German—military intrusions. During the U.S. occupations, U.S. leaders focused above all on creating powerful new militaries that would ensure "order" and serve U.S. interests. In both countries, these armed forces would support post-occupation dictators who ruled for decades in the twentieth century, Trujillo in the Dominican Republic from 1930-1961, and the Duvaliers in Haiti from 1957 to 1986.[12] It was thanks to the new militaries that the U.S. had built that Trujillo was able to execute the genocidal massacre in 1937.[13]

Since the publication of our work on the frontier world of the Dominican Republic, other scholars have uncovered new histories of collaboration and unity across the island that have prevailed beyond this frontier world. Two important recent works in this vein are Anne Eller's 2016 book *We Dream Together: Dominican Independence, Haiti, and the Fight for Caribbean Freedom* and Andrew Walker's 2018 dissertation "Strains of Unity: Emancipation, Property, and the Post-Revolutionary State in Haitian Santo Domingo, 1822-1844."[14] These works show that collaboration between Haitians and Dominicans characterized even the very moments that anti-Haitian Dominican intellectuals and some Dominicans at-large have claimed as the historic origin of Dominican anti-Haitianism, however incorrectly; that is, the Haitian "invasion" and "domination" of the Spanish-speaking side of the island in the early and mid-nineteenth century.

Elite Dominican intellectuals and others have long explained Dominican anti-Haitian sentiment as the justifiable outcome of the Haitian government ruling the Spanish-speaking side of the island between 1822 and 1844.[15] Of course, this argument was never logical. The Dominican Republic was first colonized by Spain in 1492, then briefly by France in the early 1800s, re-annexed for several years by Spain in the 1860s, militarily occupied and subjected to foreign government by the U.S. between 1916 and 1924, and invaded again by the U.S. in 1965. Yet we do not see similar prejudices against the French, Spanish, and Americans as against Haitians. Put even more simply, 1844 was a long time ago.

Furthermore, Eller and Walker show how Haitian annexation of the Spanish-speaking side of the island was more a unification than an occupation. Dominicans overall variously sought, accepted, and benefited from annexation in 1822. It was, technically, a military takeover at first, but it was embraced for the most part by the former Spanish subjects. Even though Dominican leaders had carried out a military coup and declared independence from Spain only a few weeks prior, there was substantial support for union with Haiti. Particularly in light of the conservative pro-slavery politics among Dominican independence leaders, those held in slavery (some 10 percent of society) perceived in Haitian rule the chance for liberty, and the overwhelming majority of Dominicans, who were of African descent, looked forward to racial equality.[16]

Over time, the Haitian annexation did produce escalating resistance and opposition among ordinary Dominicans, Walker stresses, but this was for economic, not cultural or imagined racial, reasons. Important works by Quisqueya Lora and María Cecilia Ulrickson substantiate these conclusions. Ranchers who composed a large part of the country's better-off population had seen in Haitian annexation prospects for free trade, which was especially attractive due to onerous taxes on cattle exports to Haiti imposed by Spanish colonial authorities in recent years. But for the Dominican majority, the Haitian state's promotion of large-scale agriculture collided with their aspirations and traditional mode of existence based on small farming and collective use of woods and pasture for hunting and stock raising. To most people's chagrin, Haitian authorities sought to impose cash-crop production and wage labor that would have taken away their economic autonomy, much as Spanish colonial leaders had earlier sought and failed to do. On both sides of the island, though the Haitian state pursued its model of export-oriented agriculture with the backing of many elite Dominicans as well as Haitians, Walker explains. And in the east, as in the west, the population overall resisted.[17]

Many Haitians and Dominicans ultimately refused to suffer the economic and political policies of the island's then president, Jean-Pierre Boyer, and, working together, they overthrew his government. In its place, some Dominicans envisaged a Haitian-Dominican confederation with a single and more liberal constitution, reducing the power of the president and the army and boosting that of the legislature.[18] It was when this liberal project failed to come to fruition that those on the Spanish-speaking side of the island moved definitively toward independence. This was achieved in 1844.

Yet not everyone on the Spanish-side of the island, Lora stresses, was on board right away with the transition to independence from Haiti. The Haitian government had freed a significant portion of the population from bondage and terminated the legal racial inequality that had prevailed during Spanish colonial rule. Annexation to Haiti had safeguarded those victories for the Afro-American majority, some of whom appear to have feared a return to the slave system and racial order that had prevailed under Spanish control. In the town of Monte Grande, for instance, local leaders refused to accept the new Dominican government until the president and vice-president negotiated an agreement there with "a group of people fearful of the intentions" of the new regime. Lora recounts that "Monte Grande had been home to an important population of slave origins, many of whom had been liberated in 1822." The day after the confrontation in Monte Grande, the government "issued a decree reiterating 'that slavery is gone forever from the territory of the Dominican Republic.'" Another independence leader, José María Imbert, declared that "everyone, of whatever color they may be, are brothers and free, and the Dominican Republic recognizes no distinctions among men based on color, but rather on their virtues."[19] Leaders of the new republic felt compelled to proclaim their commitment to universal freedom and racial equality, it seems, in order to ensure popular Dominican support for separation from Haiti. Seeming to dramatize elite white acquiescence to political reality, a few years later Buenaventura Báez, the son of a woman who had once been kept in bondage, became president.

After the island was again split politically in two, Haiti took both military and diplomatic actions to regain what was now the Dominican Republic. Haitian leaders were driven, in part, by legitimate fears that an overseas power, now especially the United States, might gain control over the Dominican Republic and threaten or compromise Haitian sovereignty from there.[20] In 1851, Haiti reportedly proposed to Dominican leaders, through the British consulate, a type of Haitian-Dominican confederation under the Haitian flag. "But in this moment," Lora writes, a union ruled by Haiti "was unacceptable to the dominant sectors of the Dominican Republic."[21] In 1855, Haiti made its last attempt to annex the Dominican Republic with a botched and quickly repelled invasion of the country.[22] It was during this era that some state and church leaders, including President Báez, broadcast resentful and disparaging rhetoric against Haiti, surely in part to galvanize the Dominican population to oppose and, if necessary, fight militarily against Haitian re-annexation.[23]

In 1861, Haitian fears of an imperial power establishing itself on the island again became a reality when Spain recolonized the Dominican Republic. But while it had taken more than twenty years for Dominicans to rebel against Haitian rule, popular armed resistance was almost immediate against Spain. Contrary to the implications of the work of anti-Haitian Dominican intellectuals during the mid-twentieth century, Eller shows, race played a major role not in the fight for Dominican separation from Haiti in 1844 but rather in the revolution against Spanish annexation in 1863. One of Eller's most original contributions is her discovery of widely circulating rumors of Spanish plans to make slavery legal again in Santo Domingo and even to enslave some free Dominicans during the 1863 war against Spain. These rumors, she argues, were probably the most powerful rallying cry of this independence war, even while some of its leaders conceded that the threat of enslavement was not a literal one. That this rumor was so galvanizing speaks volumes to the ways this was a popular revolution made by and for people of African descent—indeed by a population composed largely of descendants of people who had escaped from slavery. It is also noteworthy that the Spanish ruling Santo Domingo were popularly referred to as "the whites," as U.S. occupiers would be fifty years later.[24]

An important element in the Dominican victory over Spain was that Haitians provided Dominican rebels with a haven across the border where they could gather arms and organize their forces. Eller highlights how such collaboration translated also into an impressive discourse of fraternity among Dominicans and Haitians in these years. Leading Dominican and Haitian figures spoke of Haitians and Dominicans as "two peoples composed of the same race," in the words of one Dominican writer at the time. Members of the provisional Dominican rebel government, Eller recounts, even "proposed an outright federation" between Haiti and the Dominican Republic. The post-revolutionary Dominican government, though, tragically shifted course. Dominican leaders abandoned a politics of solidarity with Haiti, and old elite groups engaged only more strongly in racist critiques of both Haitians and the rural Dominican masses.[25]

It turns out, then, that Haitian-Dominican integration in the northern Dominican frontier provinces prior to the Massacre was not so exceptional in the long history of Haitian-Dominican relations. Collaboration more than conflict was the norm, it seems, until 1937. Dominican anti-Haitianism at the popular level developed as a major phenomenon only subsequently and in the context of the rapidly expanding dependence on Haitian migrants to cut Dominican cane. Sugar plantations had taken over a large portion of the region immediately to the east of Santo Domingo (the provinces of San Pedro and La Romana) and a far smaller area in the southwest (Barahona) during the 1880-1930 period, but it was only during the U.S. occupations of Haiti and the Dominican Republic that migrant laborers from Haiti rather than the British and French Caribbean became the backbone of the sugar economy.

In this light, the origins of contemporary Dominican anti-Haitianism seem in many ways part of a global phenomenon. Since the late nineteenth century, agricultural firms have recruited immigrants to generate profits, and particularly to exploit them for difficult, low-paying jobs, while subjecting them to mistreatment and increasingly denying them rights.[26] In a vicious cycle, popular prejudices against migrants then flow from the resulting degradation and marginalization. Because migrants are employed on exploitative terms from which national workers may be somewhat protected, migrant laborers become prejudicially associated with those inferior conditions—a version of blaming the victim.[27] The extremity of popular Dominican anti-Haitianism in recent decades has reflected, then, as much as enabled the severity of Dominican abuse of Haitian-descended workers in this period. Both the genocidal violence of the Haitian Massacre and the brutal exploitation of Haitian-descended workers have in many ways led, we have argued in our work, to anti-Haitianism—certainly broadened and intensified it—even more than vice versa. Although the experiences of Haitians and Haitian-Dominicans in the northern Dominican frontier provinces and those of Haitian laborers on sugar plantations are not one and the same, they are linked in this way and often, as a result, tethered to one another in the popular imagination.

In 2013, the Dominican citizenship of a vast population of Haitian descent born in the Dominican Republic was revoked by the Dominican government. The Dominican Supreme Court has upheld this denial on grounds that few outside observers have found legally tenable. It asserted that their families had been admitted to the Dominican Republic only temporarily for seasonal work and that they were therefore legally excluded from birthright citizenship because their ancestors had been "in transit" at the time of their birth.[28] The casting off of great numbers of people of Haitian descent into statelessness and rightlessness continues to echo in contemporary history and not only in the Dominican Republic. Historian Naomi Paik has stressed, for instance, how by establishing what she calls "spatial exceptions" or "internal zones of exclusion," U.S. leaders have not infrequently placed large numbers of people altogether beyond rights, from the 1980s carceral quarantine of Haitian refugees to the United States to the contemporary use of private detention facilities without effective governmental oversight.[29]

The Dominican government's recent—and in truth unconstitutional—exclusion of people of Haitian descent from the Dominican nation and their rights to citizenship is a chilling repetition of aspects of Trujillo's genocidal violence in 1937. The Dominican courts have abrogated Haitian-Dominicans' legal existence, thus facilitating their hyper-exploitation, just as the 1937 Massacre literally abrogated people of Haitian descent lives and with it, deep histories of collaboration as well as conflict between Haitians and Dominicans.

Notes

1. Rita Dove, "Parsley," *Museum* (Pittsburgh: Carnegie Mellon University Press, 1983), reproduced at Poetry Foundation, https://www.poetryfoundation.org/poems/43355/parsley. For powerful fictional treatments of the Massacre, see also Edwidge Danticat, *The Farming of Bones: A Novel* (New York, NY: Soho Press, 1998); and René Philoctète, *Massacre River* (New York: New Directions, 2005).

2. The Trujillo government did make an increasing effort to enforce the migration tax and the identity card fee, making the latter obligatory for both citizens and migrants. And in 1937, prior to the Massacre, the central government developed a secret plan to target Haitian immigrants in the southwest who had not paid these fees for corvée labor—an obligation also imposed on, but in this case applied less stringently to, all Dominicans in lieu of cash payment for the road tax. But this secret plan was contested by local authorities and abandoned. See Amelia Hintzen's essay on this intriguing history, "'A Veil of Legality': The Contested History of Anti-Haitian Ideology under the Trujillo Dictatorship," *New West Indian Guide* 90 (Spring 2016): pp. 28-54. On the system of corvée labor imposed on Dominicans, see Richard Lee Turits, *Foundations of Despotism: Peasants, the Trujillo Regime, and Modernity in Dominican History* (Stanford: Stanford University Press, 2003), esp. pp. 13, 106-107, 300-301 n. 100.

3. Bridget Wooding, "Haitian Immigrants and Their Descendants Born in the Dominican Republic," *Oxford Research Encyclopedias: Latin America History,* William Beezley, ed., Oxford University Press, 2018, https://oxfordre.com/latinamericanhistory.

4. Indeed, ecclesiastical records indicate that the massacre wiped out two-thirds of the parish of Dajabón at first and as much as 90 percent in nearby areas, such as Loma de Cabrera. log book, October 1937, L'École des Frères, Ouanaminthe, Haiti.

5. For a treatment of this world, see Richard Lee Turits, "A World Destroyed, A Nation Imposed: The 1937 Haitian Massacre in the Dominican Republic," *Hispanic American Historical Review* 82, no. 3 (August 2002): pp. 589-635. See also a detailed oral historical account of the socioeconomic practices of this frontier society by a Haitian man living there in 1937, which was given fifty years later: Isil Nicolas, "An Oral History of a Massacre," in *The Haiti Reader: History, Culture, Politics,* ed. Laurent Dubois et al. (Durham: Duke University Press, 2020): pp. 267-75. For the original Kreyòl version of this testimony, see Lauren Derby and Richard Lee Turits "L'histoire orale d'un massacre: entretien avec Isil Nicolas Cour," in Lauren Derby and Richard Lee Turits, *Terreurs de frontière. Le massacre des Haïtiens en République Dominicaine en 1937,* edited and preface by Watson R. Denis (Port-au-Prince: Centre Challenges, 2021). On the rural economy and land tenure in the Dominican Republic at large in the early twentieth century, see Turits, *Foundations.*

6. This anti-Haitianism was variously driven by political convenience and, increasingly perhaps, racism against what elite Dominican figures considered the putative inferiority of popular practices associated with Africa (among both Haitians and Dominicans). See Anne Eller, *We Dream Together: Dominican Independence, Haiti, and the Fight for Caribbean Freedom* (Durham: Duke University Press, 2016), pp. 10, 31, 235-36; Turits, *Foundations,* p. 150. After the massacre, anti-Haitianism was made into an official discourse by the Trujillo regime through history texts authored by figures within his cabinet charged with justifying this genocidal slaughter to the Dominican public and the world at large, such as Joaquín Balaguer, *La isla al revés: Haití y el destino dominicano* (Santo Domingo: Fundación José Antonio Caro, 1983).

7. In much of the central frontier region, such as Bánica and Elías Piña, we have observed something analogous in recent years, with only sporadic state control over the movement of people and goods across the border beyond the few official checkpoints.

8. See Lauren Derby, "Haitians, Magic, and Money: *Raza* and Society in the Haitian-Dominican Borderlands, 1900–1937," *Comparative Studies in Society and History* 36, No. 3 (July 1994): pp. 488-526.

9. As the sugar and later ginger economies declined and ultimately collapsed during the first half of

the seventeenth century, the enslaved escaped in massive numbers, most into the island's vast untamed lands and hills. Their flight to freedom launched a perhaps unique trajectory in the African diaspora: a nation forged primarily by free people of African descent in a colonial society with a comparatively poor white elite, but also with continuing racial slavery—on a smaller scale—and elaborate racist laws and legal racial inequality. Richard Lee Turits, "Par-delà les plantations. Question raciale et identités collectives à Santo Domingo." *Genèses* (Paris) 66 (March 2007), esp. pp. 52-53, 59-62; Juana Gil-Bermejo García, *La española: Anotaciones históricas, 1600-1650* (Sevilla: Escuela de estudios hispano-americanos; 1983), 63-64, 63n23, 66; Michel-Rolph Trouillot, "Culture, Color, and Politics in Haiti." On colorism in the Dominican Republic, see also Ginetta Candelario, *Black Behind the Ears, Dominican Racial Identity from Museums to Beauty Shops* (Durham: Duke University Press, 2007); David Howard, *Coloring the Nation: Race and Ethnicity in the Dominican Republic* (Lynne Rienner Publishers, 2001), pp. 85-90; H. Hoetink, *Caribbean Race Relations: A Study of Two Variants* (London: Oxford University Press, 1971). On colorism elsewhere in the Caribbean and Latin America, see Colin A. Palmer, "Identity, Race, and Black Power in Independent Jamaica," in *The Modern Caribbean*, ed. Franklin W. Knight and Colin A. Palmer (Chapel Hill: Univ. of North Carolina Press, 1989), pp. 112-114, 124-126; Jack Alexander, "The Culture of Race in Middle-Class Kingston, Jamaica," *American Ethnologist* 4, no. 3 (Aug. 1977); Clara Rodríguez, "Challenging Racial Hegemony: Puerto Ricans in the United States" in *Race*, ed. Steven Gregory and Roger Sanjek (New Brunswick: Rutgers Univ. Press, 1996), pp. 131-145 and 146-174; Edward Telles, "Mixed and Unequal: New Perspectives on Brazilian Ethnoracial Relations," *Pigmentocracies: Ethnicity, Race, and Color in Latin America* (Chapel Hill, NC: University of North Carolina Press, 2014), pp. 172-217. For interpretations of race and racism in terms of constructs of *mestizaje* in diverse Latin American spaces, see Norman E. Whitten and Arlene Torres, "Introduction," *Blackness in Latin America: Social Dynamics and Cultural Transformations*, vol. 1, ed. Norman E. Whitten and Arlene Torres (Bloomington: Indiana University Press, 1998), pp. 3-33.

10. See Sabine Cadeau, "Natives of the Border: Ethnic Haitians and the Law in the Dominican Republic, 1920-1961" (PhD dissertation, Univ. of Chicago, 2015). Superb new research has been done in recent years on the Haitian Massacre, the frontier provinces, and anti-Haitianism in the Dominican Republic, such as Edward Paulino, *Dividing Hispaniola: The Dominican Republic's Border Campaign Against Haiti, 1930-1961* (Pittsburgh: Univ. of Pittsburgh Press, 2016) and Lorgia García-Peña, *The Borders of Dominicanidad: Race, Nation, and Archives of Contradiction* (Durham: Duke Univ. Press, 2016). See also *Masacre de 1937, 80 años después: Reconstruyendo la memoria*, ed. Matías Bosch Carcuro (Santo Domingo: Fundación Juan Bosch, 2018).

11. Richard Lee Turits, "Slavery and the Pursuit of Freedom in Sixteenth-Century Santo Domingo," *Oxford Research Encyclopedias: Latin American History*, 2019; Domingo Fernández Domingo Fernández Navarrete, "Relación de las ciudades, villas y lugares de la isla de Sancto Domingo y Española," April 30, 1681, in *Clío* (May-June 1934), 91-95; Turits, "Par-delà les plantations"; Laurent Dubois and Richard Lee Turits, *Freedom Roots: Histories from the Caribbean* (Chapel Hill: Univ. of North Carolina Press, 2019), chaps. 2 and 4; Turits, *Foundations*, chaps. 1-3.

12. Dubois and Turits, *Freedom Roots*. See also Peter Hudson, *Bankers and Empire: How Wall Street Colonized the Caribbean* (Chicago: University of Chicago Press, 2017).

13. See Turits, "A World Destroyed." On the Trujillo regime, see Turits, *Foundations*, and Lauren Derby, *The Dictator's Seduction: Politics and the Popular Imagination in the Era of Trujillo* (Durham: Duke University Press, 2009).

14. Anne Eller, *We Dream Together: Dominican Independence, Haiti, and the Fight for Caribbean Freedom* (Durham: Duke University Press, 2016); Andrew J. Walker, "Strains of Unity: Emancipation, Property, and the Post-Revolutionary State in Haitian Santo Domingo, 1822–1844" (PhD diss., Univ. of Michigan, 2018).

15. See, for instance, Emilio Rodríguez Demorizi, *Invasiones haitianas de 1801, 1805 y 1822* (Ciudad Trujillo: Editora del Caribe, 1955) and Manuel de Jesús Troncoso de la Concha, *La ocupación de Santo Domingo por Haití* (Ciudad Trujillo: La Nación, 1942).

16. Walker and Eller's work draws upon and substantiates the portraits of popular backing for Haitian annexation on the Spanish-speaking side of the island offered by the important Haitian intellectual Jean Price-Mars in the 1950s and by Dominican historians Emilio Cordero Michel and Franklyn Franco the following decade. See Jean Price-Mars, *La República de Haití y la República Dominicana: Diversos aspectos de un problema histórico, geográfico y etnológico* (Port-au-Prince: publisher not identified, 1953, 1958; Emilio Cordero Michel, *La revolución haitiana y Santo Domingo* (Santo Domingo: Editora Nacional, 1968); Franklyn Franco, *Los negros, los mulatos y la nación dominicana* (Santo Domingo: Editora Nacional, 1969, 1984). The first full-length treatment of the annexation period was Frank Moya Pons, *La dominación haitiana: 1822-1844*. Santiago, Dominican Republic: Univ. Católica Madre y Maestra, 1978). Those Dominicans who opposed annexation surely made the decision not to resist with arms for two reasons: lack of popular support for resistance and the strength and prestige of the Haitian armed forces that had defeated all the major armies of Europe (British and Spanish as well as French) during the Haitian Revolution.

17. Price-Mars, *La República de Haití*, esp. pp. 141-142; María Cecilia Ulrickson, "'Esclavos que fueron' in Santo Domingo, 1768-1844" (PhD diss., University of Notre Dame, 2018), chapter 5, esp. p. 182; Quisqueya Lora H., *Transición de la esclavitud al trabajo libre en Santo Domingo: El caso de Higüey* (Santo Domingo: Academia Dominicana de la Historia, 2012). On the traditional way of life and aspirations of the Dominican peasantry for free access to land and for a counter-plantation economy and society, see Turits, *Foundations*, chapters 1 & 2.

18. Eller, *We Dream Together*, p. 25.

19. Quisqueya Lora H., "La construcción de Haití en el imaginario dominicano del siglo XIX," in *República Dominicana y Haití: El derecho a vivir*," ed. Juan Bosch et al. (Santo Domingo: Fundación Juan Bosch, 2014), 188-189 [quotations]; Víctor M. Puente Adames, "José María Imbert, líder de la 'Batalla' de Santiago," *El Caribe*, March 26, 2021.

20. Laurent Dubois, *Haiti: The Aftershocks of History* (New York: Metropolitan Books, 2012), 147-49.

21. Lora H., "La construcción de Haití," 200.

22. Dubois, *Haití*, 148-49.

23. Lora H., "La construcción de Haití," 174-75, 182-185.

24. Eller, *We Dream Together*; Rodríguez Demorizi, *Invasiones haitianas*; Troncoso de la Concha, *La ocupación*; Anne Eller, "Rumors of Slavery: Defending Emancipation in a Hostile Caribbean," *American Historical Review* 122, No. 3 (June 2017): pp. 653-679; Turits, "Slavery and the Pursuit of Freedom"; oral histories conducted by Richard Turits in the Dominican Republic, 1992.

25. Eller, *We Dream Together*, pp. 200-201.

26. Edward D. Melillo, "The First Green Revolution: Debt Peonage and the Making of the Nitrogen Fertilizer Trade, 1840-1930," *American Historical Review* 117, No. 4 (October 2012): pp. 1028-1060.

27. Ginger Thompson, "Immigrant Laborers from Haiti Are Paid with Abuse in the Dominican Republic," *New York Times*, Nov. 20, 2005; Aida Alami, "Between Hate, Hope, and Help: Haitians in the Dominican Republic," *New York Review of Books*, NYR Daily, Aug. 13, 2018; Amy Serrano, *The Sugar Babies* (Miami: Siren Studios, 2007); Amelia Hintzen, *De la Masacre a la Sentencia 168-13: Apuntes para la historia de la segregación de los haitianos y sus descendientes en República Dominicana* (Santo Domingo: Fundación Juan Bosch, 2017). On the power and intensity of racial, ethnic, or religious prejudice flowing from its associations with "other socially significant cleavages in society," see Verena Martínez-Alier, *Marriage, Class and Colour in Nineteenth-Century Cuba: A Study of Racial Attitudes and Sexual Values*

in a Slave Society (Ann Arbor, Univ. of Michigan Press, 1974), pp. 6, 75-76. See also see Barbara Fields, "Slavery, Race, and Ideology in the United States of America," *New Left Review*, 181 (May-June 1990): pp. 95-118.

28. Wooding, "Haitian Immigrants;" Amelia Hintzen, "Historical Forgetting and the Dominican Constitutional Tribunal," *Journal of Haitian Studies* 20, no. 1 (Spring 2014): pp. 108-116; Jennifer L. Schoaff, "The Right to a Haitian Name and a Dominican Nationality: *La Sentencia* (TC 168-13) and the Politics of Recognition and Belonging," *Journal of Haitian Studies* 22, No. 2 (Fall 2016): pp. 58-82; Alami, "Between Hate, Hope, and Help." See also Linda Kerber, "Stateless in the Americas," *Dissent*, Nov. 12, 2013.

29. A. Naomi Paik, *Rightlessness: Testimony and Redress in U.S. Prison Camps since World War II* (Chapel Hill: University of North Carolina Press, 2016), esp. pp. 6. See also Paul Farmer, *AIDS and Accusation: Haiti and the Geography of Blame* (Berkeley: University of California Press, 2006); Paul Farmer, *Pathologies of Power: Health, Human Rights, and the New War on the Poor* (Berkeley: University of California Press, 2004); Carl Lindskoog, "How the Haitian Refugee Crisis Led to the Indefinite Detention of Immigrants," *Washington Post*, April 9, 2018 and his *Detain and Punish: Haitian Refugees and the Rise of the World's Largest Immigration Detention System* (Gainesville: University of Florida Press, 2018); and Melanie Díaz and Timothy Keen, "How US Private Prisons Profit from Immigrant Detention," Washington, DC: Council on Hemispheric Affairs, May 12, 2015, http://www.coha.org/how-us-private-prisons-profit-from-immigrant-detention/.

Azúcar Amargo

Rosa Iris Diendomi Álvarez

INTRODUCCIÓN

Es tan rico tomar una taza de café, o de té endulzado con azúcar, es azúcar extraído de la caña que con su dulce sabor nos anima a iniciar el día, a continuar la jornada o sólo recibir un poco más energía.

Ese dulce que provocó que poderosos poderes económicos movieran miles de hombres y mujeres de la parte poniente de Hispaniola a la parte del oriente, con el fin de saciar la ambición de algunos enriqueciéndolos con el amargo dolor que dejaba la venta del dulce azúcar de caña.

Se puede ver cómo a través del tiempo y la historia un pueblo reniega de sus raíces y se perpetúa el estigma y discriminación a una determinada población y sus descendientes por creerlos inferiores, haciendo uso de todos los mecanismos posibles para normalizar y legalizar tales prácticas desde los distintos espacios del Estado, y acentuándose más en determinados gobiernos, es la opinión desde el testimonio de una descendiente de migrantes, activista y defensora de derechos humanos.

En medio de esa amarga historia, se encuentran espacios de solidaridad, que fortalecen y abren puertas de acompañamiento y lograr hacer posible que las voces de miles de invisibilizados esté presente en espacios internacionales, es una bendición del universo y la fuerza que nos dan nuestros ancestros.

Con este breve ensayo quiero compartir un testimonio desde lo más profundo del alma, el precio de aquel dulce con sabor amargo en nuestras vidas.

Este dulce amargo que crecía en comunidades aisladas, que durante 6 o 8 meses del año mantenía encendidas las chimeneas de los ingenios azucareros que producían toneladas del dulce que era exportada al extranjero, ese dulce que fue la base de la economía de la República Dominicana por décadas. Sin importar el amargo proceso por el que pasaban aquellos hombres de piel negra, piel que era bañada por el rocío de la madrugada, esa piel negra tatuada por las heridas de las filosas hojas de caña, que la única cura que recibía era ser amarrada con un pedazo de trapo y seguir la jornada.

Sí, esos hombres que bajo el refulgente sol elevaban sus brazos, machete en mano, para cortar cada tronco de caña, hasta convertirlo en toneladas, aquellos que en sus frentes bañadas de sudor brillaba el sol, miraban a lo lejos a ver si veían venir por el carril a la mujer o su hija con el bocado de harina batida, o los víveres con pica pica o arenque, o tal vez la vendedora con el pan con mamba (mantequilla de maní) con el trago de café, ese café que era endulzado con el resultado de su arduo trabajo. Cuando caía el sol así iba cayendo el silencio en los cañaverales, y el camino de regreso a casa se convertía en la congregación de hombres en caravana al batey, sin importar que una pequeña habitación podía estar compartida hasta por diez o más hombres, si tenían familias (esposas, hijos) una o dos habitaciones representaban toda su casa (sala, cocina, dormitorio etc.).

Se escucha el rechinar de la lima sobre el machete, sobre la mocha (*cript, cript, craft*) preparando la herramienta para el siguiente día de trabajo, largas filas en la única toma de agua, los galones en sus manos, conversaciones de como fue el día, uno dice que hoy la caña no pesó, otro cuenta de cómo su compañero perdió dos dedos en un accidente mientras cortaba caña, pero el capataz solo le dijo que los médicos no volvían hasta el lunes y apenas era viernes, así contando sus tristezas se preparaban para enfrentar un nuevo día de trabajo.

No había mucha diferencia entre un día y otro en el batey, llegar al campo de caña entre las 3:00 y 4:00 de la madrugada para levantar, o cortar uno o más viajes de caña, mientras los gritos del capataz "¡vamos a trabajar, haitianos!," "la brigada de Tipiti, terminen, que se van con el mayordomo para otra división del batey Porvenir"... así disponían de la vida y el trabajo de los haitianos en el batey, algunos eran vigilados mientras cortaban la planta del dulce amargo, para evitar que se escaparan.

Así se fue tejiendo la historia de nuestros ancestros haitianos, traídos a la República Dominicana para buscar mejor vida, bajo ese acuerdo entre gobernantes donde eran prácticamente vendidos de una manera vulgar.

Y años después fueron acusados de invasores, ese mismo Estado que compró la mano de obra de esos hombres, no les importó que eran negros, pobres, poco letrados para explotar su fuerza de trabajo. Ese Estado y las empresas azucareras olvidan que fueron ellos mismos quienes trajeron a los migrantes haitianos, y los confinaron en bateyes para enriquecer al Estado con la producción de azúcar, sí, esa azúcar que ha costado tantas vidas, sangre y sudor.

Ese dulce que ha costado sueños, vidas suspendidas y al final ha dejado un amargo en nuestras vidas. El Estado, que detrás de cada plantación de caña tenía un batey, hoy rechaza a los descendientes de esos migrantes negros haitianos, olvida que llegó a un punto que, en lugar de cumplir con su contrato de devolver a los braceros a su país, prefirió moverlos de un ingenio a otro durante décadas, sintiéndose dueño de esos hombres y mujeres negro/as. Pero no se conformó con eso, en más de una ocasión sigue con la idea de blanquear la raza, ignorando los propios orígenes de los perpetradores, creyéndose blancos europeos en un país de mayoría negra, descendientes de negros africanos traídos por la fuerza a la Isla de La Española.

La nueva generación tiene un reto ante la discriminacion estructural y el juego de una historia mal contada.

LA MATANZA DEL PEREJIL EN 1937

El país dominicano (República Dominicana) ha crecido en medio de una sociedad con múltiples complejos que poco ayudan a la inclusión y respeto de lo diferente. Es un país donde la dignidad humana en ocasiones parece inexistente, y el poder se impone a las leyes y al derecho. La realidad está que, en la década de 1937, costó miles de vidas de migrantes haitianos y sus descendientes sin olvidar que murieron también miles de dominicanos bajo el mandato del entonces gobernante, el dictador Rafael Leónidas Trujillo.

El exceso de poder combinado con aires de superioridad (al creerse blanco europeo) provoca que al tirano se lo ocurrió querer blanquear la raza, sin importar el costo humano, una orden plagada de prejuicio, alimentada con el discurso de una supuesta invasión por presencia de migrantes haitianos en la zona fronteriza entre la República Dominicana y Haití.

La orden fue dada. Se armó la cacería, un despliegue de militares salen en nombre de la patria a avasallar a negros indefensos, que el color de su piel y su rasgo afro fueron el principal medio de identificación, o la famosa frase PEREJIL. Miles de hombres y mujeres que cruzaron la frontera para trabajar les quitaron la vida por el "delito" de ser negros y pobres.

Ese dictador quien sólo quería congraciarse más con la élite de la época no la pensó dos veces, no le importó que el también era descendiente de haitianos, de negros, tal vez no recordó a su abuela. Fue la noche del genocidio inolvidable, cuantos huérfanos, cuantos huyeron para salvar sus vidas, cuantas familias separadas, algunos con apellidos afrancesados los dominicanizaron o españolizaron. Aún se respira la crueldad de ese momento.

A más de 80 años no se ha reparado el daño, ni el Estado ha sido sancionado por un crimen que cobró miles de vidas, un crimen de odio racial, que tiene a un País condenado a rechazar sus orígenes, a desconocerse. La matanza de 1937 creó dos grupos en la parte oriente de Hispaniola.

Octubre debería tener un día para declararlo de luto nacional en honor a los miles que cayeron a manos del racismo y la discriminación; la nueva generación conoce muy poco esta parte de la historia.

Tenemos una República Dominicana que se inventa tantos colores de piel como sea posible, pero no acepta el negro. Al menos el negro es tratado diferente y en las escuelas se reproduce el patrón en función del color de la piel; le dicen trigueños, indios, jabao, morenito cepilla'o, entre otros, pero muchas veces se refieren al negro en términos despectivos.

Dos pueblos hermanos que comparten una isla, con una historia que los une por siempre, hoy están minados de odio, intolerancia y prejuicios. Hablar de los derechos del migrante haitiano y sus descendientes en la parte oriente de la Hispaniola es estar condenado a ser un traidor a la patria, es ser señalado como pro-haitiano. Es tan increíble que los niveles de intolerancia al día de hoy puede hasta costar la integridad física. Tal es el ejemplo de Tulile, un migrante haitiano que fue colgado en el parque Ercilia Pepín de Santiago en 2014.

PARALELOS ENTRE EL 1937 Y EL 2013

La justificación de la matanza de 1937 fue la supuesta invasión haitiana, por lo que el dictador Trujillo quería "blanquear la raza" sí, aquella que es producto de una mezcla, aquella que rechazan por el color de su piel, que es el de la mayoría de sus habitantes, hombres negros y mujeres negras, descendientes de esclavos africanos de hace más de 500 años.

La Masacre del Perejil es un capítulo triste, de luto y mucho dolor en la República Dominicana, lástima que la mayoría ignora este hecho y más de 80 años después se continúa con la negación de nuestra negritud.

En aquel momento la banda de Trujillo distinguía entre el dominicano y el haitiano por el color de la piel, repetir la palabra de "perejil", no ha cambiado mucho la práctica, al día de hoy, el argumento sigue siendo el mismo.

La muerte por cuestión de origen o color recobra vida desde las alta esferas del Estado en septiembre del año 2013, cuando el Tribunal Constitucional le quita la nacionalidad dominicana a más de 200,000 dominicanos de ascendencia haitiana. Esta vez el genocidio es civil contra los descendientes de quienes sufrieron el genocidio físico.

El Tribunal Constitucional llamado a tutelar y proteger los derechos fundamentales de todos los ciudadanos, el 23 de septiembre 2013, volvió a imponer el "blanqueo de la raza" eliminándolos del registro civil. Y es curioso que en un país producto de mezcla de varias nacionalidades solo resulten perjudicados los descendientes de migrantes haitianos. Los hijos y nietos de aquellos que fueron traídos por Trujillo y otros gobernantes para cortar la caña de azúcar, los mismos que no fueron regresados a Haití, y el Estado dominicano los movía como esclavos de un batey a otro, de un ingenio a otro (factorías de azúcar). Fueron los hijos de aquellos que estaban confinados en el batey para producir riquezas y mantener la economía de la República Dominicana en los años dorados del azúcar.

Esos jóvenes, que por tener apellidos "raros," les negaban un duplicado de acta de nacimiento o les negaban la inscripción para su cédula al cumplir mayoría de edad. Ellos no podían continuar con sus estudios secundarios o universitarios, los mismos que la sentencia dijo que no son dominicanos los nacidos desde 1929 al 2013.

No fue con los descendientes de españoles, o con los descendientes de árabes, o palestinos. Solo fue contra nosotros, por el origen de nuestros padres o abuelos, nosotros, los que éramos bajados de los autobuses (guaguas) si no presentábamos la cédula, los que éramos detenidos por la policía o migración por tener perfil sospechoso (negro y benbóm). Fue contra los que no podíamos registrar a nuestros hijos porque la Junta Central Electoral secuestró nuestros documentos. Fue contra los descendientes de haitianos a quienes se sometieron a ser extranjeros en su propio país.

Esa imposición de la arbitrariedad, de querernos dañar, desproteger y seguir violando nuestros derechos; llamó la atención del mundo, la comunidad internacional volcó su atención a la República Dominicana.

El dulce por el que trajeron a los migrantes haitianos había cesado, ahora solo queda lo amargo de envejecientes indocumentados, sin una pensión, "sin derechos", solo los sueños truncados de sus hijos y nietos que son tratados como el bagazo de la caña de azúcar.

Se repite lo sufrido en la matanza, por un Estado que ha promovido y permitido un racismo estructural por décadas.

Al amparo de reclamos y protestas, la nueva generación procura la reinvindicación de sus derechos, y pese a los ultranacionalistas y el Estado indiferente, ellos continúan la lucha para devolver la nacionalidad a los descendientes de haitianos, que desafortunadamente tras la sentencia 168-13 deja en condición de apátridas a más de 150,000 personas.

Nos han dividido en diferentes grupos para confundir a la opinión pública y seguir diciendo que somos extranjeros, pero mientras más nos dividen para negarnos una solución, más nos multiplicamos en conciencia y tomamos acciónes para revertir nuestra situación. La resiliencia es una de nuestras cualidades.

UN GRAN ENCUENTRO

En la primera semana de octubre 2014, el padre Mario Serrano se comunica con el Movimiento Reconoci.do y le informa de un encuentro en Santiago en el que debían delegar a dos representantes para asistir al encuentro. Fueron comisionadas Epifanía St. Charles y yo, Rosa Iris Diendomi. Ese domingo conocimos a Frontera de Luces, junto a otros compañeros de luchas, y también conocimos a Rana, Kimberly, Julia Alvarez y su esposo, y a DeAndra; después recordaré a otros integrantes que sus nombres se me escapan por el momento.

Al conocer que hacen, por qué estaban en la República Dominicana y su interés en conocer el espacio que articula a la mayoría de los desnacionalizados, fue el inicio de un ciclo de caminar juntos de la mano.

Justo un año después de la sentencia 168-13, nos tocó compartir con Frontera de Luces la realidad de ser desnacionalizados y como el ser apátridas tiene repercusiones en nuestras vidas. Fue un gran encuentro lleno de solidaridad, de escuchar y de empatía. . . . Las lágrimas al compartir lo que vivía nuestra gente, lo complicado de entender lo que estaban haciendo las autoridades, llenó la mañana de ese domingo de propósitos y unidad.

Los profundos silencios en medio de cada testimonio y después de otro, mostraban la indignación y el dolor, miradas cargadas de deseos de aportar una solución, era realmente de hermanas y hermanos que sentían ese dolor y la desesperación que vivíamos en ese momento.

Seguido con preguntas y ver qué acciones se podían seguir desarrollando, allí se sembraba una semilla que muy pronto comenzó a dar sus frutos, ya no estábamos solo/as, se sumaban más voces, posiblemente más acciones que podrían ir más allá de nuestras fronteras. Recibimos cada abrazo, cada palabra, sabiendo que ahora podríamos hacer más. Ya no éramos los casos aislados que decía el gobierno, ahora los muchachos del batey quienes estaban sufriendo lo amargo de aquel dulce tenían más apoyo. Ahora nuestras voces transcenderían las fronteras.

NO FUE CASUALIDAD

Me considero muy creyente, y sé que todo sucede con un propósito, no fue una casualidad conocer a Frontera de Luces, en aquel octubre de 2014, que marcó una alianza de colaboración incondicional y de hermandad.

Para la última semana de octubre del 2014, la Comisión Interamericana ya tendría una sección y uno de los temas era la situación de los dominicanos de ascendencia haitiana en la República Dominicana. Allí estaría la sociedad civil y el Estado, pero sin embargo los afectados no tenían posibilidad de participar en ese espacio. No contábamos con los recursos económicos ni visado para participar y las organizaciones locales no tenían la posibilidad de apoyar en esa ocasión.

El 16 de octubre de 2014, Epifania y yo decidimos enviar un correo a Rana Dotson, una de las representantes de Fronteras de Luces, explicando nuestro interés y la necesidad de participar en ese espacio.

La respuesta fue "vamos a buscar apoyo para que puedan estar presentes" y fue sorprendente ver que, en menos de dos semanas, con el apoyo de Fronteras de Luces fue posible dar nuestro apoyo en la audiencia temática en Washington D.C.

Dos mujeres descendientes de haitianos que ni siquiera tenían una visa . . . con el apoyo y la solidaridad de la hermandad de Fronteras de Luces, nuestras voces en representación de nuestro pueblo, de nuestra gente, fueron escuchadas. El Estado ha tenido que ver que no estamos solo/as, que hoy nuestras voces son escuchadas más allá de los límites que tradicionalmente se imponían.

Frontera de Luces estuvo con nosotros, nos acompañó en cada acción, en reuniones, al impartir discursos, y cabildeo. No fue casualidad. Había un propósito; el universo nos juntó para cumplir con una de tantas misiones que juntos hemos desarrollado y continuaremos desarrollando. Este es sólo uno de varios testimonios que podríamos citar sobre la colaboración recibida de parte de Fronteras de Luces.

En Dios, no existen las coincidencias. Hay propósitos de unir, fortalecer y caminar juntos buscando el bien común libre de prejuicios, estigmas y discriminación.

CONCLUSIÓN

Se han logrado cambios a costa de un alto precio, pero el desafío continúa, hasta que no nos libremos de los fantasmas que nos hacen ver en el "negro": al enemigo, al peligroso, al ser inferior. Continuarán matando a sus compatriotas y negando la libertad y el respeto a aquellos que solo han aportado para hacer al país, la República Dominicana, más rica, no sólo económicamente, sino también en cultura, identidad y diversidad.

Si tan solo el Estado y sus élites pudieran entender que la diversidad nos enriquece, que la República Dominicana es un país de mayoría negra, aunque pase otro siglo más, negándoselo a sí mismos.

Al final la sentencia 168-13, aún nos deja esta tarea pendiente de restituir la nacionalidad plena a los dominicanos de ascendencia haitiana quienes han sido divididos en los siguientes perfiles:

Grupo A: los inscritos en el registro civil no les permiten acceder o niegan devolverles sus documentos.

Grupo A1: hijos de personas de grupo A que no han podido ser registrados porque el Estado les retiene los documentos de los padres, pese a que han pasado más de 6 años de una ley que ordena la devolución pura y simple.

Grupo B: hijos de padre y madre haitiano que no fueron inscritos en el registro civil. (163,000 según la ENI 2017)

Grupo B PNRE: 8,755 aplicaron al plan de naturalización especial, solo se les dio un plazo 180 días para registrarse; cuatro (4) años después, aún no han recibido respuesta. (El Estado dominicano les entregó un carnet que dice: "nació en República Dominicana, pero es de nacionalidad haitiana").

Grupo C: inscritos en el libro de extranjería. Les entregan una acta que no indica nacionalidad, por ende están en un limbo. (Según la ENI 2017 son aproximadamente 75,000)

Grupo D: los hijos de parejas mixtas que no deberían tener ninguna limitación, pero cuando la madre es haitiana o no posee documento, el niño no puede ser registrado (aproximadamente 81,590 según la ENI 2017).

Dada la situación actual, el Estado no presenta mecanismos para resolver dicha situación. Es más que evidente que existe apátridía en la República Dominicana.

Juntos podemos hacer los cambios que nuestra sociedad necesita: desaprender para aprender y abrazar la inclusión, respetar los derechos humanos—y amarnos con orgullo y sin miedo.[1]

Nota

1. Gracias a cada integrante de Frontera de Luces que hacen posible seguir adelante, quienes abrazan el amor, la solidaridad y el compromiso. He tenido el placer de tratar de cerca a Rana Dotson y a Edward Paulino, quienes dejan en lo que hacen la impronta de continuar adelante. Gracias, Edward, por extender la invitación a compartir con este testimonio, y por ser tan motivador y admirable. El título de este ensayo, "Azúcar Amargo," está intencionalmente mal escrito. La ortografía correcta, gramaticalmente, sería "Azúcar Amarga." El término surgió así, con la "o," entre el 2007-2008 cuando yo y otros trataban de defender las vidas de nuestros antepasados como trabajadores explotados en los bateyes; así exigiendo que el gobierno dominicano les pague las pensiones a ellos y también a los de mi generación quienes a través de leyes y sentencias han tenido sus derechos de ciudadanía dominicana abrogados paulatinamente.

Construir memoria, hacer pedagogía del futuro

Una apuesta por la emancipación en el mismo trayecto del sol[1]

Matías Bosch Carcuro

UNA ISLA ENTRE LA SOLIDARIDAD Y LA IDEOLOGÍA DEL ODIO

El pueblo dominicano y el pueblo haitiano comparten lazos de perenne y resistente solidaridad. Aunque la independencia de 1844 con que fue creada la República Dominicana se hizo en separación y guerra contra el poder haitiano, ello no limitó ni antes ni después ese vínculo profundo.

La isla entera, conquistada por el naciente imperialismo de España en 1492, sufrió los embates del colonialismo. Los cacicazgos—disposiciones territoriales de la sociedad taína que abarcaban a toda la isla—enfrentaron la violencia conquistadora, padeciendo sus consecuencias.

Al respecto relató Bartolomé de las Casas[2]:

(. . .) Los cristianos, con sus caballos y espadas y lanzas comienzan a hacer matanzas y crueldades extrañas en ellos. Entraban en los pueblos ni dejaban niños, ni viejos ni mujeres preñadas ni paridas que no desbarrigaban y hacían pedazos, como si dieran en unos corderos metidos en sus apriscos. Hacían apuestas sobre quién de una cuchillada abría el hombre por medio o le cortaba la cabeza de un piquete o le descubría las entrañas. Tomaban las criaturas de las tetas de las madres por las piernas y daban de cabeza con ellas en las peñas. Otros daban con ellas en ríos por las espaldas riendo y burlando, y cayendo en el agua decían: "¿Bullís, cuerpo de tal?". Otras criaturas metían a espada con las madres juntamente y todos cuantos delante de sí hallaban. Hacían unas horcas largas que juntasen casi los pies a la tierra, y de trece en trece, a honor y reverencia de nuestro Redentor y de los doce apóstoles, poniéndoles leña y fuego los quemaban vivos. Otros ataban o liaban todo el cuerpo de paja seca; pegándoles fuego así los quemaban. Otros, y todos los que querían tomar a vida, cortábanles ambas manos y dellas llevaban colgando, y decíanles: "Andad con cartas," conviene a saber: "Llevá las nuevas a las gentes que estaban huidas por los montes".

Comúnmente mataban a los señores y nobles desta manera: que hacían unas parrillas de varas sobre horquetas y atábanlos en ellas y poníanles por debajo fuego manso, para que poco a poco, dando alaridos, en aquellos tormentos desesperados se les salían las ánimas. Una vez vide que teniendo en las parrillas quemándose cuatro o cinco principales señores (y aun pienso que había dos o tres pares de parrillas donde quemaban otros) y porque daban muy grandes gritos y daban pena al capitán o le impidían el sueño, mandó que los ahogasen, y el alguacil, que era peor que verdugo, que los quemaba (y sé cómo se llamaba y aun sus parientes conocí en Sevilla) no quiso ahogallos, antes les metió con sus manos palos en las bocas para que no sonasen, y atizóles el fuego hasta que se asaron de espacio como él quería.

Yo vide todas las cosas arriba dichas y muchas otras infinitas, y porque toda la gente que huir podía se encerraba en los montes y subía a las sierras huyendo de hombres tan inhumanos, tan sin piedad y tan feroces bestias, extirpadores y capitales enemigos del linaje humano, enseñaron y amaestraron lebreles, perros bravísimos que en viendo un indio lo hacían pedazos en un credo, y mejor arremetían a él y lo comían que si fuera un puerco. Estos perros hicieron grandes estragos y carnecerías. Y porque algunas veces, raras y pocas, mataban los indios algunos cristianos con justa razón y santa justicia, hicieron ley entre sí que por un cristiano que los indios matasen habían los cristianos de matar cien indios.

La Isla de La Española (Hispaniola) era entonces parte de la frontera imperial española. Los esclavos traídos desde África—una vez exterminados los pueblos originarios— emprenderían sublevaciones muy pronto, en el siglo XVI. En la región de la isla que hoy es República Dominicana ocurrió la primera rebelión, a punto de cumplir 500 años de realizada.

También establecerían *manieles*, comunidades de esclavos que se liberaban y apartaban del dominio conquistador, estableciendo sociedades autónomas y autorreguladas. En 1697, con la negociación mediante la cual España cedió la parte oeste de la isla a Francia, empieza el trazado de nuevas fronteras a lo interno de la isla, con sus determinaciones económicas, lingüísticas, raciales y políticas.

La República de Haití, independiente desde 1804, empezó a gobernar en toda la Isla en 1822. Antes, el lado este, que había estado en poder de España y de Francia, se había independizado a fines de 1821 y se autodenominó Estado del Haití Español, y luego buscó afiliarse a la Gran Colombia impulsada por Simón Bolívar. No hubo consenso en qué tipo de independencia y en relación con qué bloque establecerla. En 1822 se izó la bandera haitiana e inició el gobierno de Boyer en toda la isla.

El régimen de Boyer, que llevó la abolición de la esclavitud a todo el territorio isleño, fue derivando en el abuso del poder tanto en el Oeste como en el Este, combinado con su colapso económico. La declaración de independencia dominicana y lo que se conoce como la guerra domínico-haitiana, llevada a cabo en cuatro campañas entre 1844 y 1856, en realidad no fue una guerra entre pueblos, sino entre caudillos y ejércitos. Incluso no hubo enfrentamientos violentos hasta entrado el mes de marzo de 1844.

El historiador dominicano Franklin Franco explicó que era imposible que el ejército dominicano, recién constituido, derrotara con tanta ventaja al ejército haitiano en las primeras batallas de 1844, dado que este era más numeroso, mejor entrenado y armado. La explicación, para Franco, reside en que la soldadesca haitiana no tenía convicción ni voluntad para hacer esa guerra, hastiados de los abusos del régimen de Boyer, y que fueron arrastrados simplemente por sus jefes y los intereses de estos. Los dominicanos, por su lado, estaban motivados por el objetivo de la independencia (Franco). Ya un año antes, en 1843, el presidente Boyer había sido derrocado en la sublevación del Sur de Haití: el rechazo al régimen imperante atravesaba toda la isla.

En Haití Boyer fue derrocado; Juan Pablo Duarte y los independistas dominicanos impulsaron de manera definitiva la independencia dominicana, que más tarde quedaría tensionada por las visiones contradictorias de caudillos, intereses y potencias extranjeras. Los tres Padres de la Patria dominicana serían víctimas de esas pugnas: Duarte sería condenado al destierro, Sánchez sería fusilado y Mella moriría en plena guerra de la Restauración, mientras Bobadilla y luego Santana y Báez administraban el poder y el país sería anexado a España. A su vez, Estados Unidos desplegaba sus intereses en ambos lados de la isla (Price Mars).

Mientras tanto, se desarrollaba lo que según Moya Pons podría llamarse un "antihaitianismo histórico," que luego mutaría a un "antihaitianismo de Estado" (Moya Pons).

El primero, según Moya Pons, surge y se sostiene con la evolución real de las dos naciones, empezando con "las malas relaciones que sostenían franceses y españoles en el siglo 18 en la isla de Santo Domingo". Con la guerra de Independencia, que abarca más de una década de sucesión de conflictos bélicos, aparece el antihaitianismo de Estado, ya que

> el Estado dominicano hace uso de la memoria colectiva, de los temores de la guerra y de los horrores de las invasiones de principios de siglo, y convierte esa memoria en material de propaganda de guerra para sostener vivo el espíritu bélico dominicano que lucha por su independencia.

Pero, como advertiría el poeta nacional e historiador dominicano Pedro Mir, el verdadero problema puede estar en otro lado, especialmente en los intereses de quienes, luego de las independencias, tomaron el poder y, en el caso de la República Dominicana, mientras se presentaban como nacionalistas y antihaitianos perseguían la anexión del país a España o a Estados Unidos:

> Las luchas contra Haití representaron un doble papel: al mismo tiempo que frustraban o entorpecían las tentativas anexionistas, servían a la acción anexionista dominicana como bandera para reclamar ardientemente la injerencia extranjera, en base a una supuesta incapacidad del pueblo dominicano para sostener su soberanía, a pesar de las reiteradas y concluyentes victorias militares contra las huestes haitianas.

Más tarde, Haití, el primer país independiente de América y la primera república negra del mundo, ayudaría a los dominicanos en su lucha por la Restauración de la independencia ante España y contra la tiranía de Pedro Santana entre 1861 y 1865. El presidente

Geffrard ofreció colaboración, y allí encontraron acogida tanto Gregorio Luperón como Francisco del Rosario Sánchez (Paraison).

Los guerrilleros y luchadores nacionalistas contra la primera ocupación norteamericana (entre 1915 y 1934 en Haití y entre 1916 y 1925 en la República Dominicana) colaborarían entre uno y otro lado de la frontera. El héroe internacionalista dominicano Gregorio Urbano Gilbert intentaría unirse a los combatientes haitianos *cacos* en 1915, y luego se destacaría enfrentando a los invasores norteamericanos en su ciudad de San Pedro de Macorís el 10 de diciembre de 1916 (McPherson).

En 1947, el gobierno haitiano ayudó con dinero y equipos al proyecto armado del exilio antitrujillista que saldría de Cayo Confites, en Cuba. En 1965, cuando Estados Unidos volvió a invadir a Santo Domingo, combatientes haitianos tuvieron una valiosa participación y aportaron varios mártires caídos en suelo dominicano, recordándose a Jacques Viau Renaud como poeta y defensor de la soberanía dominicana, junto a Lionel Vieux, Jean Sateur, entre otros, destacándose en la armería de la Revolución constitucionalista, el comando B3 (*El Día*) y la Operación Lazo de rescate del Palacio Nacional el 19 de mayo de 1965.

Más tarde, en 2010, al ocurrir el terremoto devastador en Haití, la ayuda dominicana fue la primera en llegar. En un conmovedor mar de solidaridad, miles de dominicanos se movilizaron a través de la frontera para asistir a las víctimas, y la República Dominicana fue el primer y más grande centro de acogida de los desplazados. El presidente haitiano, René Préval, en aquel trágico momento declaró:

> El presidente dominicano, Leonel Fernández, ha sido el primero en presentarse y llegó con un gran contingente de apoyo. Además de la importante cooperación humanitaria, se comprometió a ayudarnos en lo que ahora constituye una de nuestras prioridades que es reestablecer las telecomunicaciones, la energía eléctrica y la comunicación terrestre. Gracias a los esfuerzos del gobierno dominicano hemos comenzado a reestablecer estos servicios. (*Diario Libre*)

Pero el odio, el miedo y la sospecha entre ambas sociedades han sido cultivados al punto de haber sido convertidos en una doctrina, de la cual se nutre un rentable negocio de las élites políticas, mediáticas y económicas, muchas veces indistinguibles una de otra, como suele pasar en las sociedades dependientes y subordinadas, con oligarquías pequeñas y estrechamente fusionadas y supeditadas históricamente a las potencias.

Del lado este (República Dominicana) ese odio tiene un punto de origen histórico y también una clara naturaleza ideológica. Sobre el particular, resulta esclarecedor el informe que en 1931 redactó Francisco Henríquez y Carvajal, ministro de Trujillo en Haití, dirigido a la cancillería dominicana. Rafael Leónidas Trujillo, militar entrenado por EE. UU. y jefe de la guardia creada en la ocupación, iniciaba entonces una larga tiranía sanguinaria de 30 años. Dice Henríquez y Carvajal:

> Lo que precipitó sobre nuestro país la gran masa de inmigrantes haitianos fue la realización parcial del postulado financiero que sirvió de base económica a la ocupación

del territorio de la República Dominicana por las fuerzas navales norteamericanas. Ese postulado, no publicado, pero sí perfectamente conocido, fue: "tierras baratas en Santo Domingo, mano de obra barata en Haití". Y la conclusión: adquirir las tierras en Santo Domingo y trasegar hacia nuestro país la población de Haití. Ese plan empezó a ejecutarse, por un lado, con la fundación del gran central "Barahona," y por otro, con la construcción de la Carretera Central; derramándose luego por todo el país agrícola, y en todos los oficios urbanos, la gran inmigración haitiana ...

Pocos años después, el antihaitianismo de Estado, según Moya Pons, resurgiría con la masacre de 1937, y

a partir de este momento, el Estado recoge todos los contenidos del antihaitianismo histórico y los convierte en el material fundamental de la propaganda antihaitiana. Se elaboran entonces nuevas doctrinas antihaitianas, y el Estado trujillista convierte el antihaitianismo en un elemento consustancial a la misma interpretación oficial de la historia dominicana.

Explicaciones como las que ofreció Pedro Mir develan algo muy importante: la doctrina del miedo y el odio a Haití encubre y sirve como elemento de alienación del pueblo dominicano de su propia condición y sus luchas históricas; de distracción ante la verdadera agenda de intereses y propósitos de la élite que condujo política y económicamente al país al poco tiempo de conseguida la independencia, y en distintas coyunturas históricas posteriores. Permite por tanto adentrarse en el armazón y la esencia de la anatematización y estigmatización antihaitiana producidas por las élites.

Para ejemplificar lo anterior, respecto de los problemas fronterizos, diría Franklin Franco:

Tanto en la República Dominicana como en Haití, el conflicto fronterizo domínico-haitiano fue manejado de manera sutil y perversa por los intelectuales antinacionales de ambas repúblicas.

Cada vez que ocurría un incidente (...) a sus pueblos les transmitían la alarmante idea de que ello conformaba parte de todo un plan de invasión, ya de parte de los dominicanos hacia Haití o viceversa.

La reiteración de esta imagen malvada cuidadosamente manejada por los ideólogos conservadores haitianos y dominicanos, ha hecho un daño terrible a las relaciones domínico-haitianas, pues este estereotipo (el de las invasiones) fue transmitido constante y sistemáticamente durante más de años a dos pueblos compuestos por analfabetos, más de un 85 por ciento en ambos casos.

(...) Ni el pueblo haitiano ni el pueblo dominicano tuvieron nada que ver en ello; aquel fue un conflicto entre terratenientes grandes, medianos y pequeños, haitianos y dominicanos (...) quienes por décadas se disputaron, pulgada a pulgada, las tierras de la zona fronteriza.

LA MEMORIA COMO EJERCICIO NECESARIO

Septiembre de 2019. En dos lugares del mundo se prenden velas, tal vez en algunas casas, tal vez en espacios públicos. En Nueva York y en Santiago de Chile, la fecha se conmemora con el dolor de quienes vieron y recuerdan la aparición de lo más bestial de nuestras posibilidades como especie y de nuestra vida en sociedad.

En Nueva York se conmemora la muerte de miles de personas bajo un ataque terrorista que conmocionó a la Humanidad en 2001. Un ataque cuyos orígenes y propósitos todavía hoy se desconocen en buena medida, y que hizo estremecer de terror a Estados Unidos y, a través de los medios de comunicación de masas, expandir el pavor al mundo entero.

Ese terror fue inteligentemente utilizado por el aparato neoconservador para disciplinar el mundo, justificar y avalar guerras e invasiones, y el reordenamiento del poder de la administración Bush en su país y a escala internacional. El gran negocio empresarial-pentagonista, y la apropiación de riquezas extranjeras, cobró fuerza arrolladora de un solo golpe en la dirección política.

Hoy, bajo otros signos y etiquetas, como la defensa de la industria nacional, la seguridad interna o los recursos y servicios, se emprende una ofensiva en Estados Unidos que tiene como blanco a los migrantes, la escalada sobre Venezuela y Cuba, y la guerra simbólica con China. Momentos distintos en la lucha de clases que suelen tener expresión en la disputa política y, por tanto, en la disputa de sentido.

En Chile, las velas se encienden por el golpe de Estado efectuado hace 46 años. En ese acontecimiento, militares sediciosos, captados hábilmente desde el centro del poder norteamericano—el mismo que usó el terror del 11 de septiembre de 2001—bombardearon el palacio de gobierno, cayendo en combate el presidente Salvador Allende, e iniciando una ola de matanzas de dirigentes, artistas, activistas, militantes políticos; invadiendo barrios y poblaciones; deportando y desterrando; y plagando el país de campos de concentración, cárceles y centros de aniquilamiento.

Fue el proceso de disciplinamiento social. Luego, una casta civil se insertó en la estructura del gobierno golpista y paso a paso fue instaurando un orden económico y social neoliberal, bajo la égida doctrinal de la Escuela de Chicago, entregando las riquezas del país, privatizando y mercantilizando todos los bienes fundamentales, y convirtiendo la política sencillamente en imposible: la administración del Estado despojada de toda deliberación, puro carácter autoritario y cupular. Todo bien colectivo y derecho fue convertido en actividad mercantil y financiera para la acumulación de capital.

El diseño constitucional—fraudulentamente establecido—y el pacto que se fue ejecutando en la llamada "transición a la democracia" fue hábilmente pensado para que esa política se prolongara bajo la vestidura democrática: nada de lo realmente importante podría ser removido ni cambiado. *Gatopardismo* con rostro humano y progresista. La hegemonía plena del capital.

Ya Julio Anguita, extinto dirigente político de España, caracterizó al hoy gobernante Partido Socialista Obrero Español (PSOE)—fruto de la deriva socialdemócrata neoliberal y el eurocomunismo—como el brazo progresista o "columna izquierda" de la restauración capitalista, monárquica y consecuentemente neoliberal, post Franco. Y ha dicho que en

España existía un franquismo sin Franco; el "Caudillo" le puso nombre, rostro y cuerpo a ese espíritu, que entró en el momento clave en que se podía definir el rumbo revolucionario o reaccionario de aquel país en los años treinta (Anguita).

En Chile, el Partido Socialista aliado a los demás partidos de la llamada "Concertación Democrática," el mismo partido del presidente mártir Salvador Allende, fue pieza en el aparato partidario "progresista" y "políticamente correcto" para darle continuidad a la restauración de las oligarquías y el imperialismo en Chile, con ideología neoliberal y Estado residual-subsidiario.

El golpe de Estado—como dijo Julio Anguita para el caso español—y la transición "democrática," con su democracia "de mínimos," fue realmente la restauración del orden social que estuvo amenazado por la Unidad Popular, el gobierno de Allende y por la organización-movilización del pueblo.

Las elecciones se volvieron un fraude legalizado bajo la regla del "sistema binominal" que calculadamente provocaba el empate entre derechas y centroizquierda, y garantizaba la continuidad neoliberal, ya como neoliberalismo progresista, tolerante y prometiendo la "igualdad de oportunidades," *cualquerizando* el concepto de la igualdad en clave capitalista: la vida como carrera en la que competimos y nos "rascamos con nuestras propias uñas," suerte de cada quién el resultado final. Cualquiera que representara una contraposición o antagonismo relevante fue eliminado, sacado del juego o cooptado.

Tal como en otros casos, incluido el español, el "retorno de la derecha" fue y ha sido el gran ogro o fantasma de los cuentos infantiles, para que el juego electoral pareciera siempre una ocasión de salvación nacional, el llamado "voto útil" que cíclicamente se presta a "no abrir la puerta al monstruo" o las "ultraderechas," mientras se hace "justicia en la medida de lo posible" y las reivindicaciones y agendas se reducen a la búsqueda de la "equidad" (atenuar, compadeciéndose, el dolor ajeno).

Los efectos nocivos de esta democracia viciada y vaciada, de "modernización" institucional y material mediante el fortalecimiento de los Poderes Ejecutivos con capacidad de transnacionalizar la acumulación global del capitalismo, prescindiendo de los "pesados trámites" parlamentarios y la participación social, en base a entramados de normas supranacionales, acuerdos comerciales y reglas ad-hoc (Fiallo), mientras las personas son lanzadas a la guerra de sobrevivencia y se sostiene un discurso "bien pensante" sin los pueblos, han sido la sensación de desamparo, la inestabilidad y la precariedad permanentes.

El hecho de que, al contrario de lo que pasa en la relación de los agentes del poder estatal con las cúpulas, "en relación con la sociedad civil, con los lugares de los pobres y capas medias, la relación es vertical, discursiva, sustitutiva, neutralizadora y desarticulada" (Fiallo, 2020), fortalece el declive del compromiso democrático, porque con toda lógica dan motivos para pensar que la mentada democracia es un fraude, y que la "mano dura," y protección de un "benefactor," *páter familia*, adquiere plena vigencia. En virtud de ello, en muchos países se vive un momento populista, respuesta en lo político a un problema nodal irresuelto, y

En su centro, la globalización capitalista (...); la erosión planificada del Estado nación y la desnaturalización de la soberanía popular percibida por las poblaciones como pérdida de una democracia efectiva, de derechos y libertades reales, impotencia de una ciudadanía sin poder. Solos, débiles y sin futuro. La creación consciente del miedo, es decir, de individuos aislados, sin derechos y vínculos genera inevitablemente demandas de protección, seguridad, justicia y orden en las sociedades" (Monereo).

Por su parte Mario Tronti (citado por Anguita y Monereo) señala:

Lo culturalmente correcto y su primo, lo políticamente correcto, han realizado juntos un desarme unilateral de las ideas antagonistas que han asegurado lo que se ha llamado con razón y no por casualidad, el orden constituido, el estado actual de las cosas.

Como profecía autocumplida, el progresismo sin sustancia ha ido gestando a su mejor cómplice para hacerse necesario: el fundamentalismo de derechas, religioso y retrógrado.

Que Trump o Bolsonaro aparezcan como valientes rebeldes, como "incorrectos," en similitud al nazismo y el fascismo del siglo XX europeo, y luego ganaran elecciones, retrata esta amarga consecuencia de las democracias fosilizadas (así llamadas por Álvaro García Linera a las que contrapone las "democracias plebeyas"). Y también se convierten -no obstante, sus perniciosas consecuencias para el presente y lo inmediato- en el chantaje perfecto de retornar y sostener un *status quo* sin antagonismos de fondo al proyecto histórico de los grandes vencedores.

Pero la añorada "aquiescencia" y "gobernabilidad" no es posible de apretar entre las manos; el conflicto de clases, entre oprimidos y opresores, dominados y dominadores no cesa; aunque no aparezca aún la "clase" o los "sujetos" "para sí," que disputen "con voluntad de gobierno y de poder en una perspectiva de ruptura con el capitalismo," como dicen Anguita y Monereo.

Por ejemplo, todo comenzó a estallar -aunque el estallido no genere una crisis histórica- cuando en Chile unos jóvenes escolares empezaron a movilizarse a mediados de 2006. Luego vinieron las marchas estudiantiles de 2011 y 2012 contra la privatización de la educación y el endeudamiento de las familias. Posteriormente la irrupción electoral de nuevos actores y propuestas. En 2016 las grandes movilizaciones contra la privatización de las pensiones, y en 2018 la toma feminista de las universidades.

Comenzó a estallar, hemos dicho, pues será lento el rescabrajamiento de un modelo instaurado en el miedo, luego en el chantaje, y la ilusión de una "chilean way" al desarrollo (¡desarrollo en un país que se despoja de sus principales riquezas como materias primas baratas para las grandes transnacionales!), como núcleo de la hegemonía cultural del neoliberalismo. Chile, en gran medida, se había mantenido ausente de la ola antineoliberal y nacional-popular que recorrió y sacudió América Latina desde 1998, y hoy aparece recobrando bríos en México, Argentina y, a su modo, en Puerto Rico.

Pero, insistimos, el resquebrajamiento ha empezado, y las velas se encendían en la noche del 11 de septiembre de 2019 en el Estadio Nacional (recinto que fue convertido en campo de concentración), en los sitios donde Víctor Jara fue atrapado y posteriormente mutilado y asesinado; en múltiples puntos del país sudamericano.

La sociedad norteamericana, por su lado, se remece en fenómenos como el asesinato de

George Floyd y las protestas multitudinarias que se convierten en mundiales; la irrupción política de Bernie Sanders y Alexandra Ocasio-Cortez; las movilizaciones contra las invasiones y contra la negación del cambio climático. Empiezan a plantearse reivindicaciones socialdemócratas progresistas que en 2001 parecían impensables. El presente salda cuentas con el pasado y propone futuros hipotéticos.

En 2019, apenas un mes más tarde de aquellas velas de septiembre, iniciaría en Chile lo que ya se conoce como el Estallido Social, bajo la consigna que se no se trataba de un aumento de los pasajes del metro: "No son treinta pesos, son treinta años." Se referían a los treinta años desde 1989, cuando se anunció con bombos y platillos "la alegría ya viene" y que llegaba la democracia. Aquel Estallido Social ha abierto las puertas a un Proceso Constituyente sencillamente impensable, clausurado, impedido con candados durante décadas. Y todo cambió de pronto. "Sigan sabiendo que más temprano que tarde de nuevo abrirán las grandes alamedas ..." dijo el presidente Salvador Allende en su último discurso al pueblo de Chile.

FRONTERAS DE LUZ Y LA PEDAGOGÍA DE LA MEMORIA

Mientras, en "un país en el mundo," la República Dominicana, "ubicado en el mismo trayecto del sol," como dijo el poeta nacional Pedro Mir ¿qué pasa con el pasado? ¿A qué presente se enfrenta y con qué mirada del futuro?

El Premio Nobel de Literatura chileno, Pablo Neruda, dijo en su "Versainograma de Santo Domingo" en 1966:

> Aunque hace siglos de esta historia amarga
> por amarga y por vieja se la cuento
> porque las cosas no se aclaran nunca
> con el olvido ni con el silencio.

Por su parte, el reconocido narrador y pensador uruguayo, Eduardo Galeano, en su obra "Patas arriba. La escuela del mundo al revés" planteó la siguiente reflexión:

"¿La historia se repite? ¿O se repite sólo como penitencia de quienes son incapaces de escucharla? No hay historia muda. Por mucho que la quemen, por mucho que la rompan, por mucho que la mientan, la memoria humana se niega a callarse la boca. El tiempo que fue sigue latiendo, vivo, dentro del tiempo que es, aunque el tiempo que es no lo quiera o no lo sepa" (Galeano).

En una sociedad profundamente atravesada por la impunidad; donde los ideales de democracia, igualdad y libertad han sido llevados a su versión más reducida y administrada; donde la desmemoria es cultivada y construida, generalmente en beneficio de que causantes de brutales crímenes nunca sean sometidos al examen de la justicia y del pensamiento libre y crítico, y el orden social instaurado nunca sea cuestionado, ni se deje de ver como invariable ... en ese contexto ejercer la memoria es vital como acto reconstructivo y regenerativo.

La sociedad dominicana (y en general las latinoamericanas, esclavizadas, colonizadas, patriarcales, racializadas, sometidas y oprimidas) está hondamente marcada por las ideas, ideologías y marcos morales que en cada momento justificaron el atropello, el abuso, los vejámenes, la explotación sin límites, la privación y negación de derechos y el sometimiento al poder, y la aceptación de mínimos, bajo la denominación que se use en cada ocasión y la "razón" que se invoque a conveniencia. Y esto nunca es unilateral: el orden de dominación y opresión construye hegemonía y consensos; produce apropiación e internalización de sus valores por parte de los oprimidos y dominados.

Reencontrarse con la memoria tiene que significar reconocerse, y verse como un ser que se produce históricamente, que se constituye en el proceso de su vivir y su experiencia, encontrando los hechos y fuerzas que han condicionado ese proceso, y esto es central en un esfuerzo emancipatorio. Como dice Fiallo:

> Memoria e imaginación se articulan para potenciar posibilidades de iniciativas y creaciones, de manera tal que el aprendizaje tenga unas dimensiones integrales (para la vida) y sea constructor de la condición de ser humano (oficio de hombre) y no en una pretendida vocación unilateral de las exigencias del desarrollo capitalista de las élites en su competitividad destructora.
>
> (…) El aprendizaje para la vida implica el construir sujetos *y superar la condición de alienado, subordinado, instrumento de la mayoría popular*, lo que implica protagonismo, es decir, condición de ciudadanía en un nuevo territorio.
>
> Ello nos obliga a reflexionar críticamente sobre las prácticas actuales y articular adecuadamente momentos y recursos, de manera tal que seamos efectivos a partir de pensar cómo hacemos nuestra práctica educativa cotidiana.

Así que hacer memoria es ajustar cuentas con el trujillismo no superado y sus crímenes contra la Humanidad; es poner en cuestión la cultura y las relaciones políticas en contra el propio pueblo dominicano, para subyugarlo y doblegarlo; es recuperar la historia de luchas por la libertad, dignidad e igualdad; y el verdadero sentido de la transformación democrática que el pueblo dominicano ha buscado afanosamente, muchas veces en medio de confusiones y falsas ilusiones.

La nación dominicana necesita salir de la negación o de la deformación de la Historia construida para alienarla, es decir, para que actúe contra su identidad, sus intereses y necesidades. Necesita salir de la aceptación o validación de los mitos tiránicos, de sus silencios y acuerdos impuestos. Necesita reconocerse, reconciliarse consigo mismo y reconstituir su ética de vida.

Para ello, es preciso apoyarse en las tres columnas de la reconciliación: memoria, verdad y justicia histórica, que contribuyan a zanjar las heridas abiertas, a superar culturalmente esas marcas e impedir que se sigan replicando hechos de similar brutalidad, en cualquier modalidad que se presente. No se trata en todo caso de la tosca y manipulada visión de la "verdad" que se usó en la "justicia transicional" en muchos países latinoamericanos. El "nunca más" no es un mero repudio a actos del pasado, desconectado de una comprensión histórica de por qué ocurrieron y de que el horizonte no es solo la no repetición, sino la emancipación de las opresiones que unas veces usan la fuerza brutal y otras veces la tergiversación de la democracia.

"Un pueblo sin pasado es un pueblo sin futuro" se ha dicho, y no es mandato nostálgico. Es parte clave de aquello de ser "en sí" o "para sí": de saber quién se ha sido, qué ha tenido que enfrentar, cómo se ha llegado hasta aquí, y cuáles serían las rutas de una transformación de la vida.

Genocidio, coloniaje improductivo, ocupación extranjera y capitalismo despótico, transnacionalización, rentismo y corrupción, han sido las formas principales de la producción y reproducción social dominicana, en un entramado ideológico de difuminación de los sujetos subalternos y creación de enemigos internos y externos que, además, le arrebatan al propio oprimido dominicano y dominicana su condición de colectividad empobrecida, negra, discriminada, migrante, negada y sometida.

La política de las últimas décadas se caracteriza por una notoria ausencia de sujetos productores de reivindicaciones, sentido y proyectos populares (trabajadores, habitantes de barrios y campos, mujeres, marginados, campesinos) y una valoración sobredimensionada —otra vez— de caudillos, productos mercadológicos y ofertones electoreros.

Alguien podría pensar que el pasado es un tema que preocupa a los derrotados. Los vencedores no tienen pasado, su asunto es el presente, el futuro y la victoria; no gastan tiempo en hurgar en las victorias morales sobre lo que ocurrió o pudo ocurrir.

Parcial verdad. Si la política se hace mirando hacia el pasado, tratando de ganar las batallas sobre la memoria y lo sucedido, asume un papel eminentemente testimonial. Pero si la política se hace sin memoria, si la acción sobre el presente y el futuro carece de ella, se vuelve no sólo estúpida e ingenua, sino también capaz de traicionarse permanentemente, revisionista, se torna oportunista, presa fácil de la demagogia, las "lisonjas fugaces" de las que habló Víctor Jara y la instrumentalización.

Si la vida y la política se hacen sin memoria, pierden su ubicación histórica: sin saber qué se es, qué se ha sido, qué ha logrado, qué se le ha opuesto y cuáles han sido sus antagonistas, los sujetos son esclavos del presentismo. Son aquella "sangre nueva" sin representar nada propio ni nuevo, salvo para el marketing y la comercialización de los relatos. Líquido sin sustancia que se va por cualquier poro, haciendo hemorragia, o contaminando con parásitos o células malignas todo órgano vital.

La República Dominicana adolece de falta de memoria, de una organización intencional y deliberada de la desmemoria. Memoria golpeada, destruida, desmontada, perturbada, confundida, distorsionada. La memoria enfermada como aspecto clave y estratégico de una identidad enajenada, de sujetos neutralizados para no ser "para sí," *zombificación* histórica, escopolamina en grandes dosis para anular la voluntad propia, y bajo una ficción de libertad personal y de emprendimiento propio; vivir negándose bajo la voluntad de unas minorías voraces.

El gobierno celebrando que la población dominicana es mayoritariamente "de clases medias" y con meras estimaciones de aumento del consumo de "kilocalorías" festejándolo como disminución de la subalimentación, en pleno siglo XXI, y como si ello significara disminución del hambre, mejor nutrición y salud.

Mientras tanto, el haitiano inmigrante funciona como "invasor," "pérdida del territorio," y de "la identidad," causante de los déficits de puestos de trabajo, de salarios decentes y de servicios dignos de salud y educación. Las haitianas como "portadoras" de la "invasión" en tanto la tasa de mortalidad materno-infantil es escalofriantemente alta, entre las peores de América Latina. Asimismo, rendimientos escolares bajísimos y salarios miserables que, junto a impuestos injustos, hacen que los trabajadores y trabajadoras sólo participen de un 30% de la riqueza producida a través de sus ingresos, y casi la mitad de la población viva bajo la línea de pobreza laboral. Pero el "enemigo" creado durante más de un siglo permite explicarlo todo.

Alguien ha dicho que sólo hay problemas con los antecedentes de invasión cuando el sujeto en cuestión es haitiano. El español y el norteamericano, que ocuparon repetidas veces el país, son amigos y sus fiestas nacionales se celebran hasta con ofertones de tiendas. El haitiano que estuvo en el este durante 22 años en que no existía aún un Estado dominicano, es congénitamente un enemigo que extirpar y detener con una muralla. Racismo en su acepción más estricta: una población es enemiga sólo por el hecho de existir . . . salvo para construir los grandes edificios de la burbuja inmobiliaria y trabajar la tierra, traficados y explotados por empresarios y funcionarios públicos que nadie persigue, acusa ni sanciona.

De igual modo, el derecho de los seres humanos a vivir en relaciones de igualdad—con el apoyo de la categoría teórica género—es visto como "amenaza" a l a la familia y a la niñez. La violencia de género y el machismo haciendo estragos, destruyendo vida de hombres, mujeres y niños. Los negros y los pobres como "peligro" para la buena sociedad. La "gente sin clase" como algo a mantener a distancia. La admiración al inglés, a lo hispanófilo y lo estadounidense. La semi-esclavitud en una serie de ocupaciones como el cuidado del hogar, la vigilancia y limpieza, son realidades normalizadas.

En definitiva, la enajenación de quién se es como pueblo, como individuos y como conglomerado histórico, en términos de género, etnia, clase, posición geopolítica y geo-económica, naturalizando la vida infrahumana de las mayorías, la colonización de la vida, la opresión de la mayor parte de la dominicanidad, e incapacitando la comprensión de las causas reales y del enfoque del dominador.

Es ahí donde las velas se tienen que encender. Y Fronteras de Luz juega un papel peda-gógico, constructor de memoria, reconstructor de identidad, de sentido, liberador y descolo-nizador. Fronteras de Luz como posibilidad de encontrarse entre hombres y mujeres que no reconocen al haitiano como enemigo, y además disputan la elaboración ideológica de la razón de ser de la dominicanidad y su relación con los demás, su relación consigo mismos y mismas, como las causas de la vida deshumanizante no sólo de los inmigrantes sino de la mayoría nacional.

Fronteras de Luz como experiencia concreta de toda labor de reencauzamiento histórico: sacar en la oscuridad de la domesticación, y de la normalización de una identi-dad violenta, desigual y deshumanizada, la nobleza profunda que habita en los hombres y mujeres, su capacidad de reencontrarse con el otro y, en ese espejo, reencontrarse consigo mismo. Recuperar las resistencias que—no ajenas a contradicciones e incluso disociacio-nes—habitan en la vida social, en el territorio "de abajo," y darles dignidad histórica, cat-egoría cultural, poder transformador, potencial político.

Personalmente, conocí Fronteras de Luz en 2017, a 80 años de la masacre de 1937—que en realidad se prolongó hasta 1938—y así como mi madre y mi hermana en Chile hicieron muchas veces con mi sobrina, llevándola a participar en el encendido de velas cada 11 de septiembre, en los cacerolazos de las protestas estudiantiles, en las conversaciones en la mesa donde fuera y cuando fuera que se tratara la dignidad fundamental de todo ser humana, así hice yo con mi hijo y con mi hija, llevándolos aquella noche en Dajabón, donde recorrimos con velas el pueblo hasta el borde del río Masacre.

Mis hijos, con velas en las manos, vieron por sí mismos la reja coronada por alambres de púas; vieron la materialidad de la deshumanización y de la cultura de la opresión, de la división, "del punto y raya para que tu hambre no se junte con mi hambre" que dicen Aníbal Nazoa y Juan Carlos Núñez; la reificación del espacio del Estado-nación como territorio de control y superioridad falaz, burlada mil veces por los mismos que ordenan y pagan esas rejas.

Pero también vieron que tras esa reja había árboles, los mismos flamboyanes y matas de un lado y de otro. La misma tierra que moja el mismo río. Y el manantial de seres humanos que del otro lado llegaban a la otra orilla, con sus velas encendidas, y cómo entre un lado y otro del mundo, separado por una reja, empezaban a hablar las personas. Cada grupo en sus idiomas, y en un solo idioma que supera las particularidades de las lenguas. El tono de la bondad, el candil de la ternura, la sed de verse, escucharse y tocarse.

Todo lo opuesto a lo que la escuela -como bien explicara en su tiempo Franklin Franco- enseña: el racismo pedagógicamente organizado y al mismo tiempo ¡negado!, teniendo como primer blanco la enajenación de los niños y las niñas de la República Dominicana, que aprenden a que son "mezcla," "indios" o "morenos," combinación de españoles (que nos legaron "el idioma y la cultura"), africanos y taínos, como un licuado de frutas, donde lo noble, inteligente y productivo es aportado por el conquistador.

El acto, el hecho, aquella noche de velas, confrontaba a la ideología, y ayudaba a construir sentido nuevo.

La tarea es fundamental porque al populismo derechista hay que oponer la memoria, de nuevo, interpelada a hablar con el hoy y el mañana, como praxis, invitada obligada a la conversación. Oponer, como dicen Anguita y Monereo:

> (...) bloques históricos sociales que construyen pueblo, patria y soberanía. El internacionalismo solo será real si se opone a los nacionalismos excluyentes, a la globalización y defiende unas clases trabajadoras que convergen en una humanidad radicalmente diversa.
>
> Cuesta creer que defender estas cosas pueda ser entendido como una provocación. Hay nostalgia, sin duda. La nostalgia de un siglo XX que puso contra la espada y la pared al capitalismo imperialista. Esta herencia de éxitos y fracasos es la nuestra y, sin ella, nunca edificaremos un futuro de liberación social y nacional ...

En la República Dominicana hay una trayectoria gloriosa de luchas. Hay una lucha cotidiana también, la de sobrevivir a tantos atropellos concatenados. Hay una brecha, una grieta en la muralla del desencanto, la resignación y la ideología de la derrota convertida en pequeñas ambiciones individuales alrededor del mundo, donde se nos invita a enfrentar una pandemia con mascarillas, alcohol y "distancia social," como si nada más condicionara la salud, la enfermedad y la posibilidad de vivir.

La memoria, como dice Galeano, vive: "El tiempo que fue sigue latiendo, vivo, dentro del tiempo que es, aunque el tiempo que es no lo quiera o no lo sepa."

En pleno septiembre de 2019 en Santo Domingo, un número no pequeño de personas llegó frente al edificio que aloja a la Suprema Corte de Justicia y la Procuraduría General de la República. Decenas de dominicanos y dominicanas se reunieron allí indignados por el feminicidio que se llevó a la joven profesional Anibel González, mientras su expareja se suicidó luego de matarla, y las tres hijas de ambos quedaron huérfanas.

La rabia sacudía y sacude aún porque se ha develado todo un entramado de privilegios y contubernios en los que hombres formados en el machismo enfermo y violento, maltratadores y feminicidas, logran burlar la impartición elemental de la justicia con prebendas, sobornos, amistades e influencias. Una muestra en microscopio del orden institucional dominicano, con el resultado de una muerte ofensiva, cruel, de una tragedia que marcará la vida de tres criaturas, en la más absoluta impunidad, con el Estado como cómplice del crimen.

Mientras, una élite pequeña de oscuros personajes ha impedido que se pongan en marcha—con formalidad, sistematicidad e institucionalidad—políticas de educación y de prevención sobre la desigualdad y la violencia de género, así como impiden políticas migratorias racionales y razonables, y obstaculizan cualquier avance en materia de derechos humanos y sociales que reviertan la "naturalidad" de su poder y sus influencias en nombre de "preservar la nación y la familia."

En ese encendido de velas participaron varios niños y niñas. Entre ellos, de nuevo, mis hijos e hijas. Y vieron de frente la foto de Anibel, y supieron del edificio que, debiendo administrar justicia, gestiona la violación de derechos y de leyes, administra favores y componendas, y supieron que existe complicidad e impunidad permitiendo que opresiones diversas sigan maltratando la vida de esta sociedad.

Al hacerlo, al estar encendiendo las velas ante la foto de Anibel, como en la frontera, estaban haciendo ejercicio de la memoria, no testimonialismo. Estaban resignificando la vida social con lo que muchos y muchas han querido, entregando sus fuerzas, sus años y energías para que sea distinto a lo que existe. Estaban además construyendo memoria para sí mismos, para sí mismas, para quienes le rodean; experiencias concretas a compartir desde otra perspectiva de la existencia y de la convivencia.

Poco después, les tocó ver la Plaza de la Bandera, aquel monumento faraónico construido por el gobierno de Balaguer, (personaje que décadas después fue designado "padre de la democracia"), llena de después designado "padre de la democracia," llena de jóvenes, especialmente de los barrios populares, reclamando el fin de los fraudes electorales, de la impunidad, de la democracia burlada y exigiendo derechos, también con velas y cacerolas, banderas y pancartas. Exigiendo desde esa plaza todo lo distinto a lo que Balaguer y sus cómplices y continuadores han edificado.

Frente a la masacre de 1937, al golpe de Estado en la República Dominicana y Chile, al terrorismo de agrupaciones fundamentalistas y de Estados, a las guerras de saqueo y desposesión, al cercenamiento de derechos, a la ausencia de democracia y la abundancia de privilegios, no nos debe bastar el "nunca más." Tampoco con reparaciones y cambios simbólicos. Eso es demasiado poco, demasiado domesticable y administrable; demasiado inofensivo.

La derecha populista hasta habla contra el neoliberalismo, pero en clave represiva y opresiva: se trata de recuperar el poder estatal sobre las personas y los territorios, no de sujetos y dignidad. Como dice Tronti (en Monereo): "No me preocupa la democracia iliberal. Para combatir el autoritarismo existen muchas personas con buen sentido. Me parece más peligrosa esta democracia liberal totalizadora, impolítica y antipolítica que encuentra cada vez más personas que la asumen."

Por encima del "nunca más," ya de por sí esencial y elemental, nos parece necesario concientizar, organizar, movilizar y educarnos, en la recuperación del proyecto histórico pendiente, que con ejercicio de memoria tendrá que hacer el ejercicio de presente y de futuro.

Una gran disputa por la hegemonía. Construir el proyecto histórico que en el siglo XXI y los venideros, para nuestros hijos, hijas, en su más amplia y extendida acepción, dispute el sentido de la vida y la convivencia, seduzca con nuevos horizontes, recupere la dignidad y los derechos, construya una ética y una vida libres de opresión, dominación y explotación, y la enajenación vinculada a estas. El proyecto inconcluso de "Sed justos lo primero, si queréis ser felices" de Juan Pablo Duarte, de los hombres y mujeres que han luchado, del ejemplo luminoso de 1965.

Atrevernos, en esa dirección, a hacer como señala Paulo Freire: denunciar el mundo injusto en que vivimos, y anunciar en una esperanza realizable el mundo que vamos a construir:

(. . .) las mujeres y los hombres interfieren en el mundo mientras que otros animales sólo se *mezclan* en él. Por eso, casi no tenemos historia, sino que hacemos la historia que, igualmente, nos hace y nos convierte, por tanto, en históricos.

(. . .) Con la metodización de la curiosidad, la lectura del mundo puede incitar a trascender la pura *conjetura* para alcanzar el *proyecto de mundo.* (. . .) El proyecto es la conjetura que se define con claridad, es el sueño posible que ha de canalizarse mediante la acción política (Freire).

Reinstituir un patriotismo, humanista pleno y amplio, como lo pensó Martí; Estados como territorios democráticos para las mayorías y los pueblos; los derechos humanos entrelazados con los derechos de la Humanidad, como los planteó Fidel Castro en la ONU (Castro). Una sociedad no racista, no colonialista, no capitalista y no patriarcal, como han pensado Angela Davis y Rosa Luxemburgo, para no tener al ogro autoritario y criminal chantajeando el voto útil, sino que lo supere históricamente, construyendo una sociedad de igualdad y justicia. Nunca más atrocidades. Siempre, de nuevo, abrir las grandes alamedas por donde pasemos juntas y juntos para construir la liberación y la emancipación humana y del mundo del cual somos consciencia viva y actuante.

Notas

1. Este texto ha sido escrito primero en septiembre de 2019 y terminado en julio de 2020, en Santo Domingo, República Dominicana, atendiendo a la invitación y exhortación de Edward Paulino, co-coordinador del libro. Nos hemos limitado a indicar algunas referencias bibliográficas, apelando a la comprensión de los lectores de que otras referencias están ausentes, pero al menos se dan los nombres y temas, cuya pista se puede seguir y encontrar en internet, como en otros formatos y soportes.

2. La cita tiene como fuente una edición a cargo de José Miguel Martínez Torrejón, que mantuvo y modernizó la redacción en el castellano de la época, considerando ediciones del siglo XVI y XVII. En la nota a la edición en la fuente citada, Martínez Torrejón explica con detalles su labor al respecto.

Obras citadas

Anguita, Julio. Entrevista con Daniel Ramírez. *El Español*, "Quiero una Tercera República transversal, ni de derechas ni de izquierdas," 30 sept. 2018, https://www.elespanol.com/opinion/20180930/julio-anguita-cataluna-presos-politicos-venezuela-comunes/341467142_0.html

Anguita, Julio y Manolo Monereo. "Un mundo grande y terrible." *Cuatro Poder*, 2019, https://www.cuartopoder.es/ideas/2019/08/19/un-mundo-grande-y-terrible/

Castro, Fidel. "Discurso pronunciado ante el XXXIV Periodo de Sesiones de la Asamblea General de las Naciones Unidas." Consejo de Estado, 1979, http://www.cuba.cu/gobierno/discursos/1979/esp/f121079e.html

de las Casas, Bartolomé. *Brevísima relación de la destrucción de las Indias*. Editado por José Miguel Martínez Torrejón, Editorial Universidad de Antioquia, 2011,

http://www.cervantesvirtual.com/descargaPdf/brevisima-relacion-de-ladestruccion-de-las-indias/

Fiallo Billini, José Antinoe. *Pensamientos sociales y procesos sociohistóricos: Tomo I*, Archivo General de la Nación, vol. CCCLXI, Editora Búho, 2020, http://colecciones.agn.gob.do/opac/ficha.php?informatico=00108436PI&codopc=OUDIG&idpag=1491463183&presenta=digitaly2p

Franco Pichardo, Franklin. *Sobre racismo y antihaitianismo (y otros ensayos)*. Mediabyte, Segunda Edición, 2003.

Freire, Pablo. *Pedagogía de la indignación*. Ediciones Morata, 2001.

Galeano, Eduardo. *Patas arriba. La escuela del mundo al revés*, 2009, https://resistir.info/livros/galeano_patas_arriba.pdf

García Linera, Álvaro. "Diálogos por la emancipación (en 4 partes)." Televisión Pública de Argentina, 2015, https://www.youtube.com/watch?v=w2WhUe6pA-k

Henríquez y Carvajal, Francisco. "Informe de Francisco Henríquez y Carvajal sobre las causas de la inmigración haitiana, 1931." *República Dominicana y Haití: el derecho a vivir*, Fundación Juan Bosch, 2014.

Marte, Germán. "Lionel Vieux, otro haitiano que luchó por soberanía dominicana," *ElDía*, 25 jul. 2015, https://eldia.com.do/lionel-vieux-otro-haitiano-que-lucho-por-soberania-dominicana/

McPherson, Alan L. *The invaded: how Latin Americans and their allies fought and ended U.S. occupations*. Oxford UP, 2014.

Mir, Pedro (1983). *La noción de período en la historia dominicana. Tomo II*. Universidad Autónoma de Santo Domingo, 1983, https://www.issuu.com/aquilesjulian/docs/pedro_mir_-_la_noci__n_de_per__odo__26ccb0afcf32ee/139

Monereo, Manolo. "¡Que se vayan todos! El retorno del "momento populista" que nunca se fue." Cuatro Poder, 2019, https://www.cuartopoder.es/ideas/2019/07/29/manolo-monereo-que-se-vayan-todos-el-retorno-momento-populista-que-nunca-fue/

Moya Pons, Frank. "'La diáspora ennegrece al dominicano' o 'Antihaitianismo Histórico, Antihaitianismo de Estado': El Futuro de las Relaciones Domínico-Haitianas." Vetas, núm. 8, 1996, http://vetasdigi-tal.blogspot.com/2006/07/frank-moya-pons-la-dispora-ennegrece.html

Nazoa, Aníbal y Juan Carlos Núñez. "Punto y raya," *CNT*, núm. 286, 2003, http://archivo-periodico.cnt.es/286ene2003/cultura/cultura_archivos/ocioc01.htm

Neruda, Pablo. "Versainograma a Santo Domingo." Ediciones Cielonaranja, 1966, http://www.cielonaranja.com/neruda2.htm

Paraison, Edwin (2018). "Luperón y la Confederación Dominico Haitiana," *Acento*, 2018, 17 ago. 2019, https://acento.com.do/opinion/luperon-la-confederacion-dominico-haitiana-8597562.html

"Préval valora ayuda recibida de República Dominicana," *Diario Libre*, 18 enero 2010, https://www.diariolibre.com/actualidad/prval-valora-ayuda-recibida-de-repblica-dominicana-LJDL231129

Price-Mars, Jean. *La República de Haití y la República Dominicana: Diversos aspectos de un problema histórico, geográfico y etnológico*. 1953, Industrias Gráficas, traducido por Martín Aldao y José Luis Muñoz, 1958.

Border of Lights Historical and Personal Narrative

Rana Dotson and DeAndra Beard, *las hermanas Beard* (the Beard sisters)

We are caught in an inescapable network of mutuality, tied in a single garment of destiny. Whatever affects one directly, affects all indirectly.

—DR. MARTIN LUTHER KING, JR.

Written by Rana Dotson

It had been a delirious few days. I didn't know how I would make the trip to Rutgers University alone, sleep deprived and exhausted, driving with my breastfeeding infant. I had been attempting to make the three-and-a-half-day conference, but sunrise on the last day found me at home in Maryland in bed, still feeling depleted. Then a thought struck me with crystal clarity: *You're going for the meeting after the meeting.* My eyes flew open and my feet hit the floor.

The preceding eight years had been a whirlwind for me and my husband Julian grinding-out young newlywed start-up status: navigating the Washington DC-metro area as "transplants" while completing graduate school, securing gainful employment, finding the house we would call home, starting what would become our family of five. The grind had included wrapping up a master's degree in Public Policy, specializing in International Security and Economic policy, from the Maryland School of Public Policy, UMD College Park. I had spent a semester at the Inter-Agency Consultation on Race in Latin America (IAC), whose secretariat was based at The Inter-American Dialogue (IAD) in Washington D.C. Under the leadership of Judith Morrison, the IAC worked to address issues of race discrimination, social exclusion, and other problems confronted by people of African descent in Latin America. I began researching my capstone paper on the implications of the DR-CAFTA Trade Agreement for the most marginalized communities in the Dominican Republic which was being debated in Congress.

I knew there were important missing perspectives. In that debate which so often spoke of higher tides lifting all boats, I wondered about those who lived by the sea and possessed no boats. I had learned so much more than classroom variety political science and economics in the undergraduate semester years earlier (1999) at the Pontificia Universidad Maestra y Madre (PUCMM) in Santiago, Dominican Republic: my dark-brown-skinned, natural-haired presence was not the norm on campus. Though I developed close friendships and a love for many aspects of the culture that hosted me, a semester spent experiencing Black invisibility in an overwhelmingly African-descendant country had also been disorienting and traumatic. Subtle and overt racism forced me to relive the most difficult racial traumas of my Indiana childhood, with the script flipped in a dystopian twist. The same racist ideas and expressions originating from the historically Klan-influenced area of my youth were now being deployed by people who looked like my own, brown-skinned family members against other brown-skinned people. Some of the milder experiences ranged from being loudly berated by old men in the streets: *Get out the sun; you're already dark enough!* To being startled from deep sleep on my sister's shoulder to the sight of towering armed guards demanding our I.D. to disprove what our dark-skin implicated: we were Haitians sneaking into the Dominican Republic on the bus line heading from the Dominican-Haitian border back towards Santiago. Then there were the fellow public transportation passengers who debated my ethnic heritage as if I were an inanimate object sitting idly by: *She's Haitian, that's why she never takes care of her hair. She speaks English because her Haitian parents moved to the US and taught her English.* Never mind that I would have proudly claimed blood-line from the world's first Black-led republic if I could. The foundation of the ludicrously constructed fantasy these men built to remake my identity was laid upon their idea that anything Haitian was undesirable and unworthy: a ubiquitous, ever-present racist founda-tion which years later would become the springboard for the official reconstruction of the identities of hundreds of thousands of Dominicans of Haitian-descent in the country.

These daily experiences testified to the reach, depth, and legacy of anti-Black economi-cally motivated ideas that had driven the slave trade throughout the Americas centuries before; persistent economic and political inequalities guarded by complex racial and eth-nic norms still enforced an iron-clad system of racial social hierarchy. I found little solace knowing that my U.S. citizenship shielded me from the most punishing effects of the racial caste system in that country. The understanding only pronounced the dread and powerless-ness to defend others, some friends, who looked like me but lacked any such protection. It was devastating to confront the pernicious capacity of racist ideologies to innovate for particular cultural contexts. The vastness of that system, exported to every place European colonizers had landed, was daunting. I had learned in my Afro-Caribbean History and Culture class, taught by Natacha Calderon, that in the case of the Dominican Republic, it was the darkest-skinned Dominicans and Dominicans of Haitian-descent whose Haitian identity stood as proxy for "Black" and "undesirable immigrants," it was they who bore the brunt of the racial hierarchy. My being judged to belong to either category meant being treated accordingly, for better or for worse, by the people I met. The worst treatment was often divvied out by Dominican men. Yet, it was a young Dominican man who passionately challenged me to act in solidarity with Dominicans who were engaged in a struggle for true freedom and racial healing. Recalling the Black freedom struggle which had made my life in the United States a possibility, he looked me dead in the eyes, and asked, "Why don't you (all) do something?" The reality was complicated; Black Americans in the United States were overwhelmingly unaware of the struggles within the diaspora, and we all had work to do to develop the experience, skills, and knowledge to make meaningful contributions. But his question was a call to action that stung.

Ana María Belique (Reconoci.do lead activist) would tell me pointedly years later, "the only difference between you and me is that my ancestors' ship stopped before yours at a different place." Her words uplifted our common story of African heritage, survival and resistance and the cosmic fine hair-splitting difference of events that led to her being born Black in the Dominican Republic and me being born Black in the United States. My sister DeAndra Beard and I were born in a white, semi-agricultural, blue-collar industrial Midwestern town and raised within a deeply nurturing and protective community of extended family, replete with dozens, if not hundreds, of real and play aunties and uncles common within Black American kinship networks. This included the deeply rooted and extended family network within the church our maternal and paternal great-grandparents had established on the heels of the last wave of the Great Migration in the early 1930s. These were people who two generations from slavery had come north from points south to set down roots, purchase land, and eventually raise the beams of the church edifice with their own hands. They navigated the boundaries between our immediate community and the majority white surrounding community, forging bonds of respect.

The lessons we learned growing up within this pioneering, spiritually attuned, industrious and mutually supportive community has been the bedrock foundation grounding us in our work within the Dominican Republic, Haiti and beyond. In our navigating the boundaries within our own community, we had come to understand that "the other" was not always the enemy. Our families had worked to cultivate deeply meaningful relationships with white community members, and even while the Klan demonstrated openly in our town square, an overwhelming counter-rally was attended by Blacks and whites standing shoulder-to-shoulder. DeAndra had been a leader in that work. I had also cut my teeth in activism as a teenager, after a group of students suffered police brutality that ended with the police chief personally apologizing to me and my family and instituting racial sensitivity training for the local police department. Both DeAndra and I followed the footsteps of our oldest sister, Devona, who modeled the intellectual curiosity and moral courage that landed us within the pages of Malcolm X's story, Hurston, Giavonni, Baldwin, Angelou, Rustin, among others, and which led each of us to complete undergraduate studies at Historically Black Colleges and Universities (HBCUs). For the first time, on those hallowed grounds, we were truly free to learn. For the first time we found intellectual homes where were not made to feel encumbered but rather liberated by our state of Blackness.

In the course of my draft paper on trade issues being circulated from the IAC to congressional staffers it became clear that more in-depth research would be needed to get a full understanding of the dynamics and challenges faced by the most marginalized communities within the Dominican Republic. I had assumed policymakers crafting trade policies should have known and considered human insecurity and potential disparate implications of these policies for these more vulnerable communities. Yet, the longer I followed the issue, the more disappointed I grew at the apparent lack of inclusion. So, after a few years of preparation, supported by funding from the National Security Education Program (NSEP) David L. Boren Graduate Fellowship, I went to the Dominican Republic to explore these issues. My sister DeAndra had recently returned from Brazil, living on a settlement while doing field research on the educational strategies within the landless worker's movement (Movimento dos Trabalhadores Rurais Sem Terra (MST)). She left her breastfeeding one-year old at home to join me, then several months into a pregnancy with my second child, in the Dominican Republic. We quickly formed a local research team which included a research methods and statistics professor; (the late) Arelis García, headmaster of Isla Instituto Language School, and several Haitian students studying medicine at a local university. By the time we were to depart the country in late summer of 2007, our core team understood there was much more at stake than a research paper. We understood having heard those whose stories had been pushed to the margins of history that we carried a responsibility to *do something*. The meagerness of our own possessions or resources was a weak excuse. We had made only promises we could keep: to never forget, to carry and amplify their stories, and to give back however and wherever possible. Memory of the eyes and voices of those we had met through our research- agricultural workers and their families in impoverished, isolated rural communities known as *bateyes* held us accountable. We formed the Organization of Dominican Haitian Cooperation (OCDH) with medical students like Lesly Manigat who went on to become doctors working in partnership with batey communities and carrying out cross-border medical support in the aftermath of the 2010 earthquake, which affected many community residents.

On October 26, 2011, I met Sonia Pierre. She had come to Georgetown University Law Center to speak at the *Conference on Statelessness and the Right to Nationality in the Dominican Republic* about the growing crisis. This crisis would eventually culminate in the Constitutional Tribunal's Sentence 168-13, stripping thousands of Dominicans of Haitian descent of their nationality and effectively rendering them stateless, as Sonia direly warned all in attendance that day. She passionately entreated us to take action. We intersected in the atrium after she had stepped out for a smoke break and I had stepped out to calm my three-month-old third child whose voice echoed in the quiet auditorium. She cooed at the baby while I thanked her for her enormous work. My nervous words did not measure up to the gratitude I felt. We chatted a bit and she gave me her card. I returned to the auditorium and was caught up in a lively conversation with a contagiously enthusiastic woman named Nehanda Loiseau (now Julot) at the program's end. We chatted all the way to the bus stop where I dropped her off for her ride back to New York. Little did I know, Nehanda would later help lead a panel discussion at the Transnational Hispaniola II Conference at Rutgers University and would become a co-founder and lead coordinator for the first Border of Lights and develop The Border of Lights Monologues event in New York City. When news of Sonia's untimely death came, five weeks after that fateful Georgetown meeting, I would find her card still in my wallet. It was as if she had said to us, "keep it; it's your turn."

You're going for the meeting after the meeting. The April 12-15, 2012 Transnational Hispaniola II conference brought together activists, scholars, and students passionate about a re-imagined future for the Dominican Republic and Haiti—one that focused on commonality rather than division. My adrenaline took the wheel as the disappointment I felt at having missed all of the multi-day event was overwhelmed by the thought that kept ringing: *you're going for the meeting after the meeting.* I arrived, with nine-month-old nursing baby in a sling wrap, just after the closing words. Barely breaking my stride, as the throngs were exiting, I walked to the front of the auditorium and stood, looking around expectantly. Seconds later a young woman, whose name I would later learn was Cynthia Carrión, stepped up to the front. She elevated her voice above the chatter to beckon those who might be interested in helping with an idea to honor the victims of the Haitian Massacre: the meeting after the meeting. I found myself in a circle of about ten earnest souls, pegging the name "Border of Lights," to the idea of bringing people to the Massacre River to pay homage to the victims of the 1937 Trujillo-ordered genocidal slaughter of tens of thousands of innocents at the DR-Haiti Border. Those innocents had been killed and brushed aside by history, but we gathered there, vowing to breathe life to their stories and properly lay their memories to rest.

I later discovered I had walked into a circle of leading activists, artists, and scholars. But the small organization DeAndra and I had co-founded with Lesly Manigat in 2007, the Organization of Dominican Haitian Cooperation (OCDH), joined the collaborative effort to continue elevating the plight of Haitian-descendants in the DR. Even my husband Julian was involved in those early days, as it was all hands-on deck: he designed the border of lights logo, t-shirts, fliers, and program for the Border of Lights Monologues. We soon learned that the Border of Lights project was inspired by Julia Alvarez and Michele Wucker, two authors whose work had been pivotally important to us along the way. We had all been leading in our own ways, committed, and had been called together.

We felt the weight of the responsibility to honor the unknown victims of the genocide; unknown to us but well-known to the beloveds left in the wake of their brutal killings. We felt urgency in calling attention to the freedom struggle Sonia Pierre fought so hard for until her untimely death. The mantle of her work fell upon us. We, whose ships had just stopped at different places, at different times were connected by a common legacy within a shared diaspora. We had navigated borders for survival and for thriving. Our people had migrated to strange lands, fleeing terror to build solid homes with our own hands. We knew something of the steady driving forces behind complex manifestations of anti-*them.* So beneath that heavy mantle, we toiled to take another step down the long road of inclusion for Haitian-descendants, for Dominicans of Haitian descent, and for the full embrace of African-descendants of all hues living in the Dominican Republic and beyond. We pushed forward toward greater magnitudes of healing for ourselves, our past, and our future.

Construyendo puentes, no muros[1]

Jésula Blanc

La historia de le República Dominicana y Haití ha sido marcada por muchos momentos significativos y dentro de ellos han construido muros y puentes. El hecho de construir muros ha sido repetido a lo largo de los años, y uno de los muros más aterradores lo estamos recordando hoy, no con la finalidad de fomentar otros muros, sino con la conciencia y la convicción de que tenemos que cambiar la historia *construyendo puentes*.

En 1697, España perdió la parte del lado poniente de la Isla de la Española (Hispaniola) a Francia, donde trajeron negros y negras de África para trabajar arduamente de día y de noche, en condiciones inhumanas. Los trataban como animales y los separaron de sus familias y de su cultura. Los esclavos se sublevaron a partir de una ceremonia organizada por Boukman el 14 de agosto de 1791 en Bois-Caimán. Ellos y ellas lucharon hasta lograr la victoria el primero de enero de 1804 con el liderazgo del emperador Jean Jacques Dessalines. Así fundaron la «Primera República Negra». La República Dominicana también luchaba para ganar su independencia y Haití ha ayudado en esa lucha.

Ambas naciones tenían buenas relaciones y convivían. Pero de repente, pasó una tragedia terrible. El dictador Rafael Leónidas Trujillo ordenó que el ejército dominicano matara a los haitianos y a las haitianas y así estableció un muro muy fuerte. En la gobernanza de Jean Pierre Boyer su forma de gobernar puso otro gran muro. Pero todos estos muros están construidos por las élites y eso es una herencia de los españoles y los franceses transmitida de generación tras generación. La decisión de la corte constitucional contra 200,000 dominicanos de ascendencia haitiana (TCO/168-13) ocurrió 70 años después de la masacre. La forma de deportación es inhumana.

Por eso, el monumento que construimos en Dosmond, Haití, cada vez que lo miremos nos haga recordar el daño causado por personas sin escrúpulos y perversas de ambos países, uno por dar la orden de ejecución y el otro por beneficiarse de la sangre derramada.

¿A qué nos lleva la construcción de muros?

Evidentemente, la construcción de muros como sistema de defensa nos hace creer que eso es lo perfecto, lo mejor, nos vestimos con fuerte armadura y no somos conscientes de que al construir un muro humano nos impedimos respirar el aire del amor fraterno y de solidaridad.

Con los muros, lo que logramos en realidad es que nuestras heridas se infecten. Entonces, cerramos la historia con esa persona o con ese país, colocando el candado que mata cualquier posibilidad del encuentro y del apoyo mutuo.

¡Cuántos muros encontramos levantados por el odio, el rencor, la enemistad, la indiferencia y por creernos superiores o mejores que las y los demás!

¡Qué ridículo y aterrador se ve una puerta encima de un puente!

Nos pertrechamos instalando muros de todo tipo—muros visibles y muros invisibles; en lugar de mostrarnos como personas o como pueblos vulnerables.

Somos vulnerables y necesitamos la historia en todos los momentos.

Por eso, cuando levantamos un muro estamos pensando en los que quedan fuera.

Construir puentes, no es sinónimo de permitir que los acontecimientos marcados por muros se repitan. Eso, ¡NUNCA MÁS!

Puentes:

+ Haití ayudó a los dominicanos en la batalla de La Restauración; grupos de dominicanos y haitianos pasaron por Capotillo.
+ Puentes entre los vecinos, las comadres, los compadres, y las parejas de ambas naciones.
+ El asilo dado a los haitianos en 1991 después el golpe del Estado de Jean Bertrand Aristide
+ La creación de la Mesa de Dialogo Transfronterizo (MDT)
+ La creación del Comité Intermunicipalidad Transfronterizo (CIT)
+ La ayuda humanitaria de la República Dominicana en 2010 cuando ocurrió el terrible terremoto
+ La ayuda humanitaria de la República Dominicana después del Huracán Mateo en 2016

Entonces, ¿Qué nos parece si dejamos de levantar muros y nos animamos a construir puentes?

¡Vamos a quitarle al corazón el candado! ¡Animémonos a construir puentes!

Puentes que nos ayudan a conocernos mejor, a mirarnos a los ojos, a soñar y construir esperanzas.

¡Cuántos puentes se han levantado a lo largo de la historia de este espacio insular! ¡Cuántos puentes se construyeron en el año 1937 cuando familias dominicanas arriesgaron sus propias vidas para proteger a personas y familias haitianas que hoy permanecen en nuestras comunidades!

Seamos portadores y portadoras de la buena noticia de los puentes que sí se construyen y que no se publican por los medios de comunicación.

No estamos ahí para quejarnos y llorar lo que nos ha pasado sino para ver el presente y el futuro. Ustedes, los jóvenes, son el motor del cambio del mundo y hay que dejar de transmitir el odio. Los padres de familia y parientes también deben dejar de imponer una mala imagen de los dos países de la isla. Los medios de comunicación no resalten las buenas convivencias ni los hechos loables para que los sepa el público.

Las preguntas que podemos hacernos hoy serían las siguientes: ¿Construimos muros o puentes? ¿Qué beneficio podemos obtener con la construcción de muros? ¿Cuáles beneficios aportan y apoyan la construcción de puentes?

Sabemos que el corazón tiene sus propios espacios y hay que administrarlos bien para poder acoger las buenas ideas que nos invitan a construir una historia distinta y no nos dejen llorando del pasado.

Para construir puentes hay que limpiar el corazón y la mente. Hay que arriesgarse a soñar y detener a quienes quieren derribar nuestros sueños.

Si lo logramos, encontraremos la paz interior, que nos impulsará a trabajar para el bien de las generaciones del futuro y para un país y una isla más habitable. Hay que mirar hacia el frente sin volver la espalda.

Hay que limpiar la mente también y abrir el corazón de los dirigentes y de la sociedad civil de ambos lados para que haya una cultura de paz en la isla. ¡Es pa'lante que vamos!

Muchas gracias.

Nota

1. Este ensayo fue escrito para una conferencia en Dajabón para conmemorar los 82 años de la masacre de 1937.

Jacques Viau Renaud

Icon of Solidarity between Haiti and the Dominican Republic[1]

Sophie Mariñez, PhD

In the Dominican Republic, few subjects are more divisive than those of the relations between Haiti and the Dominican Republic and the treatment of Haitians on Dominican soil. These subjects separate families and end friendships, as many hold different views on history. For more than a century, Haitians have gone to the Dominican Republic to work in the sugar cane industry, laboring under slave-like conditions. Most recently, they have come to work in a variety of other industries, including construction and domestic service. In spite of their contribution to the national economy, they are often portrayed by right-wing politicians as a menace, a population that is taking jobs away from Dominicans and polluting the nation with their presence. Although it is reactivated anytime it seems politically expedient, this view was used in 1937 as a tool to justify a massacre perpetrated that year by dictator Rafael Trujillo against tens of thousands of Haitian migrants and their Afro-Dominican descendants.

The relationship between the Dominican Republic and Haiti—which share the island indigenous people called *Ayiti*, later on named Hispaniola—has not always been one of conflict, mistreatment, and massacre. Indeed, long before the existence of the present-day nations, the island often witnessed solidarity between very different people. During a period when all of Hispaniola was united under Haiti (1822–44), slavery was abolished on the entire island, turning it into a haven for hundreds of freed slaves from the United States who migrated to start new lives on Hispaniola. After the separation of the nations in 1844, which led to the founding of the Dominican Republic, solidarity continued. This was particularly clear in the 1860s, as Haitians helped Dominican leaders regain their independence from Spain (to which Dominican conservatives had annexed the new nation, returning it in 1861 to its former colonial status) through ammunition, supplies, trade, housing, and protection of refugees. Some Haitians even joined the expeditions against Spanish troops (Eller). In the twentieth century, while both nations were under the control of dictators—Trujillo in the Dominican Republic, François Duvalier in Haiti—leftist militants on both sides of the island also understood the continuing need to be allies and learn from each other. When Dominican president Juan Bosch was elected in 1962, hundreds of Haitians fleeing the Duvalier dictatorship took refuge in the homes of Dominican families. Most of these families were members of the left that had helped bring Bosch to power. When Bosch was overthrown in 1963 by a right-wing coup, Haitian exiles joined the Comando Haitiano, which helped the Constitutionalistas in their fight against the U.S. Marines sent in 1965 to ensure Bosch would never come back to power. Many died in combat (Vieux).

According to Lionel Vieux, who was part of this alliance, solidarity and friendship between leftist Haitians and Dominicans was the most natural thing in the world. The tacit understanding was that once Bosch was restored to power, Dominicans would help Haitians overthrow Duvalier. It was a notion of solidarity in which your gain is seen as my gain. Rather than acting to "save" someone in need, this solidarity was an agreement between equals, whereby the welfare of the other meant the welfare of the self, and fighting for the other was, in a way, fighting for oneself.

No one captured the era's Haitian-Dominican solidarity better than poet Jacques Viau Renaud. Born in Port-au-Prince in 1941, he was part of a modestly middle-class family that moved to Santo Domingo in 1948. As a young man, Viau met the artists, writers, and poets of the Generación del Sesenta (the Sixties Generation), known for their progressive inclination. His poetry was shaped by major aesthetic and political movements taking place at the time, including emergent Afro-affirming, anticolonial literary and philosophical scenes led by Aimé Césaire and Frantz Fanon; and second, by the Marxist and internationalist views espoused by his compatriot Jacques Stephen Alexis, a celebrated Haitian novelist. The artists of the Generación del Sesenta whom Viau knew as a young man—including Antonio Lockward Artiles, Miguel Alfonseca, and Silvano Lora—shared these internationalist and anticolonial ideas, a pride in African heritage, and a rekindled notion of Haitian-Dominican friendship. They organized in groups with such telling names as El Puño ("The Fist") and La Isla ("The Island"). La Isla, led by Viau's close friend Antonio Lockward Artiles, in particular, actively promoted solidarity between Haiti and the Dominican Republic.

These radical views informed Viau's poetry, which also addressed events taking place beyond the island. The poem "A un líder negro asesinado" (To a Murdered Black Leader), for example, was written in homage to U.S. civil rights activist Medgar Evers upon his assassination in 1964. It offers poignant testimony to a pan-Africanism that was in tune with events beyond Haiti and the Dominican Republic, and shows the impact that the U.S. civil rights movement had outside the United States. It also reflects an international current of writers and artists who engaged politically and used their art and literature as tools for political rebellion. In regard to Haitian-Dominican dynamics, Viau had a particularly privileged position as he belonged to both sides of the island. Born in Haiti, he saw himself as Haitian-Dominican and wrote exclusively in Spanish. His friends were Dominican poets and yet he also read Haitian authors and knew very well the history of Haiti. His poems emphasize a solidarity that manifests itself most concretely through the use of two terms: "nosotros" (us/we) and "patria," a term that can be translated as "country," "homeland," or, most literally, "fatherland," depending on the context See, for instance, this excerpt of the poem "Se va amontonando el silencio" (The Silence Is Piling Up):

> Camaradas, en nosotros está la alborada,
> quieren matarla
> matándonos,
> quieren guardarla en cajas de acero,
> asesinarla.
> Camaradas, no os dejéis asesinar,
> alcémonos en nombre del pueblo con el pueblo.
>
> Volved las espaldas a la noche
> gritad: Patria, te amamos . . .
> Patria te arrancaremos de los barrotes.
>
> *Comrades, the dawn lives within us*
> *they want to kill it*
> *by killing us,*
> *they want to keep it in cages of steel,*
> *murder it.*
> *Comrades, don't let them murder you,*
> *let's rise in the name of the people with the people.*
>
> *Turn your backs against the night*
> *shout: Fatherland, we love you . . .*
> *Fatherland, we will free you from the jail bars.* (2015, 70, my translation)

Viau's use of the collective pronoun "nosotros" is consistent with the poetry of his generation, which consciously used its art to further a political project of collectivity, inclusiveness, and unity. I would argue that Viau's use of the term "patria" is intended to be equally expansive. Instead of wondering whether he meant Haiti, his birth country, or the Dominican Republic, his adopted country, I suggest that he meant both but also more than that: patria as an *idea* of a nation, an imagined community of oppressed people—be they on the island or in the rest of the Americas—who are comrades, partners, and fellows sharing the same fight for freedom. *This* was his beloved patria, and he was willing to die for it, as he ultimately did.

When the Marines invaded the Dominican Republic in 1965, Viau joined the rebel unit Comando B-3, and soon became a sub-comandante. Hit by a mortar on June 15, he died a week later, on June 21, when he was only twenty-three. Hundreds of people attended his funeral. Although Dominicans had already adopted him as one of them, Constitutionalist president Francisco Caamaño formalized this adoption by issuing a decree granting him posthumously Dominican nationality for defending with his life the nation's democracy and sovereignty.

Since 1965 the Dominican concept of "patria" has shifted considerably from the solidarity community imagined by Viau's generation. While the fall of Duvalier in 1986 led to a rapprochement between the two countries well into the end of the past century, the adoption of neoliberal economic policies has accompanied a shift in values, giving priority to self-interest, competition, and individual success instead of solidarity. The party Bosch created almost a decade after the 1965 revolution, the Partido de la Liberación Dominicana (PLD), has been in power since 1996, with a short hiatus between 2000 and 2004. Yet it has turned its back on Haitians, erasing their contributions to Dominican history and implementing constitutional policies that culminated, in 2013, in the infamously anti-Haitian court ruling 168-13. This ruling strips of their nationality multiple generations of Dominicans of Haitian descent who had been entitled to Dominican nationality by virtue of birthright citizenship. The ruling provoked local and international outrage, galvanizing protests by activists, journalists, writers, and scholars. Worldwide solidarity flourished to unprecedented levels, broadcasting the message that many Dominicans do not agree with a notion of *dominicanidad* (Dominicanness) that excludes the poor and blacks. At the same time, another front emerged, protected by the PLD, to discredit, intimidate, and marginalize these activists. This divided Dominican society into, on the one side, those who defended an idea of an ethnic state, and, on the other, those of us who emerged as critics and dissenters, supporters of an expansive definition of Dominican society. The once-unifying concept of "patria" became the ultimate tool for dividing the nation.[2]

Several years ago, I was able to interview journalist Juan José Ayuso, who also participated in the 1965 revolution. When I asked him about Viau, with whom he had been close friends, he responded, with tears running down his face: "¿Para qué patria fue que peleamos? Para esto? Mira en lo que nos hemos convertido!" (For which country did we fight? For this? Look at what we've become!) Like Ayuso, I have a broken heart but I try to not let despair take over. New generations of artists, writers, and activists are rising and following in the footsteps of Viau and his generation, a sign that not everything is lost, and that hope and solidarity are alive, after all.

Notes

1. An earlier version of this article was originally published under the title of "Looking for Solidarity" in *The Boston Review* (May 24, 2019).

2. At the time of this essay's revision (July 10, 2020), the PLD has been officially replaced by the Partido Revolucionario Moderno (PRM), which won the elections held on July 5, 2020. It is unclear, however, whether the new regime will make it a policy to reverse anti-Haitian measures established by the PLD.

References

Eller, Anne. *We Dream Together: Dominican Independence, Haiti, and the Fight for Caribbean Freedom.* Duke University Press, 2016.

Meï, Siobhan Marie & Nathan Dize, "*J'essaie de vous parler de ma patrie* by Jacques Viau Renaud, a *Haiti in Translation* interview with Sophie Maríñez, Amaury Rodríguez and Raj Chetty. H-Haiti.

Viau Renaud, Jacques. *Ma Patrie, mes deux patries, mon île*. Translated by Jean-Marie Bourjolly. Cidhica, 2018.

Viau Renaud, Jacques. *J'essaie de vous parler de ma patrie*. Edited by Sophie Maríñez and Daniel Huttinot, with the collaboration of Raj Chetty and Amaury Rodríguez. Mémoire d'encrier, 2018.

Viau Renaud, Jacques. "I'm Trying to Tell You of My Country." Translated by Raj Chetty and Amaury Rodriguez. *The Black Scholar* vol. 45, no. 2, 2015, pp. 61–64.

Viau Renaud, Jacques. *Y en tu nombre elevaré mi voz: poesía y homenaje a su gesta*. Edited by Ángela Hernández. Fundación Juan Bosch, 2015.

Viau Renaud, Jacques. "The Permanence of Weeping." Translated by Patrick Rosal, *Connotation Press* vol. 4, no. 8, 2010.

Viau Renaud, Jacques. *Poesía completa: Jacques Viau Renaud*. Edited by Miguel D. Mena. Cielonaranja, 2006.

Viau Renaud, Jacques. *Permanencia del llanto: El XX aniversario de la insurrección de Abril*. Editora Universitaria, 1985.

Viau Renaud, Jacques. *Permanencia del llanto*. Publicaciones del Frente Cultural, 1965.

Vieux, Lionel. *Tertulia: Testimonio de un combatiente haitiano del comando B-3 (Guerra de Abril de 1965)*. Museo Memorial de la Resistencia Dominicana, 2018.

Pilgrims of Humane Remembrance at the Borderlands

Silvio Torres-Saillant

Early in October, since 2012, a gathering of parents, children, students, teachers, members of the clergy, community organizers, cultural activists, artists, and scholars have convened at a series of sites that straddle the arrondissement of Ouaminthe in Haiti's Nord-Est Department and the Dominican city of Dajabon. They have come from various places on both sides of the River Massacre on the island of Hispaniola as well as from numerous cities overseas, especially throughout the United States, the home of large diasporic communities of Dominican and Haitian ancestry. They have come to participate in peaceful acts of subversive remembering. During a two-day program of activities (discussion sessions, readings, arts and crafts exhibitions, prayers, performances, and community service), they commune with their neighbors across the borderline. They assert their human sameness over the national difference that the political partition of the island prescribes and its governments emphasize. Through various reflection-inducing tasks, they commit to remembering the past with an eye on increasing their chances of realistically envisioning a future of wholeness for Haitians and Dominicans. Their yearly pilgrimage seeks to forge sites of constructive remembrance that put memory to the service of healing on what could otherwise be milestones of rancor. They gather here to come to terms with and transcend a most ghastly chapter in the history of horror in the hemisphere. They call what their gathering achieves a Border of Lights, which they rightly oppose to the border of darkness that has often marred communication between the two polities that share the island.

The intersection of Ouanaminthe and Dajabón, where Dominicans and Haitians of good will have gathered every October since 2012, stands out among the key border points that in October 1937 witnessed the slaying of some 15,000 men, women, and children of Haitian ancestry, immigrant and Dominican-born alike. It was the seventh year in the three-decade-long rule of Dominican dictator Rafael Leonidas Trujillo. Machete-wielding soldiers and hired civilians hewed lives wholesale quietly, and—one imagines—messily, in order to avoid the noise that firearms would make if used. Despite the stealth, the Dominican government's genocidal violence shocked many in the hemisphere, and several Pan-American conferences ensued soon thereafter to address the inevitable crisis. Arbitration occurred among the region's heads of state, and an accord emerged that required Trujillo to make amends even without formally admitting to having committed the horrendous villainy. The Dominican government agreed to pay reparations to the administration of Haitian president Sténio Vincent. As "arbitrated" on the negotiations, the Vincent government would receive $750,000 for spending in a series of "colonies agricoles" for accommodating Haitian refugees who had escaped from the slaughter across the border.

Literature has done a fine job of urging the peoples of Hispaniola and the rest of the world to contend with the memory of the horror that took place on the island's borderlands in 1937, a time when, still counting on US support, the Trujillo regime literally got away with murder, specifically mass murder. Literary texts have pointed to the Vincent government's odd interest in maintaining a cozy relationship with the Dominican dictator, thereby failing to press hard enough to secure the justice that the victims of the massacre deserved. *Les semences de la colère* (1949), the novel by Anthony Lespès, tells the story of the "colonies agricoles" in a way that leaves readers filled with a sense of the despair endured by the refugees upon their return to Haitian territory. They generally had to fend for themselves in the face of obstacles stemming from the impromptu choice of the area assigned to them, the climate, the suitability of the soil, and the overall institutional neglect. In his review of the novel by Lespès, the African American scholar Mercer Cook observed that when he lived in Haiti in the early 1940s, it was widely known that Trujillo had ended up paying less than the $750,000 "arbitrated" in the negotiations and that even the absurd amount actually disbursed did not all reach the refugee camps (Cook 1949: 474).

The revolutionary Haitian literary artist Jacques Stéphen Alexis chose the bloodshed at the Haitian-Dominican border in 1937 as the context in which to bring to closure the difficult lives of his main characters Hilarion and his wife Claire-Heureuse in part 3 of his gripping debut novel *Compère Général Soleil* (1955). After surviving earlier trials, they see their infant son Désiré die in the attack by Trujillo's henchmen and their dogs. When they finally reach the Haitian border, Hilarion derives some satisfaction from dying in Haiti, "the domain of Ayiti Toma. He closed his eyes and smiled," whereas, "She was alone" (Alexis 290). Professor Carrol F. Coates, who translated Alexis's novel into English, observes that the "'missing' third subsection of part 3 might logically have been an exposé of the reasons for Vincent's failure to protest the massacre or a glimpse of Claire-Heureuse's return" (Coates xxxi). Coates notes that the novel gives signs of the author's awareness of secret correspondence between Trujillo and Vincent. In addition to his owing major favors to Trujillo, Vincent had other apprehensions that inhibited his public response to the mass killings. In a letter to his compatriot Elie Lescott, Vincent explained: "Having attested before the Haitian people to the sincerity and the solidity of our relations with the neighboring State and also to my personal friendship with President Trujillo, I admit that I am rather embarrassed by this sad event which, in all conscience, seems to me to go beyond ordinary border matters" (Vega 446 as cited by Coates xxxviii).

The 1989 novel *Le peuple des terres mêlées* (1989) by the avant-garde Haitian poet and literary path-finder René Philoctète evokes the horrors of 1937 in a manner that invites reflection on the cultural fusion and the border-bending practices of the people living in those cities and towns at geographical points where the two countries of Hispaniola meet and diverge. The French adjective *mêlée*, stemming from the verb *mêler*, which translates into English as *blend*, *combine*, or *mix*, may also in its noun form denote a *clash* or *skir-*

mish between combatants, or may even suggest the confusion of a *free-for-all*. These various valences all seem to apply to the variegated and asymmetrical cosmos inhabited by
the characters in Philoctète's novel, beginning with the protagonists, the Dominican labor
organizer Pedro Brito and his Haitian wife, Adèle Benjamin, a native of the commune of
Belladère in the arrondissment of Lascahobas. A leader, with his celebrated compatriot
Franketiénne, of Spiralisme, a Haitian literary school that upheld poetics characterized by
narrative defiance of logical progression and a mode of utterance that makes no conces-
sion to common sense, Philoctète tells the tale of the carnage in a manner that allows the
magical to reign supreme. We encounter machetes that seem bent on doing the killing on
their own as well as an oversized raptor-like bird that hovers over the sky in the Dominican
province of Elías Piña, as if supervising the affair and providing support to the perpetrators on the ground. The bloodshed takes on a nightmarish form in scenes like that of Pérez
Agustín de Córdoba, a local boss of Elías Piña who serves as captain to murderous gangs
and as killer himself. In a frenzy, Agustín charges against the powerless Haitian throng,
stabbing and maiming the bodies before him while recreating in his mind moments of
memorable sex with his former Haitian mistress Emmanuela. Through the thick fog of
the horror, however, the love story of Pedro and Adèle shines forth with irrevocable clarity.
Their tragedy too stands out in a plainly painful way as Pedro, in the end, fails to save his
beloved from the cruel blades of his own compatriots.

In her preface to *The Massacre River* (2005), the English translation of *Le peuple des
terres mêlées*, Haitian-American fiction writer Edwidge Danticat draws attention to the
way in which Philoctète's novel lingers on the struggles of the people living in the borderlands, the points where the two nations of Hispaniola come together while drifting apart.
She reflects on her own findings about those lands, on her realization that, "sandwiched
between the two borders was a group of people who tried to make a new world, people
who were as fluid as the waters themselves, the people of the Massacre River," who, like
Pedro and Adèle, not only suffer but they also sing, as they do in the pages of Philoctète's
novel (Danticat 2005: 8). By the time she penned her preface, Danticat had already become
widely known as the author of *The Farming of Bones* (1998), her own successful novel evoking the genocidal onslaught of 1937. Danticat's text explores plights and complex quanda-
ries of normal people who were not always henchmen of the dictatorship but who often
found themselves involved in horrors due to circumstances not of their own making.

The story of *The Farming of Bones* privileges a focus on individuals variously connected to Amabelle Désir, the narrator who survives the genocide by escaping to Haiti
before it is too late. We learn of Amabelle's beloved, Sebastien Onius, her acquaintances,
and the Dominican family she lived with up until the unfortunate events. We take an
especially close look at Doña Valencia, the lady of the house, *la dueña*, whom Amabelle
comes back to visit in later years. It is clear to Amabelle that Doña Valencia wishes she
had something satisfactory to say about the killings years back. We see it in her nervous
attestation to the individual Haitians whom she claims to have protected from imminent death: "I hid many of your people. I hid a baby who is now a student at the medical
school with Rosalinda," referring to her daughter, whose birth Amabelle had assisted in
(299). Señor Pico, the señora's husband, now dead, had actively partaken in the exter-

mination, and she knew that Amabelle had him in mind. As if answering an impending, though unasked, question, Dona Valencia says, "Amabelle, I live here still. If I denounce this country, I denounce myself. I would have had to leave the country if I'd forsaken my husband. Not that I ever asked questions. Not trusting him would have been like declaring that I was against him" (299).

In dramatizing Amabelle's journey to Haiti with the gang of refugees that formed itself spontaneously as they all sought to escape the carnage, Danticat's novel offers a critical view of the condition of the characters whether on one side of the island or on the other. Without a state to back them, they must fend for themselves. Yves, a member of the gang, resents the apparent impunity with which the Dominican government has harmed them. "Tell me, why don't our people go to war because of this?" he asks rhetorically, adding "Why won't our president fight?" (197). Already on the Haitian side, while standing in line to offer the testimonials that would qualify them for whatever pittance the survivors of the horror can apply for in keeping with the government's negotiations with the Trujillo regime, the refugees receive a disdainful treatment. The narrator observes the similarity of military garb on both sides of the island: "The soldiers from the Police Nationale . . . , the same khaki uniforms as the Dominican soldiers – a common inheritance from their training during the Yanki invasion of the whole island" (234). They get to look at a giant photograph of President Sténio Vincent, "a sophisticated looking man," wearing "a gentleman's collar with a bowtie, the end of which touched the shiny medal of the Grand Cross of the Juan Pablo Duarte Order of Merit, given to him by the Generalissimo as a symbol of friendship between our two people" (236). Danticat's novel, which in many ways pays tribute to *Les semences de la colère* by Lespès and *Compère Général Soleil* by Alexis insists on evoking the horror of the massacre in a way that retains the humanity of victims and perpetrators, staying clear of caricature representations of good and evil. In that respect, her novel takes full advantage of the artistic and moral caliber characteristic of figurations of the 1937 horrors in the literature of Haiti and its diaspora.

On the other hand, the first and best-known literary text by a Dominican author exploring the same genocide at the border, namely *El Masacre se pasa a pie*, a tale allegedly composed in 1937 and kept in concealment for 36 years by Freddy Prestol Castillo, a magistrate sent to the border during the massacre, deviates from the Haitian model of humane remembering. When the author found it safe to publish his story, and it appeared in print in 1973, the Dominican literati read Prestol Castillo's text as a novel and praised it as a text that presumably exposed the genocidal crime perpetrated by the Trujillo dictatorship. This came as a strange credit to a novel that, upon closer inspection, generally justifies the genocide of 1937, carping on the thievery of Haitian marauders on the border regions. In a nightmarish state of mind, the narrator recreates in his dreams all the elements of fundamentalist anti-Haitian historiography as he witnesses the actual massacre. His mind turns the machete wielding killers into avengers for the butchery that the schoolbooks taught him to impute to the troops of Jean-Jacques Dessalines in 1805, as they withdrew from the eastern part of the island, which had fallen under French military control. The 1802 Napoleonic invasion of Saint-Domingue had come to Hispaniola to crush the insurrection of the enslaved population originally led by Toussaint Louverture. The rebels had defeated and expelled the French forces from the western side of the island and had created there the Republic of Haiti, but the anti-French resistance lacked the human resources to expel them also from the eastern side, hence Dessalines's 1805 withdrawal. Through a narrator whose imagination works as if programmed to find in the remote past an act of Haitian violence against Dominicans for every atrocity committed at the present moment before his very eyes by Dominicans against Haitians—never distinguishing between Haitian foreigners from Dominicans of Haitian ancestry—the novel conditions the reader to accept the claim by the character who in the midst of the killing says: "we are collecting on an old debt" (Torres-Saillant 2011: 83). Apart from his aberrant observations that animalize those he perceives as ancestral others, saying things such as "the feet of Haitians, like those of cattle, are hoofs," the narrator relegates them to a lower rung of the human species when referring, for instance, to "the alphabet of smells of this primitive race" (Torres-Saillant 2011: 83).

El Masacre appeared in 1973 under the imprint of Editora Taller, at the time managed by José Israel Cuello, a leftist who still claimed affiliation to a socialist creed, and a quarter century later, in 1998, the Socialist Bloc long gone, Cuello's press reissued the novel as one of the distinguished titles that merited inclusion in a sort of permanent canon of Dominican letters, placing it in the series Biblioteca Taller Permanente. This elevation of Prestol Castillo's tale occurred when already several literary scholars had read the text closely, revealing its fraudulent status as an exposé, chiefly Diógenes Céspedes, Iván Grullón, and Elissa Lister (Torres-Saillant 2011: 83). In *On the Edge* (2018), a cultural history of representations of the Haitian-Dominican border in literature and other art forms, University of Essex scholar Maria Cristina Fumagalli has accomplished an insightful and admirably balanced reading of Prestol Castillo's text. Staying clear of indictment or praise, she offers *El Masacre* as a text to be valued primarily for the conflict and contradictions that seem to plague the mind of the author, as reflected in the psychopathology of the narrator (Fumagalli 2018: 141). Here as well as in her foreword to *You Can Cross the Massacre on Foot* (2019), the recent English translation of *El Masacre*, Fumagalli urges us to consider political and moral impasse as central to the tale that Prestol Castillo set out to tell (Fumagalli 2019: xv). Like the character of Doña Valencia in Danticat's novel, Prestol Castillo is trapped. A magistrate serving, as everybody else on the government payroll, at the pleasure of Trujillo, he apparently lacked the political will of those conscientious objectors who chose to go into exile. He had nowhere to go if he denounced the regime. But it seems that he was not devoid of the degree of sensibility necessary to respond to large-scale pain massively inflicted on innocent victims. He did recognize the evil perpetrated by the regime, hence the narrative ambivalence of his utterance, the structural disarray of the writing, and the morally fraught stance of an author who seems simultaneously to commemorate and blame the victims of the horror at the hands of a regime that he seems unwilling and unable to embrace fully or resolutely reject (Fumagalli 2018: 141).

The agony of Prestol Castillo's text to a large extent epitomizes the difficulty that the memory of the massacre has entailed for Dominicans. Still eight decades after the horrors, the task of engaging in salutary remembering remains an aspiration of the part of the citizenry that wishes to dismantle the historical sensibility inculcated in the population by the pedagogy and literacy of the Trujillo regime, which continues to reign supreme in the country until the present day. This aspiration forms the kernel of the seminar "80 Years after the Massacre: Reconstructing the Memory" held in Santo Domingo in October 2017 and of the published volume gathering the proceedings of that event. The editors of the volume articulate the aspiration in a paragraph that bears quoting *in toto*:

> The nation needs to delink from the negation or deformation of its history. It needs to stop accepting or validating each tyrannical myth and imposed silence or consensus. It needs to refrain from venerating false heroes and taking despicable crimes as patriotic epics. It needs to recognize itself, become reconciled with itself, and reconstruct its ethical system. To do that, it must contend with three pillars of reconciliation: memory, truth, and historical justice, which can help close our open wounds, culturally transcend the scars, and prevent them from continuing to replicate acts of brutality in whatever modality of the present. (Bosch Carcuro, Acosta Matos, and Pérez Vargas 2018: 13)

Remembering the killings of 1937—*el corte* (the slashing) in Dominican parlance, *kout kouto-a* (the stabbing) in Haitian creole, and the Vísperas dominicanas or *Vêpres dominicaines* in Trujillista diction—has been as hard for Dominicans as it was complicated for Prestol Castillo to navigate it. A footnote on the vespers could illustrate the mnemonic obstruction that the citizenry has had to contend with. Adopting the term vespers served the scribes of the Trujillo regime to align the mass murder of innocent and unarmed people on the border with a historical episode in European history that they could construe as a precedent of patriotic indignation. They seized upon the "Sicilian Vespers," the name conventionally given to the 1282 bloody uprising of residents of Sicily against the French-born King Charles I, who had ruled the kingdom without local support since 1266. The rebels proceeded by seeking to kill indiscriminately every French person on the land, civil servants and members of the clergy included, leaving an approximate toll of 3,000 deaths. The currency of the term in the arsenal of Trujillista discourse is acknowledged by historian Bernardo Vega, who mentions "Vísperas" in his amicable exchange with Edwidge Danticat as they debated minor disagreements concerning some details of verisimilitude in her novel's depiction of the logistics of the genocide (Vega and Danticat 2004). Carrol Coates refers several times to the "Dominican Vespers" in his critical annotations to his translation of *Compère Général Soleil* (Coates viii, xv, xxx, and 295). The epithet appears in the title of an article by an author who posits the massacre as among the root causes of Dominican migration to the United States (Jenks 1997). "Vêpres dominicaines" occurs also in a 2010 review of *Le peuple des terres mêlées* (Mobraz 2010). Given the Eurocentric pretentions of the *intelligentsia* that operated as scribes of the dictatorship, with no room for a dissenting opinion by anyone living in the country, the Sicilian precedent served as a vehicle for ennobling the carnage, rendering it patriotic, and, therefore, turning it into something that the people ought to embrace. Whether or not the rhetorical move to glorify the mass murder worked, the fact remains that there was no alternative discourse to refute it. Without a sturdy national press that had the slightest semblance of autonomy, the truth of the events at the border was the truth of the murderous Trujillo regime. Ironically, while the government never admitted that the carnage had been a state action, ascribing it to the spontaneous indignation of peasant farmers in the borderlands, the massacre somehow provided the intelligentsia with a platform for systematically disparaging Haitians racially, culturally, morally, religiously, and as a people incapable of sustaining an organized society. The writings of the Trujillo intelligentsia incessantly dehumanized Haitians, weaving a tale that represented Dominicans as waging an ongoing war to save their civilization from the encroachment of Haitian barbarians. In that respect, in their aggregate discourse, they committed overtly to a most virulently racist anti-Haitian dogma, in addition to voicing a blatantly negrophobic creed despite the overwhelmingly African descent of their country's population. The names of Joaquín Balaguer, Manuel Arturo Peña Batlle, and Emilio Rodríguez Demorizi resonate because they are best known by virtue of their proximity to Trujillo himself. But they represented only the tip of the iceberg. The discursive enterprise of the regime operated as a "total war" or a gigantic trolling campaign that seeped into the media, the schoolbooks, the church sermons, the political speeches, and every other arena relevant to socialization and the construction of public memory. In Dominican society, then, remembering the past meant to retrieve the narrative woven and disseminated by the Trujillo regime.

Even today it remains difficult for the citizenry to extricate themselves from the influence of what can appropriately be called *trujillismo cultural.* That is not because of the persuasive power of the discursive regime of the dictatorship, but rather, because its legacy has remained practically unchallenged institutionally in Dominican society. During the 1960s and 1970s, from their platform at the Autonomous University of Santo Domingo and other progressive outposts, a new *intelligentsia* came into their own to rectify the deformation of historical memory sponsored by the dictatorship. They made available quantitatively and qualitatively impressive bodies of discourse that effectively refuted the historical disinformation that the Trujillo intelligentsia had engaged in for thirty years. But Trujillo's substitute, the most influential and most powerful politician after the dictatorship, happened to be none other than Balaguer, perhaps the most vulgar anti-Haitian and the most militant negrophobe from among the scribes active in the dictator's court. During the twenty-two years of Balaguer's rule after the death of the tyrant, *trujillismo cultural* continued to reign supreme in Dominican public discourse, with the new knowledge produced by progressive scholars and thinkers since the 1960s onward remaining relegated to the classrooms of left-leaning university professors and alternative fora for self-selected audiences and interlocutors. The Balaguerato, an ideological extension of the Trujillato, with the Catholic Church by its side, ensured the continuation of the assault on public memory perpetrated by the dictatorship about the massacre and about the ethnological constitution of the Dominican people.

New and younger political leaders have come to the helm of the Dominican State in last four decades. Politicians from the Partido Revolucionario Dominicano (PRD), a party founded in New York in 1939 by the anti-Trujillo resistance, governed for three 4-year terms (1978-1986 and 2000-2004), and the ideological offspring of the progressive Juan Bosch in the Partido de la Liberación Dominicana (PLD) ruled for the remaining presidential terms until August 2020. Neither of them, however, saw it fit to seek to rehabilitate public memory from the deleterious deformation inculcated by the dictatorship. During a PRD government, the Minister of Culture gave the National Book Award (2002) to a negrophobic, anti-Haitian tract that warned that the Haitian presence in Dominican society represents an imminent threat to the national and cultural identity of the Dominican people, a threat compounded by the return migration of *domicanyorks*. Similarly, during a PLD government, the Ministry of Culture gave the literary life-achievement award to Roberto Marcallé Abreu, the author of a trilogy of novels that offers a vision of future Dominican greatness after resolving the "Haitian problem" by means of the genocidal extermination of large portions of the Haitian population in the country, combined with the sterilization and deportation of the remainder of them, making no distinction, again, between Dominicans of Haitian ancestry and Haitian immigrants (Victoriano-Martínez 2020: 191–207).

There is no way to overestimate the value of what those pilgrims do, who have come to the Ouanaminthe-Dajabón borderlands every year at the beginning of October since 2012 to propose salutary ways of remembering the horrors of the past whether we are the descendants of victims or of perpetrators. Unlike non-racist Germans, who, with widely broadcast public displays such as the Trials of Nuremberg, had occasion to look with scorn at what the Third Reich had done in their name when it orchestrated its "final solution," Dominicans of good will who have not had privileged exposure to humane remembering find themselves at a loss for things to say when they see their country indicted for the 1937 massacre. Unless they are historically "in the know," Dominicans have no way of saying in retrospect to the Trujillo regime, "no, you did not do that for me. You did it for yourself to satisfy your own perverse, criminous, dark desires: In fact, you did it against me because you have soiled the very idea of Dominicanness by linking it with mass murder and malevolent cowardice. You are fundamentally anti-Dominican." When the Dominican government withdrew the citizenship of over 250,000 compatriots of Haitian ancestry, many Dominicans of good will were at a loss for things to say when the international community began to indict their country. Many reacted instinctively by defending the Dominican government. They thus spoke as supporters of an action that, had they been asked, they would not have approved. Dominicans of good will would not support a government's decision to place a large segment of their country's population in a stateless limbo, turning them into foreigners in their own birthplace, vulnerable to the whim of any *guardia* who could grab them by the hand and drag then to the nearest border point for deportation to Haiti, a country which may be entirely alien to them and whose languages (French or Créole) they may not speak. Humane remembering can warn us about those ultra-nationalists who act in ways that we know are inimical to our ethics of national identity and belonging. Whoever invokes Dominicanness to justify or enable harm done to others, whether they are foreigners or compatriots of other ancestries at home, smears Dominicanness and is, of necessity, anti-Dominican even if it is the Dominican government itself doing it. We should owe no loyalty to rulers who invoke our name in vain to perpetrate evil while advancing perfidious ends.

The liberal governments that came after Balaguer did not commit to delinking from the tenets of *trujillismo cultural* probably because they are too useful. The paradigms therein involved could come in handy at key political junctures. They can, at any time, translate into good political capital that could help particular sectors win elections, stay in power, or elicit support for corrupt schemes. Anti-Haitianism worked in electoral campaigns that kept the PLD in power, and the denationalization law of 2013 bears every resemblance to a voter suppression scheme. One can trade in hatred not only for hatred's sake, but one might resort to it simply because it is sure to work in a ploy that might be motivated primarily by economic or political gain. The problem, though, is the resulting legacy for the future, the climate of social relations that such a ploy might be left to our children and their children in turn.

There is nothing to guarantee that the carnage of 1937 will not come back. For as long as *trujillismo cultural* remains alive, no one can assure us that Trujillo will not come back with another name or even with the same. Ramfis, the grandson of the murderous dictator, was able to establish himself as a viable candidate in the Dominican political market for the 2019 election cycle, and he did so without delinking from the legacy of his grandfather. Ramfis vowed to set the record straight about his grandfather, whom he views as having unfairly suffered too many years of slander by people in Dominican society. He did not win a major nomination this time around, but we have not yet heard the last thing about him. Suffice it to glance at the highly active website dedicated to promoting his candidacy and to refute all charges made in recent scholarship against his grandfather, apart from publishing articles and documents that highlight the generalissimo's great virtues while maligning those he regards as his grandfather's foes, be it Juan Bosch, the CIA, or the people involved in killing him (*trujillodeclassified.com*). In the United States, the traffic of hatred brought to the White House a candidate who declared himself the enemy of immigrants of non-European Christian origins and labeled Mexicans as "rapists" and "murderers." In Brazil, the open indictment of people of African descent and indigenous origins in addition to celebrating the ominous dictatorship of years past put the current president in the national palace. There is really no way to overemphasize relevance of what those pilgrims do, who have come to the Ouanaminthe-Dajabón borderlands every year at the beginning of October to propose salutary ways of remembering the horrors of the past in hopes of contributing to a new humane logic of social relations in Hispaniola and elsewhere.

Works Cited

Alexis, Jacques Stéphen. *Compère Général Soleil*. Paris: Editions Gallimard, 1955.

Balaguer, Joaquín. *La isla al revés: Haití y el destino dominicano*. Librería Dominicana, S.A., 1984.

Bosch Carcuro, Matías, Eliades Acosta Matos, and Amaury Pérez Vargas, eds. *Masacre de 1937, 80 años después: Reconstruyendo la memoria*. Fundación Juan Bosch/CLACSO, 2018.

Byrd, Christopher. "A History of Carnage." *The American Prospect: Ideas, Politics & Power*. 30 December 2005, *prospect.org*.

Coates, Carrol F. "Introduction." *General Sun, My Brother: A Novel* by Jacques Stéphen Alexis, translated by Carrol F. Coates. U of Virginia P, 1999, pp. ix-xxxviii.

Cook, Mercer. Review of *Les semences de la colère* by Anthony Lespès. *The Journal of Negro History*, vol. 34, no. 4, October 1949, pp. 474–75.

Cortés, Zaira. "Nieto de Trujillo propone muro . . ." www.telemundo47.com, 29 March 2018.

Danticat, Edwidge. *The Farming of Bones*. Soho Press, 1998.

Danticat, Edwidge. "Preface." *The Massacre River* by René Philoctète. Translated by Linda Coverdale. New Directions Books, 2005, pp. 7–9.

Fumagalli, Maria Cristina. *On the Edge: Writing the Border between Haiti and the Dominican Republic*. Liverpool, 2018.

Fumagalli, Maria Cristina. "Foreword." *You Can Cross the Massacre on Foot* by Freddy Prestol Castillo. Translated by Margaret Randall. Duke UP, 2019.

Jenks, Kevin. "The 'Dominican Vespers': The Cultural Roots of US Immigrants from the Dominican Republic." *The Social Contract*, summer 1997, pp. 268–75.

Lespès, Anthony. *Les semences de la colère*. Editions Henri Deschamps, 1949.

Morbraz. "*Le people de terres mêlées* de René Philoctète (1989)." Blues dans le Sud. Philmorbraz.blogspot.com, 13 Feb. 2010.

Pereyra, Emilia. "El enfático interés del nieto de Trujillo . . ." www.diariolibre.com, 7 Dec. 2017.

Philoctète, René. *The Massacre River*. Preface by Edwidge Danticat. Introduction by Lionel Trouillot. Translated by Linda Coverdale. New Directions Books, 2005.

---. *Les peuples des terres mêlées*. Editions Henri Deschamps, 1989.

Prestol Castillo, Freddy. *El Masacre se pasa a pie*. Editora Taller, 1998.

Torres-Saillant, Silvio. *El retorno de las yolas: ensayos sobre diáspora, democracia y dominicanidad*. Ediciones Librería La Trinitaria y Editoria Manatí, 1999.

---. "Elogio del irrespeto." *El Caribe*, 11 May 2003, p. 9.

---. "La herencia criminal." *El tigueraje intelectual*. Foreword by Franklin J. Franco Pichardo. Editora Mediabyte, S.R.L, 2011, 79–85.

Vega, Bernardo. 1988. *Trujillo et Haití*. Vol. 1, 1930-1937. Translated by Guillermo Piña Contreras and Françoise Mironneau. Fundación Cultural Dominicana, 1995.

---. "Bernardo Vega y Edwidge Danticat discuten la matanza de 1937". *Periódico Hoy*, 5 June 2004.

Victoriano-Martínez, Ramón Antonio. "The Black Plague from the West': Haiti in Roberto Marcallé Abreu's Dystopia." *Racialized Visions: Haiti and the Hispanic Caribbean*. Ed.

Valdés, Vanessa K. Afro-Latinx Futures Series. New York: SUNY Press, 2020, 191–207.

To Dajabón, with Love

Cynthia Carrión

As I sit at the border crossing of Dajabón, DR I am amazed that a river which takes less than 50 steps to cross has witnessed so much bloodshed, heartache and despair. Getting our supplies ready for our crossing one more time before tomorrow's event, I am met with panic. If a genocide happens and no one speaks of it can it be erased from memory? I am still confronted with people that ask me why are you not talking about "lo bueno de Trujillo." To that I say I am not here to talk about the good of Trujillo, I am here because all humans no matter what side of a river they come from deserve respect and dignity. 75 years is a long time to wait for the world to lend its ear, its heart and its memory to this tragedy. Please help get the word out #borderoflights.

CYNTHIA CARRIÓN (VIA FACEBOOK), **OCTOBER 3, 2012**

To be part of the Border of Lights movement has been an honor of a lifetime. Never could I have imagined all that it would involve when I told Julia Alvarez I was interested in helping organize what she had called a "border of lights." I am forever changed by the friendships with fellow BOLers and the town of Dajabón that both welcomed and challenged me. Below are excerpts of the communications sent during 2012 as we commemorated the seventy-fifth anniversary of the Haitian Massacre. We were, and still are, a group of volunteers doing the best we can with what we have. At the heart of BOL is to bring together as many people as possible to be involved (to know and remember) and ensuring that those most impacted are at the center of decision making and calling for justice.

2/5/2012 (Email to contacts)
Dear Friends, A few months ago, I heard author Julia Alvarez speak about the need to raise our voices in honor of those who brutally died of injustice during the 1937 Haitian Massacre. She planted a seed in me that I can no longer ignore. October 2012 will mark the 75th year of the Haitian and Haitian-Dominican massacre that occurred on the border town of Dajabón, Dominican Republic.

Will you join me in helping to plan, attend, and/or spread the word about this historic moment? Our first planning meeting will be held this Friday, February 10th at 8:30pm Yip-pie Cafe: 9 Bleecker Street
To RSVP and for more information: www.facebook.com/events/303755133007105/

There is no set agenda or plan for a gathering, only the need for our island and people to heal. For me this is a crucial moment to acknowledge the loss of life and a declaration that we are brothers and sisters on both sides of an island. Professor Edward Paulino (John Jay College) and I have begun having conversations about what this day could be and want to include as many people as possible from the Dominican Republic, Haiti, US, and beyond in making this a meaningful, impactful, and realistic event.

I am calling on us all to come together and share our thoughts, ideas and energy on how to form a Border of Lights from October 2- 6, 2012.

Let's come together to plan, envision and build a movement!

As author Julia Alvarez states:For many years, in talking about the hard and difficult relationship between Haiti and the Dominican Republic, and [about] the Haitian massacre in 1937, I have been saying, that people – forget government, forget institutions – that *people* should come to the border on October 3rd (the anniversary of the Haitian Massacre of 1937), and create a border of light. Have musicians, singers, actors, writers reading, poets reciting, just people coming together and lighting a candle, making a border of light and saying, "You know what? We can create an alternate way of being neighbors and being human beings together." (*Manhattan Times* article, October 14, 2011).

Please feel free to contact me if you have any questions or would like additional information.

In solidarity, Cynthia

April 26, 2012, 2:40 PM (email correspondence between Mario Serrano and Cynthia Carrión)

Gracias Mario por tus respuestas.

Estoy de acuerdo con todo lo que escribiste. La gran pregunta es ¿cuál es la mejor forma o cómo podemos hacer esto con los actores locales de Dajabon? Queremos apoyar los esfuerzos.

Estoy disponible el sábado a las 11 (hora dominicana), o el domingo después de las 5 de la tarde.

¡Si guía, yo te sigo!
Cynthia

Reminder: Border of Lights Working Group:

BOL Weekly Conference Call starts at 10:00PM EDT on Wednesday, 13 June 2012
As the creator of this conference call, you can moderate participants from this link:
http://wiggio.com/moderate_call.php?callid=2267072&uid=1056402
To join the call, dial 1 (702) 589-8240 and enter access code 5145356.
Scheduled by: Cynthia Carrión

On **Sat, September 8, 2012** at 11:32 PM, Cynthia Carrion <cm.carrion@gmail.com> wrote:
Dear Friends,

For the past few days, I have been struggling with how best to write this email, which shares one of my deepest passions while also asking for support. On September 27th, I will be leaving for the Dominican Republic to help organize a solidarity event along the Haitian-Dominican Republic border to commemorate the 75th anniversary of the 1937 Haitian Massacre, (also known as the Parsley Massacre), an ethnic cleansing meant to exterminate the Haitian population on the Dominican border.

Between 10,000 and 20,000 Haitians and Dominicans of Haitian descent were slaughtered by the Dominican army and conscripted civilians. The orders were given by the dictator Rafael Trujillo. Dominican authorities have never truly acknowledged the mass murder nor given adequate compensations to victims' families. I am a part of a collective called Border of Lights (BOL), which is looking to honor those who died in this tragedy and to shine a light on the ongoing injustices that those of Haitian descent continue to face in the Dominican Republic. Members of our volunteer collective include Dominican author and activist Julia Alvarez, Haitian author Edwidge Danticat and other dedicated organizers, teachers, students, and artists. Many I speak with support our efforts, some think I'm crazy or it's too dangerous and others have no idea what I'm talking about.

I need your help in proving that this is not crazy, that the world cares and that change is possible. We are currently raising funds for a peace walk, vigil, park clean-up/beautification, art installation and community teach-i ns from Oct 4-6th. We are also collaborating with other community-based organizations to support a mural at the border that honors those lives lost and calls for unity.

Growing up I would spend my summers in the Dominican Republic, more specifically Santiago de los Caballeros. When I was nine, I remember asking my grandmother why there was so much hate among Haitians and Dominicans. She took a deep breath and told me it was because the island was too divided and we didn't know how to be neighbors. Twenty (plus) years later, I'm asking that its finally time to become neighbors.

To learn more about our work (and get resources to teach about the massacre) visit: www.borderoflights.org and to make a contribution to our efforts please go to: http://www.kickstarter.com/projects/borderoflights/border-of-lights (every dollar is appreciated)!

We are also in need of filmmakers, organizers, folks with time to help us out, so please don't be shy in reaching out or sharing this with your networks.

With love and in solidarity,

Cynthia

9/29/2012 (email to friends and supporters)
I'm in Santiago staying with my Abuela while we make FINAL preparations for our events along the border. At 88 years old and with a cane she calls her novio, my grandmother has been an incredible partner. All day she has been by my side as I rented a car, bought supplies in the mega hardware store of Beller (think Home Depot) and tried to navigate the streets of Santiago. She's even allowed me to store all our compras including a lawn mower, paint accessories and hedge cutters in her living room. I should also mention she opened her home and hospitality to my ad-hoc organizing meetings in the patio. She wouldn't be my Abuela if in the middle of all this, she wasn't also preparing me my meals and remind-ing me that on an empty stomach nothing can be resolved. In return I've promised to attend a festival at the nursing home she volunteers at later today.

Please allow me to gush over my family just a little bit longer. My Tia Yadira gave our project a shout out during her morning television program in Santiago and has equipped me with a cell phone fully stocked with minutes. With the support of my mother, I have been able to buy many of the supplies we need, not to mention she worked with me on my Spanish talking points. Dave has added international roaming to our phone plan and taken my panic calls.

I am so humbled by friends near and far who have donated funds, ideas and encouragement to Border of Lights.

Our kickstarter project ends tomorrow at 11:59PM. We have nearly doubled our initial goal, which has allowed us to support commemoration events in other border towns and a community mural. With more funds we can do even more so the call is still on going.

At the heart of this project is an awareness campaign. To bring attention to a horrific tragedy and to show solidarity with those who work to end discrimination and injustice against Dominicans of Haitian descent and Haitians; remnants of the massacre. Please let me know if there is anything I can do to get these stories out.

Stay tuned for NPR's "Tell Me More" program on Monday which will have Dominican author Julia Alvarez and Haitian author Edwidge Danticat speaking about the project. There is even talk that *Time Magazine*, the BBC, and CNN might be joining us as well on Thursday. Fingers crossed.

For our full program, please visit www.borderoflights.org "Get involved" section or "news" for the press release (share widely).

Thank you all for getting us to this point. Hope you don't mind my updates.

In solidarity, Cynthia

PS: apologies in advance for any typos as working from my phone has a few limitations. Cynthia Carrion / 917.447.0991 /cm.carrion@gmail.com

10/5/2012

Where do I begin? Yesterday was one of the most amazing days of my life on every level. By passion and profession I am a community organizer and to be a part of Border of Lights/Frontera de Luces was the ultimate experience of seeing communities come together. While I am grateful that the events we planned for Thursday were a success, we were also reminded of the work that remains.

Yesterday started with a 7:30 am interview on Radio Marién. Padre Guillermo Perdomo hosted the morning program and invited Padre Regino (Solidaridad Fronteriza), Eddie and I to discuss our project. The hour long interview was kind, honest and a lot of fun. We talked about my raíces dominicanas and how my Abuela made me mangú con cebolla before leaving for Dajabón. The conversation of course transitioned to the importance of our gathering.

During our interview, Padre Regino mentioned that in the 38 years that he has been working on the border he has never publicly spoken of the massacre. That it is our silence of this tragedy that is hurting us all. It was a safe and welcoming space to share our thoughts and vision of peace and awareness.

In contrast, our interview on Beller Digital's program with Juan de Dios Liberato was more aggressive. At the last moment, the host decided he was not going to be a part of the interview and sent his producer. This time Eddie and I did not have Padre Regino, we took on questions of "why are you doing this knowing it is going to unleash old wounds" and "don't you know Haitians hate Dominicans too." They thought I was from Chile for some reason, I think it was easier for them to see us as outsiders. Just as I was thinking we shouldn't be here, I was whispered a message from a young man working master control.

"I am Haitian and Dominican. I know the importance of your work." With that, I took on the questions with greater vigor. As soon as we finished we were told we needed to leave immediately, no time for handshakes or a thank you.

Later in the afternoon the producer came down to the park where we were setting up our postcard action to further discuss, with the facts, with Dr. Edward Paulino.

Between interviews, we were setting up supplies, getting lunch arrangements, and doing our best outreach for the vigil at the border on both sides.

Occupy Parque Duarte: by 1pm, we began our interactive art installation in the middle of Parque Duarte at the heart of Dajabón. Using rope and clothes pins, we clipped over 200 post cards around the gazebo that read: "*1937 - República Dominicana y Haiti - cuéntanos*", tell us what you know. We then went around asking everyone to share with us what they heard knew or wanted to say about that time.

What came back was astonishing. Everything from "we are brothers" to "it was an invasion that the President Trujillo ordered to stop." We have messages of hope and messages of hate. This is the first step in any healing process to share, put it out there to be called out. We had students from Doulas school, DREAM volunteers and even Julia Alvarez taking to the street and asking members to share. We asked old men sitting in the park, limpiazapatos (shoeshine boys), baseball teams, street vendors, and military police; even Miss Dajabón participated. The cards were filled anonymously so people felt open to honestly share. The cards came back in Spanish and Kreyòl. For those that could not write or preferred to just talk, we recorded it for them.

At 3:30, Eddie had everyone gather, by then we were joined by 35 Mariposa Foundation students, The Hub for Santiago, and many others. We discussed what we saw and Eddie had students act out in silence the different forms of injustice they saw portrayed on the cards.

It was then off to the vigil (with a quick stop for dinner). Prior to the peace walk and vigil there was a community mass. Over 300 people gathered and the team of priests shared the importance of this moment.

October 7, 2012

I'm still taking it all in. These last few days have been an incredible experience. I leave a piece of my heart in Dajabón, and in return I've been given friendships, courage and a new spirit for justice. Silence when used as a weapon of oppression can be as powerful as a gun. This weekend silence retreated and we left hopeful that light will replace darkness on the border.

"Nourishing the Palm of Liberty"

Jacques Viau's Haitian-Dominican *Insularidad*

Raj Chetty and Amaury Rodríguez

Throughout the twentieth century, the more recalcitrant sectors of the Dominican elite—recalcitrant as in racist and reactionary—concocted a series of lies and fabrications with the aim of erasing the strong emotional, cultural, and political bonds that unite Haitians, Dominicans, and rayanos.[1] To that end, the US-backed Trujillo dictatorship (1930–1961) was the main vehicle that facilitated the spread of the old anti-Haitian hatred incubated in the minds and social circles of a dominant, foreign, white, and European elite who saw the emancipatory seal of the Haitian Revolution (1791–1804) as a threat to their economic interests, and ultimately, as a threat to their own existence. To be sure, the United States had already been pushing narratives of Dominicans' relative racial and cultural superiority over their Haitian neighbors, particularly during the periods of overlapping US occupations of both nation states on the island, from 1914–1934 in Haiti and 1916–1924 in the Dominican Republic. These narratives stood in marked contrast to the practices of soli-darity between Haitians and Dominicans, particularly at moments of immense historical and social rupture, such as the Haitian Revolution from 1791–1804, the founding of the republic in 1844, the Dominican War of Restoration in the 1860s, the US occupations referenced above, the Trujillo and Duvalier dictatorships, the 1965 Revolución de Abril, and the devastating 2010 earthquake in Haiti.[2]

In the early twentieth century, the role of the sugar barons in the spread of racism and anti-Haitian hysteria was instrumental. Relying primarily on a foreign labor force, the sugar industry created a segregated labor system that sought to divide the working class along ethnic lines, and further domesticate Haitian sugar cane laborers (Martínez). Beyond the dictatorial period, there was a continuity of the elite project of domination with the erasure of the history of Haitian-Dominican solidarity. With the defeat of the 1965 Dominican democratic revolution by US Marines, the political rehabilitation of some of the closest collaborators of the Trujillo regime gave the upper hand to the forces of reaction, led by Joaquín Balaguer. During the *trujillato*, Balaguer had been a close collaborator of the Tru-jillo dictatorship, and he played a critical role as a racist pamphleteer and an apologist of the 1937 Haitian massacre carried out by Trujillo and his henchmen. Francisco Rodríguez de

León argues that Trujillo was the personification of terror and violence that characterized his regime, while Balaguer was the *letrado* intellectual who rhetorically and discursively created justifications for state repression, including the 1937 genocide.[3] After Trujillo's death, the US-backed "election" of Balaguer in 1966 inaugurated a twelve-year counter-revolution (1966–1978) that strengthened the repressive apparatus by not only persecuting left-wing activists but also keeping in check labor activists and organizations that made a series of efforts toward the organization of Haitian sugar cane workers. Balaguer's regime also collaborated with the Duvalier dictatorship and its persecution of Haitian exiles.

Balaguer's commitment to maintaining the status quo as well as his anti-black hatred toward José Francisco Peña Gómez, a Dominican politician of Haitian descent, were exemplified in a number of racist campaigns throughout the 1970s, 1980s, and 1990s. In the 1990s, Leonel Fernández, of the Partido de la Liberación Dominicana (PLD), came to power with the support of Balaguer and others, contributing to the rehabilitation of both trujillismo and balaguerismo. With the aid of both Balaguer and Vincho Castillo, another well-known trujillista, and the blessing of Juan Bosch, founder of the PLD in 1973, anti-Haitian racism, the elite's preferred political weapon of choice, not only was rehabilitated, but became normalized.

Today's conservative intellectuals in the Dominican Republic spread anti-Haitian racism and conservative nationalism, playing a similar role as that of their predecessors during the Trujillo regime. The need to prevent the emergence of organized popular resistance to colonial violence in Hispaniola is the central rationale behind this orchestrated erasure of *insularidad*. That is, to maintain the system of exploitation and oppression which are essential pillars of capitalist rule by local elites and their powerful imperialist allies. Thus, while "insularity" carries the negative connotation of being provincial or isolated—we mean *insularidad* in this context to describe a progressive attempt to forge an imagined community in solidarity across the Haitian-Dominican border, tying together Dominicans, Haitians, Dominicans of Haitian descent, and rayanos.[4] Our use of "imagined community" here resonates with Sophie Maríñez's deployment of the phrase in her *Boston Review* article on the importance of Viau's poetry.[5]

THE POET OF *INSULARIDAD*

The preceding brief overview provides a historical frame to understand Jacques Viau Renaud, whose life and poetry exemplify the idea of *insularidad*, particularly in the two poems we include below. In addition to being a poet, Viau was a revolutionary militant and martyr of the 1965 Dominican revolution. Born in Haiti in 1941 and murdered by US marines in Santo Domingo in 1965 during the Dominican Revolución de Abril, Viau left a legacy of immense significance for Dominicans, Haitians, rayanos, and Dominicans of Haitian descent. This last group, descendants of Haitian migrants, in some cases with multiple generations born in the Dominican Republic, have been engaged in a struggle to retain the political recognition, as Dominican citizens, guaranteed to them by the pre-2010 Dominican Constitution. Their citizenship has come under assault through various legal and constitutional mechanisms, buttressed by the longer history discussed above and the social conditions that history has spawned.

State anxiety over this group—people of Haitian descent born in the Dominican Republic, the children of Haitian migrant laborers—extends back to Balaguer's rule during the Doce Años. As Amelia Hintzen has pointed out, in the mid- to late-1970s, "El gobierno de Balaguer buscaba una manera de resolver el 'grave problema' de que los hijos de haitianos tuvieran derechos como dominicanos . . . ya en los años 70 el gobierno estaba intentando revocar los derechos establecidos de los residentes haitianos con la manipulación de [la] idea de 'en tránsito'" ("Extranjeros en tránsito" 230–31). Though those efforts were largely unsuccessful at codifying legal or constitutional efforts to erase Dominicans of Haitian origin from citizenship and its benefits—e.g. voting rights, access to identification cards necessary for social services, higher education, and birth and marriage registration—they paved the way for subsequent efforts that did.

The contemporary form of exclusionary state repression against Dominicans of Haitian origin has developed and evolved since the 1980s, accelerating in the 2000s via a series of court cases and juridical and constitutional measures that culminated in the Tribunal Constitucional's infamous Sentencia in 2013 (Sentencia TC/168). These measures included a new emphasis on universal documentation, a state administrative practice promoted by international development agencies (Hayes de Kalaf). The ruling effectively put into question the citizenship status of hundreds of thousands of mostly Haitian-descended Dominicans.[5]

To be sure, large numbers of Dominicans, Haitians, rayanos, and Dominicans of Haitian descent have consistently resisted these efforts, and the opposition within the Dominican Republic to TC/168 was forceful. This resistance brings to the contemporary moment the form of solidarity Viau forged through this poetry and sealed with his blood in 1965, in defense of Dominican sovereignty.[6] In "Patria" ("Homeland"), penned in 1963, Viau casts a glance, at once forlorn and hopeful, at Haiti from the Dominican Republic. Forlorn because of the ravages of poverty and the imperial necropolitics that perpetuate and deepen it, but hopeful because of the revolutionary potential in the worker, the one who intimately knows the Caribbean soil. In spite of having lived in the Dominican Republic for most of his shortened life, Viau evocatively writes, "Patria / he sentido como corres a través de mi sangre / agolpándote en my garganta / golpeándome la nuca / acudiendo a gritos a mi canto" ("Homeland / I have sensed how you course through my blood / congealing in my throat / striking at my nape / in an uproar, converging upon my chant"). Here, Haiti is not only located inside of the poet, but it also moves with his poetic chant and causes this chant to move it. The lines capture a powerful dialectic between the homeland, Haiti, and the poet living in exile, Viau in the Dominican Republic. By the end of the poem, this dialectic unites the poet's chant of the opening stanzas with the "canto de prole vegetal, mineral y humana" ("proletarian chant, vegetal, mineral and humane") in the final lines of the poem.

While Viau remains at the level of indirect metaphor in "Patria"—he never names Haiti explicitly in the poem—in "Pobre del que no comprenda" ("Pity the One Who Does Not Understand"), Viau invokes Haiti more directly, though still without naming it. Across the poem, the poet apostrophically calls an unnamed "amiga" not only to hear her voice, but to participate actively in facilitating the poet's ability to raise her voice, give her heart, blood, lungs, entrails, and vision to benefit "mi pueblo / tu pueblo" ("my people / your people"). At the center of the poem, the poet desires that his blood specifically be used for "nutriendo la Palma de la libertad (de 1804)" ("nourishing the Palm of liberty (from 1804)"). In this one economical, poetic phrase, Viau captures the revolutionary struggle of the Haitian Revolution that successfully established an independent Haiti in 1804, free from racial slavery, and the idea that revolution did not finish in 1804, but needs nourishing in Viau's 1960s, for both nations on the island. It does so via the symbolic richness of the Caribbean palm that graces the center of the Haitian flag and whose leaf appears in the Dominican one.

The "Palma de la libertad" is particularly resonant as a symbol for *insularidad*. In the opening of *We Dream Together: Dominican Independence, Haiti, and the Fight for Caribbean Freedom*, Anne Eller shares the following story during the Dominican "Guerra de la Restauración" (War of Restoration):

> After dark on a late spring night in 1864, an anonymous group toppled a towering palm tree, the Tree of Liberty, in the town square of Santo Domingo. Planted by officials from Jean-Pierre Boyer's administration four decades earlier, the tree represented a celebration of Dominican emancipation, independence, and the unification of the former Spanish colony with the revolutionary Haitian state. Those who won abolition in 1822 called themselves "freedmen of the Palm." (1)

Viau undoubtedly draws from this understanding of the Palma as a unifying symbol that brings together Haitian and Dominican revolutionary struggles for freedom from slavery and European colonial control. In the wake of Trujillo's *ajusticiamiento* and in the light of the early years of Duvalier's dictatorship, as Dominican society is convulsed by struggles between forces for democracy and forces to maintain trujillista ideological and political control, Viau poetically invokes the Palma to point his readers toward histories of Dominican-Haitian solidarity with a symbol that they would all recognize.

The two poems we present here, in their original Spanish and with our translations to English, are representative of Viau's artistic vision and the sort of *insularidad* structuring the work of Border of Lights.[7] During his tragically shortened life, Viau denounced the Trujillos and the Duvaliers of his time. Viau wrote so we won't forget Trujillo's genocidal crimes in 1937 and afterwards. Viau wrote so we won't forget the crimes of the Duvalierist army in his beloved Haiti. The poet of Haitian-Dominican *insularidad*, Viau's vision and commitment span the entire island, speaking truth to power.

Homeland

Homeland
I have sensed how from your hungering latitude
surges my people through sonorous essences
and palpable respirations.

Homeland
I have sensed how you course through my blood
congealing in my throat
striking at my nape
in an uproar, converging upon my chant.

I have been present at your anguish from afar
cresting in the crown of the trees
exploding in the fruits
in the migratory birds
that inhabit the naked extension of your
fallen tear.

I have encountered your voice
elevated by the aroma of my lament
and of my sweat
the sweat of the peasant
and of the laborer
felled like ancient creole pines.

You I have viewed flowing over the cheeks
of our young women fighters

Patria

Patria
he sentido cómo desde tu hambrienta latitud
sube mi pueblo a través de sonoras esencias
y palpables respiraciones.

Patria
he sentido como corres a través de mi sangre
agolpándote en mi garganta
golpeándome la nuca
acudiendo a gritos a mi canto.

He presenciado desde lejos tu angustia
crecida en la copa de los árboles
explotando en los frutos
en las aves migratorias
que habitan tu desnuda extensión de
lágrima caída

He escuchado tu voz
levantada por el aroma de mi llanto
y de mi sudor
del sudor del campesino
y del obrero
talados como viejos pinares montañeses.

Te he visto correr sobre las mejillas de
nuestras jóvenes luchadoras

discovering the definitive form of death.
I have encountered your cry, mother of phthisic children
phthisic yourself
fecund mother
pauperized by those who rob your limpid aluminum
as the tears of a child
and dissolve the steel of your entrails
in the intense ashes of hatred
robbery and crimes of petty kings for hire.

Oh homeland
my homeland
each time I pronounce your name
a wound opens in my heart
and from there your eyes watch me
and watch the world
and watch América

and the Antilles divided for the dollar
and the bracero maimed for the dollar
and the woman destroyed in the shantytowns
or in the brothels
too often for the dollar,
that arrives at our beaches dressed in linen
in grand gray suitcases
enormous catafalques that transport to our América,

hallando la forma definitiva de la muerte.
He escuchado tu grito madre de niños tísicos
tísica tu misma
madre fecunda
pauperada por los que te roban el aluminio limpio
como lágrimas de niño
y disuelven el acero de tus entrañas
en las intensas ascuas del odio
el robo y el crimen de reyezuelos a sueldo.

Oh patria
mi patria
cada vez que pronuncio tu nombre
se abre una herida en mi corazón
y desde allí tus ojos me miran
y miran al mundo
y miran a América

a las Antillas divididas por el dollar
al bracero manco por el dollar
a la mujer destrozada en los arrabales
o en los prostíbulos
también por el dollar,
que arriba a nuestras playas vestido de lino
en grandes maletas grises
catafalcos enormes que traen a nuestra América

along with rehearsed smiles,
death.

Oh homeland
droplet of blood
from the center of your lament
you I await
you I hear
and you I chant.

Perhaps, my homeland
you are contemplating me
or my friend Juan or Pablo
fallen for you
severed
over the yellow sunrise of the cornfields
where the sun multiples in grains[.]

You weep, homeland,
you bleed, you suffer,
but we
destitute construct each minute
the dreadful advent of justice.
You weep, homeland,
but we will not delay destroying the cords that bind your song,
We will set ablaze with a new fire,

junto a las sonrisas ensayadas,
la muerte.

Oh patria
girón de sangre
desde el centro del llanto
te espero
te escucho
y te canto.

Quizás Patria mía
estás pensando en mí
en mi amigo Juan o en Pablo
caídos por ti
cercenados
sobre la amarilla sonrisa de los maizales
donde el sol se multiplica en granos[.]

Lloras, Patria,
sangras, sufres,
pero nosotros
desnudos, estamos construyendo a cada minuto
el advenimiento terrible de la justicia.
Lloras, Patria,
pero no tardaremos en destruir las cuerdas que atan tu canto.
Incendiaremos con un fuego nuevo

climbing and insistently climbing,
over the bruises on the peasant's torso
where the Sun, eternally falling on his back,
rests.
Oh homeland
you will rise
you will be rising already.

The hunger of the people
the hatred of the people
turned to rage and call
insatiable thirst
dreadful shuddering of this orb
irredeemable collapse of the dollar
will reconstruct deliberately
grain by grain
each ear of corn robbed from our hope.

Homeland
those who are not born
we who have been born and rise
and are born and rise again
always
in each minute
axe, pole, and pick
knife and club in our hands
without a single garment

---

que crece y seguirá creciendo
sobre las magulladuras del torso campesino
donde el Sol siempre a sus espaldas cayendo
descansa.
Oh patria
crecerás
estarás creciendo ya.

El hambre del pueblo
el odio del pueblo
tornado grito y cólera
sed insaciable
estremecimiento terrible del orbe
caída irremisible del dollar
reconstruirá lentamente
grano a grano
cada mazorca robada a nuestra esperanza.

Patria
los que no han nacido
nosotros los que hemos nacido y crecemos
y volvemos a nacer y a crecer
siempre
a cada minuto
hacha, palo y pico
cuchillo y garrote en nuestras manos
sin ninguna indumentaria

desnudos
trocaremos la vegetación
haremos de esta tierra
nuestra tierra
morada del trabajo y la justicia
canto de prole vegetal, mineral y humana
hollando la faz de la tierra antillana
hoy cadalso del hombre caribe.

destitute
we will transform the vegetation
we shall make of this earth
our earth
dwelling place of work and justice
proletarian chant, vegetal, mineral and humane
treading the face of the Antillean earth:
today the gallows of the Caribbean man.

Pity the One Who Does Not Understand

Pity the one who does not understand your love
for my mountains and for my valleys
for my people
your people.

Listen to my voice, friend,
listen to it,
and if crying or rage imprisons my scream
open my chest
puncture my lungs:
It is vital that my scream breaks glass windows
shut from hunger.
Open my chest
take my heart and launch it into the furrow of our
thirst
of the thirst of my land
your land,
and may it bloom into lilies and rifles,
lilies for your forehead
rifles for our hands.
Take my blood

Pobre del que no comprenda

Pobre del que no comprenda tu amor
por mis montañas y mis valles
por mi pueblo
tu pueblo.

Escucha mi voz, amiga,
escúchala,
y si el llanto o la cólera aprisiona mi grito
abre mi pecho
perfora mis pulmones:
Es preciso que mi grito rompa los cristales de las
ventanas
cerradas del hambre.
Abre mi pecho
toma mi corazón y lánzalo al surco de nuestra sed
de la sed de mi tierra
tu tierra,
y que florezca hecho lirios y fusiles,
lirios para tu frente
fusiles para nuestras manos.
Toma mi sangre,

launch it to the wind so it rains on my homeland
drowning the farmers of death
nourishing the 'Palm of liberty (from 1804)
Take my arms
launch them north of my land
so that they return multiplied,
determined to be seed again.

Launch my eyes to the south
so that my land becomes a fountain of stars.
Throw my entrails into the valleys
so that they flourish into unshakeable pinewood
and let my breath turn
into hurricane wind.
But keep for you, my love,
For yours, my love,
For your land, my love.

lánzala al viento para que llueva sobre mi patria
ahogando los labradores de la muerte
nutriendo la Palma de la libertad (del 1804)
Toma mis brazos,
lánzalos al norte de mi tierra
para que renazcan multiplicados,
decididos a ser simiente de nuevo.

Mis ojos, lánzalos al sur
para que mi tierra sea un surtidor de estrellas.
Tira mis entrañas a los valles
para que florezcan hechos pinar inconmovible
y deja mi aliento convertirse
en viento huracanado.
Pero guarda para ti, mi amor,
para los tuyos, mi amor,
para tu tierra, mi amor.

Notes

1. The term "rayano" derives from the term "la raya" for the Dominican-Haitian border and refers to residents of the border region. For more on the figure of the rayano, see Victoriano-Martínez and García Peña.

2. Recent work in English on these landmark historical conjunctures has foregrounded Dominican-Haitian solidarities. On the Haitian Revolution, see Nessler; on 1844, see Tavárez; on the War of Restoration, see Eller; on the US occupations of both nations, see García Peña; on the 1937 massacre, see Hintzen, "A Veil of Legality."

3. On the use of the term, "genocide," to describe the 1937 massacre, see Paulino.

4. In this formulation of *insularidad* we draw from the group of independent journalists from the island organized under the name, "Espacio Insular." In addition to critical news stories, Espacio Insular provides media workshops for activists, especially Dominico-Haitians, and collaborates with Haitian independent media and activists. They also transmit over an independent radio station, called Radio Cimarrona. See www.espacinsular.org.

5. Maríñez's article is reprinted in this volume as "Jacques Viau Renaud: Icon of Solidarity between Haiti and the Dominican Republic" (88–92).

6. For more on the specifics of this ruling, see in this anthology the articles by Rosa Iris Diendomi Álvarez ("Azúcar Amargo") and Deisy Toussaint ("El racismo, una causa encubierta"), and the interview with Padre Regino Martínez Bretón. See also Amézquita. For a juridical argument against it, see Rodríguez and Pujals Suárez.

7. Viau's poetry has been published in book form across various decades. His collected poetry was published in 2006 by Cielonaranja, and there are translations of his work into English and French (see the entries under Viau in the Works Cited).

Works Cited

Amézquita, Gloria. "Imaginary Narratives about *Dominicanos* of Haitian Descent: Media Debates concerning Sonia Pierre and Juliana Deguis." *Pan-Caribbean Integration: Beyond Caricom,* edited by Patsy Lewis, Terri-Ann Gilbert-Roberts, and Jessica Byron, Routledge, 2018, pp. 138–50.

Eller, Anne. *We Dream Together: Dominican Independence, Haiti, and the Fight for Caribbean Freedom,* Duke UP, 2016.

García Peña, Lorgia. *The Borders of Dominicanidad: Race, Nation, and Archives of Contradiction.* Duke UP, 2016.

Hayes de Kalaf, Eve. *Making Foreign: Legal Identity, Social Policy, and the Contours of Belonging in the Contemporary Dominican Republic.* 2018. University of Aberdeen, PhD dissertation. British Library EThOS.

Hintzen, Amelia. "'A Veil of Legality': The Contested History of Anti-Haitian Ideology under the Trujillo Dictatorship." *New West Indian Guide,* vol. 90, 2016, pp. 28–54.

---. "Extranjeros en tránsito: La evolución histórica de las políticas migratorias en la República Dominicana." *República Dominicana y Haití: El derecho a vivir,* edited by Angela Hernández, Fundación Juan Bosch, 2014, pp. 213–31.

Maríñez, Sophie. "Looking for Solidarity." *Boston Review,* May 24, 2019. http://bostonreview.net/arts-culture/sophie-marinez-jacques-viau-renaud

Martínez, Samuel. *Peripheral Migrants: Haitians and Dominican Republic Sugar Plantations,* University of Tennessee P, 1995.

Maríñez, Sophie. "Looking for Solidarity." *Boston Review*, May 24, 2019. http://bostonreview.net/arts-culture/sophie-marinez-jacques-viau-renaud

Nessler, Graham. *An Islandwide Struggle for Freedom: Revolution, Emancipation, and Reenslavement in Hispaniola, 1789-1809*. University of North Carolina P, 2016.

Paulino, Edward. *Dividing Hispaniola: The Dominican Republic's Border Campaign against Haiti, 1930-1961*, University of Pittsburgh P, 2016.

Rodríguez, Jaime Luis and Bartolomé Pujals Suárez. "Sentencia TC/168/2013 del Tribunal Constitucional Dominicano: Radiografía de una sentencia constitucional notoriamente inconstitucional." *República Dominicana y Haití: El derecho a vivir*, edited by Angela Hernández, Fundación Juan Bosch, 2014, pp. 301–30.

Rodríguez de León, Francisco. *Trujillo y Balaguer: Entre la espada y la palabra*, Nostrum, 2004.

Tavárez, Fidel. "The Contested State: Political Discourse during the Independence of the Dominican Republic, 1844." *Transnational Hispaniola: New Directions in Haitian and Dominican Studies*, edited by April Mayes and Kiran Jayaram, University of Florida P, 2018, pp. 44–66.

Viau Renaud, Jacques. "I'm Trying to Tell You of My Country." Translated by Raj Chetty and Amaury Rodríguez, *The Black Scholar*, vol. 45, no. 2, 2015, pp. 61–64.

---. *J'essaie de vous parler de ma patrie*. Edited by Sophie Maríñez and Daniel Huttinot, Mémoire d'encrier, 2018.

---. *Ma Patrie, Mes Deux Patries, Mon Île / Mi Patria, Mis Dos Patrias, Mi Isla*. Translated by Jean-Marie Bourjolly, Les Éditions du CIDIHCA, 2018.

---. "The Permanence of Weeping." Translated by Patrick Rosal, *Connotation Press: An Online Artifact*, vol. 4, no. 8, 2010, www.connotationpress.com/featured-guest-editor/may2010/418-jacques-viau-renaud-poetry-translated-by-patric-rosal. Accessed 10 July 2020.

---. *Poesía completa*. Ediciones Cielonaranja, 2006.

Victoriano-Martínez, Ramón Antonio. *Rayanos y Dominicanyorks: La dominicanidad del siglo XXI*. Insituto Internacional de Literatura Iberoamericana. Universidad de Pittsburgh, 2014.

Mujer Rayana

Solidarity and Womanism in the Dominican-Haitian Border

Amanda Alcántara

The border between the Dominican Republic and Haiti is often described as a region with many contradictions, namely a history of ongoing violence, coupled with the cultural porosity of the area. Harvard Professor Lorgia García Peña describes those of the area as having "Rayano consciousness" (border-citizen consciousness) in her book *The Borders of Dominicanidad: Race, Nations and Archives of Contradictions*, pointing out several examples, including Sonia Marmolejos, a rayana woman who received a lot of international attention after she nursed babies to health with her breast milk following their rescue during the 2010 earthquake that devastated Haiti.

This consciousness exists amid a history of anti-Haitianism in the Dominican Republic, one that caught international attention in 2015 when the government enacted a campaign attempting to grant documents to workers of Haitian descent, followed by threats of deportation for those who did not obtain them by the set deadline. It was close to one year after this campaign when I traveled to Dajabón, a Dominican province in the northern side of the border, asking: What about the women of this region?

So much of the historiography of the border and news reports surrounding the area and the issues around Haitian immigration in Dominican Republic lack a feminist perspective that centers on women.

In 2016, I began to study the history of women in Dajabón and how the region's contradictions manifest in the lives of working-class Dominican women, Haitian women, and those with mixed national identity. For the project, twenty-seven women who were either of Dominican descent, of Haitian descent, or both, were interviewed.

What I found was that women in Dajabón contributed tremendously to the regions' entrepreneurship and economic development, driving them, for example, to form women-centered organizations which seek to educate women, raise awareness in the community, and protect worker's rights.

The fact that women are centered in this work gives space for womanist thought. Alice

Walker describes womanist as, "A woman who loves another woman, sexually and/or non-sexually. She appreciates and prefers women's culture, women's emotional flexibility . . . [she] is committed to the survival and wholeness of an entire people, male and female. Not a separatist, except periodically for health . . . loves the spirit . . . loves struggle. Loves herself" (Walker). Womanism is often used to specifically discuss feminism that centers on black women (Rodriguez).

Yet, even as what as a womanist thought exists in the region, the very conditions that create the need for such women-centered groups and organizations, in addition to entrepreneurial unprotected work, affects such efforts for solidarity.

RACE IN THE DOMINICAN REPUBLIC AND ITS EFFECTS IN DAJABÓN

During the recent global debates surrounding anti-Haitianism in the Dominican Republic and the nation's history with anti-blackness, one fact is traditionally ignored: anti-blackness is not inherent to Dominican culture or society. Rather, it is a result of a nation economically controlled by elites, a nation with a history of international pressure to divest from black nationalism. As Kimberly Eison Simmons reminds us, "[. . .] Dominicans have been denied their blackness by the state." Often when people discuss the roots of anti-blackness in Dominican Republic, they begin with the dictatorship of Rafael Leónidas Trujillo and the 1937 massacre of Haitian immigrants. Yet, as several historians and academics have pointed out, including García Peña, the history of anti-Haitianism in the Dominican Republic precedes the Trujillo Era and is largely influenced by US foreign intervention and policy. In 1906, for example, when contraband and exchange along the Dominican-Haitian border was the norm, the US intervened to stop it (Moreta). The current rhetoric not only ignores this, but also fails to acknowledge how the black Dominican population also faces economic struggles.

Furthermore, the form of racism that exists in the Dominican Republic today must be understood in relation to the nation's history of oppression and the resistance to it, in addition to the nation's role in post-slavery struggles within the larger Latin American, Caribbean, and North American context. In his *Introduction to Dominican Blackness*, Silvio Torres-Saillant writes about Dominicans' evolving perceptions of blackness and the historic movements to reclaim blackness in opposition to the state's anti-Haitian campaign. He notes that much Dominican historiography leaves out grassroots anti-racist struggles in favor of promoting the oppressive (and ultimately colonial) perspectives of the elite.

> The intellectual elites [. . .] monopolized the conceptualization of Dominicanness as the ideological descendants of the Spaniards and white creoles who directed the colonial system in Santo Domingo. When they imagine Dominican history and the Dominican people only the experience of their ancestors comes to mind, the experience of all others, meaning the majority of the population, receiving only tangential, if any, treatment. Thus, the actions, the suffering, and the dreams of black Dominicans are

largely ignored by José Gabriel García (1834–1910), the reputed founder of Dominican historiography. The December 1522 slave rebellion, for instance, matters to him only as an illustration of the ills that befell the administration of Governor Diego Colón. (Torres-Saillant 38)

For women living in the Dominican Republic, as a disenfranchised and marginalized group inhabiting the intersections of blackness and womanhood (Crenshaw 1244), such anti-blackness is even more marked. Perceptions of blackness in the Dominican Republic affect women in a very specific way—from perceptions of beauty that lead to chemically altering one's hair[1] to the over-sexualization of women's bodies.

In her book *Borderlands/La Frontera: The New Mestiza*, Gloria Anzaldúa describes how, for Chicanas who grew up in border towns, material and symbolic borders function as open wounds. Black women's bodies are places of exploitation, embodying the border as a harshly contested site between vying systems of power. For Haitian women—as a disenfranchised group—the border often passes from being symbolic into becoming a concrete and violent threat that offers no protection from the state against gender violence.[2]

My research shows that while there are clear points of similarity in experiences, national identity also plays a role in the relationships between Haitian women, Dominican women, and Dominican women of Haitian descent, thus becoming a barrier to building solidarity.

Nonetheless, there are many organizations and groups in Dajabón seeking to empower women on both sides of the border regardless of the racial and ethnic background of the women involved. These organizations provide a framework to approach womanist thought. Oftentimes, though, the work of such organizations is met with many challenges such as a lack of sustainability in the long term given that many of the organizations rely on grants, some of which are international.

There are *Centros de Madres* in every *municipio* of the province that provide workshops for women and families. There are also different initiatives that seek to teach women entrepreneurial skills like a group of women doing artisanal work with recycled materials which are later sold, the growth of peanuts through shared crops in the community of El Pino (these peanuts are harvested by women, and sold generating income), the Centro Pon/Puente which provides workshops, Solidaridad Fronteriza which deals with violations of human rights, and la Red Janok Siksé which promotes the defense of human rights, among other entities.

Of the women that I interviewed, particularly women of Dominican descent, most of them shared that they had not been discriminated against and some tied discrimination to low-self-esteem. One woman, forty-seven years of age, shared that she had experienced discrimination based on her dark skin color, but she also added "If you catalog yourself as discriminated, then you will be. It's something personal. When your self-esteem is as low as the ground, anything they tell you will make you upset."[3] Because the state does not provide a definition of racism that is widely understood, there is no basis by which to understand racism as a systemic ill as opposed to a personal one. Cultural anthropologist Yadira Perez Hazel argues that different types of racism are recognized by different censor markers: "In the Dominican Republic, the human sense of touch, smell, hear, taste and sigh are called upon to mediate, evaluate, legitimate, and negotiate day-to-day encounters and occurrences."

Similarly, a twenty-six-year-old Haitian woman who travels to Dajabón everyday shared that she has never felt discriminated against by Dominicans and she repeated the words of the other woman who I interviewed almost verbatim, "A person who feels discriminated because of his or her skin color is a person with low self-esteem, and I wasn't born that way." When asked specifically if she has ever been discriminated against, she said that she hadn't ever experienced discrimination against her by a Dominican person, yet later on she shared a story of being discriminated against by the military agents who did not want to allow her to enter the country despite the fact she worked at the organization Centro Puente. She shared that one time a guard also tried to touch her inappropriately.

The role of the US also affects perceptions of race today on an interpersonal level especially as international actors are ever-present either via nongovernmental organizations, non-profits, or religious missionary work. Several of the women whom I interviewed, especially those with visibly dark skin, expressed that they felt pride in their skin color because "a los gringos les gusta" ("American white men like it").

When speaking about their natural hair, one Dominican woman said, "I'm of the kind that lives like this, without any shame . . . the majority of foreigners like it natural." Another woman of mixed ethnic descent (that is half-Dominican, half-Haitian) said, "I feel proud of my color, I find that Americans are very attached to us. To this color. From any of those countries, they find someone with my skin color and they're very proud of that color."

The lack of framework by which to understand racial discrimination against black women reflects in the thoughts expressed by some women doing solidarity work. Perez Hazel writes about the boundaries of blackness: "I argue that the Dominican state is invested not only in controlling the boundaries of blackness and Dominican identity but in maintaining this existing ambiguity and state of precarity as a means of manipulating power." Blackness is simply perceived as a color, not a race; it is everyone and it is no one.

Centro Pon/Puente, a binational organization that works in Dajabón and Ouanaminthe, hosts different workshops for and by women, including classes on self-esteem, hygiene, cooking (Dominican cooking for Haitian housemaids), human rights classes, and more. The women who attend these meetings are mostly living in poverty, therefore finding new forms of sustenance is empowering. I was able to interview two of the women working in this organization, one of Dominican descent, whom we shall call Carmen, and another of Haitian descent, whom we shall call Jean.[4]

Carmen shared with me her story of significant hardship. She was given away as a child to another family where she had to work hard to fend for herself. She married very young and says that finding Padre Regino (a Jesuit priest who started Solidaridad Fronteriza) changed her life. She shared that she was able to finish school and get into social work with the organization that she is in now. She shared with me that the first workshops led by Centro Pon/Puente were binational, and even remarked that sometimes Dominican women had to travel to Haiti and even share a bed with Haitian women when attending events together. When asked about the relationship along the border between Dominican and Haitian women, she said, "It's mandatory. You either have a relationship with them

[Haitian women] or you're screwed." When asked what she thinks of Haitian women, she answered, "They tolerate a lot. Here they kill more [women], but over there they beat them more." She added, "We have to tolerate all business matters, 'you may not speak my language, but I need you.'" She shared several times that she believes Haitian women tolerate too much and mentioned again that there is machismo in the Dominican Republic, but in Haiti it is worse.

Jean lives in Ouanaminthe, but she travels to Dajabón to work with Centro Pon/Puente. Her work involves recruiting women in Haiti to participate in the different workshops. Jean shared that there's racism in the Dominican Republic, and she added "but in Haiti, too." When asked if she has ever been mistreated because of her own skin color, she said that she had not. Jean travels every day from Ouanaminthe to Dajabón and the trip takes her about an hour. She shared, however, that one time she was in the market, and because of the packed conditions there and the large traffic of people, she witnessed how a pregnant Haitian woman was sexually assaulted by a Dominican man.

NEOLIBERALISM AND MARKET COMPETITION

Over the past century, the Dominican Republic has seen an economic shift which has greatly affected the entire community and has encouraged entrepreneurship but has negatively affected black women. An article titled "Small Entrepreneurs and Shifting Identities: The Case of Tourism in Puerto Plata" (Northern Dominican Republic) focuses on the way small entrepreneurs in this area have had to shift their labor strategy and their identities in order to cope with the ongoing changes that began in the 1980s.

On the one hand, it has been noted that tourism is often approached as a means for progress for developing countries. On the other hand, the effectiveness of this industry to provide a steady income for local entrepreneurs and residents is limited. Therefore, these entrepreneurs and residents are increasingly unsatisfied about their (lack of) possibilities to participate in the 'processes of modernization" (Roessingh and Duijnhoven).

The Heritage Foundation states: "In 2015, a streamlined bankruptcy law was adopted. A liberalized investment regime has facilitated growth around free trade zones and contributed to economic expansion of about 5 percent annually over the past five years." Given that this economic shift prioritizes free markets, black Dominican women have inevitably suffered.

Most, if not all, of the women I interviewed expressed incredible pride in their work, while at the same time referencing its hardships from lack of worker and workplace protection to a lack of recognition given that the region's market brings hundreds of shoppers from around the island. This pride in their labor as a marker of worth is tied to the view of racism as a choice in that it seeks autonomy within the confines created by the current systems. The labor conditions under a neo-liberal system that prioritizes free markets promotes this belief of self-worth attached to work. "The ideological appropriation of a myth of a racial democracy and myth of a male breadwinner, and the imposition of neoliberal Structural Adjustment Programs (SAPs) on the Dominican Republic in the early

1980s . . . the intersection of both these myths creates a foundation of internalized racism and machismo, among Afro-Dominican working-class women, which serves as nourishment for the evolution of neo-liberal Structural Adjustment Programs (SAPs)" (Rodriguez). SAPs—international loans—often require the implementation of free market programs vs. building local sustainable economic models.

During my first day in Dajabón, I met a woman who does solidarity work with Haitian women migrants and Dominican *pepeceras*. *Pepeceras* are women who sell "pepes" or used clothing. Maricela Elena, the President of the Asociación de Mujeres la Nueva Esperanza Dajabón, known more commonly as ASUMONEDA, shared with me that the selling of pepes began in the eighties and nineties when Dominican Dajabóneras would cross to Haiti to purchase clothing that had been donated by international communities. ASOMUNEDA was formalized on April 25, 1993 in order to fight for the rights of the women engaging in this work; the first *lucha* pursued was to legalize the selling of pepes. Women would travel to Haiti then return to the Dominican Republic to sell the clothing items, often in larger towns in the Central and Eastern parts of the island from Puerto Plata to Santo Domingo. Maricela Elena shared with me that because this market was initially illegal, the women would often have the clothing taken from them (often by border patrol agents who would then sell it themselves). "During that time, we were abused, and many times they even sent us to jail."

She also said that they often faced sexual violence while purchasing clothes in Haiti. Eventually, however, the women united to form ASOMUNEDA and won the fight to make the work legal. Maricela Elena said that "ASUMONEDA came about to protect women, we accomplished that today pepes are no longer contraband."

I argue that a womanist thought indeed is emerging in the consciousness of many of the women living in the border region. Some of the quotes from women I interviewed reflecting this include:

+ "Us Haitian women have courage. We work a lot. There's an economic violence against us that forces us into these conditions."
+ "We do not let ourselves be left as cowards, we always find a way of stimulating our self- esteem."
+ "Dominican women are so strong in this life, that if her husband leaves and she has no food left to eat, she finds garbage, and turns on a fire to cook and feed her children."
+ "Us women are so strong, because despite the programs that we have, we still push forward."
+ "Us women are better with money and as administrators. We are not wasteful nor bad spenders. If a man earns two thousand pesos and gave one thousand to the household, he feels that he doesn't owe anymore."
+ "We are smarter; we think before we act. Men need to be taught too as well."

Despite such examples of womanist thought, neoliberalism and anti-Blackness in the Dominican Republic—functioning together—effectively disarm black women by disavowing their shared blackness as a heritage that could serve to connect them. Instead, a myth of racial equality exists that does not view race as a unifier. When asked what they think of the word "Negra," Dominican women responded:

+ "I think when someone says negra, they mean color but aside from that, I see no other distinction because as a woman I have the same thing that another woman may have. Because we are all Dominican, but we're not Dominican, we're a mixed race, we don't know what we are."
+ "People think the word negra is an insult. Negra isn't an insult."
+ "I use the word negra for affection."

ASUMONEDA has about 300 members across the border of the Dominican Republic and Haiti, and it functions as an organization in the Dominican Republic, (it is not binational). When asked how the organization has changed over the last several years, one member complained that the market has been taken over by Haitian women. "They took the business from us" she said. "It is impossible to compete with them because their prices are too low." In Ouanaminthe, one of the women who I interviewed there shared that she actually hated travelling to Dajabón because of the bad treatment that she received, but also precisely because of these cheap prices. She noted that she has to "sell more" in Dajabón. Another Haitian woman who I interviewed in Ouanaminthe shared that she too dislikes going to the market, specifically employing the word "economic abuse" to describe how the precarious living conditions in Haiti force her and other women to travel. "When a Haitian woman can't eat or meet her necessities, many times she goes to bed without eating . . . that's economic abuse, Haitian women suffer from that." She also shared that in the space where the market is held, Dominican women get to have the spots that are inside and sectioned off, while Haitian vendors have to sit outside on the floor. When the market closes and it is time for them to leave, she also confirmed that the workers are treated badly by CESFRONT.

Market competition, accompanied by a national identity enforced by the state, then push Dominican and Haitian women in this region apart, despite similarities in struggle ranging from economic violence to domestic violence. Thus, Haitian women are then subjected to an added layer of state violence.

VIOLENCE AGAINST WOMEN IN DAJABÓN

Systemic racism and sexism work hand-in-hand to prevent true solidarity work in the border, reflecting the need for an intersectional approach when considering the region. Hilda Peña, the director of an organization called la Red Janok Siksé, explained that there are situations of sexual violence in the border region against both Dominican and Haitian women. When trying to open a new Centro de Madres in one of the local towns, the men fought back until they were invited, they were very ambivalent at first and this caused many women to stop attending the meetings. Many men forced their wives to stop going. One woman shared: "Many times the woman does everything in the household, and yet the man comes home and asks, 'You still haven't cooked?' That's prejudice." She also shared that many men believe women have to live below them, and they started getting upset when women began to learn at los Centros de Madres that they can exist side-by-side with their partners, not below them. "The moment you explain to him that you're to live side-by-side, he befriends another female."

During the first quarter of 2016, Dajabón was the region with the largest index of feminicides in the Dominican Republic (OPD: Observatorio politico dominicano). Of all the women that I interviewed, twelve had been victims of domestic violence, some still actively living with their abusive partners. When I returned to Dajabón to present on this research, during the Q&A a man complained that it is the women's fault that they do not stand up for themselves. "They like it," he said.

Furthermore, Haitian women are also subjected to violence by state officials or people with whom they work. Peña, who at the time was also the past director of Solidaridad Fronteriza, shared that when someone is undocumented the authorities do not want to take her case. Cases of human rights violations against Haitian women happen often in the border region, particularly as women try to enter the country to work in the binational market. Solidaridad Fronteriza, an organization that itself had to pick the name "Fronteriza" instead of "Solidaridad BiNacional" to ensure funding, takes on complaints against border patrol agents and seeks to bring them to justice.[5] One particular complaint was of a Haitian woman, Marie (name changed), whom I interviewed. She shared that she was in the market when a CESFRONT (Specialized Border Security Corps) guard approached her and asked her for money. Marie runs a money pool, so she had the day's money on her when she was stopped. When she refused to give it up, the CESFRONT guard slammed her against the wall and started taking her belongings. Her daughter who she pointed to, no older than eleven years, was there and she took out her cell phone to record. At that moment, the CESFRONT guard grabbed the girl by the neck and took her phone. "I jumped to fight him, so he let her go and in that moment, he grabbed me and threw me against the wall. I returned to grab her so that he would let her go and she was also fighting so that they would return the cell phone. In that moment they grabbed me and hit me . . . all I could say was that 'this isn't going to end like this.'" She was not able to recuperate all of the money taken from her, but they did return the money from her sales that day, and her merchandise. CESFRONT did not return the money pool money.

Other cases show the limitations in place when seeking to bring justice to cases of sexual violence. One particular complaint shared with me was one where a Haitian woman defended herself from a sexual attack where the guard also stole money from her. Peña shared with me that having the border patrol steal from these women is not uncommon; "CESFRONT picks them and takes their merchandise . . . they take everything." In the example of the woman who defended herself from sexual violence, they were able to seek some form of justice by having CESFRONT return the woman her money. The proof required the guard to show his genitals. She claimed that he had tried to force her into performing oral sex on him, and she bit him. When they made him take off his pants, the bite marks were there. Yet the sexual violence committed against her was not addressed or brought to justice, showing how violence against women (particularly sexual violence) continues to be seen as interpersonal and private, and therefore not something that the state can confront or address.

Fifty-five percent of violations against human rights in the border are against women, according to a report by Solidaridad Fronteriza. "Uno se siente impotente," Peña said ("One feels helpless").

According to an extensive qualitative research report put together by Colectiva Mujer y Salud and Mujeres del Mundo (Collective Women and Health and Women of the World), Haitian women are subjugated to sexual violence, violations of labor rights, *macuteo* (the act of "shaking down" for money), and other forms of abuse. The research states: "Haitian migrant women, as well as those who have been displaced or who are in transit on the Dominican-Haitian border, find themselves at risk of suffering violence against women (VAW) in various contexts . . . There are high levels of routine violence against women in the region, which takes on various forms: physical, sexual, economic, and verbal/psychological violence, as well as high risks of illicit human smuggling and trafficking, including for purposes of forced sex work" ("Making Visible").

THE SOLIDARITY WORK CONTINUES DESPITE CHALLENGES

Because of the importance of financial independence and the women's shared experience of living in poverty or being working class, much of the solidarity work in the region centers on selling products. Women come up with creative ideas to get ahead in light of the economic hardships that they face on a daily basis.

In the summer of 2016, women organized a fair where they sold artisanal products made from recycled material—a trade taught by a workshop given by a local Dominican woman. The fair was organized with the support of different local organizations. The women were up early in the morning getting everything ready; they had been planning for months and I was lucky enough to witness the final product. The goal of the fair was to showcase and sell their art. With recycled materials, mostly plastic bottles, the women make candlestick holders, figurines, pencil holders, and other items. With natural materials, like higüera, they made lamps. The group included about twelve women from different towns in Dajabón, some of them of Haitian descent. I interviewed one of the women who said that she was married to a Dominican man. She was abandoned as a child and raised by an uncle who abused her before coming to the community of Los Indios in Dajabón "en los tiempos de Balaguer" (during the Balaguer years). She shared: "I've been through a lot of hardships . . . now I'm learning to make artisanal products with this woman," she said, pointing to the instructor.

The name of the group is "Domay artesanias/atizana," a combination of the words Dominicana and Ayiti. The card that you receive when you purchase artisanal products from this group is in both Spanish and Haitian Creole. The card reads: "The Border Network of Women Artists is an organization of women from different communities in the northern border of Haiti and the Dominican Republic . . . thanks to the activities of the network, we're improving our participation in our family's decisions and in our communities."

While the women of the region continue pushing for solidarity work, regardless of the national barriers, the region is filled with contradictions. As some of the Dominican women say things like "you have to work with Haitian women"—at times resentfully—moments of solidarity also emerge, including expressing concern in moments where racial consciousness seems to defy the state's teachings and an urge to learn Haitian Creole for many locals.

One of the last interviews I conducted was with a woman, Laura, from a community called Los Indios. Given the fact that this community is said to have been a home of Taínos, and the national identity of the Dominican Republic is often explicitly tied to a Latin Americanist indigenous romanticism, I admit that I expected Laura to center indigeneity in her beliefs. Yet, she surprised me when I asked her what she thinks of the word *negra*: "I say we all have dark skin, except some of us have lighter skin, and others darker."

Author's note: This essay is adapted from my master's thesis for the Center for Latin American and Caribbean Studies, New York University, submitted May 2017. Special thanks to Nancy Albamira Rijos, to my primary advisor, Katherine Smith, and to my secondary advisor, Edward Paulino.

Notes

1. Discussed in detail in Ginetta E.B. Candelario, *Black behind the Ears: Dominican Racial Identity from Museums to Beauty Shops*.
2. See Allison J. Petrozziello and Bridget Wooding, *Fanm Nan Fwontyè, Fanm Toupatou*.
3. All translations were done by Amanda Alcántara.
4. This article uses pseudoynms for some of the interviewed women to respect their privacy.
5. Now called Centro Montalvo.

Works Cited

Anzaldúa, Gloria. *Borderlands/La Frontera: The New Mestiza*. Aunt Lute Books, 1987.

Candelario, Ginetta E.B. *Black behind the Ears: Dominican Racial Identity from Museums to Beauty Shops*, Duke UP, 2007.

Collins, Patricia Hill. "WHAT'S IN A NAME? Womanism, Black Feminism, and Beyond." *The Black Scholar*, vol. 26, no. 1, 1996, pp. 9–17, www.jstor.org/stable/41068619.

Crenshaw, Kimberle. "Mapping the Margins: Intersectionality, Identity Politics, and Violence against Women of Color." *Stanford Law Review*, vol. 43, no. 6, July 1991, 1241–99.

García Peña, Lorgia. *The Borders of Dominicanidad: Race, Nation, and Archives of Contradiction*, Duke UP, 2016.

"Making Visible the Violence Against Haitian Migrants, In-transit and Displaced Women on the Dominican-Haitian Border." In "Women in Transit," Colectiva Mujer Y Salud and Mujeres Del Mundo as Part of the Project, 2012.

Moreta, Angel. *Capitalismo y Descampesinización en el Suroeste Dominicano*. Archivo General de la Nación, Volumen LXXXI, 2009.

Perez Hazel, Yadira. "Sensing Difference: Whiteness, National Identity, and Belonging in the Dominican Republic." *Transforming Anthropology*, vol. 22, no. 2, 2014, 78–91.

Petrozziello, Allison J. and Bridget Wooding, *Fanm Nan Fwontyè, Fanm Toupatou: Making Visible the Violence against Haitian Migrant, In-Transit and Displaced Women on the Dominican-Haitian Border; Qualitative Research Report Commissioned by the* Colectiva Mujer y Salud *and* Mujeres del Mundo *as Part of the Project "Women in Transit." Colectiva Mujer y Salud*/Observatory Migrants of the Caribbean, 2012, http://www.globalmigrationpolicy.org/articles/gender/Fanm%20nan%20fwontye%20 Violence%20against%20Haitian%20migrant%20women%20Petrozziello%20WOODING%20 2012.pdf.

Rodriguez, Griselda. "Mujeres, myths, and margins: Afro-Dominican women within a capitalist world-economy," 2010. Syracuse University, PhD dissertation.

Roessingh, Carel and Hanneke Duijnhoven, "Small Entrepreneurs and Shifting Identities: The Case of Tourism in Puerto Plata (Northern Dominican Republic)." *Journal of Tourism and Cultural Change*, vol. 2 no. 3, 2005, pp. 185–202.

Simmons, Kimberly Eison. *Reconstructing racial identity and the African past in the Dominican Republic.* UP of Florida, 2009.

Torres-Saillant, Silvio. *Introduction to Dominican Blackness.* CUNY Dominican Studies Institute, 2010.

Walker, Alice. *In Search of Our Mothers' Gardens: Womanist Prose.* Harvest, 1983.

Hasta la Raíz

cine documental por el derecho a la nacionalidad en RD

Juan Carlos González Díaz

Desde que me mudé a la República Dominicana en 2011 tardé varios meses en entender la situación que padecían las personas negras en el país, especialmente las dominicanas de ascendencia haitiana.

Yo no era precisamente un recién llegado a las diversas manifestaciones de la discriminación que se practican en el Caribe, ni un extranjero en búsqueda del exotismo del "buen salvaje"[1] latinoamericano. Sentía que mi conocimiento con el racismo[2] y el clasismo en Venezuela me daba un bagaje inicial para mirar esta nueva realidad.

Al principio, pensaba que la discriminación afectaba únicamente a la población haitiana. El baño de fuego para constatar este tipo de discriminación ocurrió pronto en la intersección de la Avenida 27 de Febrero con Avenida Duarte de la capital.

Cualquiera que haya pasado un tiempo en Santo Domingo sabe que a las seis de la tarde de un día de semana esa intersección de avenidas es un caos de personas, vehículos privados, transporte público y vendedores ambulantes. La gente que frecuenta esa zona es mayoritariamente de extracción popular.

Ese día del que hablo había un tapón infernal. Los vehículos avanzaban pocos metros a duras penas mientras el calor veraniego golpeaba sin clemencia. De pronto, el ruido dio paso a un sonido más enfocado, y el movimiento interminable pero pausado del lugar fue interrumpido por la veloz carrera de un hombre negro, cuidadosamente trajeado y calzado, que abrazaba su maletín mientras zigzagueaba entre la gente, alejándose a toda prisa de algo que tardamos poco en identificar.

Enseguida vimos bajar por la Avenida Duarte una guagua destartalada, y el bullicio que se había suspendido hasta un segundo antes, volvió con más fuerza, como abriéndole paso a los agentes de Migración que flanqueaban el vehículo mientras buscaban identificar a más "morenos"[3] entre una población mayoritariamente afrodescendiente.

Al vehículo, corroído por el óxido, se la habían adaptado rejas en las ventanas, por cuyas rendijas se asomaban manos, otra vez negras, resignadas ante lo inevitable.

Solo un grito rompió la procesión. Un hombre de unos cincuenta años, que viendo la escena soltó socarrón: "¡quemen a esos haitianos!"

LA HISTORIA DEVELADA

El episodio de la guagua de Migración en la Duarte con 27 de Febrero abrió mis ojos a un tipo de discriminación, instrumentalizada principalmente desde el Estado dominicano, que basaba las redadas del cuerpo oficial en perfiles fenotípicos. Pero todavía tardé un poco más en dimensionar cómo esa discriminación se extendía a los descendientes de esos mismos migrantes.

Antes, conocí a algunos de los jóvenes dominicanos de ascendencia haitiana que se empezaban a organizar para exigir la devolución de sus documentos. La mayoría eran personas que tenían actas de nacimiento, cédulas y hasta pasaportes expedidos por el Estado dominicano. Todas tenían en común ser hijas de migrantes haitianos.

Yo no noté ninguna diferencia en el habla y las costumbres que ya observaba en el resto de los habitantes de República Dominicana.

Junto a ese grupo de jóvenes, ideamos una campaña que pudiese dar cuenta de la problemática central: eran dominicanos, nacieron en el país, tuvieron documentos hasta que un día la Junta Central Electoral[4], a partir de la Resolución 12-07 (https://www.youtube.com/watch?v=Rukj6D1Oxvs), decidió en la práctica y de forma discrecional suspender la emisión de esos mismos documentos de identidad.

Les acompañé a las primeras manifestaciones públicas que organizaron frente a la Junta Central Electoral para exigir la devolución de sus documentos y el cese de la política discriminatoria. Pero no fue sino hasta cuatro días después del repentino fallecimiento de Sonia Pierre[5] cuando vi claramente la necesidad de contar la historia que luego se convirtió en *Hasta la Raíz*.

Aquel jueves de diciembre en 2011, todo estaba listo para realizar la primera gran manifestación de personas dominicanas de ascendencia haitiana en el país. Paradas frente a la Suprema Corte de Justicia, el inmenso grupo proveniente de diversos bateyes del interior lucía camisetas con el rostro de la recién fallecida Pierre.

Cuando todo estaba por empezar, un pequeño contingente de policías intentó evitar la actividad con el argumento de que no contábamos con los permisos oficiales para estar ahí. Luego de una breve discusión, recuerdo como Ana María Belique—una de las activistas del movimiento—tomó el micrófono y con algo de la rabia contenida por ese nuevo intento de abuso policial (y quizás por muchas otras razones) pronunció el inicio de un discurso que logré grabar con mi cámara y que años más tarde se convertiría en parte del documental.

Dirigiéndose a la multitud dijo:

"Yo nací en este país, igual que muchos de ustedes. Mis padres son haitianos—y orgullosamente lo digo y no lo niego—pero yo nací aquí, en este país (. . .) ¿Qué tiene que decidir la Junta si yo soy dominicana? ¿Cuántos de aquí somos dominicanos? Y vamos a luchar por nuestro derecho (. . .) En la mano de nosotros está si vamos a permitir que sigan pisoteando a nuestros ancestros, si vamos a permitir que sigan pisoteando lo que somos."

EL CAMINO ANDADO

Producir *Hasta la Raíz* tomó poco más de cinco años desde el momento que Ana María pronunció esas palabras hasta el estreno en Santo Domingo. En el camino, muchísimas cosas sucedieron en la lucha por el derecho a la nacionalidad en República Dominicana. Algunas de ellas están recogidas en el documental.

Recuerdo por ejemplo la concentración de marzo del 2012, en la que las personas que se manifestaban resistieron pacíficamente a un intento de amedrentamiento de la policía. Detenidos por un contingente de jóvenes funcionarios a mitad de la Avenida que separa la Plaza de la Bandera del edificio de la Junta Central Electoral, las mujeres y hombres del movimiento Reconoci.do se plantaron firmes, cantaron, gritaron consignas, expresaron su indignación a la prensa y, casi sin planificarlo, se cohesionaron como grupo.

También viene a mi mente el encuentro que las personas dominicanas de ascendencia haitiana sostuvieron ese mismo año en el Congreso Nacional con legisladores de la talla de Guadalupe Valdez. O la Vigilia de marzo de 2013 y la Caminata desde San Pedro de Macorís hasta la capital en abril de ese mismo año.

En todos esos episodios, fui testigo de primera fila del temple que fueron mostrando los jóvenes activistas mientras recibían algunos insultos y muchos apoyos de personas desconocidas que les veían manifestarse. Mientras caminaban podían escuchar tanto un "¡depórtenlos a todos!" gritado desde un vehículo como un abrazo de personas que se acercaban a mostrar su solidaridad.

Algunos de esos acontecimientos se muestran en *Hasta la Raíz*. Durante el proceso de edición del documental, parte del esfuerzo fue tratar de hacer memoria con esas movilizaciones sociales, dejando un rastro de la organización y vocación no-violenta de estas manifestaciones.

Pero en *Hasta la Raíz* también hubo una intención política, en el sentido de ejercicio de derechos y denuncia de arbitrariedades de funcionarios del Estado, amén de una breve cronología de los pasos seguidos por distintos gobiernos dominicanos para negar la nacionalidad a los descendientes de migrantes haitianos nacidos en el país.

El más estrambótico de esos pasos dados por el Estado dominicano fue por supuesto la Sentencia 168-13, ampliamente denunciada a nivel nacional e internacional. Esa sentencia fue el resultado de al menos cuarenta años de esfuerzos sistemáticos de estos sucesivos gobiernos y funcionarios por negar el derecho de los dominicanos de ascendencia haitiana, pero también el de sus padres migrantes, quienes por décadas fueron explotados en los campos de caña del país bajo contratos leoninos otorgados por el mismo Estado, sin seguridad social ni prestaciones laborales, en el mejor de los casos[6].

ALGUNOS LOGROS Y REVESES DE *HASTA LA RAÍZ*

Desde que fue estrenada en marzo de 2017 y hasta octubre de 2019, la película ha sido proyectada públicamente más de 100 veces, con una audiencia que supera las 3,500 personas de once países y treinta y cinco ciudades y pueblos. Además, fue seleccionada para ocho festivales de cine documental en diversas partes del mundo:

1. Dominican Film Festival (2017). New York, EEUU
2. Festival de Cine por los Derechos Humanos (2017). Medellín y Bogotá, Colombia
3. Kunta Kinté (2017). Turbo y Cartagena de Indias, Colombia
4. Festival Insularia (2017). Islas Canarias, España
5. Human Rights Film Festival (2017). Madrid, España
6. Real Action/ Real Change (2017). Los Ángeles, EE. UU.
7. Censurados Film Festival (2018). Lima, Perú
8. Women Deliver Film Festival (2019). Vancouver, Canadá

Se organizaron presentaciones en centros comunitarios, escuelas públicas y colegios, organizaciones no gubernamentales, universidades, centros culturales, además del recorrido de festivales ya mencionado. También se presentó en salas comerciales de la República Dominicana, específicamente en Santo Domingo y Santiago de los Caballeros.

La distribución del documental despertó el interés de algunas universidades de los Estados Unidos, Brasil, Chile, Colombia, Canadá y España especializadas en estudios sobre identidad, racismo, Caribe insular, Latinoamérica, y otros. Estas universidades han organizado proyecciones de *Hasta la Raíz* como forma de generar conversación sobre la realidad dominicana, pero también como espejo de las realidades particulares de cada país.

El documental también fue incluido en la conferencia mundial sobre Apatridia e Inclusión en La Haya, Holanda de 2019.

Hasta la Raíz no solo fue concebida como una pieza cinematográfica, sino que también se pensó como una herramienta de sensibilización y reorganización del colectivo de personas dominicanas de ascendencia haitiana.

Parte del éxito que ha tenido la película en término de número de proyecciones y personas que han podido verla, se debió a la forma de involucrar al liderazgo de este movimiento. Casi siempre que es posible, la proyección del documental finaliza con la participación y testimonio de alguna protagonista, dando la oportunidad de contar la actualidad del tema.

Todavía hoy en día, luego de más de dos años después de la premiere, las personas dominicanas de ascendencia haitiana continúan realizando proyecciones de la película en comunidades bateyeras y organizando espacios de debate.

Pero hasta el momento, *Hasta la Raíz* no ha sido presentada a ninguna autoridad con poder de decisión sobre el derecho a la nacionalidad en República Dominicana. Esto probablemente tiene que ver con la incapacidad de tender un puente entre el gobierno y las personas afectadas.

Esta relación, siempre tirante y precaria debido a la política discriminatoria y discrecional que muchos funcionarios estatales de diversos rangos aplicaron a la población dominicana de ascendencia haitiana, nunca tuvo espacios formales de conversación o negociación en la que se pudiera proponer una agenda de trabajo común.

Y aunque en el período inmediatamente posterior a la sentencia 168-13 se logró acercar momentáneamente las posiciones, y tuvo gestos públicos de reconocimiento del "drama humano" que significaban sus efectos, hoy en día no existe voluntad política para aproximar a las partes y abordar la inmensa tarea pendiente con la aplicación de la ley 169-14.

Por algunas de esas razones, la película no ha podido ser presentada en el Congreso

Nacional, ni en el Ministerio de Interior y Policía, por poner dos ejemplos: porque ¿quién puede fungir como interlocución con esas instancias? ¿qué capacidad tienen los funcionarios gubernamentales para procesar *in situ* las críticas al Estado que se derivan del documental, así como el testimonio vivo de sus protagonistas y activistas?

La llegada al cine comercial en República Dominicana fue quizás el punto más alto del esfuerzo de distribución. Para ello, fue diseñada una campaña digital para Facebook e Instagram, incluyendo publicidad pagada. Aunque la afluencia de público a las salas no fue satisfactoria, si quedaron aprendizajes importantes sobre lo costoso del proceso y la necesaria inversión publicitaria que ha de realizarse para así atraer audiencias diversas, no vinculadas directamente a la problemática ni a las organizaciones sociales.

La distribución aún necesita valorar estrategias como la venta por catálogo de películas educativas, la venta a canales de televisión, y el *pay per view* de plataformas digitales.

En la República Dominicana, el cine documental todavía tiene mucho espacio para crecer, pero los productores necesitan pensar más cuidadosamente las estrategias de distribución e inserción en los espacios comerciales, donde compiten con las películas de ficción, en un entorno cultural aún no acostumbrado a ver un documental en las salas de cine, y una oferta de películas que compiten con una importante inversión de *marketing*.

REFLEXIONES FINALES

Por último, pero no menos importante, quisiera sugerir algunos de los cambios sociales en la vivencia de la negritud que he podido verificar en estos ocho años viviendo en la República Dominicana. Por supuesto, esta es una apreciación hecha desde la subjetividad de un hombre mestizo (pero "rubio" para los estándares de la sociedad dominicana), que disfruta de los privilegios de ser "blanco" en la RD, matizado por el hecho de pertenecer al colectivo de migrantes venezolanos que, al menos desde el año 2015, ha visto crecer su número hasta convertirse en el segundo colectivo migrante más numeroso del país, luego de los haitianos[7], y que ha padecido también—aunque en menor medida—episodios de discriminación, aporofobia y persecución por parte de las autoridades de migración dominicanas.

En lo político, la situación de las personas dominicanas de ascendencia haitiana todavía no se ha resuelto. El gobierno dominicano ofrece cifras distintas a las de las organizaciones sociales y de derechos humanos que trabajan el tema y, como dijimos antes, no existen espacios de interlocución para trabajar de forma conjunta la resolución, caso a caso, de las personas que aún se encuentran en riesgo de apatridia.

Pero parte de los argumentos que durante todos estos años han esgrimido las personas dominicanas de ascendencia haitiana para denunciar la discriminación que padecen también describen las prácticas racistas y negadoras de la herencia afro y haitiana en la sociedad dominicana.

En este sentido, en el último lustro es posible enumerar el surgimiento de un significativo número de iniciativas y personalidades que públicamente celebran alguna de estas herencias, como por ejemplo: la reivindicación del actor Jean Jean de su identidad dominico-haitiana, la creación de salones de belleza especializados en tratamiento del cabello afro—destacando la estilista Carolina Contreras y su salón Miss Rizos—la fusión afro-caribeña del grupo musical La Gran Mawon, la propuesta mágico-religiosa "Afro-ink" del pintor Eddaviel, y el activismo antirracista-feminista de la población LBTQ organizado en el colectivo Afritude.

También en estos últimos cinco años es posible constatar las denuncias a diferentes situaciones de discriminación: como la de la periodista a la que le negaron el cambio de su cédula por llevar el cabello rizado, o la reflexión sobre el racismo sufrido en su propio país por parte del medallista olímpico Luisito Pie; el caso de discriminación ejercida por la Ministra de Educación Superior contra la politóloga Nicky González, o los diversos análisis sobre racismo institucionalizado en las escuelas o en las empresas privadas.

Con esto no quiero decir que antes de la irrupción en escena de la población dominicana de ascendencia haitiana la lucha anti-discriminación no existiera, pero resulta llamativo que la exposición pública que consiguió el movimiento por el derecho a la nacionalidad en la República Dominicana (sobre todo en el período 2012–2014), incluyó siempre, como parte de sus ideas, fuerza al derecho de la no discriminación por motivos de raza u origen nacional.

No es el objetivo de este ensayo ahondar en la correlación entre esta exposición pública de las personas dominicanas de ascendencia haitiana y sus posibles efectos invisibles en el resto de la sociedad dominicana en términos de auto-aceptación e inspiración para combatir las prácticas discriminatorias en el país, pero podría ser una interesante hipótesis de estudio para los científicos sociales.

Complementariamente, creo que también es importante prestar atención a la reconfiguración en todos estos años—que van desde esa primera gran manifestación en honor a la memoria de Sonia Pierre en diciembre de 2011 hasta el presente—de los diferentes movimientos autodenominados "ultranacionalistas", que aunque inicialmente atomizados y casi siempre muy vociferantes, han logrado en fechas más recientes alinearse a diversas estrategias que van desde la auto-organización de tipo paramilitar hasta el impulso de candidaturas presidenciales.

Todos estos movimientos tienen como elemento común el rechazo a las demandas esgrimidas por la población dominicana de ascendencia haitiana, un ataque frontal a las figuras que lideran el movimiento—especialmente Ana María Belique—o quienes lo apoyan de forma solidaria, incluyendo amenazas de muerte a través de las redes sociales como Facebook, Twitter o Instagram (redes que por cierto han hecho caso omiso a las peticiones de eliminación de las cuentas que promueven estos discursos de odio).

¿Están estos grupos ligados de alguna manera a la estructura estatal en cualquiera de sus niveles? ¿Existe alguna posibilidad de negociación de estas posturas antagónicas entre quienes defienden el derecho a la nacionalidad de las personas dominicanas de ascendencia haitiana y los grupos ultranacionalistas? En caso de que no, ¿cuáles son las estrategias de presión de la sociedad civil organizada para que el Estado garantice la seguridad e integridad de las personas activistas y la justa exposición de sus demandas sin temor a represalias?

Notas

1. El término de "Buen Salvaje" lo tomo del significado atribuido por el autor Carlos Rangel en su libro *Del Buen Salvaje al Buen Revolucionario* (Monteavila Editores, 1976). En su obra, Rangel critica el mito europeo que ve en los latinoamericanos personas buenas pero corrompidas por la sociedad occidental que ha destruido sus valores originales y de la que habrá que liberarse por medio de revoluciones que restablezcan una identidad perdida y distinta de la occidental.

2. Para leer más sobre algunas de las caracterísiticas del racismo venezolano, ver: http://elestimulo.com/climax/la-venezuela-multicultural-aun-esconde-racismo/

3. Palabra que se usa en República Dominicana para referirse a las personas negras, especialmente de tez muy oscura y/o provenientes de Haití.

4. En República Dominicana, la Junta Central Electoral es la institución del Estado responsable de emitir actas de nacimiento y cédulas de identidad. Además, controla el Registro Civil y organiza los procesos electorales.

5. Un breve perfil de esta líder social puede leerse en: https://rfkhumanrights.org/people/sonia-pierre

6. Diversas investigaciones también describen los sistemas de control policial y migratorio implantados en los bateyes aledaños a los ingenios azucareros controlados por el Estado dominicano. Ver, por ejemplo: LISTER, Elissa "El Batey, aproximación a sus realidades y representaciones desde la colonialidad." *Hacer Ciencias Sociales en América Latina: Desafíos y Experiencias de Investigación.* FLACSO, 2019.

7. Según la Encuesta Nacional de Inmigrantes (2017) cifra del número de venezolanos en la RD en 25,872 y se proyecta que para finales del año 2020 puedan llegar a ser más de 40 mil migrantes.

Building a Future of Reconciliation

Small Rebellions and the *Dominicanidad* of Tomorrow

Saudi García

BORDER OF LIGHTS VIGIL OCTOBER 2019

We found ourselves walking, shoulder-to-shoulder, two to three people at a time, toward the *Masacre* River. The church had just finished its service, a beautiful multicultural gathering that brought a choir from Haiti to Dajabón to commemorate the eighty-two years since the 1937 massacre of Haitians in the Dominican Republic. The event known as *El Corte*, or *Kout Koutou* as it is known in Kreyòl, attempted to reframe the borderlands into a controlled space where Haitians and Dominicans could be surveilled, distinguished, and separated. The project of remembering is lonely. In the lead up to this year's Border of Lights event, only one radio show in the Capital city of Santo Domingo mentioned anything about the events that unfolded in 1937. As I stood in that early October evening with candles and white calla lilies pressing into my hands, I was reminded of the gentle texture of the lives that were lost, the brilliance of their souls, and the emptiness that nested itself in communities torn asunder by grief that has been left to fester, unrecognized and untreated.

Our solemn parade left the park and crossed a few streets to the sound of Calle 13's *Latinoamérica*. Once we were close to the river, we were confronted by a barricade of border guards. Their grey uniforms were splattered by the lights of their pickup trucks, which defied us to take one more step. I was shocked, and the excuse that this *cordón* of officers was "for our safety" simply did not satisfy. Something in me longed to see the river, though I had seen it in the daytime earlier when I crossed to Ouanaminthe on the back of a *moto* to see the 2019 Border of Lights-supported mural painted by Mouvement Azueï. The ease with which I was able to cross is a huge privilege, and the feeling of having our mobility restricted on a day like this, a day for creating a portal between the ancestors whose lives were destroyed and us, still here, still breathing, still alive, felt violent. I checked in with the organizers, trying to understand. They had never done this, restricted us like this, one said. I looked with longing toward the river, just a few blocks away. A circle formed, the crowds held on to their candles, and the ceremony began. We sang, we listened, we prayed; we made some peace with a history that rightfully still haunts us today.

The 2019 Border of Lights vigil was a portal of feeling, a necessary ritual, a space to cradle the smallness of the gestures and the emotions that were meant to be stifled by El Corte. It was a space of transgression in the simple act of normalizing the ways that Dominicans and Haitians are so very alike, so very human. We need more spaces like this—spaces of encounter, transgression, normalization, unity, and cooperation—if we are to change the conditions of aggression that Dominicans have allowed to flourish, both in their name and in the name of their nationalism. The present moment calls for it, and that call has been answered in a variety of ways over the past six years in the Dominican diaspora.

LINEAGES

I am a Dominican-born, US-based anthropologist, writer, and activist thinking about the possible futures of the place that saw my birth: An island of many mountains divided by violence, greed, corruption, and deep wells of pain. I am a dark tan color, yet decidedly lighter-skinned. My hair is what would be considered "good," and sometimes in my Santo Domingo neighborhood *y en el monte*, and because "race" is relative, they call me "*rubia.*" I speak Spanish, some French, and I am beginning to learn Kreyòl. It matters that I place my body in this story because light-skinned Dominican bodies like mine enjoy the privilege of invisibility in the island of Ayiti: we have been forcibly constructed as the "norm" and generally don't experience race-based violence for looking how we do. This body teaches me much as I relearn to feel deeply, to not follow orders, to break through pain, to let myself cry and heal.

I came into the work that led me to that riverside immediately after graduating college, when I moved to New York City to serve Spanish-speaking youth in the Bronx and noticed Dominicans organizing with the collectives We Are All Dominican and Rights for All D.R. I had graduated from college from one of those ultra-liberal elite East Coast schools where I quickly realized that my version of Black Lives Matter was global, that it encompassed Black people all over the world. Since then, I have found kinship with those living in Hunts Point, New York, the hills of Cotuí and Monte Plata (where I currently am completing my dissertation research on mining and pollution) and the beleaguered cities of Haiti, where a population in revolt seeks to make true on the promises of humanism, democracy, and liberation for all. I inherited a tradition of struggle, of seeking joy and permanence, of holding calla lilies and candles at the riverside.

After TC 168-13 irrevocably altered the lives of hundreds of thousands of Dominicans of Haitian descent, I felt it my duty (really the least I could do) to amplify their struggles and support them however I could. Working with We Are All Dominican, we organized, we marched, we *flyered*, we protested in front of the Dominican consulate, we talked to family members intent on perpetuating anti-Haitian sentiment. As this work was unfolding during my first few years of graduate school, I simultaneously began the work of undoing my own racist bias in community alongside other Dominican women whom I didn't have to explain anything to, who understood. It became evident to me that the state project of bordering Dominicanidad, as Lorgia García Peña writes, extends into the diaspora in significant ways in the digital age. At the same time, generational shifts, increased understanding about race and racism, and the desire to make visible other visions of Dominicanidad contribute to a continuation of the diasporic unraveling of Dominicanidad, spearheaded by people like Silvio Torres-Saillant in the 1990s.

There isn't a lineage or guidebook for how to be an anti-racist Dominican, however, as Ibrahim X. Kendi writes, it's not possible to be "not racist." You are either racist or you are anti-racist. For young Dominicans who have been raised with ethno-racial phobia against Haitians, the work of undoing racism is the work of undoing colorism *and* anti-Haitianismo while being bombarded with a barrage of messages dissuading us from doing this work. Some things I've personally encountered include: "Dominicans cannot be racist against Haitians because they, too, are Afro-descendants;" "Why are you so obsessed with racism? That's a US-based way of thinking about things;" and, of course, "*Tu eres una Afro-enferma y Afro-Nazi.*" Conveniently excluded from this conversation is the fact that the Dominican Republic is a society captured by white power and privilege, a capture so nearly perfect that hatred of the Black, the Haitian immigrant, and the poor passes as our social and cultural norms. The Republic's Spanish and European-descendant citizens have racialized Haitians, Afro-Dominicans and their culture from their positionality as white people and have ensured that their racist, capitalist, and anti-humanist values and attitudes permeate every aspect of national "Dominican" culture. Only when I was ready, when I began to understand how this covert white supremacy dynamic hid behind "Dominican culture" and shaped me, could I actually begin to be in true community and solidarity with Haitians. That's where In Cultured Company comes in.

BIRTH OF IN CULTURED COMPANY (ICC) AND OUR FIRST YEAR

In late August of 2018, I was invited to participate in an experiment, an innovative space bringing together Dominicans and Haitians in the diaspora to have in-person encounters and conversations. I was excited by the possibility to have that deep level of offline engagement, the kind that can result in the birth of a new movement and the creation of authentic relationships to counter the psychic power of generations of anti-Haitian hate and fear among Dominicans. While I did not know the founder of the new collective, France François, I trusted her dedication to this mission, her deep competency in the study of peace, justice and development, and her long-term commitment to the well-being of Haitians around the world. In telling the story of her ideation of ICC and its eventual birth, France says that she noticed the curiosity that Dominicans had about Haiti, a curiosity that was expressed in hushed, almost-taboo tones. She eventually realized that because of the Dominican Republic's economic and political interests—the same ones that orchestrated that genocide in 1937—Dominicans and Haitians may never get to a state-led solution for the current conditions of inequality that plague these relations. However, people-centered, people-led solutions that begin from our own active choices to dismantle oppressive narratives and build new relations could eventually bring about necessary transformations. In Cultured Company is unique in that it brings Dominicans and Haitians together in order to learn our history, undo the damage of nationalist historical narratives, and imagine potential solutions to the contemporary pressing problems that our island faces. However, other groups, such as We Are All Dominican, the Dominicans Love Haitians Movement, and Mouvement Azueï continue to uplift a vision of unity, solidarity, and care between Dominicans and Haitians.

More than a year into our process, we have held three separate workshops and one community fundraiser. Our first workshop was held at New Women Space, a radical feminist collective space where we hosted more than sixty participants. We did not know if the people who signed up—half Haitians and Dominicans—would come, yet they did. Each time we have hosted the Decolonizing Hispaniola workshop, it has morphed and grown. Our second time around, we invited musicians and spiritual leaders Alexandra Jean Joseph, Sky Meneski and Bembesito Akpon to share their knowledge of Dominican and Haitian music and spirituality. On the stage of the First Spanish United Methodist Church, which the Puerto Rican activist group the Young Lords took over on December 28th, 1969, they harmonized and improvised, exemplifying the naturalness of Dominican-Haitian sonic and aural relations. We have hosted a fundraiser, a public education series with Dominican and Haitian scholars called "Summer Schooled," and we sustain an active social media presence on Instagram, Twitter and Facebook that provides avenues for public education and lively exchanges. The COVID-19 pandemic forced our work to take place online exclusively, and while online engagement is vital, being in the live workshops and sharing space with our island peers is a magical and necessary experience that we look forward to having once more.

Each of our workshops has been dynamic and yet structured around a similar formula: we gain an understanding of the island's complex history, we learn about the present-day consequences of allowing white supremacy to run rampant in the D.R., we learn about the nature of historical trauma, our island's Afro-derived spiritual traditions, and ways that we can begin to experience more healing in our bodies, our relationships, and ourselves. Above all, we create a space for complex feelings, one of resonance, joy, and connection. If our Dominican participants don't remember a single historical date, what matters is that they come to a space of deeper self-awareness, empathy, and connection with humans whom they had been raised to either hate or ignore.

In Cultured Company does not hold all the answers for how to move from violence and continued oppression toward a space of reconciliation and deeper belonging. Such a massive process of decolonization and reprogramming will take a collective and organized effort across different sectors of society. However, in over a year of participating in this labor of peacemaking for Dominican and Haitian racial equity, I have gathered four lessons for how to move forward into a future of reconciliation and greater solidarity. To move forward, I suggest we need:

A) *Reinvigorated and Critical Understandings of the Meaning of History, Historical Narrative and Nationalist Myth-Making*
B) *Reforming Collectivity and Depth of Feeling among Dominicans*
C) *The formation of a Complex Apology and Reparations program*
D) *The Fostering of Relations of Deep Care, Cooperation, Mutuality and Belonging.*

While it can be argued that the Dominican Republic did not have the formalized systems of apartheid and Jim Crow, contemporary socioeconomic inequality, denationalization, and acts of violence against Haitian immigrants, their children, and dark-skinned Dominicans constitute similar forms of oppression that need immediate addressing. More than improving relations between Dominicans and Haitians, undertaking this peace-work as labor that is focused on process, as opposed to results, can help build a new Dominicanidad that is less grounded in the anti-black, anti-poor, and discriminatory attitudes. Such attitudes are currently at the center of our national identity narratives and they negatively impact poor, rural, and urban Afro-Dominicans. Racial Equity Peacemaking can be a pillar of a renewed Dominicanidad and can draw inspiration from similar work all over the world, most crucially South Africa and the United States.

FOUR LESSONS ON HISPANIOLA'S POLITICS OF DECOLONIZATION

Reinvigorated and Critical Understandings of the Meaning of History, Historical Narrative, and Nationalist Myth-Making

Despite the many changes that In Cultured Company's process has undergone in over a year of experimentation, the public education components of our work are central to all the possibilities that can unfold from our workshops. We spend considerable amounts of time on a presentation about Dominican and Haitian history because historical revisionism, myth-making and, increasingly, disinformation on social media, have created Dominican "histories" that do not at all resemble the complexity, vibrancy, and importance of the historical relationship between Dominicans and Haitians. We want participants to understand that Dominican history has been told by the victors, in other words, by the very same people who refuse to acknowledge the acts of violence committed in 1937. Through close readings of texts like *The Borders of Dominicanidad* by Lorgia Garcia Peña (2016), *We Dream Together* by Anne Eller (2017), *Dividing Hispaniola* (2016) by BOL organizer Edward Paulino, and others, we offer ways of approaching Dominican history that take flight into a space of Black transnational solidarity, possibility, and cultural identification. "Imagine," I tell participants, "Two small nations of Afro-descendants that dared to live free of chattel slavery nearly fifty years before their kindred in other parts of the hemisphere would fight for freedom. Imagine a space of black freedom so magnetic that it attracted thousands of African Americans seeking a place to call home. Imagine . . ."

Through our public education platform, we dismantle some of the myths and misconceptions about our island's shared history. Some of the most prominent ones that come up include: "There was no slavery on the Eastern side of Hispaniola;" "Haitians enslaved Dominicans;" "El Deguello de Moca was a massacre in which Haitians killed hundreds of Dominicans;" and, "Dominicans have racially-mixed looking features because of the Taíno and Spanish mixture." Due to the lack of a radical and widespread public school curriculum teaching Dominican and Haitian (and generally Caribbean) history in New York City and the Dominican Republic, the youth of the island and its diaspora are pedagogically underserved.

Misunderstandings and distrust have flourished in that space. For example, in our first workshop's small circle discussion, a Dominican participant asked, "do Haitians hate Dominicans?" She had been taught that this was the case by her community. The Haitians in the room replied that this was not the case—they simply did not think about Dominicans and understood that Dominicans simply "did not like Haitians." This exchange caught my attention because of the relief that the Dominican participant experienced at understanding that in fact the story she had been told—a story that was indeed a justification for violence against another group—was in fact not supported by evidence. She was not "hated," and therefore need not harbor feelings of anger, resentment, suspicion, or hate. Something else could flourish with the mental and emotional energy that had been previously dedicated to those feelings. This micro-moment was so powerful for me because it illuminated the power of contact, presence, and sharing perspectives to uplift our humanity and seek fuller versions of historical "truths."

Telling the story of the 1937 genocide is a punctum, to use Roland Barthes' term in reference to photography, a gathering point that connects storytelling, feeling, and reckoning. We listen to testimonies from some of the living survivors of the massacre, which were collected by NPR into a short video available on YouTube. I watch myself and I watch the audience experiencing stories of fleeing, stories of Dominican people who refused to follow orders, stories of those who barely escaped death. More times than not, my eyes well-up, my chest tightens and I begin to cry. Instead of hiding my tears, I let them flow because it's crucial that people understand that this is something to indeed mourn over—all these years later. This "something" is a wound that requires tending, and because they have now heard the story, they too are responsible for its healing. This is by no means a deliberate strategy of emotional manipulation. Instead, the emotional response happens spontaneously because of the weight of knowing a version of the truth in which me and my people are not racially innocent, that the imagined community that I belong to, the people who claim me, were capable of world-shattering violence and continue to cause great harm in the highly unequal, apartheid-like society that is the Dominican Republic. The desires for change, care, reparation, and reconciliation that grows from that space of collective knowing—feelings that can spontaneously be felt arising from the audience—are worth the discomfort and the pain that might be initially experienced. Feeling, rather than simply knowing, is the starting point, the fuel that can generate the will to explore alternative possibilities for the future. This leads to a second lesson I've garnered from doing this work.

Reforming Collectivity and Depth of Feeling among Dominicans

While undergoing the social labor of facilitating peace and reconciliation between Dominicans and Haitians as I began my doctoral research, I have noticed how decades of neoliberal capitalism and lack of engagement with social histories of fascist trauma have fostered individualism, competition, and isolation in contemporary Dominican society. When politicians fan the flame of *antihaitianismo* to create a sense of panic and scarcity, they do so to mask the inequality at the center of the country's model of governance and economic development. At the same time, the international public image of Dominicans is completely dissociated from the lived reality of the fierce struggle for survival, dominance, and perpetuation of the white, neoliberal, and elite status quo. The nation is instead portrayed as a space of friendliness, openness and cooperation; such portrayals hold grains of truth, but ignore how decades of privatization have left many Dominicans numb and struggling to survive while also silently benefitting from the labor and economic contributions of Haitian immigrants in the country.

The fascist, racist, and patriarchal characteristics of Dominican society that were left unchallenged after the Trujillo dictatorship haunt the aspirational sense of plurality and openness that is enshrined in the country's constitution. This is evident in the lack of coercive legal measures to prevent discrimination and the application of exclusionary laws like TC 168-13. Therefore, when Dominicans celebrate the joy and resilience of our culture, when we savor the scrappiness of our survival, but fail to acknowledge Haitian contributions to it or participate in political demands structural change, we are unfortunately complicit in a system of oppression that has transformed our culture from one of communal living to one of fierce individualism, consumerism, social disintegration, and ethno-racial oppression. Returning to the sense of shared humanity at the center of our cultural being is crucial to even beginning the process of offering an apology, reparations and reconciliation to our Haitian peers. In a future scenario of reconciliation, what can formerly oppressive populations abundantly offer if we are not doing the labor of regenerating these negative cultural dynamics within our own communities?

When examining the lessons that emerged from South Africa's peace and reconciliation process, Timothy Murithi found that in this process "a key step [was] to find a way for members of these communities to 're-inform' themselves with a cultural logic that emphasizes sharing and equitable resource distribution" (27). This cultural logic was "Ubuntu," a sense that my person, dignity, well-being, and humanity are inextricably tied to those of the people around me. The words of Archbishop Desmond Tutu are worth quoting at length:

> I am human because I belong, I participate, and I share. A person with Ubuntu is open and available to others, affirming of others, does not feel threatened that others are able and good; for he or she has a proper self-assurance that comes with knowing that he or she belongs in a greater whole and is diminished when others are humiliated or diminished, when others are tortured or oppressed, or treated as if they were less than who they are. (5)

It would be inappropriate to simply apply the cultural paradigm of Ubuntu to Dominican society, yet I hold fast to the belief that reconciliation begins by experiencing relationships, models of governance, and economies that are grounded in collectivity and that reinvigorate the feelings of mutuality, cooperativism, and unity that have historically been central to Dominican social life. For example, *Convitismo*, a term derived from the word *convite*, or communal work parties in rural communities, is a version of Ubuntu that can guide a "re-informing" of Dominicanidad aligned with community and care. Belonging in *Convitismo* may not be rooted in constructs like "nation" or "race," but in the interconnectedness that emerges from mutuality at the most basic levels: the neighborhood, the town, the city. After learning an alternative history of the island of Hispaniola, our hope is that participants are able to enter into a deepened sense of community with each other, taking their engagement from the digital realm into their everyday lives. This level of cultural realignment toward collectivity is necessary to move toward a process of apology, reconciliation, and reparation.

The Fostering of Cross-Cultural Relations of Deep Care, Cooperation, Mutuality, and Belonging

The sustainability of the transformations that Dominicans are experiencing in their relations to colorism and to their Haitian peers cannot flow from a space of guilt, a desire to be politically correct, or other coercive factors. They instead have to come from a space of care, spontaneity, and authentic relationships. I use the word "care" not in an emotional and undefined way. I understand care as necessarily grounded in service and in action, both of which get to be joyful and empowered. Following re-owned culture-shifter Adrienne Maree Brown, I hold the belief that the individual body reflects the social body, which means that our personal transformations can have momentous consequences when scaled up to the level of community. Humans, the social worlds we have created and the nature of which we are a part of, are organized in a fractal fashion. Therefore, the positive personal shifts occurring among the members of In Cultured Company's community to regenerate a sense of shared humanity and connection resonate on a larger scale. Regaining depth of feeling and a sense of shared humanity across social class, nationality, gender, and sexual preference is central to the process of reconciliation.

In the Winter of 2019, In Cultured Company had a chance to glimpse a future in which Dominicans and Haitians actually sustain equitable, loving, and care-filled relations. On February 27, 2019, we launched our first social media campaign, #RealDominicansAreNotAntiHaitian. One photo inspired more than 1,000 posts and reposts and a conversation spanning three languages, the Caribbean, and the United States, marking a clear desire to tell a different story about Dominican-Haitian relations. An assortment of images was shared, yet the ones that were most striking were images of Dominicans and Haitians in deep relationship: Parents holding their children, partners holding each other, and friends expressing more than solidarity. Joy, care, and belonging were present in ways that were as transgressive as they were necessary. Returning to the theme of belonging—Ubuntu, if you will—it's crucial to understand that interpersonal solutions are only a piece of what it might take for Dominicans to enter into a right relation with our Haitian peers. Protecting ourselves from the backlash against this work and forging systemic solutions to problems like *apátrida* (denationalization), lack of social security for retired sugarcane workers, and police brutality remain central aspects of the work.

The Formation of a Complex Apology and Reparations Program led by Dominicans

After recognizing ourselves as part of a group that is a perpetrator of violence, the responsibility of Dominicans is to lead efforts for formal and complex apologies. These apologies are complex in that they acknowledge that harm is both historical and ongoing.

While there currently isn't a cultural institution that can lead such a process, such as the Xhosa Inkundla/Lekgotla group mediation and reconciliation forums used during post-Apartheid reconciliation processes, the responsibility of a new generation of Dominicans is to lead that process ourselves. There is no official precedent in Dominican society for a "trial event"—a five-stage process of fact-finding, repentance, forgiveness and mercy, compensation, and reconciliation—for harm (whether committed during the Trujillo dictatorship or over decades of structural violence against Haitians). In fact, today there is an institutional failure to recognize that racism is a problem in the Dominican state, and that Haitian immigrants' human rights are being violated.

Despite these obstacles, the work of In Cultured Company is laying the groundwork for Dominicans to lead this process through an understanding of our history, our roles as part of a group that has perpetrated violence (and has also experienced violence from a powerful elite), and our responsibility of participating in an ongoing restorative justice process. Some aspects of this process will necessarily include the return of nationality to Dominicans of Haitian descent, an end to police brutality faced by Haitian immigrants and the granting of pensions to sugarcane workers, among many other solutions for greater equity and social harmony. A broader vision would see Dominicans and Haitians returning to the mountainous countryside from which they have been expelled to work the land together and forge climate-resilient, sustainable communities supported by a progressive and anti-racist state.

SMALL REBELLIONS BY WAY OF CONCLUSIONS

It's late evening in Dajabón, and the crowd has dispersed and begun to make its way back home. A few Border of Lights organizers and I carry a white paper box with a candle to the riverside. We get as far as we can on the dusty road framed by a concrete canal. A burly border guard tells us that we cannot go to the water, that he's following orders, that if his boss sees the flickering light he would know that he disobeyed. Fascism is following "orders" for the sake of "peace" and "structure." It's how El Jefe, Trujillo, would have wanted it: A militarized society where men in boots and uniforms force feed us spoonfuls of violence and call it "order(s)." We plead and we are allowed to leave a candle on the roadside, against a metal chain link fence. I leave my *calla* intertwined between the melded pieces of iron, so that whichever spirit comes tonight knows that someone cared.

Acts like these are small, yet magic lives in the moments of recognition that Dominicans and Haitians experience when they realize their bodies move the same to the rhythm of drums, and that this is not by accident. It is the same swaying lullaby that broke out in me when I heard a *Dajabonera* woman speak that distinctive mixture of kreyòl and Spanish. It's the feeling of tattooing my body with the whole of this island because it matters that the story be told in full and in blood, not in the bitter, petrified pieces Dominican nationalism taught me to chew. It's a rebellion carried in the whispers of the *luas* that spills over with hope and possibility upon learning how to tell the island's *full* story from a space of empowerment, empathy, and with eyes alighted toward more possible futures.

The following images are from In Cultured Company events, courtesy of Jay Espy Photo.

Works Cited

Brown, Adrienne M. *Emergent Strategy: Shaping Change, Changing Worlds.* AK Press, 2017.

Eller, Anne. *We Dream Together: Dominican Independence, Haiti, and the Fight for Caribbean Freedom.* Duke UP, 2016.

García Peña, Lorgia. *The Borders of Dominicanidad: Race, Nation, and Archives of Contradiction.* Duke UP, 2016.

Murithi, Timothy. "Practical peacemaking wisdom from Africa: Reflections on Ubuntu." *The Journal of Pan-African Studies*, vol. 1, no. 4, 2006, pp. 25–34.

Paulino, Edward. *Dividing Hispaniola: The Dominican Republic's Border Campaign against Haiti, 1930–1961.* University of Pittsburgh P, 2016.

Invocación vigilia

In memoriam 1937, El Corte

4 de octubre, 2019

Padre Regino Martínez Bretón

La sabiduría popular aprende, se nutre de la vida y nos enseña para que aprendamos a vivir. "El palo dao ni Dios lo quita." Lo acontecido en 1937, la matanza de negros en la frontera del norte, Dajabón, no se resuelve lamentándonos, ni acusando, ni quedándonos de brazos cruzados. Si hoy hacemos memoria de "El Corte" es para que tengamos presente el futuro; ese futuro que se define en el presente. Ahora, definiendo nuestros sueños, nuestras esperanzas, nuestros desafíos fronterizos que no pueden empolvarse. Sólo unidos y organizados podemos hacer que se hagan realidad esas soluciones que benefician a todas las personas fronterizas de aquí y de allá.

Las autoridades de la República Dominicana y de la República de Haití tienen una responsabilidad porque administran nuestros recursos; pero nosotros también somos doblemente responsables de lo que acontece en la frontera porque somos la memoria de nuestras autoridades manteniendo viva nuestra unión organizada como comerciantes, como artesanos, como juntas de vecinos, como madres, como agricultores, como ciudadanos, como sociedad civil ...

En los primeros cinco años del dos mil, las organizaciones comunitarias de Dajabón y Wanament insistíamos en que el mercado es binacional; además, solicitábamos un puente peatonal para evitar los desesperantes tapones de motores, carretillas, buses, patanas y gente a pie, todos queriendo pasar al mismo tiempo. Hoy, después de más de diez años vemos casi terminada la construcción del mercado mellizo en Wanament y el puente peatonal terminado sin estrenar ...

Solo la unión organizada pasa la noche con el Pueblo que sufre necesidades y violaciones de sus derechos; es por eso, que el Pueblo no olvida y le recuerda a las autoridades políticas. Los políticos primero ven sus necesidades personales y resuelven con lo que es nuestro. La sociedad civil unida y organizada le recuerda y exige a las autoridades su misión en la sociedad.

Hoy seguimos soñando con un marco jurídico fronterizo binacional que regule el control al cruzar la frontera de aquí para allá y de allá para acá; como dos repúblicas en una isla. Que nada se haga por debajo de la ley y que nadie le pase por arriba a la ley. Para la ley todos somos iguales. El control individualizado es corrupto, represivo y violador de los derechos humanos.

El control individualizado, violento y corrupto nos trae recuerdos indeseables. Sólo la justicia y la legalidad hace presente la paz, la armonía y el 'Buen Vivir' que todos deseamos. Ahora es el momento de comenzar a construir el futuro de justicia y legalidad para que "nunca más" se violen nuestros derechos inalienables en nuestra isla.

La vida es un regalo que nos compromete a defenderla y cuidarla como a la propia vida de cada persona. Yo solo no voy a ninguna parte . . . unidos y organizados nos hacemos sentir a nivel binacional y nos beneficiamos todos y todas. ¡¡Aquí y allá!! ¡¡Justicia y legalidad!! ¡¡Nada por debajo de la ley!! ¡¡Nadie por encima de la ley!! Así seremos luz para las fronteras de las naciones.

¡Dios nos bendiga y fortalezca nuestra unión organizada!

Border of Lights

How Memory Activism Re-Imagines National Belonging

Robin Maria DeLugan

Since 2012, the borderland between Haiti and the Dominican Republic has hosted annual commemorations organized by the Border of Lights collective of an infamous episode of state-sponsored violence in 1937. Comprised in large part of members of the diaspora from the Dominican Republic and Haiti who currently live in the United States, Border of Lights coordinates annual activities on the Caribbean island of Hispaniola in conjunction with local activists and organizations who seek to improve cross-border relations between Haiti and the Dominican Republic. By bringing attention to the 1937 violence demanded by Dominican dictator Rafael Trujillo and the estimated 15,000 lives that were lost, the aim is to raise awareness of the deep legacies of xenophobia against Haiti and the anti-black racism that motivated the violence and continues to afflict the Dominican Republic today. Memory activism aptly describes the historical memory projects that seek to transform such deep-seated prejudices and promote a more inclusive society. Through commemorations, Border of Lights and their solidarity networks connect the Dominican Republic's difficult past of state violence and dictatorship to present day exclusions of Haitians, Dominicans of Haitian descent, and dark-skinned Dominicans. The collective goal is for commemorative practices and community outreach to change exclusionary meanings of *Dominicanidad* (what it means to be Dominican) by fostering instead a vision of a more just and tolerant society. The long-distance, transnational involvement of Border of Lights and other faraway supporters illuminates the powerful way in which migration and diaspora influence the ongoing project to imagine and reimagine national belonging in the Dominican Republic. It was my privilege to attend the annual 1937 commemorations in Dajabón in 2014, 2016, and 2017, and this experience has influenced my understanding of the complex way that memory activism is engaged with the ongoing process of nation-building in the Dominican Republic today.

The Massacre River, named for a colonial era act of violence, geographically divides Haiti and the Dominican Republic, the two nation-states that share the Caribbean island of Hispaniola. The area where the border towns of Ounaminthe and Dajabón flank this river is regarded as the epicenter of the notorious 1937 massacre of thousands of people (mostly Haitians, but also dark-skinned Dominicans). Then and there, locals from both nations had lived together and cooperated. They commonly understood themselves as "*Rayanos*" (border dwellers). Despite the traditions of this fluid communal border region, and intending to stave off the perceived encroachment of Haitians and to pursue a project of "whitening" the nation, Dominican dictator Rafael Trujillo ordered the mass killing of black bodies that was carried out by machete. The years that followed the genocidal violence were accompanied by the slow and steady fortification of the physical border which aimed at separating the Dominican Republic from Haiti. This was matched by the ideological project of nation-building that reinforced an idea of Dominican uniqueness by crafting the significance of *Dominicanidad* against the negative "Otherness" of the people from Haiti. Though the animus was born in earlier colonial times, the modern nation was forged by reaffirming a hierarchy based on difference.

Following the 1937 massacre and throughout much of the twentieth century, authoritarian rule continued to shape Dominican society. (Trujillo was assassinated on May 30, 1961, yet many policies persisted under his successors.) Among the impacts of authoritarianism was the consolidation of the dominant idea that being Dominican meant being non-Haitian and non-Black. This enduring conception of national identity emphasized who belonged by fostering xenophobia against Haitian ethnic difference and adding force to long-standing anti-black racism. Thus, by defining the nation's identity, it also established its margins and limits. These margins not only outlined the territorial borders that separated the two nation-states, but also imposed upon the domestic population. To understand how in a society comprised predominantly of people of mixed Spanish, indigenous Taíno, and black African descent, certain Dominicans were negatively subjected to the racism that stigmatized blackness, the scholarship of Dominican historian Franklin Franco is essential reading. In 2015, Franco's 1969 classic *Los negros, los mulatos y la nación dominicana* was translated into English.[1] Despite racial discrimination and the absence of modes of cooperation between the governments and people of Haiti and the Dominican Republic, throughout history there have been other ways of imagining "*Dominicanidad*." In *The Mulatto Republic: Class, Race, and Dominican National Identity*, April Mayes's principal argument is that in the nineteenth century, and even during the US military occupation (1916–1924), there were different representations of *Dominicanidad*, and not all of them were anti-black or anti-Haitian. As with Border of Lights today, people of both nations have in the past imagined a closer unity. Recent books from Anne Eller and Maria Cristina Fumagalli explore a history of inspiring cross-border union and collaborations on Hispaniola.[2]

Antagonisms have also shaped the national experience. Following the 1937 atrocity, during the twentieth and now early twenty-first centuries, as plantation and other labor exchange brought migrating Haitians into the Dominican Republic, Haitians were addressed as the nation's "Other." Their children, born and raised in the Dominican Republic, legally earned birthright citizenship. As Dominicans of Haitian descent, many went on to raise Dominican children of their own. Unfortunately, this generational process of migration and adaptation did not undo the discrimination against Haitians that was codified by the 1937 state violence and the decades that followed. On January 12, 2010,

when Haiti suffered a devastating earthquake that caused 200,000 deaths and left 1.5 million Haitians homeless, many migrated to the Dominican Republic. The economy of the
Dominican Republic, stronger than that of Haiti, was a magnet for migrants who filled low
wage labor sectors such as construction (Jayaram). This recent influx of Haitians into the
Dominican Republic exacerbated long-standing tensions against Haitians. The Dominican Republic's 2017 immigrant census tallied 751,080 Haitians, who comprised 7.4% of the
population in the Dominican Republic.[3]

In their important 2017 article, "*El antihaitianismo en la República Dominicana: ¿Un
giro biopolítico?*", Samuel Martínez and Bridget Wooding offer a comprehensive explanation
of how, dating back to at least to the 1990s, the government of the Dominican Republic
steadily sought legal means to prohibit Haitian migration. One of the techniques of government was to refuse to issue national identity cards (*cédulas*) to Dominicans of Haitian
descent. *Cédulas* are required in the Dominican Republic to work legally, marry, register for
high school or university, open a bank account, obtain a driver's license, passport, or vote.
In other words, it is an essential identity document for full participation in society. With
time, this refusal of the government of the Dominican Republic to provide identity cards
to its citizens has intensified. Legal challenges ensued, and in 2013, changes to the national
constitution reaffirmed by the Constitutional Tribunal, the Dominican Republic's highest
court, not only removed birthright citizenship for Haitians but made it retroactive to 1929.
This devastating legal maneuver immediately stripped an estimated 200,000 Dominicans
of citizenship. Most of these people remain stateless today.

To understand the activities leading to the crisis of statelessness, many people point
to the case of Juliana Deguis Pierre. Ms. Pierre was born in the Dominican Republic of
Haitian parents who migrated there in the 1960s, when they were contracted to work in
the sugarcane fields. Juliana's birth was entered into the civil registry, and she received a
Dominican birth certificate. In the 1990s, the *Junta Central Electoral* (JCE), the government office that authorizes birth certificates, marriage certificates, and national identification cards, ruled against providing birth certificates and *cédulas* to people "suspected of
being Haitian." The JCE and many (but not all) branch offices refused to issue identity
documents to those targeted as Dominican citizens of Haitian descent. In 2008, when
Ms. Pierre attempted to apply for a *cédula*, she was informed that she was not eligible, and
her birth certificate was confiscated. She and other plaintiffs sued the government of the
Dominican Republic.

Over the next few years, the case wound its way to the Constitutional Tribunal. In
its ruling, TC/0168/13, now popularly referred to as *la sentencia* (the Sentence), the court
found that under international law every state has the sovereign right to determine its
nationality policies. The ruling revoked Pierre's citizenship, declaring that at the time of
her birth her undocumented parents were "in transit" and therefore she and others in her
situation were not entitled to receive birthright citizenship. Previously, "in transit" was
understood as applying to diplomats and tourists who were in the country for fewer than
ten days. The new court ruling expanded "in transit" to apply to Haitian migrant workers
who for decades had worked in the Dominican Republic's sugar plantations. The court
ordered the government's civil registry to make an audit of its records going back to 1929

to identify persons irregularly entered as citizens. This reinterpretation of the national constitution, retroactive to 1929, immediately impacted thousands of Dominicans of Haitian descent who overnight were classified as "foreigners" rather than "nationals." Stripped of citizenship from the only nation they know, and despite international outcry and feeble attempts by the government to restore citizenship to a handful of cases where more extensive documentation allowed the restriction to be abrogated, most of those affected continue to remain in a condition of statelessness (*apátrida*). In the early unfolding of this grim context of heightened anti-Haitian sentiment in the Dominican Republic, the Border of Lights collective was formed. As members of the Dominican and Haitian diaspora, they demonstrated their personal ties to original homelands. Further, as members of immigrant families themselves in the United States, they had first-hand experiences with systems of racialization. They were motivated to participate in efforts to contest such marginalization, both in the United States and on Hispaniola.

As outlined above, while government action in the Dominican Republic demonstrated anti-Haitian bias, there was also a rise in popular anti-migrant sentiment. The border patrol became extra-vigilant, capturing and returning unauthorized migrants back to Haiti. Organizations such as the Jesuit-run *Solidaridad Fronteriza* (Border Solidarity) advocated to protect the human rights of migrants. Border of Lights, informed by the lessons of history and determined to not let history repeat itself, directed fresh public attention to the 1937 massacre to examine how this difficult violent chapter of the Dominican Republic's history continues to impact the nation. Today, through annual commemorations, victims and survivors of 1937 are being remembered. The public is reminded about how the logic and legacies of Trujillo's violence continue to shape the nation. This contemporary effort to bring attention to the Dominican Republic's difficult past should be seen as essential to the ongoing process of nation- building. Common understandings of the nation and national identity are being examined and re-examined. In the process, we can ask, is the nation being reimagined anew?

FORGING NATION-STATES AND NATIONAL IDENTITY

Thinking about the construction of Dominican national identity, we can step back and consider a worldwide process that has resulted in today's array of distinct modern nations. Beginning in the late eighteenth century, struggles for independence from colonialism, monarchies, and imperialism brought a new political form: the nation-state. Establishing the nation-state means more than delimiting sovereign geographical territory and installing a centralized government. In recent decades, scholars have devoted much attention to studying the processes that also aim to unite the population around a common sense of culture, history, and identity. The need for common identity and an emotional and patriotic commitment to the nation depend on forming what Benedict Anderson famously dubbed "imagined communities" (7). The national community is considered "imagined" in at least three ways: (1) it involves constructing a social identity that aligns with the emerging nation-state form; (2) it is "imagined" in that despite the fact that most people will never have the chance to know most of their compatriots through the process of nation-building, they will have a shared sense of belonging to the nation; and (3) the national community is "imagined" as coexisting in a world with other nations where the nation-state form defines the core political and collective identity of modern society. Seeing nation-building in this way helps us understand the power of the nation-state and how representations of national identity can anchor one's very sense of being and belonging in the world today. It is important to view nation-building beyond a one-time historical event coinciding with the birth of an independent nation-state. Even while the nation may seem durable and fixed, its continued existence involves an active ongoing process of nation-building. Through promotions of history, symbols, commemorations, and rituals, the national community participates in reinforcing the meaning of the nation and its importance. Consider, as examples, how the flag, national anthem, museums, monuments, and the celebration or recognition of key individuals and historical events can unite many in the nation and foster emotional ties of allegiance and patriotism and belonging.

A critical view of any historical and ongoing project of nation-building must examine the complex working of power that necessarily accompanies the dynamic process. As a dominant way to represent and define the nation is imagined, what other ideas are thereby discarded or ignored? Who was included and who was left out of the historical and ongoing process of nation- building? What silences are manifested? Does ideology about a shared connection to national history and culture obscure understandings and encourage inequality? In nations, such as the Dominican Republic, how did foundational social and racial hierarchies introduced by colonialism continue to influence the nation's modern definitions of status and belonging?

On the island of Hispaniola, the Dominican Republic's path from being a colony of Spain to independence involved occupation by Haiti as that nation attempted to unify the island (1822–1844), renewed occupation by Spain (1861–1865), and occupation by the United States in 1916. External but also internal actors and influences, then and now, continue to shape the process of nation-building. Before describing my experiences in Dajabón as a participant in three of the annual 1937 commemorations coordinated by Border of Lights, I want to advance a bit further our understanding of nation-building. A more global lens can help us understand why historical memory about 1937 is salient today. We can start by considering the context for nation-building in the 1930s, the interval between the two world wars. This period immediately followed the upheaval of the global economic depression. At this historical juncture, the defining and redefining of many nations in the world happened under authoritarianism and totalitarianism. Writing about Latin America (including making specific reference to the Dominican Republic), Jean Franco describes this as a period of "Cruel Modernity" because efforts of nation- building were accompanied by repression and violence, not to mention economic disparity, and these social forces mark society well into the present day (2). During this time, dictatorships and military regimes prevailed, often supported by United States' imperialistic and capitalistic interests. They perpetuated foundational ideas about nationalism, especially those, for the purposes of this discussion, that reinforced ethnic and racial boundaries. Franco links the turbulent 1930s to the decades of violence and unrest that followed. Throughout much of the twentieth century in Latin America, what transpired was a process of "failed" nation-building. We are familiar with histories of state violence, rebels and insurgency, repression, torture, and other severe acts against humanity. Despite these legacies that weigh upon national society, ongoing democratization and adherence to international human rights, standards, and norms have also become forces that are influencing nations and their futures. In democratizing societies, rights and recognitions may have been inscribed in the nation's founding, and they can foster solidarity. However, when lacking or not uniformly applied, they can also be stark reminders of inequality. This discrepancy can foment discontent and motivate efforts to challenge the status quo. In the Dominican Republic, memory activism about 1937 involving the Border of Lights collective, when linked to heightened contemporary exclusions against Haitians, offers an important illustration of how and why past violence is being brought to the public's attention today.

MIGRATION, DIASPORA, AND TRANSNATIONAL BELONGING

One last discussion about nations and nation-building is essential to a better understanding of the Border of Lights collective's commitment to bringing attention to the 1937 violence, its victims, and its survivors. We have already explored how the emergence of nation-states involved a process of establishing discrete territories that also required populations to share an identity as an imagined community. I also mentioned that in the historical process, some populations within the territory were marginalized from the dominant views of national identity and those who belonged (e.g., racial, ethnic, religious, and other minorities). But national populations are dynamic, not static. This is particularly true when we consider the effects of migration. When new people immigrate into a nation, what is the process of their incorporation into the nation? Are they relegated to the margins? How does their presence transform the meaning of the nation and national belonging? In the United States, a nation largely forged by immigration, not just racial categories but hyphenated identities can mark an immigrant's distinction. Immigrants are often tied to their national origin transposed into an ethnic identity descriptor attached to their "Americanness." The fact that the Border of Lights collective was formed by valiant people in the United States who primarily identify as Dominican-American or Haitian-American, by citizens who care about justice in the Dominican Republic and Haiti, is not a coincidence. It speaks to the uneasy way that the United States incorporates newcomers, especially racial and ethnic minorities, where a sense of belonging may reside more with original homeland affiliations. It illustrates the enduring ties that Dominican-Americans and Haitian-Americans have to their families' original homeland or homelands in a world that is shaped by migration. We might ask, to what extent does one's experience as an immigrant or as children of immigrants influence a sense of belonging to distant homelands? It also highlights the power behind the construction of national identity—which can inspire connections across time and space or can relegate some to the margins—and communicates the fundamental compelling resonance of national belonging.

Today we increasingly speak of the impact of migration as tied to processes of globalization. As the world becomes more interconnected, migration becomes a norm. With recent advances in technology, migrating populations can more easily stay connected to original homelands. Rather than seeing migration as a one-way ticket, we can recognize how people forge simultaneous links to multiple nation-states. The useful concept of "diaspora" has long been used to describe how people from one original homeland can be dispersed throughout the world and still maintain a sense of common identity, of belonging to that homeland. Diaspora involves a collective identity that links people in the world from one original location to a sense of common community. While "diaspora" continues to have relevance, the newer concept of "transnationalism" better explains what is unique about contemporary phenomena. The foundational research of Nina Glick Schiller et al. provides an analytical framework for transnationalism that continues to motivate scholars today (14). Transnationalism emphasizes how the boundaries of nation-state are expanded by migrants and immigrants who, for example, through enhancements in transportation, banking, and communications technology are able to stay closely involved with and connected to original homelands. Today the modern world system precisely illustrates where global and national economies are pushing people out and where other, stronger economies serve as magnets for newcomers. Of course, there are also political and social reasons that motivate the specific movement of people, including the desire for refuge from political strife. History, too, has a role, and we can see how past political relations can influence people from former colonies to migrate to metropoles, to the former colonizing centers, due to legacies of language, culture, and other mutual associations. Governments of migrant-sending nations, especially those on the periphery of the world economy, increasingly find the migration of their citizens to be a resource that can bolster the flailing national economy. By sending money back to families via remittances and by transferring other resources and influence, be it monetary or social capital, "transmigrants" contribute to the families they left behind. Their assistance alleviates the pressure on governments to solve the economic conditions that can motivate migration in the first place. Today, governments value their faraway citizens and invest resources designed to develop the migrants' ties of belonging to the original homeland. Beyond economic aid, faraway citizens can also be committed to improving national society in other ways. Consider the power of national identity: like so many aspects of culture, it becomes common property and we take it for granted. When, however, the dominant view is also one that discriminates, marginalizes, or otherwise harms others, it may take effort to see it as a particular product of history and as one that can be re-examined and transformed.

Scholars such as Wendy Roth, who writes specifically about migration from the Caribbean to the United States, argue that it is through the experience of migration that many are able to see the construction of the nation through fresh eyes (97). Perhaps the challenges of being an immigrant and struggling to be accepted in a new society raise consciousness about how nations construct borders and boundaries of belonging. Or it may be through the process of one or more generations of families born from immigrant ancestors that the ongoing project of nation-building becomes less theoretical and more of a lived experience. In the case of Dominicans migrating to the United States, it is the harsh reality that while they are viewed as "Latino," they are also generally considered to be "Black." This goes against the norms of national identity in the Dominican Republic that, as described above, place a negative value on "blackness." While being newly categorized as Black can be seen as a negative in light of the history of African Americans in the United States, it can also be a liberating identity that motivates Dominican (and Haitian and other) citizens to contest racism and marginalization. This energy is not only productive for transforming the United States into a more inclusive and just society and encouraging diasporic and transnational ties, but also has re-directed this same quest for equality and inclusion toward the immigrants' original homelands. Whether such long-distance involvement is welcomed or appreciated by national governments and society is an open question. As will be described below, while this may be seen by some as an importation of an unwelcome desire to remake the nation, the Border of Lights collective has allied with people and entities in the Dominican Republic and Haiti to support the efforts on the ground on Hispaniola to imagine a more humane and inclusive world.

In 2013, prior to my participation in the Border of Lights commemoration, I traveled to the Dominican Republic for the first time to learn more about the historical memory attention to the 1937 atrocity. From the capital Santo Domingo, I travelled to Dajabón. Dajabón feels very much like a frontier town, with much commercial and social activity in the streets. Many genres of Caribbean music (especially from Haiti and the Dominican Republic, but also from Puerto Rico and Cuba) blare from passing cars and open shops. It is hot and humid. I also experienced Dajabon's famous market. On Mondays and Fridays, the border is open from morning to dusk, and Haitians are able to visit the bustling market without a visa. Haitians are the primary consumers of market goods, which range from fresh produce and live poultry to housewares and clothing. It is wonderfully chaotic. I visited staff at *Solidaridad Fronteriza* (Border Solidarity), well-known for defending Haitian migrants. They are a partner organization in the annual 1937 commemoration.[4] Here I learned more about the work accomplished by the Border of Lights collective. During the visit, I saw the mural on the wall outside the *Nuestra Señora del Rosario* Catholic Church which was commissioned by Border of Lights following the first commemoration in 2012. The mural emphasizes bi-national friendship and cooperation. In 2017, the mural was restored, and a commemorative plaque was installed alongside it to mark the 80th anniversary of the massacre. I vowed to return to Dajabón to gain firsthand experience of the 1937 commemoration.

In 2014, 2016, and 2017, I participated each year in the two days of planned activities that took place on the Dominican Republic side of the bi-national commemoration. Reaching Dajabón from California involved a cross-country flight to arrive in Santiago, the Dominican Republic's second largest city. From Santiago, a two-hour bus ride through the picturesque countryside brought me once again to the border town. When I attended the Border of Lights commemorations, I stayed at the same hotel as most of the organizers, which was far from luxurious. Each year, during late summer/early fall, the key members of the Border of Lights collective plan the year's upcoming events from the comfort of their homes in the United States. For the designated weekend, they arrived from Florida, Massachusetts, New York, and elsewhere. Dominican-American historian and activist-scholar Dr. Edward (Eddie) Paulino has been my primary connection to the annual activities. He is passionate about the work and generous with his time. Each year, the days are broadly structured in a similar manner, but the program always offers new events. Typically, the Friday before the commemoration involved completing last-minute details, with the planners regrouping in the evening. Saturdays featured art, culture, or sports activities to involve local youth and youth from other towns who arrived via bus; their attendance was supported by nonprofits dedicated to educating and empowering young people on the island, especially young women.[5] The central park across from the *Nuestra Señora del Rosario* church was the primary site for public activities. On Saturday evenings a special mass took place in this church to commemorate the victims of 1937. Prior to the Catholic mass, a local restaurant provided dinner for the hundred or so people participating in the pre-commemoration activities. The lead clergy of the church was an important partner. During the evening mass, local parishioners were nearly overwhelmed with the many newcomers who arrived for the commemoration. All who were present received a history lesson about the 1937 massacre, and it was emphasized that in its aftermath Dominicans were encouraged only to see their divisions from Haitians, and how this negated a history of cooperation and coexistence and common humanity. The sermon advocated for solidarity with Haitians and with Dominicans of Haitian descent, a message that resonated in the current challenging political landscape and abuse of human rights.

Following the church ceremony, a procession formed. Based on my three years of experience, I estimate an average of one hundred people participated in the procession. Carrying hand-held candles balanced inside wax paper cups, and spontaneously singing songs of faith and solidarity, the procession wound through the mostly dark streets of Dajabón until reaching the closed border gate. Here, we shared brief testimonials about the impact of the massacre on both Dominican and Haitian society and identity. We mounted the candles that lit the way through the dark procession on the ledge of the steel border gate. Everyone peered into the darkness to see the flickering lights on the other side of the river where the simultaneous procession in Ouanaminthe, Haiti, was taking place to mirror the activities in Dajabón. Once the commemorative march and gathering in solidarity were done for the evening, the crowd dispersed, and people made their way back to their homes and hotels.

My observation is that many local residents of Dajabón did not yet actively participate in the commemorative events, but instead watched with curiosity or possibly ambivalence from the sidelines. In 2017, in an effort to draw more local attention and participation, a mobile deejay van was hired to not only play music loudly along the procession route and at the border gate, but also to amplify the poignant spoken reflections and testimonials that were shared. With its colorful, flashing lights, the "disco" truck was an eye-catching novelty, but the attention- grabbing truck did not seem to measurably influence more local community participation that evening. Each year the organizers conduct outreach and design activities that are intended to resonate with local residents.

Following the procession, some of the Border of Lights crew moved operations to the city of Santiago. There, at a restaurant, the crew conducted an online "global vigil" via the website maintained by Border of Lights. This creative use of technology invited people from around the world to send photographs that represent their virtual participation in the annual commemoration. People posted photos such as lighting candles and shared personal words about why it was important for them to remember the 1937 violence. While a digital divide may preclude many on Hispaniola from joining in this online practice, this dimension of the annual commemoration importantly allowed others, in particular members of the diaspora, to participate long-distance.

The following morning, there were gatherings with local activists, some of whom travel hours from Santo Domingo. The get-together provided an opportunity to not only debrief about the previous day's activities but for Border of Lights members to get important updates about the ongoing conditions in the Dominican Republic. It was a special privilege to be invited to sit in on these meetings and to learn first-hand about the social justice work happening in the Dominican Republic and in Haiti. This gathering of activists also made explicit the efforts to link remembering the 1937 massacre to current conditions of racism, xenophobia, and exclusion on the island.

Between my first visit to the Dominican Republic in 2013 and my latest visit in 2017, while traveling to and from Dajabón, I observed a noticeable intensification of the guarding of the border region. Whether traveling from Dajabón by private car or public bus, during the closest thirty miles to the border, there were frequent stops at numerous checkpoints manned by the military. The checkpoints sought Haitians who may have stowed away or who were otherwise unauthorized to be in the Dominican Republic. At each checkpoint, I observed groups of detained young men, presumably Haitian, huddled together on the side of the road. I was told that at the end of the day, they are returned to the border and ordered back into Haiti. Historically in 1937, and still today, the border region between Haiti and the Dominican Republic is ground zero for the government's anti-migrant, anti-Haitian policies.

By organizing annual 1937 commemorations, Border of Lights intervenes through memory activism as educational and cultural activities aim to illuminate history and raise consciousness about the connections between past state violence and the violence imposed on Dominicans of Haitian descent and Haitian migrants today. Through their memory activism, Border of Lights and their solidarity networks in the Dominican Republic emphasize the negative legacies of 1937 that continue to shape exclusionary ideas about national belonging. By bringing the past into the present in this way, their aim is to challenge the status quo and transform the meaning of national belonging in the Dominican Republic, instead of repeating divisions from the past, and to imagine a more just and inclusive nation.

Notes

1. See Franklin J. Franco. *Blacks, Mulattos, and the Dominican Nation.* Translated by Patricia Mason. Routledge, 2015.

2. See Anne Eller's *We Dream Together: Dominican independence, Haiti, and the fight for Caribbean freedom.* Duke University Press, 2017; and Maria Cristina Fumagalli. *On the Edge: Writing the Border Between Haiti and the Dominican Republic.* Oxford University Press, 2015.

3. *2ª Encuesta Nacional de Inmigrantes* (ENI-2017). Santo Domingo: Oficina Nacional de Estadística. April 2018.

4. In February 2018, four highly-regarded Jesuit social action centers in the Dominican Republic—Centro Bonó, Solidaridad Fronteriza, CEFASA, and Servicio Jesuita Con Migrantes-Jimani—consolidated organizationally under the umbrella Centro Montalvo www.centromontalvo.org.

5. Participating youth-serving organizations included: The Mariposa DR Foundation (https://mariposadrfoundation.org); DREAM Project (https://www.dominicandream.org); and Yspaniola. (http://yspaniola.org).

Works Cited

Anderson, Benedict. *Imagined Communities: Reflections on the Origin and Spread of Nationalism*. Verso, 1983.

Franco, Jean. *Cruel Modernity*. Duke University Press, 2013.

Martínez, Samuel and Bridget Wooding. "El Antihaitianismo en la República Dominicana: ¿Un giro biopolítico?" *Migración y Desarrollo*, vol. 15, no. 28, 2017, pp. 95–123.

Mayes, April J. *The Mulatto Republic: Class, Race, and Dominican National Identity*. University Press of Florida, 2014.

Roth, Wendy. *Race Migrations: Race and the Cultural Transformation of Race*. Stanford University Press, 2012.

Schiller, Nina Glick; Basch, Linda; Blanc-Szanton, Cristina. "Transnationalism: A New Analytic Framework for Understanding Migration." *Annals of the New York Academy of Sciences*, 1992, pp. 1–24, doi:10.1111/j.1749-6632.1992.tb33484.x.

Memorialization, Solidarity, Ethnically Mixed Couples, and the Mystery of Hope

Mainstreaming *Border of Lights*

Maria Cristina Fumagalli and Bridget Wooding

October 2019 marked the eighth anniversary of the *Border of Lights* commemoration of the 1937 massacre of Haitians and Dominico-Haitians on the Dominico-Haitian border. As the website of the initiative explains: "This is why Border of Lights came to be . . . to commemorate the lives lost and affected by the 1937 Parsley Massacre, to uplift the narrative of historical and ongoing collaborations between two peoples at the Dominican Republic (DR) and Haiti border, to continue in the struggle for justice, with hope in our hearts."[1]

Border of Lights is therefore both a laudable and necessary initiative because across-the-border exchanges on Hispaniola have often been framed as being characterized by conflict and violence. The first border clashes between the Spanish and the French colonizers took place in the seventeenth century, before the French colony of Saint Domingue was officially established in 1777. The warfare produced by the 1791 revolt and Haitian Revolution, during which the border between the two sides often shifted or disappeared altogether, the Haitian occupation of the Spanish side between 1822 and 1844 and, more recently, the 1937 massacre of Haitians and Haitian-Dominicans in the Dominican borderland, have all contributed to cast the island and borderland as sites of violent confrontation. Yet, border relations have also been characterized by many collaborative linkages and productive exchanges between the two peoples which have been minimized routinely and occluded by ultranationalist discourses which have been invested in hiding, justifying, or denying the horrors of the 1937 massacre.

Over the years, *Border of Lights* has stubbornly continued to commemorate the massacre, reminding us that solidarity and communality have played, are playing, and can continue to play an important part in border relations and that they need to be persistently brought to the fore and nurtured in order to counteract powerful ultranationalist narratives. In what follows, we will show how we have built on the example set by *Border of Lights* when we organized a series of activities in Comendador in October 2017 in close collaboration with associates on both sides of the border. We will conclude by suggesting how the lessons learnt from the *Border of Lights* experience could be usefully mainstreamed into activities relating to Dominico-Haitian relations on a more permanent basis, so that positive spin-offs of the annual commemoration may have a ripple effect on and in island society.

Underlining cultural continuities and collaboration between Haitians and Dominicans has clearly become particularly urgent since September 23, 2013, when the Dominican Constitutional Court ordered that all birth registries from 1929 should be audited for people who had been (allegedly) wrongly registered as Dominican citizens. This put at risk of denationalization (and, in some cases, expulsion) 133,000 Dominicans of Haitian ancestry. Also, long-term migrants, born in Haiti, have faced an uncertain future under a pioneer regularization plan for undocumented migrants in which 250,000 long-term migrants have received temporary status rather than residency in the country.

Since 2013 local civil society organizations have continued to demonstrate against nationality stripping, plead their case in the media, and use all the legal means at their disposal to restore the fundamental rights of those affected by the ruling, but for human rights activities to gain traction it is vital to challenge ultra-nationalist propaganda from a cultural, not only legal, point of view. Among those affected by the denationalization crisis, for example, are ethnically mixed couples and their children born in country who are facing collateral problems for being registered as Dominicans. Working in the Dominican Republic, Observatory Caribbean Migrants (OBMICA) developed a three-year project (2016-2019)[2] aiming at realizing the constitutional right to Dominican nationality of children born to such couples in the Dominican Republic. To better understand their predicament and support them in their battle for the restoration of their right. However, it is vital to understand that ethnically mixed couples are not "exceptional" but that it is the "state of emergency" in which they are plunged that has recast them as "non-normative" families. Approaching the issue from a broader historical and cultural perspective, therefore, can be extremely valuable since mixed couples are not only well represented in literary texts, but they have often been chosen as powerful symbols of hope in literature and performance art which have put border relations at their core.

In Freddy Prestol Castillo's *El Masacre se pasa a pie*, written as the 1937 massacre was unfolding in Dajabón, for instance, victims and perpetrators are often related: Captain Ventarrón, one of the military men in charge of the killings, is utterly distressed when he suddenly remembers that his own grandfather was born in Haiti. The mixed family of Sargent Pío's illegitimate sister, who had married a Haitian-born wealthy land- and cattle-owner and had seven children with him, is spared by the Sargent who, instead of killing them as he had been ordered to do, lets them escape through the border to find refuge in Haiti. Among the main characters of René Philoctète's *Le peuple des terres mêlées* (1989), another text focused on the 1937 massacre but from a Haitian perspective, we find "the lovers of the border", that is "*el mulato Dominicano*" and labour activist Pedro Alvarez Brito and his wife Adèle, "*la chiquita negrita haitiana*". Philoctète uses Spanish to describe them in the original text in French, in order to highlight the bilingualism of the people living in the borderland, and this mixed couple embodies the idea of unity between Haitians and Dominicans conveyed by the title of this novel which identifies a "single people" ("*le peuple*") on these "*terres mêlées*" ("mixed lands").

Mis 43 años en La Descubierta, which is not a fictional text but a memoir which illustrates the life of Jesús María Ramírez in La Descubierta, a small town in the central portion of the Dominican borderland, explains how, in 1937, news of the killings which took place in the north reached the central portion of the borderland and its inhabitants were informed that, by the end of 1938, 'Haitians' living in the area would have to relocate in Haiti regardless of the fact that they might have lived for years (or were even born) in the Dominican Republic. As part of a process which became known as *el desalojo* (or 'evacuation'), ethnically mixed families were dismembered and Ramirez informs us that the majority of those who refused to go, were killed.

In his 1963 collection of poems entitled *La criatura terrestre*, the Dominican poet Manuel Rueda, who was born in Montecristi in 1921 and was fifteen when the 1936 border agreement was signed, remembers life in the northern borderland before the massacre: he famously explains that before the establishment of the borderline, his 'world was entire' and that he felt 'exiled from Eden' when the borderline was forcefully inscribed on the ground. Twenty-five years later, in the long poem *Las metamorfosis de Makandal* (1998), Rueda focuses instead on a mythological mixed couple: the mutual desire of the characters Makandal and Anaïsa, in fact, plays center stage as their flesh crawls "between Dajabón and Juana Méndez"—that is, at the very heart of the northern borderland. Makandal is a legendary figure in Haiti, a slave who had organized a massive insurrection against the French plantocracy in Saint Domingue but was captured just before he could bring his plans to fruition and then burnt at the stake. Many believed that he managed to escape by metamorphosing into a fly and he was expected to return one day to fulfil his prophecies. Anaïsa is instead a powerful spirit or *lua* of Dominican Vodú and in Rueda's poem their union is so strong that Makandal at some point metamorphoses into Anaïsa and becomes one with her ("I, the strong Makandal, / am Anaïsa!") erasing the 'self vs other' binarism enforced by the border.

A different (but equally compelling) kind of corporeal and spiritual fusion is at the core of a truly compelling visual metaphor for the island of Hispaniola which also foregrounds a "mixed couple," namely the Dominican artist Karmadavis's video performance *Estructura completa* (2010). As a blind man of Dominican origin carries in his arms a disabled woman of Haitian origin whose legs have been amputated, this mixed couple becomes a complete structure which moves along the streets of the Dominican Republic and overcomes different obstacles only through cooperation: in order to move forward the "structure" of which they are part, the woman has to pay attention to passers-by, walls, steps, traffic and communicate their presence promptly and effectively while the man has to trust her and act on her guidance. Both members of this peculiar "mixed couple" are perfectly aware of their deficiencies and of the deficiencies of their partner but they are also fully committed to make their partnership work by building on what they can offer to one another because they know that neither can go anywhere without the other.[3]

Border of Lights's positive message resonated also in the 80th anniversary of the massacre when the Juan Bosch Foundation co-organized an international seminar in which various academic, activists, writers, and institutions gathered at the INTEC University in Santo Domingo in order to break the silence surrounding the massacre and reflect on its relevance for current Dominico-Haitian relations.[4] In the same year, encouraged by the success of the *Border of Lights* initiative, we joined forces and set out to contribute to the transformation of the eightieth anniversary into an occasion to rethink and help reframe past, present and, crucially, future relations between Haiti and the Dominican Republic.

Inspired by the decision of the founders and participants of *Border of Lights* to make their presence felt in the northern borderland where the massacre was carried out (but also where solidarity between the two people has always been strong), we decided to complement their activities in Dajabón/Ouanaminthe by extending the commemoration to the central borderland, an area where the local population had also been affected by the massacre and the subsequent *desalojos* and where the cross-border towns of Belladère (Haiti) and Comendador (Dominican Republic) face one another. Working in close consultation with local civil society organizations and authorities on the border at the Comendador/ Belladère crossing, we devised a series of inter-connected activities which built on the *Border of Lights* experience. Initially instigated by diaspora actors of Haitian and Dominican ancestry, this experience has come to incorporate and be "owned" by local organizations on the ground.

On October 24, 2017, human rights concerns were put in dialog with academic research on the literary/cultural history of the massacre in a talk by Fumagalli in the Centro Cultural Juan Pablo Duarte in Comendador which targeted a young age group and made available to the local population some of the findings included in her monograph *On the Edge: Writing the Border between Haiti and Dominican Republic*, the first literary and cultural history of the border region. The talk, in French and Spanish to celebrate the bilingual and bicultural nature of the borderland, was attended by some seventy-five school children and numerous officials from Haiti and the Dominican Republic. Fumagalli's talk focused on the different ways in which literary texts and performance artists have told and retold the history of the massacre and, at the same time, foregrounded the continuous presence and relevance of mixed couples, offering a number of examples (including the above-mentioned ones) which, it was hoped, would resonate with the local population among which mixed couples feature in considerable numbers. Consecutive official reports on the numbers and characteristics of Haitian migrants and their descendants in the Dominican Republic (ONE 2013 and ONE 2018)[5] have identified some 25,000 cases where Dominican documentation has not been acquired for children born to ethnically mixed couples where one parent is of Haitian ancestry. In fact, local contacts along the border report many cases of undocumented offspring of such couples, especially in the border province of Elías Piña which is the poorest province in the country and where the chief town Comendador is located.

Fumagalli highlighted, for instance, that the protagonists of René Philoctète's *Le peuple des terres mêlées* live in Comendador/Elías Piña – the very place where we organized our activities—and are part of a transnational, bilingual, and bicultural community which was not divided or separated by the presence of a physical border. Before the massacre, as Philoctète points out, the priest of Elías Piña used to purchase his eggs in Belladère, the Dominican sergeant in Bánica bought his *clairin* in Mont-Organisé, and merchants from Jimaní, sold their wares in Fond-Parisien.

Apart from offering an account of Philoctète's reconstruction of the massacre and a crucial contextualization of the ethnically mixed couples at his core, the talk also brought in sharp relief the end of the novel, where those forcibly displaced by the massacre are of "every color, every walk of life, every belief, every character, every kind of memory and beauty." Significantly the narrator cannot tell (and does not want to know) if they are Haitians or Dominicans: all he knows is that they have "so many things in common, share so many wounds and joys that trying to distinguish the two peoples violates their tacit understanding to live as one" and their "dream of creating one people from two lands mixed together." It was pivotal, in fact, to convey the message that, in Philoctète's novel, the massacre is not allowed to abolish, once and for all, the deep connections which characterized the peoples of the borderland and that the novel contains the promise of a new beginning, of a new "world to build."

Philoctète's novel also enabled us to explore and underline, in a market town like Comendador, the historical significance of binational markets in the border region: Adèle and Pedro, in fact, met at the market of Maribaroux, according to him, or of Thomassique, according to her. The suggestion that the two cannot agree on the exact location of their first encounter signposts the fact that the markets which were held (then) on Haitian territory were visited by both Haitians and Dominicans on a regular basis and were central to the local economy and social life of the area, a fact that, as Fumagalli observed, was also underlined by Ramírez in *Mis 43 años en La Descubierta*. Fumagalli's talk, also inaugurated a photographic exhibition on the border crossing of Belladère/Comendador (October 23 to October 28) which was very well received by the local population. The exhibition especially featured Haitian market women who cross twice weekly to the Dominican Republic to engage in small-scale trading in a border market and who had been the focus of a research project by OBMICA. While the photographs, by Hillary Petrozziello, had previously been exhibited at the Centro Cultural de España in Santo Domingo,[6] this was the first time that these images were seen locally and OBMICA gifted the exhibition to our local collaborators for permanent use on the border.

The *pièce de résistance* of the activities was a concert celebrated in the market square in the evening of October 24, 2017, with the binational cultural group Azueï and with guest artist Delmas T1, a Dominican rapper of Haitian ancestry. Azueï is a movement of talented Haitian and Dominican artists initially supported by the European Union and launched in 2015, during a retreat conducted by Dominican and Haitian artists on the shores of Lake Azueï, a nature sanctuary that spans the borders of the two countries and aims to promote a culture of peace and dialog through art and culture. Significantly, further confirming the cross-pollination that this kind of activities are supposed to facilitate, Azueï's first musical album which came out in 2021, features a piece entitled "Mixed couple."[7] The outreach with the media carried out on the ground in Comendador in October 2017 involved both of us speaking with local social communicators: Wooding, for example, exchanged for an hour with the local program host Mario Alcántara, Presenter of the TV program "Good Night Elías Piña."

Mindful of the importance of turning the memorialization of the 80th anniversary of the massacre in Comendador into a permanent legacy, we organized two further activities:

first of all, two Azueï artists, the Dominican Gabriel Shak Doñe and the Haitian Olivier A. Ganthier, painted together a mural in Comendador which is aimed at reiterating solidarity, peace, and cooperation between the two countries. In relation to bottom-up attempts at cultural rapprochement between Haiti and the Dominican Republic, the group Azueï was therefore able to have not only its first musical performance but also its first mural in Comendador since, previously, their musical and artistic performances on the borderlands, supported by *Border of Lights,* had been limited to the northern border crossing of Dajabón/Ouanaminthe.

Secondly, OBMICA launched a video called "The Haitian-Dominican border past and present" on December 18, 2017, which is the annual day of the International Migrant, celebrated for when the *International Convention on the Rights of All Migrant Workers and Their Family Members* came into force in 1990. The video features reflections on the massacre and border relations by Wooding, Fumagalli, and the local cultural promoter Juan Secundino, as well as documenting the activities carried out in the central borderlands in October. Importantly, since the video is a useful milestone which evidences, from the testimonies of interviewees, the impact of the activity on the border,[8] it has also been mobilized in follow-up activities to exhort the competent authorities to urgently attend to the legal rights of the figure of the cross-border dweller (*habitante fronterizo*) – included in the Dominican Migration law of 2004. Were this regulation mechanism to be implemented, it would be easier to protect the rights of persons who cross the border routinely to work on the other side, notably Haitian women who participate in the bi-weekly *ferias,* the border markets, which today are held in the Dominican Republic.

It is now commonplace that it has been easier to memorialize the 1937 massacre from the vantage point of the Haitian and Dominican respective diasporas, especially through literary and artistic voices based in the United States. The consequences on the island of this opening of new spaces to remember the past with a view to re-inventing the future need to be further disentangled, so that local human rights actors on the ground may fully profit from this new canon abroad and use it for their own ends across Hispaniola. It is our contention that the *Border of Lights* initiative provides precisely this bridging role which needs to be even further capitalized upon on the border and elsewhere on the island by island-based organizations and activists.

Annual commemorations in October, for example, could be put in dialog with the results of the Haitian and Dominican Republic Universities' research project (OBMEC 2015–2017) focused on the environment, education, migration, and trade on the Haitian-Dominican border and synthesized in the webpage of the new Dominican Border Observatory created in late 2018. An outstanding issue is that of using island relevant texts in the school curriculum, recognizing that great strides have been made in recent years to translate pertinent texts in Spanish into French and vice versa. It is unfortunate, for example, that the title of Philoctète's novel was misleadingly translated in Spanish as *Rio Masacre,* a title which emphasizes violent conflict rather than the transnational solidarity and collaboration at the core of the novel. Paradoxically, Philoctète's narrative is rooted in the central border area and not in the north where the Rio Masacre (a name which was chosen to commemorate the slaughter of a company of French *boucaniers* and border-trespassers in 1728, when the island was still officially a Spanish colony) is to be found.[9] However, the point is that inserting such texts into the curriculum could be beneficial for schools on either side of the border and beyond. Sadly, the Q&A that followed Fumagalli's talk in Comendador revealed that the school children had not had access to literature dealing with the border and, specifically, to works focused on the 1937 massacre and local reactions to this defining event and were not even aware of the existence of Philoctète's work which is set in their hometown.

Another avenue to be further explored is that of better disseminating the existing work on the island of Dominican and Haitian artists. One such example is the Dominican performance artist Karmadavis whose *Estructura completa* has been mentioned above. For over a decade, Karmadavis has been a prize winner during the biannual Centro León art exhibitions in Santiago de los Caballeros in the Dominican Republic, but his work is not as well-known as it should be on the island nor has it been fully explored by interested parties as a means of gaining more traction on human rights issues concerning Dominico-Haitian relations. As Fumagalli has pointed out elsewhere,[10] in 2014, Karmadavis returned to the Dominican borderland where he set his performance *Comedor Familiar*, a performance provocatively informed by the desire to "look for similarities"[11] rather than positing incompatible differences between the two peoples. Here Karmadavis identifies the borderland as a place which can play a decisive role in promoting the development of national identity in relation with and not in opposition to one's neighbours whilst foregrounding the predicament of mixed couples.

For this performance, Karmadavis (who is a trained chef) placed a dining table straddling a small stream on the borderline between Haiti and the Dominican Republic, a visual reminder that the frontier often runs alongside a river—the Massacre in the north, the Pedernales in the South, and the Artibonite in the central portion of the borderland. Then, equipped with a cooking stove, he prepared a delicious lunch for a nearby family with a Dominican father, a Haitian mother, and a Haitian-Dominican child. This meal was a gastronomical fusion of ingredients and dishes typical of both nations. *Comedor familiar*, therefore, represents a "family meal" and the safe space of a "family dining room" where members of a family sit together, share food and renew their bonds of intimacy: the "mixed" family portrayed here reaffirms that such bonds can transcend the limits of national identification and nationalistic discourses. However, the table on which the family ate had only three legs to indicate the extreme precariousness of mixed families who now live not only near the border but throughout the national Dominican territory.

Karmadavis's *Comedor familiar*, however, is an ultimately hopeful work, as the epigraph to the performance explains: "when dialogue is no longer possible, what still exists is the mystery of hope." This hope has been the engine behind *Border of Lights*, Wooding's and OBMICA's work, Fumagalli's research, and is sustained by the belief that the way forward for the realization of the human rights of Haitian migrants and their descendants in the Dominican Republic is the restoration of citizenship to those Dominicans who have been affected by the 2013 ruling. More broadly, the forging of future border relations predicated on solidarity may become a lot easier when the values so valiantly championed and the inspiration afforded by the *Border of Lights* initiative are mainstreamed, creating new synergies across the island and, concomitantly, fresh grounds for hope.

Coda

As we are writing this chapter, the world is in the grip of the Covid-19 pandemic and, in line with Border of Lights, we believe that policy advocacy must support different ways of sustainably including side-lined groups, often ostracized because of their ethnicity, so that that they may fully belong in Dominican society, benefiting from risk management both now and in the future. We sincerely hope that, despite all the terrible challenges that it presents, the pandemic might also provide opportunities to improve border relations and finally address the predicament of segments of the populations in precarious legality like Haitian migrants and denationalized Dominicans of Haitian ancestry since, in order to be effective in the Dominican Republic, it is evident that the Covid-19 response ultimately has to include all those who have been routinely marginalized and neglected.

Notes

1. *Border of Lights.* October 2017. http://www.facebook.com/pg/BorderofLights/posts/. [Accessed 20 May 2020].

2. Final outputs of the project include: A Protocol for para-legals to accompany affected persons. OBMICA. *Facilitando el acceso al registro civil dominicano a descendientes de parejas mixtas: protocolo para el acompañamiento legal.* Santo Domingo, Editora Búho. 2018 http://obmica.org/images/Publicaciones/Libros/Protocolo-2018-FINAL.pdf. [Accessed 6 July 2020]. An accompanying video (in English, Spanish and Haitian Creole) OBMICA. *Libertad.* Santo Domingo, 2018. http://obmica.org/index.php/parejas-mixtas/multimedia/228-libertad-la-historias-de-las-y-los-hijos-de-parejas-mixtas. [Accessed 6 July 2020].

3. All these examples are given more sustained attention in Fumagalli, Maria Cristina. *On the Edge: Writing the Border between Haiti and the Dominican Republic.* Liverpool, Liverpool University Press, 2015 & 2018 and Fumagalli, Maria Cristina. "Foreword". *El Masacre se pasa a pie/ You Can Cross the Massacre on Foot,* by Freddy Prestol Castillo. Translated by Margaret Randall, Duke University Press, 2019, pp. v–xvii.

4. Conference papers were collected in Bosch Carcuro, Matías Eliades Acosta Matos, and Amaury Pérez Vargas, editors. *Masacre de 1937, 80 Años Después: Reconstruyendo la memoria.* Santo Domingo, Ediciones Fundación Bosch, 2018.

5. ONE. *Segunda encuesta nacional de inmigrantes en la República Dominicana, ENI-2017, Informe General.* Santo Domingo: Oficina Nacional de Estadística. 2018. https://dominicanrepublic.unfpa.org/es/publications/informe-general-de-la-segunda-encuesta-nacional-de-inmigrantes-eni-2017. [Accessed 6 July 2020].

6. Exhibition called "Haitian migrant women in the Dominican Republic," reviewed in OBMICA. "Publicaciones de parte de OBMICA" in OBMICA Boletín Informativo Year 1. Number 3. Santo Domingo, Editora Búho. December 2011. http://obmica.org/images/Publicaciones/Boletines/boletin%20obmica%20dic%202011.pdf. [Accessed 6 July 2020].

7. See Album fundraising launch in *Acento.* "El movimiento haitiano-dominicano Azuei dará a conocer la producción de su primer álbum para el que requiere apoyo económico." 26 mayo 2019, Santo Domingo. https://acento.com.do/musica/el-movimiento-haitiano-dominicano-azuei-dara-a-conocer-la-produccion-de-su-primer-album-para-el-que-requiere-apoyo-economico-8685612.html [Accessed 6 July 2020].

8. OBMICA. "Un octubre para mirar hacia delante." In OBMICA Boletín Informativo Year 7.

Number 4. Santo Domingo, Editora Búho. December 2017. http://obmica.org/images/Publicaciones/ Boletines/Boletin-Obmica-4-2017-correo-1.pdf [Accessed 6 July 2020].

9. This point was brought forward by Fumagalli and Arturo Victoriano-Martínez, during the international Santo Domingo seminar in October 2017 when it was observed that the decision on the title in Spanish had been an arbitrary one on the part of the publishing house, possibly because they may have felt it might increase their sales.

10. Fumagalli, Maria Cristina. "La massacre de 1937: adueñarse de un recuerdo tal y como relumbra en el instante de un peligro." *Masacre de 1937 - 80 años después: Reconstruyendo la memoria,* edited by Matías Bosch Carcuro, Eliades Acosta Matos, Amaury Pérez Vargas, Santo Domingo, Fundación Juan Bosch, 2018, pp. 273-294 and Maria Cristina Fumagalli, "'When dialogue is no longer possible, what still exists is the mystery of hope': Migration and Citizenship in the Dominican Republic in Film, Literature and Performance." *Border Transgression and Reconfiguration of Caribbean Spaces,* edited by Myriam Moïse and Fred Réno,London, Palgrave MacMillan, 2020.

11. Suero, Indhira. "Karmadavis entre Haiti y RD" in *Listín Diario.* 4 January 2015. https://listindiario.com/ventana/2015/01/04/351276/karmadavis-entre-haiti-y-rd-entre-haiti-y-rd [Accessed 6 July 2020].

Quisqueya Sankofa Consciousness

Ana Ozuna

In the United States, Eurocentric master narratives emphasized in textbooks reaffirm notions of otherness and xenophobia, what novelist Chimamanda Adichie denotes as the danger of the "single story" in her 2009 TED Talk. Adichie explains how the "single story" creates stereotypes, robs people of their dignity, and makes the recognition of equal humanity impossible. My childhood was marred by the "single story" of Blackness in the United States because as a child I did not see myself represented in any books used in my primary school's curriculum. I simply did not exist, and the Dominican Republic only constituted a geographic location in the Caribbean region, neither notable history nor prominent individuals worth mentioning. On the other hand, from an early age, my teachers exuberantly portrayed Pilgrims as civilizing agents, lauded the US founding fathers as emblematic figures of the Enlightenment, and celebrated US imperialism. This "single story" relegated indigenous people as tragic victims of American expansionism, African-descended people as bounded property, and nineteenth century Asians as self-sacrificial in their quest for the American dream. This reductionist characterization of American history left me questioning my heritage. Unable to discern the complexities of immigration in relation to race and ethnicity, yet craving a recognizable identity, I conceived of myself as African American although my parents were clearly *dominicanos*.

My parents made every effort to dominicanize me. They had arrived to *la gran manzana* (the Big Apple) in 1972 with aspirations of better employment and educational opportunities, opportunities that had been stifled in the Dominican Republic by the despotic presidency of Joaquín Balaguer. They lived in rented rooms with our relatives until they settled in Washington Heights on Sickles Street. The convention of open-door living among *dominicanos* required graciously receiving guests even if a *vecino* (neighbor) or family member arrived as early as 9AM and stayed for hours. In my childhood home, I heard Spanish interlaced with Dominicanismos; the smell of *sancocho* (stew), *moro* (rice and peas), *pollo guisado* (stewed chicken) and other Spanish Caribbean fare intermingled with the sounds of salsa, merengue, and bachata. All things *antillano* (Antillean) reflected in the bodegas and other local businesses resonated throughout the neighborhood as a testament to the vibrancy of this transnational community. During my early formative years, my parents nestled my sisters and me in this enclave of "Dominican-ness."

In 1979, we moved to the Bronx so that my father, Adrian Ozuna, who had been an engineering student at the Universidad Autónoma de Santo Domingo, could accept a position as a superintendent at a six-story apartment building on Morris Avenue in the Fordham Road area of the Bronx. No longer a melting pot of Irish, Italians, Jews, Central and Eastern Europeans after decades of white flight, by the early 1980s the Bronx was majority Black and Latinx. Throughout my childhood, I remember my mother's disgruntled feelings toward the Bronx. But her dominicanization efforts did not let up. She longed for Quisqueya culture in the Heights, and she made sure we visited as often as possible. By the time I was age 7, the bus trips were replaced by plane rides during the hot summer months to Las Américas airport. We spent several summer vacations with relatives in urban Santo Domingo and often travelled to small rural communities to visit distant relatives. I cherished the misty and humid air; the captivating storytelling that would go on for hours when the power went out; the distinct taste of food cooked with *leña* (wood); outings to a *río* (river) or a day spent in Boca Chica eating fried fish and home cooked *espagueti con pollo* (spaghetti with chicken); buying *pesos'* worth of cheese or salami; and sharing a bag of candy with neighborhood kids or family just because this was the norm and not thinking twice. I cherished this time away from the bellowing trains, melodramatic tenement living, and the ever-present gray, green, and brick red skylines of *Nueva York*.

My grandmother, Doña Tiolinda, was also pivotal in my parents' "Dominicanization" efforts. The matriarch of the family and a staunch Catholic who attended mass every Sunday, she arrived in New York in the 1980s and never left the Dominican enclave on Sickles Street. I remember always asking for her blessing, only eating traditional Dominican fare during our visits, and speaking Spanish in her home since she enforced a "no inglés" (no English) policy with a whack of her *chancletas* (slippers) on any offenders. She resembled the *"ganadora"*[1] vendors of the early colonial period in the Dominican Republic since she created an underground market selling many popular items for her mostly female clientele, including sheets, quilts, and clothes. A fair-skinned Dominican, her picture still reminds me of the illustration of the Spanish woman with long flowing hair on the then-popular Maja soap. She considered herself and those who achieved the "somatic norm" of Hispanic whiteness to be superior and more likely to succeed (Candelario 224). She never forgave my mother for marrying my father, a radiant dark-skinned Dominican, though she tolerated him. Similarly, my sisters and I received lukewarm affection from my grandmother unlike the warmth she expressed to my lighter-skinned cousins. I learned from an early age that physical features signifying whiteness granted privilege and superior status. My coming-of-age ritual revealed my family's adherence to colonial beauty standards that situate afro-textured hair as a bodily signifier that needs to be "fixed" and transformed to be beautiful and manageable. During the process of chemically straightening my hair, I remember feeling a combined sense of dread and relief. Although my hair abnegated any pretense of being naturally straight, refusing to blow in the wind as one would imagine the mane of the sixteenth-century Taina ruler, Anacaona, at least my stretched *greña* (hair strands) signified conformity and access to the *negra bella* characterization of *dominicanos aquí y allá* (both here and back there).

When I left home to attend college in upstate New York, I began to study the geographic, linguistic, cultural identities, and histories pertaining to African descended people. I became interested in the Black Atlantic and ultimately selected the maroon figure in Dominican literature as the subject of my PhD dissertation project. Afro-Dominican New Wave writer Blas Jiménez (1949-2009) captivated me with his exploration of Afro-Dominican identity in his writings. His 1987 poetry book *Exigencias de un Cimarron* challenged Eurocentric Dominican texts that celebrate the colonial enterprise. Jimenez's revisionist work denounced the invisibility of the colonial Blacks using forceful and assertive language:

¿Y de mí Quisqueya?
¿te acuerdas de mí?
recuerda que cuando llegó Ovando
ya yo me multiplicaba
ya había huido
ya me había rebelado
ya era cimarron

Translation: And of me Quisqueya / do you remember me / do you remember that when Ovando arrived / I was already reproducing / I was already taking flight / I had already rebelled / I was already a maroon.

Jiménez's staunch commitment to redeeming the African maroon as a key destabilizing agent of coloniality directly refutes the nineteenth century identity paradigm developed by the Dominican intelligentsia centering indigenous and Spanish roots while disavowing African heritage. I humbly heeded his call to commemorate the maroon and insert Dominicanidad within an African diasporic context. In this project I have undertaken both literary analysis and historiography spanning Hispaniola and Jamaica. Sankofa constitutes my organizing philosophical framework.

Christel N. Temple's 2010 article, "The Emergence of Sankofa Practice in the United States: A Modern History" resourcefully encapsulates the expansive expressions of what she calls this "Akan philosophical tradition." Temple denotes Sankofa's essentiality in retrieving and reconstituting African values and knowledge systems as a "Diasporan phenomenon" yet clearly centers its Ghanaian origin (127). Beyond the interpretations and critiques of Sankofa within scholarly circles, Temple hails Sankofa "as a phenomenon within Black popular culture," pointing out its ubiquity in the names of educational and cultural institutions, businesses, and products. She traces some of this attention to the excavation of the African Burial Ground in New York City and its designation as a National Historic Landmark in 1993. In the same year Haile Gerima's film *Sankofa*, which highlighted the emancipatory power of Africanist knowledge systems in fortifying enslaved communities also contributed to the increase visibility of Sankofa principles.

Within Black Studies, scholar Maulana Karenga among others (Opoku, Kwaku Ofori-Ansa, Niangoran-Bouah) conceptualize Sankofa as an Afrocentric practice of reconstituting the past by retrieving essential African wisdom to generate optimal conditions for the present and the future. Afrocentric scholar Weldon Williams offers an extended efficacy of Sankofa by affirming its utility as a method of writing history vital to liberate African descended people from "Eurocentric temporal captivity" (12). Williams explicates that the Sankofa bird concomitantly suggests the stillness and acceleration of time since it can stand still or suddenly take flight and lose track of time as when time "flies" (13). Williams's analysis of the reciprocate Adinkra communicator as a pair of logarithmic spirals which "geometrically contain infinity in finite space" reveals its expansive dimensions. As Williams wrote: "The double spiral Sankofa symbol constructs the future and past as curvilinear paths of time which mirror each other" (16). Correspondingly, Williams's treatment of Sankofa prompts the researcher to dispel the Hegelian negation of Africa as ahistorical by tapping into a time vortex of the epic memory pertaining to African antiquity and the future all at once.

My Sankofa journey led me to examine the valiant indigenous leaders who contested colonization as early as 1493 with the destruction of La Navidad fortress and how African *ladinos* joined Taino rebels in the fight against Spanish colonization and enslavement in 1503. I also learned about the centrality of the Haitian Revolution in the spreading of radical Black activism and anti-colonial movements throughout the Americas. This thirteen-year anti-colonial struggle led by formerly enslaved soldiers cumulated with the creation of the first Black Republic in the world in 1804, shifting the power dynamics of the imperial enterprise based on enslavement. I finally began to see myself in history; I saw myself in the *bozal* maroon leader, Sebastian Lemba, and the nameless enterprising Black *ganadoras* who, according to the sixteenth-century writer, Álvaro de Castro, had more freedom than Spanish residents since they "travel[led] all over the island stealing, transporting, and secreting their merchandises . . . richly dressed and decorated with gold" (Price 38–39). I saw myself in Makandal, Toussaint Louverture, in the nameless women who poisoned their masters, and in twentieth century Afro-Dominican agrarian activist Mama Tingó.

Michelle Obama describes a quest for visibility much like my own in her autobiography, *Becoming* (2018). Readers encounter an African American girl in a working-class family who lived modestly on the second floor of her aunt's house in Chicago, excelled as a student in her formative years, travelled beyond her neighborhood to attend a specialized high school, and decided to apply to Princeton University although her school counselor bluntly demonstrated her disapproval. Throughout the book, Obama offers testament to the challenges she encountered as a young professional, a working mother, and eventually as the First Lady. She notes how time and time again she overcame "invisibility," a line of resistance she attributes to her enslaved ancestors (405).

As Obama, tapping into legacy of resistance has proved vital in my identity affirmation journey. Hence, Sankofa consciousness has ultimately shifted my thinking away from non-constructive formulations of Dominican Black denial to instead consider affirming narratives of Africanidad as presented in the works of Kimberly Simmons, Edward Paulino, Silvio Torres-Saillant, Ginetta Candelario, Dawn F. Stinchcomb, Milagros Ricourt, Anne Eller, and Lorgia García-Peña among others. Their work formulates a trajectory of Africanist affirmations silenced by resounding white supremist frameworks nestled in anti-Blackness and anti-Haitianismo. In this regard, Sankofa consciousness has also heightened my adherence to decolonizing nomenclature. I now understand the profound negative implications of utterances such as negra bella (beautiful Black woman): on the surface it is a compliment, but it connotes "Black and beautiful" as an atypical pairing. Likewise, I understand that maldito negro/haitiano (damned Black person/Haitian) aligns the speaker to white supremist ideals, and thus both enact systemic racism and violence against the Black body.

After two years of settling into my first tenure-track position, I sought out opportunities to return to the Dominican Republic and contribute in a professional capacity during my summer breaks. In 2011, I settled on volunteering for the DREAM Project in Cabarete, located in the Puerto Plata Province in northern Dominican Republic. I spent six weeks working with a cohort of Dominicans, Dominicans of Haitian ancestry, Haitians, and diaspora educators dedicated to creating enriching learning experiences for at-risk students of Dominican and Haitian heritage (ages 8–15) in La Cienaga and Cabarete communities during the four-week Guzmán Ariza Summer program. I designed student-centered thematic units to promote an understanding of the shared history and intersecting cultural practices shared by Dominicans and Haitians. I remember the difficult conversations and awkward moments in the classroom when Dominican and Haitian children spewed hateful remarks based on deeply rooted racist ideas of Black inferiority. I vividly remember assigning students to work on Venn diagrams to represent Dominican and Haitian history and culture as a culminating activity. Students realized the multiple overlapping characteristics shared by the two island nations. They could see themselves and each other as one people hopefully beyond this fifty-minute lesson.

During my second summer with DREAM, Catherine DeLaura, its executive director, introduced me to Cynthia Carrión, human rights advocate, organizer, and member of Border of Lights (BOL), a nonprofit organization that supports border communities in the western region of the Dominican Republic. From Carrión, I learned about the organization's vision to foster unanimity between Dominicans, Haitian-Dominicans, and their diaspora counterparts through collaborative service projects. I greatly admired their commitment to grassroots organizing and anti-racist advocacy in the Dominican Republic and its diaspora communities.

In late 2012, I began participating in Wiggio conference calls with BOL executive members. These phone calls acquainted me with BOL's service projects, meetings, and teach-ins with local activists, artists, entrepreneurs, educators, and scholars in Dajabón, Santiago, and Ouanaminthe, Haiti. I envisioned the collaboration of DREAM Project volunteers and contacted Catherine DeLaura to get her on board. Concomitantly, I signed on to participate in the seventy-sixth-year commemoration of the Haitian Massacre coordinated by BOL. As I think back to this year, I am not sure what kept me grounded as my life changed drastically. In July 2013, I accepted a tenure-track position at CUNY and moved from Florida to New York the following month. This was the first time I lived in New York City since I left for college at the age of seventeen. I looked forward to cosmopolitan living and reconnecting with my family, but after only a couple of months I was glad to be on a plane to Quisqueya. Within hours of arriving to the hostel in Santiago, on October 3, I began to meet the BOLers whose vibrancy and individual talents resonated over the phone lines for months. As the time for commemoration events approached, they were like Marvel comic characters whose unique powers finally fully manifested at the time of action. They received me amiably and warmly: scholar-activist Edward Paulino; then–graduate student Megan Myers; Haitian medical doctor Lesly Manigat; Miami-based consultant Sady Díaz; African educators Rana Dotson and DeAndra Beard; educational consultant Kimberly Moore; and, prolific writer Julia Alvarez and her husband, Bill Eichner.

After an evening of buoyant exchanges, early morning on the following day, we travelled to Dajabón to commence day one of our commemoration activities. It was Friday, October 4, and the city buzzed as local residents prepared to celebrate their *fiesta patronal* for Our Lady of the Rosary, originally a day of rosary prayer initiated by Pope St. Pius V in 1571 to implore the defeat of Ottoman forces in eastern Cyprus. As a border town, it is an uncanny place, a place in unfixed cultural flux as Dominicans, Dominicans of Haitian ancestry, and Haitians conjoined in public and private spaces with a legacy spanning three hundred years. After settling in at a hostel, Megan and I traversed the streets until we found a *papelería* to buy necessary office materials for our upcoming activities. DREAM Project volunteers arrived later in the afternoon and participated in teach-ins with local activists and business leaders. I was surprised to learn the extent to which local employers depended on the labor of Dominicans of Haitian ancestry and Haitians. I also sensed the sincere willingness of these local Dominican leaders to promote solidarity of all residents, whether of Haitian descent or not.

BOL's diasporic and local commitment to peacemaking defied borders and the homogenizing narrative of *anti-haitianismo*. On the first evening of the commemoration, local residents, the diasporic coalition of BOLers, DREAM volunteers, and others affiliated with various NGOs attended a mass led by Father Regino Martínez at the *Nuestra Señora del Rosario* church on Avenida Duarte and 27 de Febrero. These street names implore the remembrance of the Trinitario movement that led to the creation of the Dominican Republic as a separate and independent nation no longer under Haitian rule. They are meant to foment anti-Haitian sentiment, yet in this location we came together to condemn the public lynching that occurred during the first week of October in 1937 when over 15,000 Haitians, Haitian-Dominicans, and dark-skinned Dominicans executed for their pronunciation of the Spanish word "*perejil*" (*parsley*) and thus their failure to physically and verbally uphold *dominicanidad*. After the mass, we marched west and gathered at the river shared by the two nations. Each participant lit a candle and stood in the night to honor the innocent victims who lost their lives in a violent idealization of whiteness and justification of violence against Black bodies. As the candlelights flickered, we revivified the fallen and they appeared in the glow of our faces. Some danced in the shadows to celebrate the continuation of a borderland consciousness that Rafael Leónidas Trujillo Molina had sought to destroy with various measures meant to purge the region of the Dominican-Haitian frontier culture and replace it with *antihaitanismo* (Sagás 58–59; Turits 594).

The following day we waited patiently for hours on the official border crossing point before gaining permission to enter Ouanaminthe in Haiti across the river. This was the first time I crossed a national border without an airplane. I found Ouanaminthe both clearly different in appearance from Dajabón and starkly like it. The day in Ouanaminthe started with an interactive art exhibition which entailed postcard making by local residents and the exhibition of other artwork by local, diaspora, and international artists. Blocks away, Haitian school children participated in an autobiography book-making activity and Megan and I joined DREAM volunteers in leading *Deportes para la vida*, game-based activities aimed at teaching HIV/AIDS prevention and leadership skills at an orphanage. Throughout the day, the Dajabón delegation savored local Haitian fare and engaged in leisurely conversations with local residents, leaders, activists, and educators.

In the late afternoon, we crossed back to Dajabón. There BOL members and I bid farewell to our hosts and DREAM project volunteers, thanking them. We returned to Santiago to prepare for the Global Virtual Vigil. By 8PM, BOLers had set up computers to connect with worldwide members, many of whom hosted events at their schools, universities, or local communities, and now participated in a virtual candlelit vigil connected synchronously in cyberspace through the Facebook platform. I marveled at the continuous flow of images of individuals bearing witness from all racial, ethnic, religious, and national backgrounds—in this act standing boldly against state-sponsored violence, xenophobia, and racism. This social media tool allowed us to tap into the hearts, minds, homes, and communities of like-minded people to collectively attest to our joint commitment to contest hatred.

On Sunday, October 6, 2013, we attended a powerful leadership summit to debrief and, soon after, departed evermore committed to continuing this work in our respective institutions. Exhausted, but grateful, I began to connect Border of Lights with the legacy of joint Afro-Latinx and Latinx activism and radical scholarship of the late nineteenth century and early twentieth century. Anti-colonial revolutionaries such as Dr. Ramón Emeterio Betances, Lola Rodríguez de Tió, Máximo Gómez, José Martí, and Arturo Alfonso Schomburg all developed a transnational sensibility dedicated to coalition building with their regional Antillean neighbors and those living in exile communities throughout Latin America, the United States, and Europe. Schomburg participated in anticolonial freedom struggles for Puerto Rico and Cuba while challenging systemic racism and white supremacy by promoting the intellectual heritage of African-descended people worldwide. Edward Paulino, a cofounder of Border of Lights, follows in this diasporic activist scholar tradition refuting the incessant notion of a cock fight between Haitians and Dominicans, and instead underscoring centuries-long economic and cultural interactions "from weekly food markets to marriages" on the Haitian-Dominican borderland and beyond, in spite of racist state-issued policies throughout the twentieth century delineated in his book *Dividing Hispaniola: The Dominican Republic's Border Campaign against Haiti, 1930–1961* (10). Border of Lights is a testament to the continuity of Haitian-Dominican solidarity with the active participation of its diaspora communities.

Since the inception of Border of Lights, other diaspora scholar-activists such as Julia Alvarez, Michele Wucker, Edwidge Danticat, and Junot Díaz have used their voices to contest discriminatory actions against dark-skinned members of Dominican society in conjunction with BOL and other social justice-centered NGOs on the island and its diaspora. Hence, since the 2013 Constitutional Court ruling (TC/0168/13 or *la sentencia*), diaspora-based scholar-activists and local Dominicans have denounced acts of violence and intimidation, the seizure of residency documents, and illegal deportations of dark-complexioned Dominicans of Haitian ancestry and Haitians. Julia Alvarez asserts Quisqueya Sankofa consciousness by calling for Dominicans to play an active role in denouncing the injustices against Haitians: "We, Quisqueyanos *valientes*, need to acknowledge the shameful treatment of our Haitian brothers and sisters in the past and in the present in order to co-create a brighter future" (Alvarez, "Massacre Testimonio").

Dominican-born activist, natural hair pioneer, and co-founder of MissRizos, Carolina Contreras, opened the MissRizos Salon in La Zona Colonial in 2015, creating the first space in Santo Domingo to address needs of women who dare to wear their hair naturally. Contreras disavows the limited paradigms of race and Eurocentric beauty standards in the Dominican Republic, and instead points out the nation's African roots:

> I find myself in a Black country. When I am riding the train, sitting in a public car, or walking down the streets, almost everyone around me is visibly Black. This is not the case in the US, so self-hate and denial of one's Blackness becomes really particular in a country where almost everyone is of Afro-descent. (Contreras, "Changing Beauty Standards in the Dominican Republic")

Contreras's introspection on Dominican Blackness reflects my musing on the Dominican Republic as a nation constituting the African Diaspora. Having long ago rebuked the "single story" of Blackness, I now embrace an Afro-latinx subjectivity linked to the history and intellectual heritage of the Black Atlantic, and communities of African-descended people globally. Accordingly, Sankofa Quisqueya consciousness generously continues to affirm my identity and inform my resolve to contest intersectional oppression and therefore support the work of the Border of Lights collective.

Note

1. This term refers to sixteenth-century Black women vendors who participated in illicit business.

Works Cited

Adichie, Chimamanda. "The Danger of a Single Story." TED: Ideas Worth Spreading, July 2009, https://www.ted.com/talks/chimamanda_ngozi_adichie_the_danger_of_a_single_story

Alvarez, Julia. "Border of Lights, Haiti and Dominican Republic." *Border of Lights, Haiti and Dominican Republic*. Accessed 31 Jan. 2015.

Candelario, Ginetta E. B. *Black behind the Ears: Dominican Racial Identity from Museums to Beauty Shops*, Duke University Press, 2007.

Dawson, Imani. "Changing Beauty Standards in the Dominican Republic." *Tribe Called Curl*. 05 Nov. 2014. Accessed 31 Jan. 2015.

Eller, Anne. *We Dream Together: Dominican Independence, Haiti, and the Fight for Caribbean Freedom*. Duke University Press, 2016.

García-Peña, Lorgia. *The Borders of Dominicanidad: Race, Nation, and Archives of Contradiction*. Duke University Press, 2016.

Jiménez Blas R. *Exigencias De Un* cimarrón *(En* sueños*): Versos Del Negro Blas III.* Taller, 1987.

Karenga, Maulana. Introduction to Black Studies. University of Sankore Press, 2010.

Obama, Michelle. *Becoming.* Crown, an Imprint of the Crown Group, 2018.

Ozuna, Ana. "Rebellion and Anti-colonial Struggle in Hispaniola: From Indigenous Agitators to African Rebels" Africology: The Journal of Pan African Studies. vol. 11, no. 7, (May 2018): 77–95. http://www.jpanafrican.org/docs/vol11no7/11.7-5-Ozuna.pdf

Ozuna, Ana. "Feminine Power: Women Contesting Plantocracy in The Book of Night Women," Africology: The Journal of Pan African Studies, 10.3 (May 2017): 132–148. Web: http://www.jpanafrican.org/docs/vol10no3/10.3-10-Ozuna.pdf

Paulino, Edward. *Dividing Hispaniola: The Dominican Republic's Border Campaign Against Haiti, 1930-1961.* University of Pittsburgh Press, 2016.

Ricourt, Milagros. *The Dominican Racial Imaginary: Surveying the Landscape of Race and Nation in Hispaniola.* Rutgers University Press, 2016.

Sagás, Ernesto. *Race and Politics in the Dominican Republic.* Gainesville: University of Florida Press, 2000.

Simmons, Kimberly Eison. *Reconstructing Racial Identity and the African past in the Dominican Republic.* University of Florida Press, 2009.

Temple, Christel N. "The Emergence of Sankofa Practice in the United States." *Journal of Black Studies* 41.1 (2009): 127–50. Print.

Torres-Saillant, Silvio. "The Tribulations of Blackness: Stages in Dominican Racial Identity." *Callaloo*, vol. 23, no. 3, 2000, pp. 1086–111. Accessed 31 Jan. 2015.

Turits, Richard Lee. "A World Destroyed, A Nation Imposed: The 1937 Haitian Massacre in the Dominican Republic." *Hispanic American Historical Review*, vol. 82, no. 3, 2002, pp. 589–636.

Williams, Weldon C. "African Origin of the New Age: An Astrochronology of the Black Experience." Diss. Temple U, 2002. Print.

Wucker, Michele. *Why the Cocks Fight: Dominicans, Haitians, and the Struggle for Hispaniola.* Hill and Wang, 1999.

Committed to Solidarity

The DREAM Project

Catherine DeLaura

In 2012, DREAM was contacted by Cynthia Carrión, one of the founding members of Border of Lights, to participate in the inaugural Border of Lights event commemorating, bearing witness to, and raising consciousness about the seventy-fifth anniversary of the 1937 Haitian Massacre in the Dominican Republic. The movement was initiated primarily by a committee of Dominicans and Haitians living in the diaspora. As an organization, The DREAM Project is rooted on the island of Quisqueya but also maintains strong ties to diasporic communities in the United States. The Border of Lights initiative was thus an appealing educational and cultural activity for the organization's local and international volunteers to participate in and gain a greater understanding of historical and contemporary events that shape relationships between Dominicans, Haitians, and Dominicans of Haitian descent.

The DREAM Project is an educational nonprofit organization that works along the North Coast of the Dominican Republic. Communities that partner with DREAM's schools, libraries, teacher-training initiatives, and other educational programs are a reflection of the deep historical ties of the island, with Dominicans, Haitians, and Dominicans of Haitian descent living and working alongside one another in sometimes harmonious and sometimes fraught relations. DREAM's staff also reflects the social makeup of these communities, with teachers, youth leaders, and employees representing Dominican and Haitian identities alike. Additionally, DREAM's international presence has attracted long-term volunteers and full-time staff members from the US, including many of Dominican descent, connecting the island and the diaspora. From the start, there was significant interest among staff and volunteers to participate in the Border of Lights event. As one staff member pointed out, "*vivimos en el país pero no sabemos mucho de la frontera*" (*We live in the country, but we don't know much about the border*).[1] Border of Lights was initially an opportunity for all of us to (re)learn about *la frontera*, a site often mentioned and framed as a point of division and separation. Border of Lights attempts to flip this narrative by positioning *la frontera* as a possible point of healing and solidarity or, as one staff member suggested, "*una frontera de paz*" (*a border of peace*).

Physically standing at the border, participating in border-crossings, carrying out community service in solidarity with communities on both sides of the border, and exploring the bi-national market are experiences of cross-national connection that have encouraged more staff members to attend the event each year. The educational events, candlelit march, and vigil on both the Dominican and Haitian sides of the border, a Catholic mass, and community service events have been highlights of DREAM's annual participation in Border of Lights. DREAM staff have been able to contribute their talents as educators, youth program facilitators, and community service leaders to a broad range of solidarity initiatives, including cleaning the Dajabón River on the side of Ouanaminthe, Haiti, working with children and youth in an orphanage in Haiti, organizing youth from both sides of the border to participate in sports activities, and, more recently, in the shelter for street boys founded by Padre Mario Serrano. As DREAM staff members make annual visits from Puerto Plata to Dajabón/Ouanaminthe, there has been an increasing sense of connection to the physical location along both sides of *la frontera*.

This annual trip over time has also provided a window into the economic development of both communities—with the weekly bi-national market a key symbol of this exchange relationship that also makes socioeconomic inequities visible. Though Dajabón has always had the sheen of an economically stable border town, Ouanaminthe has followed a more difficult path shaped by local, bi-national, and global policies. The first time we entered Ouanaminthe in 2012, we saw little kiosks dotting the road to which hundreds of cell phones were connected. These stations served as reliable sources of electricity, with people paying small amounts to charge their phones with vendors whose stations had batteries or generators. The vast number of phones connected to the power source signified a widespread lack of access to electricity. However, these kiosks have largely disappeared as electricity access has improved in Ouanaminthe. While in the Dominican Republic, electricity was only provided for half days at a time on alternating schedules across many communities, there were no charging kiosks as most people had at least partial access to electricity (with the exception of some rural areas). Now communities across the Dominican Republic are also being provided with more reliable electricity coverage. While both countries have seen increased access to power, visible inequities remain. Thus, the trip also provided staff members an opportunity to contextually understand economic and infrastructural development in both countries in a new light. As one staff member noted before participating in the event: *"tenía otra imagen de Haití"* (I had a different picture of Haiti). After attending Border of Lights, the same DREAM staff member shared: *"Hay más cosas que nos pueden unir que las que nos pueden separar"* (There are more things that can unite us than those that can separate us). She added: *"Creo que esta actividad nos une mucho y cambia muchas mentes después de participar"* (I think that this activity unites us and changes a lot of minds after participating).

Border of Lights also moves beyond a revisionist history of the Dominican Republic that pits the two nations and its people against one another. Attending the event, we learn not only about the history of the 1937 Haitian Massacre, but also about how this period is re-framed and silenced in contemporary times to serve agendas of division and separation. Regarding the (mis)education around this history, one staff member commented: *"Hay cosas que muchas personas todavía no entienden, tanto la parte haitiana como la parte domini-*

cana . . . este evento enseñó a muchas personas que eso fue una masacre genocidio, o sea, no fue una guerra" (there are things that many people still don't understand, among both Haitians and Dominicans alike . . . this event taught many people that this was a genocidal massacre, in other words, it wasn't a war). Many staff members agreed that this aspect of history is widely misunderstood and even taught erroneously in schools. One teacher stated: *"la historia está allí pero no se enseña"* (the history is there, but it's not taught). Another teacher added that *"nunca enseñan el 100% de la historia"* (they never teach 100% of the story). In fact, one teacher shared how this misinformation is brought up regularly in her classroom in the Dominican Republic, with students using (inaccurate) interpretations of history (i.e., invasion) and past tragedies to justify mistreatment against students of Haitian descent.

This unlearning and relearning of history was a primary motivation for attending the event for many of our educators. We want our educators to bear witness to what happened in October 1937, to unlearn myths about Haitian invasion, and to start to understand the massacre through the lens of systematic ethnic cleansing under a brutal dictatorship. As an educational organization, we value critical thinking and encourage all teachers and students alike to understand that questioning what we are told can help shape us into more informed citizens that take action to fight injustice. We need to understand who controls the flow of information and who has the power to weave narratives that frame history from a particular perspective in order to achieve divisive ends. Our engagement in Border of Lights has helped open up this discussion among our staff and has broadened teachers' knowledge so that they can introduce and address the topic and its modern-day manifestations (e.g., racism and discrimination) into their classrooms and communities.

But we also know that realizing the goals of this event requires more than physical presence at the border once per year. Dominicans, Haitians, and Haitians of Dominican descent live and work side by side on a daily basis, and often divisive imaginaries of *la frontera* are carried with them. DREAM has had to grapple with this tension for its seventeen years of existence. Miseducation about history has a strong influence on the way that students and their families interact with one another inside and outside of the classroom. For example, one summer we hired a local Haitian woman to cook meals for our summer camp program. The local Dominican teachers refused to eat her food. While they openly shared that they didn't like the flavors and seasonings she used to cook, we knew the issue was rooted in anti-Haitian sentiment. When the local government seeks to round up Haitians (but not Europeans or United States citizens) without Dominican documents in the North Coast communities where we work, we have heard whispers of agreement behind closed doors among some Dominican neighbors. These are the day-to-day issues that we, as a staff, must face head-on, and engaging with history is one place to start. Before we were invited to the Border of Lights event in 2012, our summer camp had focused on Dominican-Haitian relations. And, as one of our staff members shared, *"No solo deberíamos enfocarnos en una sola frontera. Todos los paises tienen fronteras. ¿Cómo podemos vivir en respeto y harmonía? Es un tema de derechos humanos"* (We shouldn't just focus on one border. All countries have borders. How can we live in respect and harmony? It's a human rights issue).

As an organization, we recognize that the work to address these issues in our classrooms and communities never ends. We need headline events like the Border of Lights, and we also need small scale conversations between neighbors, colleagues, and classmates.

We need new narratives in the dominant media, but we also need revised school curriculum as well as innovative and engaging classroom activities that do not shy away from engaging these topics from a historical and contemporary perspective. We also know that while showing up and attending the Border of Lights is a step towards transformation, what we really need is for our educators to take what they learned into their classrooms, into their homes, into the places they frequent, and above all, into their way of thinking. We are asking ourselves how we can provide the resources and pedagogical training necessary for our teachers to initiate and continue critical conversations with their students. For example, we are considering a book competition where students can share narratives of *solidarity, collaboration*, and *empathy*—all keywords that our staff used to describe lessons learned from the Border of Lights event. All of our teachers learned about the Border of Lights directly through their connection with DREAM, and as an organization, we have an opportunity to share new narratives with the hundreds of students that participate in our programs in the Dominican Republic on an annual basis.

But how do we ensure that students and families, who do not affiliate with these types of institutions and community organizations, can also receive critical information about Dominican-Haitian relations? We need a new *revolución educativa* in the public schools. A recently published book by Richard T. Middleton and Sheridan Wigginton, *Unmastering the Script: Education, Critical Race Theory, and the Struggle to Reconcile the Haitian Other in Dominican Identity*, examines how social science textbooks and historical biographies in the country have increasingly shifted to embrace and articulate blackness as a foundational element of Dominican identity. Despite this shift, there still remains widespread public and governmental pushback against reframing dominant narratives that contribute to anti-Haitian sentiment. This pushback becomes particularly prevalent given that nationalism is on the rise both locally in the Dominican Republic as well as globally. Yet we also know that there are many examples of solidarity, friendship, and activism that re-frame common beliefs about Haitian-Dominican relations. These moments are present in our staff meetings and youth programs, in interactions between community members, and in social justice movements initiated in the Dominican Republic as well as those with roots in diasporic communities. We start this work inspired by these small moments and large movements, and we are determined to allow solidarity to speak louder than divisive tactics. As one of our staff members reminded us: *"La palabra solidaridad tiene peso sin tener frontera"* (*The word "solidarity" carries weight without having a border*), and we at DREAM are committed to living out this solidarity in all we do.

Notes

1. These comments are from anonymous DREAM staff members and teachers who have attended Border of Lights between 2012 and 2019. A special thanks to Molly Hamm-Rodríguez and Narcisa Núñez for support in writing the article. DREAM staff and community members, who have attended Border of Lights between 2012 and 2019, participated in surveys and focus groups about its impact on DREAM and the communities we work in. The DREAM Project has been involved in Border of Lights every year since 2012 and has sent groups as large as forty individuals.

Borders as Bellwethers

Border of Lights, Transnational Hispaniola, and American Futures

Kiran C. Jayaram and April J. Mayes

> "Before I built a wall I'd ask to know
> What I was walling in or walling out,
> And to whom I was like to give offense."
>
> —ROBERT FROST, "MENDING WALL" (1914)

INTRODUCTION

In the 1990s, as increased migration from Africa and Latin America to Spain and Italy generated hostile, anti-immigrant reactions in those two countries and then across the European Union, advocates and scholars alike began to comment on "Fortress Europe," wondering if the promises of the common market and a common currency would fall under the weight of dissension over how to deal with immigration from the "Third World" to the "First World." The specter of "Fortress Europe" appeared again more recently as the world has borne witness to the tragedy of African and Middle Eastern refugees drowning in the Mediterranean Sea as they exercise their human right to flee conflict and seek sanctuary elsewhere. In the Americas, President Donald Trump incited his supporters with his anti-immigrant rhetoric and policies. In 2019 alone, President Trump leveraged the United States' economic power to bully the presidents of Mexico, El Salvador, and Guatemala into shifting his draconian immigration policy further south, from the US-Mexico border through Central America. Thousands of asylum seekers from all over the world now languish in US-Mexico border towns, in Chiapas, Mexico, and in detention centers from Tapachula to Denver, Colorado awaiting their turn in the proverbial "line." As a result, hundreds of families have been separated and dozens have died in US custody.

The need to counter these macabre bordering regimes with humane laws and policies stands before us and is, we would argue, the defining task of our present moment. In this effort, Hispaniola is quite instructive; emboldened by recent publications (Victoriano-Martínez; Eller; García-Peña; Nessler; Mayes and Jayaram; Ramírez), we can confidently assert that Hispaniola has a great deal to offer global discussions about border regimes and bordering processes, albeit not because the Haitian-Dominican border is a model of state-led cooperation and not only because the island (or more accurately, the set of islands) stands apart from most others in the world in that it hosts more than one national government.[1] We argue that the intellectual, artistic, and advocacy work of scholars and activists in Border of Lights (BOL) and the Transnational Hispaniola Collective (THC) provides a powerful counter-narrative to contemporary discourses regarding borders and border crossings.

Our own ability to draw this and other lessons from Hispaniola took shape within the intellectual social formation that is the Transnational Hispaniola Collective and by using the transnational Hispaniola framework in our scholarship. Always attentive to the historical conditions of our creation (cf. Yelvington), this chapter describes the work of THC, its relationship to the BOL project, and the moments that proved productive for imagining different forms of belonging within an interstate system from an island-wide perspective. The conclusion offers some reflections for how to continue the work in our current moment in which borders have become increasingly militarized and securitized through the Americas and around the world.

THC AND ITS ACTIVITIES

From its beginning, THC has been a collaborative effort of scholars, practitioners, activists, and artists from the island and beyond, dedicated to transforming "the dominant paradigms in Dominican and Haitian knowledge production" (Mayes et al. 26).[2] We began by promoting histories and experiences that countered the *fatal-conflict model*, the idea that Haitians and Dominicans have been destined to be antagonistic toward each other because they each share a goal of island-wide domination (Martínez). In our early work on cross-border collaborations and moments of solidarity, we spoke directly to and against the *fatal-conflict model* as a framing device that obscured more than it revealed and as a discourse that hampered social movements against racism and xenophobia. However, in organizing the major publication (2018), THC broke free of the chains of this now defunct debate. We moved away from countering that form of *negative peace* toward production of a *critical peace education*, one based upon challenging militarization, xenophobia, and the structural inequality that comes with capitalism while promoting decolonization efforts (Williams and Hantzopolous). This new conceptualization-oriented THC activities around the idea of self-determination, a counter-plantation perspective, that of "the people who, from the period of slavery until the present day, have sought out spaces of freedom and autonomy for themselves in the midst of, and in many ways against, the dominant economic and political orders in which they lived" (Dubois and Turits 2–3). Put simply, we are now interested in using the transnational Hispaniola framework to show how Hispaniola's borders and bordering processes speak to the present moment.

The Transnational Hispaniola Collective conference in Santo Domingo (THC I) started as a project of April Mayes and Yolanda Martín in conversation with Pablo Mella and Sylvio Torres-Saillant. THC I followed a traditional conference format, with plenary sessions and concurrent panels, mostly from history and the social sciences. Presentations were in the speakers' primary language, save for Jayaram's presentation in Haitian Creole (with PowerPoint in Spanish), which caused some public discussion during the event. This conference formed the foundation for subsequent THC activities.

The second event, held at Rutgers University (New Jersey, USA) included primarily arts, humanities, and social science presentations. These included plenary performances by Josefina Baez, by Gina Ulysse, a joint plenary on literature by Myriam Chancy and Ana Lara, a visual arts plenary, and a plenary musical performance with Sanba Zao, Mireille, and Toné Vicioso. Organizer Carlos Decena actively sought to address the critique that THC did not include enough Haitianists by incorporating two as co-organizers (Yveline Alexis and Kiran Jayaram) and by reaching out to the Rutgers Haitian Students Association. To handle linguistic issues, we had volunteers provide individual translations between Haitian Creole, Spanish, and English at every panel and plenary for attendees. This second conference led to the creation of a coedited volume by Mayes and Jayaram (2018), which includes both scholarly chapters and teaching syllabi.

The third THC event was planned to co-occur with the 2016 Caribbean Studies Association meetings (Port-au-Prince, Haiti). The organizational team included THC veterans (Jayaram and Mayes) with support from Darlene Dubuisson and Jhon Picard Byron. The team facilitated traditional academic presentations at CSA for THC participants, but they realized two other important accomplishments. First, the THC proposal to become an official working group of the Caribbean Studies Association was voted on and approved, thus ensuring a renewable institutional presence for THC. Second, the main THC event, held at the Plaza Hotel, was a series of *teach-ins* for 100 Haitian university students. These eight sessions, where teams of 2–5 presenters taught the audience in two-hour modules, covered anthropology and economics, political ecology, digital humanities, human rights, peasantries, border studies, feminism, activism after the 2013 Dominican Constitutional Tribunal decision, pedagogy, and Dominican anthropology. This last session led to a productive exchange between Haitian students and Dominican presenters about Haitian-Dominican relations. This research-teaching praxis model mirrors a critical peace education perspective.

In another move in the direction of a counter-plantation model, the most recent THC-inspired event was the workshop, "Island Anthropologies: Anthropological Knowledge Production in Haiti and the Dominican Republic" (Santo Domingo, 2019). This event, organized by Jayaram and Luisa Rollins-Castillo, brought together scholars to discuss the past, present, and future of social and cultural anthropology, linguistic anthropology, ethnology, and archaeology on the island. The workshop's three goals were: a) to place in conversation scholars from Haiti, the Dominican Republic, and beyond who work on anthropologies of social inequality, migration, and environment, and cultural heritage, b) to discuss the history of such inquiry and training in Haiti and the Dominican Republic, and c) to discuss how future research and teaching of anthropology (broadly understood) and archaeology within Haiti and the Dominican Republic can use south-north exchanges to contribute to broader engagements. The organizers are working to publish the proceedings in Spanish, Haitian Creole, and English. The workshop mirrored both the counter-plantation and critical peace education models through what we called a "critical ecological perspective" (Mayes and Jayaram 254), a major shift from the early days of THC and BOL.

THC AND BOL

Connections between THC and BOL started during the first stages of both projects. In 2012, the Closing Plenary of THC[2] at Rutgers University focused on those who continued to work in the spirit of Solange "Sonia" Pierre, the stalwart Dominican defender of the rights of Haitian Dominicans and of Haitians, who died prematurely in December 2011. The panel included a performance by Nehanda Loiseau, a partial screening by Eddie Paulino of a documentary about Haitian-Dominican issues, a speech by Ambassador Julissa Reynoso (US Ambassador to Uruguay), and personal reflections by her daughters, Solange and Manuela Dander Pierre, Jenny Moron, Lecedy Luiz, all representing Movimiento de Mujeres Dominico-Haitianas (MUDHA) and Ana María Belique Delva (later, of reconoci.do). Julissa Reynoso, the first Dominican American to be named a US ambassador, addressed the importance of Pierre's work in the Dominican Republic. During the reflections, tears flowed from presenters and audience members, alike. The panel concluded, and with it, the entire conference. At that moment, Eddie Paulino asked to make an announcement. He reminded the audience that 2012 marked the 75th Anniversary of the *kout kouto*, the 1937 massacre around Dajabón.[3] He asked those who may be interested to meet with him to help memorialize the incident through a project called "Border of Lights." The collaborative relationship has also allowed for members of the THC collective to participate in BOL activities. From the beginning, Paulino has given a standing invitation to any THC scholars who would like to participate in the annual BOL event at the border. More specifically, Paulino organized the creation of a plaque in 2017 that would be placed in Dajabón as part of a permanent memorial to the 1937 massacre. Kiran Jayaram agreed to help with the translation of the Haitian Creole version of the plaque. Upon its completion, Paulino wrote, "Know that you, along with a select group of translators, were instrumental in the plaque's Haitian Kreyòl version in Dajabon. Through that plaque you are bearing witness. Thank you" (Personal Communication with Kiran Jayaram, 22 Jan 2018).

BORDERS AND BORDER-CROSSINGS—A HISPANIOLA TAKE

There is no contradiction in our formulating an island-wide perspective that counters methodological nationalism while supporting efforts like BOL that brings our attention back the border. The border *is* significant to the island's history, not in the least because, as a result of European colonialism, monarchical officials, geographers, and cartographers spent centuries trying to define it while free and freed Indigenous and African-descended peoples spent centuries defying it. Its mere existence is a constant reminder of colonialism's legacies and how, at various moments of history, macroeconomic downturns and US intervention have combined with nationalism to foster xenophobia, particularly in the Dominican Republic. Borders, in these times, are like Frost's "good fences," creating and enforcing divisions among people who share blood, kinship, and economic ties. Especially when it comes to Hispaniola, one might be tempted to fall back into a fatal-conflict mode to explain the 1937 Massacre as simply what might be expected from two nations at each other's throats.

As other chapters from this volume treat that topic, we forego a discussion of the details, instead focusing on the historical political economic context. As Richard Lee Turits pointed out, the Dominican economy declined after the 1929 US market crash, which was followed by legislation that showed preference for Dominican labor nationals over the use of immigrants (Martínez 1995). At the same time, Rafael Trujillo took control of the Dominican state apparatus and promoted the idea of Haitians as an enemy that constituted "the key element of a new national identity based upon a new representation of the past" (Derby and Turits 65). Through our framework, moreover, we draw attention to another point: while the 1937 Massacre occurred at the border, the historical, material, and ideological conditions that made possible the violence that was unleashed against Haitians and border-residing Dominicans have their roots in the systematic land loss weathered by Haitian peasants and the growth of a plantation-based sugar economy in the Dominican Republic which occurred while Hispaniola was under US military governance.

The 2013 decision by the Dominican Constitutional Tribunal to question the citizenship of people born after 1929,[4] occurred at the confluence of similar factors to the 1937 Massacre. First, in 2008, the US financial markets suffered the largest drop in value since 1929. This led to stress on economies across the globe, slamming the Dominican economy (Forbes 2009). Second, as Amelia Hintzen astutely observed, this single court decision represented the culmination of decades of policy changes enacted by the right-wing coalition led by the Partido de la Liberación Dominicana (PLD). Subsequent to this legal decision, the Dominican immigration authorities implemented a process of denationalization, disparately impacting people of Haitian descent, under the banner of "registration" and "regularization" of the population. In other words, rather than part of the fatal-conflict model, we understand this event within a wider political economic crisis. Thus, these conditions legitimized antagonistic state policies toward and violence against poor border crossers and their descendants through an appeal to national borders. Moreover, as the scholar-creators of the intellectual effort, "The Otherness Triangle," asserts: "the island neighbors' conflictual relations generally reflect tensions, contradictions and inequalities rooted in global political economic and information orders."

TOWARD A CONCLUSION: GLOBAL HISPANIOLA/LÒT BÒ A

In earlier iterations of our transnational Hispaniola framework, we countered the state's coercive violence by also pointing out the spaces of hope and change have existed throughout history. Even during the 1937 Massacre, some ethnic Dominicans hid those Black and Haitian populations who were being targeted in the genocide (Derby and Turits 2006).

While these responses may elevate and express solidarity with those who lead various struggles for social justice across the island, the majority of Hispaniola's residents persist in precarity. In this context, we need to "give particular attention to . . . new modes of social justice engagement [that] are emerging or might be imagined, [in order to] to promote respectful, horizontal dialogue among Haitians [and] Dominicans" (Carey et. al. Personal Communication with the Authors).[5]

For those who remain on the island, new forms of social and political engagement are happening, but for many others, migration is their response to the island's ongoing political and economic turbulence; the need to *chache lavi* (seek a better life) beyond Hispaniola demonstrates the island's deep ties to global and hemispheric capital flows and development policies. The persistence of migration to the United States, Europe and, more recently, mainland Latin America also demands that scholars think about Hispaniola as a formation that takes place *lòt bò a*—that is, "over there." That Hispaniola refuses to be contained by territorial and aqueous limits compliments the interventions made by Victoriano-Martínez and García-Peña who, in their works of cultural and literary analysis, contend that the border and its subjects exist as an "other world" that counters exclusionary narratives of the nation. In this "other world," according to Victoriano-Martínez, *rayanos* (border residents) mirror both/and border consciousness theorized by Gloria Anzaldúa who wrote about the US-Mexican border. For Victoriano-Martínez, the *Dominicanyork* (Dominican migrant) embodies the *rayano* and the concept itself "opens a space through which to analyze new cultural paradigms that are forged by the existing tensions within binary categories such as: Dominican/Haitian; Dominican/Dominican-American; masculine/feminine; inside/outside" (61). For her part, García-Peña looks to Josefina Báez's allegory, El Nié—"neither here nor there"—as a "symbolic space . . . [that] expands our notions of borders; it displaces the location and polarity of the nation-border, instead proposing the body as the location that contains and reflects national exclusion (borders) across history and generations" (5). That is, people do not move across borders; borders move along with people.

Hispaniola has a global past, present, and future that is rendered on the landscape and through the very lived experience and movements of its people. The historically anchored, human- and ecological-centered scholarship, activism, and creative work from Hispaniola teaches us that borders are many things. They are embodied and they are wounds across landscapes, the scars of which continue to cut into the present, forcing us to "think through containment, regulation, punishment, capture, and captivity" (Sharpe 22). Hispaniola's story reminds us that borders are also sites of kinship and relation, of economic and political entanglements. Hispaniola teaches us that borders are spaces of possibility for people striving toward or claiming emancipation and self-determination (Bragadir; Dubois and Turits). Finally, Hispaniola's story challenges us to see border work as countering silencing (Trouillot), "ghosting" (Ramírez), and xenophobic nationalisms (Garcia-Peña). Following Christina Sharpe's provocative invitation, we may think of this counter-narrative as a form of "wake work," as a movement toward "inhabiting a blackened consciousness that would rupture the structural silences produced and facilitated by, and that produce and facilitate, Black social and physical death" (22). The "wake work" required in this context means seeing the relationship between the facilitation of "Black social and physical death" across the island, through violence and repatriation, with the continuous and not-so-voluntary removal of Hispaniola's people into migrant streams. Moreover, to think through Hispaniola's future means acknowledging its present coloniality as a legacy of the plantation complex. We must ask, why the first black republics facilitate "Black social and physical death"; why, even after "freedom," does violence accompany state formation and why does that violence turn against Haitians and darker-skinned Dominicans? A movement for reconciliation and reparations may be one mechanism that helps us answer these questions.

Notes

1. Other examples include New Guinea, Ireland, and St. Martin.

2. To date, THC has held four events (2010, Santo Domingo, Dominican Republic; 2012, Rutgers University, USA; 2016, Port-au-Prince, Haiti; 2019, Santo Domingo, Dominican Republic), produced a special edition of *Estudios Sociales* (2009), a scholarly article (2013), and an edited volume (2018).

3. This is called *kout kouto* in Haitian Creole or *El Corte* in Spanish.

4. This decision is commonly referred to as "La Sentencia."

5. A group of scholars who submitted two panels at THC's second meeting at Rutgers University in 2012, named their effort, the "Otherness Triangle," and continued to develop their idea at the annual congress of the Latin American Studies Association in 2014. These scholar-creators include, Henry "Chip" Carey, Karen Richman, Samuel Martínez, Pierre Minn, Marion Werner, Bridget Wooding, Jean-Marie Théodat, Lauren Derby, and Edward Paulino. The quotes here are taken from the panel abstraction, "An Otherness Triangle: Haiti, Dominican Republic, the World."

Works Cited

Bajaj, Monisha and Maria Hantzopolous. *Peace Education: International Perspectives*. Bloomsbury Academic, 2016.

Bragadir, Nathalie. "Shifting Territories: The Production of Space on Eighteenth-Century Hispaniola." *Transnational Hispaniola: New Directions in Haitian and Dominican Studies*, edited by April J. Mayes and Kiran C. Jayaram. University of Florida Press, 2018, pp. 23–43.

Centro Bonó. "Hispaniola Transnacional: por un pasado y futuro común." *Estudios Sociales* vol. 40, no. 151, 2009 [2013], pp. 7–11.

Derby, Robin L.H. and Richard Turits. "Historias de terror y los terrores de la historia: la masacre haitiana de 1937 en la República Dominicana." *Estudios Sociales*, vol. 92, 1993, pp. 65–76.

---. "Temwayaj Kout Kouto, 1937: Eyewitnesses to the Genocide." *Revolutionary Freedoms*, edited by Cécile Accilien, Jessica Adams, and Elmide Méléance. Caribbean Studies   Press, 2006, pp. 137–43.

Dubois, Laurent and Richard Lee Turits. *Freedom Roots: Histories from the Caribbean*. University of North Carolina Press, 2019.

Eller, Anne. *We Dream Together. Dominican Independence, Haiti, and the Fight for Caribbean Freedom*. Duke University Press, 2016.

Forbes. 2009. "#76, Dominican Republic." https://www.forbes.com/lists/2009/6/bizcountries09-best-countries-for-business_Dominican-Republic_CHI094.html

Garcia Peña, Lorgia. *The Borders of Dominicanidad. Race, Nation, and the Archives of Contradiction*. Duke University Press, 2016.

Hintzen, Amelia. "Historical Forgetting and the Dominican Constitutional Tribunal." *Journal of Haitian Studies*, vol. 20, no. 1, 2014, pp. 108–16.

Martínez, Samuel. *Peripheral Migrants: Haitians and Dominican Republic Sugar Plantations.* University of Tennessee Press, 1995.

---. "Not a Cockfight: Rethinking Haitian-Dominican Relations." *Latin American Perspectives,* vol. 30, no. 3, 2003, pp. 80–101.

Mayes, April, Yolanda C. Martín, Carlos Ulises Decena, Kiran Jayaram, and Yveline Alexis. "Transnational Hispaniola: Toward New Paradigms in Haitian and Dominican Studies." *Radical History Review,* vol. 115, 2013, pp. 26–32.

Mayes, April J. and Kiran C. Jayaram. *New Directions in Haitian and Dominican Studies.* University of Florida Press, 2018.

Nessler, Graham. *An Islandwide Struggle for Freedom. Revolution, Emancipation and Reenslavement in Hispaniola, 1789–1809.* University of Chapel Hill Press, 2016.

Ramírez, Dixa. *Colonial Phantoms: Belonging and Refusal in the Dominican Americas, from the 19th Century to the Present.* New York University Press, 2018.

Sharpe, Christina. *In the Wake. On Blackness and Being.* Duke University Press, 2016.

Turits, Richard. *Foundations of Despotism: Peasants, the Trujillo Regime, and Modernity in Dominican History.* Stanford University Press, 2003.

Williams, Hakim and Maria Hantzopolous. "Peace Education as a Field." *Encyclopedia of Educational Philosophy and Theory.* E-book, edited by M.A. Peters, 2017.

Victoriano-Martínez, Ramón Antonio. *Rayanos y dominicanyorks: la dominicanidad del siglo XXI.* Nuevo Siglo, 2014.

Yelvington, Kevin A. "Constituting Paradigms in the Study of the African Diaspora: 1900–1950." *The Black Scholar,* vol. 41, no. 1, 2011, pp. 64–76.

Mwen pa dyab men m ap konte moun

Évelyne Trouillot

Yo di m fòl pase m ap konte moun. Lè m te piti manman m te konn di moun pa konte moun, se dyab ki konte moun. Epoutan, mwen pa dyab men m ap konte moun.

Depi 2 jou m ap konte moun. Anvi an monte m konsa, m pa konn kote li sòti. De pitit fi mwen yo mete men nan tèt. Pitit gason mwen an di l ap mennen m kay dòktè. Mwen konnen m pa malad. Mwen granmoun, se nòmal, kò m kòmanse lage m, l ap prepare l pou l ale. Mwen gen plis ke 80 lane, se nòmal pou m bite lè m ap mache, se nòmal pou gen imaj k ap vin nan tèt mwen, gen figi moun mwen pa wè depi lontan k ap fè m siy. Se nòmal pou m vle konte moun mwen yo.

Mwen pa dyab men m ap konte moun.

Papa, tifrè mwen an Roro, matant Klodya, monnonk Gaston, papi Antwàn, Anriyèt, m poko fini, kite m konte. M tande nou di m ap radote. M tande nou k ap di fòk yo ta banm yon kalman. M pa bezwen kalman. Mwen viv lontan san m pa konte pèsonn, m janbe lanmè, male Miyami, m travay kay moun, m bourike nan restoran, pandan plis pase dis lane m santi poul lè m pral dòmi, m aprann pale angle. M aprann di *please, thank you, yes sir, yes madam, I am fine*, menm lè m pa t *fine*. M fè tou sa m dwe fè pou m te okipe pitit mwen yo, voye yo lekòl, ba yo ledikasyon, mwen fè tou sa, jodi a m rive nan yon laj kote m ap gade dèyè. Finalman, m ka sonje jou sa a. M pa t ka fè sa anvan pase chaj la te twò lou, gen chaj ou bije bliye pou ou pa efondre.

Mwen gen yon tikaye kadriye, ti kaye tankou sa mwen te konn sèvi lekòl lè me te piti. Se sou li m ap ekri non moun mwen yo. Zòt mèt di mwen fou.

Dayè sa sa fè si m ta fou, moun fou se moun yo ye tou. Epi alaj mwen si m fou, se yon fou dou mwen ye, m pa gen fòs pou m voye wòch.

M toujou renmen jwe ak wòch, genyen ki dous nan men w, lè ou manyen yo ou pa ta di se yon ti sirèt tou won k ap tann ou pase lang ou sou li. M te konn jwe ak galèt bò lasous la, m te konn jwe ak Felipe. *Vamos à jugar a las escondidas.* Lago kache, se sèl pawòl ki te nan bouch Felipe. Woy ! Eske fòk mwen mete non l sou lis la ? M kwè l te rete lakay li, lòt bo fwontyè. Banm rekòmanse konte.

Papa, Roro, matant Klodya, monnonk Gaston, papi Antwàn, Anriyèt, . . .

Anriyèt se te pitit kòmè Altagrasya a, li te konn vin jwe avèk mwen ak Felipe. Nou te konn benyen ansanm lè solèy la te twò cho sou do nou. Lè konsa figi Felipe te konn vin tou wouj, nou te konn fawouche l pase li te tankou yon oma.

Roro pa t ka vini avèk nou, li te twò piti. Se sak fè jou sa a, li te rete avèk papa. Lè bagay yo gate, Papa mete ti frè m sou zepòl li pou l kouri. Papa di m kouri mafi, kouri pitit mwen, mwen di papa, kote pou m ale ? Ale ak manman w. E ou ? E Roro ? Papa m repete kouri mafi. Manman pran men m, li di ann kouri pitit mwen, pa gade dèye, pa gade dèye. Gwo dlo ap soti nan je manman m men li kenbe men m di pou nou kouri ansanm.

Gen lontan m ap kouri, men m pa janm bliye bri kò k ap tonbe, bri manchèt, bri zo k ap kase. Bri kò k ap tonbe tankou mango mi, bri manchèt k ap kase zo tankou manchèt nan chan kann. M ap kouri, bri yo ap kouri avèk mwen. M kouri, m pa gade dèye men m te gen tan wè Anriyèt tonbe, li te gen yon ti wòb jòn, m wè jip la tou sal ak san, m kòmanse kriye. Men mwen kontinye kouri. Manman di kouri mafi. Gen lontan m ap kouri.

Nou janbe rivyè, nou kite fwontyè a dèye, men m toujou tande bri. Bri sa yo yo sonnen fò anpil pase yo chita nan tèt mwen. Lè nou rive Wanament, manman soupire epi li di « Apre tout tan sa a, se konsa m touven nan peyi m ». Mwen di « E mwen manman, kote peyi m ye ? » Manman m pa reponn, li vire tèt li men m te gen tan wè l ap kriye.

Peyi isit tounen peyi m, mwen marye, mwen fè pitit mwen yo isit. Mwen wè pitit pitit fèt nan Miyami, mwen tounen Ayiti pase se isit manman m antere. Men jodi a m sonje moun mwen yo m te kite lòt bò frontyè.

M ap konte vye moun mwen yo : Papa, Roro, matant Klodya, monnonk Gaston, papi Antwàn, Anriyèt, Altagrasya, kòme Chantal . . .

Felipe pa t vle kite m ale jou sa a, li si tèlman renmen jwe, li te kenbe ke jip mwen li di « Sofia, non, Sofia ». Manman m pran men m, li trennen m, mwen tande Felipe k ap kouri dèye nou. Manman m kouri vit. Kòmè Chantal te konn vann rapadou. Li lage tout atè pou l kouri tou.

Gen anpil wòch anba pye m. M blese, m kouri, m tonbe, m leve. Gen wòch ki bèl, men gen wòch ki frape fò, gen wòch ki fèt pou bare wout, gen wòch ki fèt pou fè san koule.

Lè m sonje jou sa, m wè bra k ap voye wòch, m wè bra k ap leve manchèt. Se pa de moun ki tonbe, se pa de bri zo kase m tande. M vle sonje tout moun pa m yo, sa ki tonbe, sa ki mouri. Mwen pa bliye sa ki te pase. Manman pa t janm vle pale de sa. Tout kò l te pran tranble lè konsa. Mwen te pito pe pou m pa fè l kriye men mwen pa bliye. Jodi a, m ranmase memwa m. Kite m konte vye moun mwen yo.

Pa di m fou, pa di m ap depale. Pawòl la lou, li granmoun menm jan avè m. Pitit mwen yo konnen, mari m tou te konnen, depi mwa doktòb rive, pa gen lenn ki ka vlope m. Tout kò m frèt pase kò a pa janm bliye. Se yon jou samdi nou te kòmanse kouri , manman avèk mwen. Menm si m pa advantis, le samdi m toujou pèdi apeti. M pa ka bliye lodè san m te wè koule. Jodi a, memwa m derefize dòmi. M bouke jwe lagokache ak vizyon kin an tèt mwen. M vle pitit mwen yo sonje, m vle pitit pitit mwen yo sonje. M pa konn si Felipe vivan toujou. Mwen ta renmen pitit Felipe ak pitit pitit li ki lòt bò fwontyè a pa bliye. Pou ankenn moun pa bliye jou sa a, pou nou sonje bri manchèt, bri kò ki tonbe, bri zòtèy ki frape nan wòch. Men tou pou n pa bliye tout jou anvan yo, jou escondidas, jou benyen ansanm, jou wòch dous kou galèt, jou lasous. Jou mwen menm ak Felipe nou te bije separe san n pa konprann pouki.

Manman m mouri depi lontan. Li mouri ak kè l grenn, gen yon doulè ki te chita anndan l ki pa janm etenn. Menm lè li wè pitit pitit li, je l toujou rete tankou de zetwal kache dèyè nyaj. Souri li yo toujou gen koulè lapli. Manman pa janm bliye Papa, Roro ak tout lòt yo. Mwen toujou panse si se pa t pou mwen li t ap mouri tou depi menm lè a. Mwen te piti se vre men mwen pa ka bliye non plis.

Kite m ekri non moun mwen yo. Se avèk yo mwen vle fè dènye bout wout ki rete m lan. Mwen vle sonje, mwen vle nou tout sonje. Non, mwen pa fou. Menm si anpil fwa m konn anvi rele. Anpil fwa m leve lannuit, m gen yon lòt lang ki monte nan tèt mwen. Se pa depale m ap depale. Mwen gen yon defile vizaj k ap pase devan je m. Mwen konnen yo pa la ankò. Nan rèv la lè m vire gade, m pa wè pèsonn. Yo tout disparèt.

Se pa dyab ase ki konte moun. M konte non tout moun mwen yo : Papa, tifrè mwen an Roro, matant Klodya, monnonk Gaston, papi Antwàn, Anriyèt, Altagrasya, Kòmè Chantal, MariWòz, Elifèt, Pedro, Kantav, Sara . . .

Si nou rasanble tout ti kaye kadriye pou nou konte valè moun ki mouri jou sa a, ala adisyon n ap fè mezanmi, ala paj n ap ranpli. Ala dlo k ap koule. Epoutan nou pa ka bliye.

M ap kite ti kaye kadriye pa m lan pou pitit mwen, pitit pitit mwen ak tout sa ki vin dèyè, pase fanmi an long, l ap grandi. Fòk li grandi byen. Timoun k ap mache aprann gade devan men yo dwe gade dèyè tou. Fanmi an long, fòk memwa a long tou. M pa fou, mezanmi, se vye moun mwen yo ki di m pa bliye yo.

Johnny Rivas

Chiqui Vicioso

Existe una tercera república en la frontera. Allí no aplican las leyes constitucionales de ninguna de las dos naciones que habitan esta pequeña isla, imperan solo la ley del más fuerte, el oscurantismo de la falta de educación y cultura, el instinto del hombre reducido a primate.

Por esas tierras reinan los productores de banano, quienes mediante una franquicia de la Unión Europea exportan aproximadamente ochenta toneladas de guineo desde el puerto de Manzanillo, como en los viejos tiempos de la United Fruit en Centro América. Por suerte para los trabajadores dominicanos y haitianos que laboran en esos campos, la Unión Económica Europea exige permisos de trabajo y condiciones de salubridad, algo a lo que se presta la Dirección de Migraciones, porque allí habla el poder de los exportadores y con eso no se juega.

A esos predios ha llegado la acción de la Red Jesuita de Solidaridad Fronteriza, Orden religiosa que todos los días trata de implementar el mandato de amar al prójimo como a sí mismo, a que se reducen todos los Mandamientos, y que le lava la cara a la iglesia en un momento en que lo que copa la atención nacional son los abusos de los curas, y Nuncio, pederastas.

Viviendo como uno de ellos, está el padre Regino, quien como ya dije antes no está interesado en loas, boatos, vajillas de plata, mansiones de lujo, suntuosidades u océanos. Su voto de pobreza y solidaridad lo lleva a compartir con los condenados de la tierra su suerte, su pan, su destino, con la ayuda de hombres como Johnny Rivas, a quien tienen preso desde hace tres meses con una acusación absurda: la de mandar a matar a una bruja haitiana, algo que el propio asesino de la señora en cuestión niega, porque no conoce a Johnny.

Hacinado, en la Cárcel de Montecristi, donde hay 150 presos (en vez de los 60 que deben alojar las instalaciones), y los jefes de la prisión cobran espacio y peaje (¿Por donde andará Roberto Santana a quien le encanta montear y cantar boleros?), Johnny permanece en la cárcel por un único delito: trabajar con el padre Regino, a quien la gente de Manzanillo teme alojar aterrorizada como está por los nacionalistas locales.

El fascismo asoma su oscura trompa cada vez que se habla de justicia social por estos predios, donde imperan el polvo, la guazabara, el cactus y los hombres y mujeres envejecen prematuramente por la falta de suavidad del ambiente y de los gobiernos, que, uno tras otro, olvidan que la gente del sur tiene derecho a la vida, a la esperanza y a la alegría. Y entre ellos, quienes practican el amor inderrotable.

"Desafíos y éxitos en la frontera"

2018 Border of Lights panel in Dajabón Municipal Hall

Jhonny Rivas

Transcribed and translated into Spanish by John Presimé

Nou salye tout otorite yo ki nan salon an, nou ranmesye nou tout pou opòtinite sa aprè midi a. Map pwofite pou'm salye ansyen konseye Jean Baptiste ak tout travayè yo ki akonpanye nou sòti Dajabon vini isit la.

Mwen rele Jhonny, mwen sòti Sizanèt, mwen rete sendomeng depi lè m fini etid mwen. Mwen te fè etid primè mwen nan lekòl Notre Damme Saint Sezanne, e etid segondè mwen nan nouvo kolèj aprè mwen te pase nan Lycée Trou Denie, Okap Ayisyen.

Aprè mwen te al rete Sendomeng menm si m pa te ale poum rete, men le mwen te vizite pou vakans mwen te viv anpil ekspresyans la ba, aprè midi sila a, mwen vini pou'm prezante nou opòtinite ak defi nan fwontyè Dominiko-Ayisyèn lan, si nou ta al fè yon prezantasyon sou sa, premye man, nou we tou de fwontyè yo, Dajabon ak Wanament ki viv antre yon mache kote yon pòtay divize yo.

Ak òganizasyon yo nou wè fwontyè nou nan lòd pa fòs lame dominikèn, migrasyon, kazèk, ak tout lòt òganizasyon kòmèsan yo ak solidarite ki estriktire pa Centro Montalvo ki se yon òganizasyon ki reyini nou kòm migran anplis konsila Dajabon lan.

Lè nou sonje nan ane ki sot pase te gen anpil pwoblèm te gen yon ONG Fondasyon Solidarite ki estrikti kounye a kòm sant Montalvo sou fwontyè a nan Dajabón kap fè anpil nan travay nan zòn fontalye a, men daprè eksperyans ak syans nou fè nan Repiblik Dominikèn nan Santiago , San Pedro de Macoris, Kapital, Mao a ak Dajabón sou Dwadelòm, mwen prezante kòm reprezantan Dwadelòm nan fwontyè a ansanm ak 46 òganizasyon nan peyi ki gen an tèt li Jesuit yo pou defann dwa yo travayè yo.

Lè nou wè fwontyè a ak wè kòman ayisyen yo ap viv, nou te panse gade dèyè yo wè ki jan lavi sa a, nan 1937 nou wè ke te gen yon touye men se pa vle se touye pawòl Bondye a mansyone pa jan nou wè Ayisyen ap viv, e nou konnen lòt nasyon renmen wè ke ayisyen yo devlope ak byen òganize nan peyi a se pou sa kòm reprezantan de Dwadelòm nou ke li nesesè pou fè yon travay an Ayiti, kòm pwofesè nou wè ke gen yon travay ki pou fètavèk Ayisyen yo ki Sendomeng lan e nou antre nan kominote travayè yo pou òganize yo ak kanpay Jeziit yo nou te fè yon travay pou idantifye Ayisyen yo pou fòme pwojè idantifikasyon ki pi gwo a avèk yo.

Nou kòmanse ak 3 asosyasyon kounnya menm, nou te benefisye 46 gwoup ki sòti nan Navarrete jiska Dajabon, nou sonje travay Solidarite te fè depi 1986 jiska 1989, te gen yon premye defilè militè te pran machadiz komèsan yo nan fwontyè a e lè nou wè travay Solidarite te konn fè se reyini komèsan yo epi fè asosyasyon kòmèsan yo.

Lè mwen li liv e mwen wè travay e mwen wè travay Jeziit yo te ekri sou sityasyon fwontyè a mwen te aprann sou kòman tan an te ye e kijan tan an ye jodi a epi ki defi nou te rankontre antre jan sityasyon te ye ayè e kijan li ye jounen jodi a.

An 1986, te gen yon ong ki te apèn kòmanse nan fwontyè, li rele nou espwa ki travay ak fanm yo. Pè Regino te ini 400 gason ak fanm pou kreye òganizasyon sila a pou'n konbat problèm yo te konn viv nan fwontyè a Ayisyen kòm Dominiken, nan moman sa pè a te reyini ak prezidan moman an ki se te Joaquin Balaguer pou mande kanpe sityasyon kote yo te konn ap jete machandiz kòmèsan yo, konsa ong sa se te Solidarite (Solidaridad) epi yo te chanje non sa li plizyè fwa.

Yo te konn reyini ak kazèk yo e yon te fonde plizyè lòt òganizasyon se pou sa nou fè yon rapèl pou yon konba ki te rele Sánchez tou pre fwontyè a, konsa gras a eksperyans sa yo nou ofri tèt nou pou travay kòm reprezantan Dwa delòm.

Mwen ekspere ke eksperyans sa sèvi ou ak pitit ou pou kapab prevent bagay sa yo demen.

Mèsi tou òganizasyon travayè yo a pati ane 2002, yo te gen kapasite pou reklame dwa yo, salè yo, asirans yo, tan konje pou vizite famiy yo. San òganizasyon sa yo travay sa pa tap posib.

Nou rekòmande tout elèv yo, fiti agwonòm, avoka, edikatè pou edike tout zanmi yo ak fanmi yo pou sa ki te fèt nan epòk masak la pa fèt ankò, sa ka pase ankò sèlman si nou pran konsyans sou sa ki alantou nou.

Pou sa jounen jodi a nou eseye wè kòman nou ka ede gen yon chanjan pou agrandi travayè ayisyen nou yo, etan Sendomeng, de peyi sa yo se tankou mari ak madanm e li difisil pou yo divòse se pou sa nou eseye sipòte de pèp yo pou nou ka viv an amoni.

Pou sa mèsi pou opòtinite sa a e nan yon pwochèn okazyon nou ka fè yon pi bon travay sou travayè nou yo etan Sendomeng. Mèsi dèske ou la avèk nou. Nou mande yon chanjman pou yon meyè konpòtman nou vle amelyore fwontyè nou ak yon pi bon vi antre de pèp sa yo kote nou ka viv an pè. Mèsi anpil.

Saludamos a todas las autoridades en el salón, estamos agradecidos por la oportunidad de esta tarde.

Aprovecho para saludar al antiguo consejero Jean Baptisté y todo el staff que nos acompaña desde Dajabón para venir hasta aquí.

Mi Nombre es Jhonny. Soy de Sizanet (en el Norte de Haiti), vivo en la República Dominicana desde que terminé mis estudios. Mis estudios primarios los hice en la Escuela Notre Dame de Saint Sezane, y mis estudios secundarios en un nuevo colegio, después pasé al Liceo de Trou Dernie en Cap-Haïtien.

Después fui a vivir a la República Dominicana sin la intención de quedarme, pero cuando fui a visitar, en unas vacaciones, tuve muchas experiencias allí y por eso me quedé.

Esta tarde, vengo para presentar oportunidades y desafíos en la frontera domínico-haitiana. Si fuéramos a hacer una presentación sobre esto primero, vemos las dos fronteras, Dajabón y Ouanaminthe, que viven entre un mercado dividido por un portón.

Nuestra frontera está ordenada por las fuerzas armadas dominicanas, la migración, el ayuntamiento, y todas las organizaciones de comerciantes y de Solidaridad que están estructuradas por el Centro Montalvo, la cual es una organización que nos reúne como migrantes, además del Consulado de Dajabón.

Cuando recordamos los años pasados, habían muchos problemas. Había una ONG (organización no-gubernamental) que era la "Fundación de Solidaridad", estructura que es ahora mismo el Centro Montalvo en la frontera de Dajabón que hace mucho trabajo en la zona fronteriza. Según la experiencia y los estudios que hemos hecho en la República Dominicana (en Santiago, San Pedro de Macorís, la Capital, Mao, y en Dajabón) sobre los derechos humanos, me represento como representante de los derechos humanos en la frontera, junto a 46 organizaciones en el país, que dirigimos con los Jesuítas para defender los derechos de los trabajadores.

Cuando vemos la frontera y percibimos como viven los haitianos, miramos hacia atrás para ver cómo era la vida en 1937. Vemos que hubo una masacre, pero no queremos que la palabra "masacre" se mencione porque vemos cómo nuestros haitianos están viviendo y sabemos que la otra nación le gusta ver que el haitiano se está desarrollando y que se está organizando bien en el país. Por eso, como haitiano y representante de los Derechos Humanos, veo que es necesario hacer un trabajo en Haití. Como profesor, vengo aquí del otro lado de la frontera. Veo que hay trabajo que hacer con los haitianos en la República Dominicana y estamos entrando en las comunidades de los trabajadores para organizarlos con la compañía de los Jesuítas. Hemos hecho un trabajo para identificar a los haitianos para formar el proyecto más grande de identificación con ellos.

Empezamos con tres asociaciones, y ahora hemos beneficiado a 46 grupos saliendo desde Navarrete hasta Dajabón. Recordamos el trabajo que Solidaridad Fronteriza hizo desde 1986 hasta 1989; había un primer reto cuando los militares cogían las mercancías de los comerciantes en la frontera. El trabajo de Solidaridad Fronteriza era reunir a los comerciantes y hacer una asociación de comerciantes.

Cuando leo libros sobre el trabajo de los Jesuítas quienes escribieron sobre la situación de la frontera, aprendí cómo era ese tiempo y como es ahora. Además de los desafíos que hemos encontrado entre aquella situación dera ayer y como está actualmente.

En 1986, había una ONG que acababa de empezar en la frontera, que se llamaba la Nueva Esperanza, y trabajaba con las mujeres. Fue el Padre Regino quien reunió a 4,000 hombres y mujeres para crear esa organización para enfrentar los problemas que vivían los hombres y mujeres, tantos dominicanos como haitianos. Se reunió con el presidente del país, quien era Joaquín Balaguer, para pedir un alto a la situación de tomar las mercancías de los comerciantes. Entonces esa organización era Solidaridad Fronteriza y fue cambiando a diferentes nombres; se reunía con los ayuntamientos y fundaron varias organizaciones; por eso hoy día hacemos un llamado a un combate que el que hubo en Sánchez, cerca de la frontera. Gracias a todas esas experiencias, nos ofrecemos para trabajar como representante de Derechos Humanos.

Esperemos que esta experiencia les sirva a ustedes y sus hijos, e hijos de sus hijos, para poder prevenir estas cosas en el futuro.

Gracias a todas las organizaciones qué, a partir de 2002, los trabajadores fueron capaces de reclamar sus derechos, sus salarios, sus seguros, y su tiempo libre para visitar a sus familiares. Sin las organizaciones, ese trabajo no sería posible.

Recomendamos a todos ustedes: estudiantes—futuros agrónomos, abogados y educadores,—que eduquen a sus amigos y familiares para que algo así, como la masacre, no vuelva a suceder, pero eso solo se va a lograr si creamos conciencia en todos aquellos quienes están a nuestros alrededores.

Por eso, hoy en día, intentamos ver cómo podemos tener un cambio a gran escala para nuestros trabajadores haitianos en la República Dominicana; esos dos países son como esposo y esposa y se les hace difícil obtener el divorcio. Por eso tratamos de apoyar a los dos pueblos para que podamos vivir en armonía.

Gracias por esta oportunidad. En una próxima ocasión podremos hacer un mejor trabajo sobre todos nuestros trabajos en la República Dominicana. Gracias por estar aquí con nosotros. Pedimos un cambio para un mejor comportamiento, queremos una mejor frontera, y una mejor convivencia entre los dos pueblos en donde podamos vivir en paz. Muchas gracias.

A Portrait in Charcoal[1]

Jake Kheel

As *Death by a Thousand Cuts's*[2] production team, we are extremely proud of our documentary's success and the great support we've received in the Dominican Republic. Following its world premiere at the Hot Docs Canadian International Documentary Festival in Toronto, the film won the Grand Jury Prize for Best Documentary at the Seattle International Film Festival and has since been screened at festivals all over the world. Audiences in Europe, Colombia, Mexico, and across the United States have been visibly moved and shocked by the precarious conditions on the border of Haiti and the Dominican Republic. The conversations that have followed these screenings are serving as a wake-up call to the rest of the world.

However, beyond the strong reactions and awareness that the film has stirred on the international festival circuit, far more important has been the powerful impact that it has had in Haiti, as well as in the Dominican Republic. Although our distribution and action plan for Haiti is still in its early stages, we see great potential for the film to generate dialog about the complex trafficking and trade of charcoal, the negative impacts of deforestation, the need to find alternative fuel sources, and the broader necessity of strengthening the working class economy for the underclass to replace charcoal trade jobs.

At the first screening we held at the Inter-American Development Bank (IDB) in Haiti, the question-and-answer session encompassed an hour-long, animated debate among the participants on Haiti's role in finding a solution to the challenge of wood charcoal use. We were surprised that when one of the participants expressed disapproval of the way the film portrayed Haiti, several participants, with decades of combined experience working in binational projects, passionately defended the balanced depiction of both nations in the film. This sort of discourse is precisely one of the film's objectives.

Meanwhile, in the Dominican Republic, *Death by a Thousand Cuts* has generated a national discussion regarding the illegal trafficking of charcoal, deforestation, and the delicate relationship with Haiti. As social documentary filmmakers, we feel that the real success of the film goes beyond prizes and festivals, in that it has succeeded in generating dialog.

As conservation photographer Eladio Fernández noted, we hope that the documentary will act as a platform or a "launching pad" for other organizations to voice their concerns about the diverse environmental issues affecting the country. We are guardedly optimistic that the Dominican government seems to be reacting to a growing public concern for the environment and so far, has expressed a newfound commitment to the natural environment. We hope this will become a lasting commitment.

But perhaps our primary achievement has been the way the general public has been deeply affected by the film. We have received positive feedback from people expressing the impact the film has had on them, but even better, we are seeing how these voices are joining the debate and the dialogue to encounter genuine solutions.

However, after several dozen screenings around the world, without fail, we almost always hear the same concern from viewers. What are the solutions? How can such a complex set of problems be overcome?

After completing five years of in-depth investigation into the charcoal issue, we have gained a unique perspective on the issue. We believe that when viewed as one large issue, the damage caused by the wood charcoal industry may appear to be too complex to solve. But if they are divided into more manageable components, there are genuine opportunities for both short and long-term solutions. The key is in tackling the problem strategically, without over-simplifying, while ensuring that the scale of the problem does not lead to paralysis from over-analysis.

I. STRENGTHEN THE DOMINICAN REPUBLIC'S PROTECTED AREAS

Any visitor to the country's protected areas is immediately impacted by the lack of available resources to protect the parks. Any pride in the number or size of the parks is meaningless if the parks don't have the resources needed to properly manage and protect them. From our first visits, we concluded that it was essential for the parks to have sufficient rangers, vehicles, tools, radios and equipment. The park system must guarantee basic and continuous support to ensure, for example, that there is enough gasoline for their vehicles and food and uniforms for the park rangers.

In addition, sufficient funds are needed to ensure that the park employees—including forest rangers—enjoy a decent standard of living and thus are less susceptible to bribes or coercion. They should receive thorough training to build morale and help create a feeling of pride as a protector of the nation's forests.

The protection of the National Parks also requires investments in infrastructure to encourage the Dominican public and visiting tourists to play a more active role in the parks. Improved infrastructure will provide incentives for opportunities to go camping, hiking, bird watching, taking photographs, research, and simply enjoy these spectacular and unique resources that are these parks. More visitors to the parks will open up employment opportunities for guides, trail maintenance, selling handicrafts for adjacent communities to participate in the economy in lieu of the charcoal trade and/or illegal agricultural operations within the park system.

Until there is a proper budget and government commitment towards these countries' protected areas, these areas will continue to be at risk.

2. CONTROL OF ILLEGAL CHARCOAL TRAFFIC

Clearly, improving facilities in the protected areas will help limit the illegal charcoal trade that takes place within the protected areas. However, the charcoal trade is not limited only to the national parks, but also in many underdeveloped and poorer areas of the country. In our research, we concluded that an approach based solely on punitive measures against charcoal producers would not be successful. Placing all the emphasis on pursuing and punishing small-scale charcoal producers is not just a waste of resources, but it does not fundamentally address the underlying issue that many of these regions suffer from high levels of poverty. Destroying their sole source of livelihood will only end up increasing their poverty and desperation, without necessarily limiting the charcoal trade.

On both sides of the border, we discovered that charcoal producers are generally the poorest of the poor. They are people who have very few economic alternatives and that they produce charcoal "rather than stealing." In desperate situations like this, punitive measures have little effect on charcoal demand and poor producers will continue to do what they can to survive and support their families.

The war on charcoal is, in this way, similar to the so-called "war on drugs." Although the growers in Peru, Bolivia and Colombia are punished for producing drugs, the demand for their product continues.

In conclusion, although we welcome the recent emphasis and attention paid by the Dominican government to the issue of illegal charcoal trafficking, we believe that the solution for slowing charcoal production has to be through economic productivity. There need to be alternative livelihoods for the producers while simultaneously reducing demand.

An example mentioned recently by Eduardo Sanz Lovatón[3] is to create economic incentives to encourage business investment in alternatives to charcoal and bi-national projects in Haiti. The private sector in the Dominican Republic is creative and entrepreneurial. Socially motivated businesses could devise new economic opportunities in the border area and in Haiti that would reduce demand for charcoal as well as poor producers' need to make it.

3. DEVELOPMENT OF SUSTAINABLE FORESTRY PRODUCTS

An increase in supervision, control and vigilance capacity of the protected areas, and control of the illegal charcoal trade will create new sustainable production opportunities for forestry products. Forest management plans, which currently lack credibility and in many cases transparency, require technical know-how in addition to planned monitoring and supervision in order to ensure that the forestry products (whether charcoal, wood or agroforestry) are legitimate and sustainably produced.

This endeavor would require tight monitoring with the government in an independent observer role to ensure that these products do not come from illegal sources, do not harm the habitats of important or endangered species, and do not enter protected areas. In some parts of the country—making the most of certain rapid growth and regeneration species—

the development of energy farms and productive forests is a possibility, as long as they are managed with complete transparency and consistent technical supervision.

4. LONG-TERM SOLUTIONS FOR HAITI

The leading cause of illegal wood charcoal production and trafficking in the Dominican Republic is, undeniably, the high level of demand from Haiti. Identifying and implementing solutions to the overwhelming demand for charcoal is a complex challenge. It will require significant investment as well as the need to confront the economic interests of certain individuals that control the charcoal trade. However, until a viable energy alternative can be established, distributed cost-effectively, and technically maintained in Haiti, the demand for wood charcoal will continue.

Already a number of international organizations are already working to address this issue. The Global Alliance for Clean Cookstoves[4] and other entities have conducted a study that identifies potential short and long-term solutions in Haiti. Interestingly, this group found that the vast majority of the consumption of wood charcoal is concentrated in the country's urban centers and cities. Working strategically, a solution could be provided for these urban areas with new options like propane gas or alternative, sustainable charcoal.

Nonetheless, it is clear that in the same way that has occurred in the Dominican Republic, a plan for introducing an alternative fuel source to Haiti's urban centers would no doubt involve a huge investment in infrastructure as well as the subsidies needed to ensure that the vast majority of the population can afford it. It is also estimated that the charcoal economy provides more than 300,000 jobs in Haiti, and economic alternatives would have to be found to fill this employment gap.

We believe it is vital and absolutely essential to find a long-term solution in the face of the high demand for wood charcoal in Haiti. But it is also important to acknowledge that a solution of this kind would be extremely complex and will undoubtedly require collaboration, cooperation and investment on the part of both countries. Yet, the environmental situation in Haiti is affecting the whole island. Both countries share the same rivers, mountain ranges, ecosystems, and natural resources. There is little doubt that a lasting solution to the challenge of deforestation will require a bi-national approach and discarding past historical fissures. With this bi-national vision for the future, we have great hope for both Haiti and the Dominican Republic—the island of Hispaniola at-large—to be able to strengthen its natural resources, economy and the lives of its citizens as a new path forward.[5]

Notes

1. Essay reprinted with permission from Jake Kheel's webpage: http://jakekheel. com/a-portrait-in-charcoal/

2. https://www.facebook.com/DeathByAThousandCutsFilm/

3. http://www.listindiario.com/puntos-de-vista/2016/10/23/440177/ haiti-muerte-por-mil-cortes

4. http://cleancookstoves.org/

5. See the following two links on vimeo with clips from the documentary: "The Life of the Charcoal Maker" https://vimeo.com/171804030, password: **carbonero** and "Politicas: Aborando la Problematica del Carbon" https://vimeo.com/189821206, password: **policy**.

El racismo, una causa encubierta[1]

Deisy Toussaint

La dictadura de Rafael L. Trujillo en República Dominicana duró desde 1930 hasta su ajusticiamiento en 1961 y es dentro de este período cuando se implanta el racismo de Estado sustentado por uno de los pilares de la ideología trujillista: el antihaitianismo— reflejado en el vehemente intento de "blanquear" la raza, desarrollando sin recato una política xenófoba. Sin embargo, y para desgracia del tirano, por mucho que se empolvara el rostro, lo cierto es que su abuela materna era haitiana a quien de alguna manera negó ignorando su existencia, razón por la que solo exaltaba los apellidos Trujillo y Molina que le acreditaban la pureza española.

Sería difícil determinar los motivos reales que le llevaron a dar luz verde para ejecutar la masacre de 1937. Hay quien sustenta que fueron las tiranteces con su homólogo Stenio Vincent, algunos argumentan que fue la imprecisión de la línea fronteriza, otros las constantes denuncias de robo de ganado en el área y otros, todas juntas, pero nadie duda que una orden así solo podría haberla dado un hombre violento, racista y vengativo.

Durante el otoño de aquel funesto año, militares, policías y convictos autorizados, mataron a cuchilladas, hachazos y machetazos a un número indeterminado de personas (entre diez y treinta mil) quienes vivían en la zona fronteriza. De la cantidad exacta no se tiene precisión, muchos fueron asesinados en el mismo lugar donde los encontraban, otros fueron llevados a zonas aisladas para asesinarlos en masa e incluso hubo grupos que fueron lanzados al mar ¿Su delito? Ser haitianos en territorio dominicano.

No hubo piedad con ancianos, mujeres o niños, ni siquiera con muchos dominicanos también negros y pobres, que fueron confundidos por no pronunciar a tiempo la palabra "perejil", recurso usado por los custodios para diferenciar a los negros haitianos de los negros dominicanos, por la tendencia que existe en el idioma Kreyòl de pronunciar la "R" como la "L". Es por eso que este episodio pasó a la historia como La Matanza del Perejil.

Una multitud de cuerpos mutilados fueron arrojados a lo largo del río Masacre, frontera natural entre los dos países y escenario de antiguas disputas entre las colonias, francesa y española, en otras épocas.

A partir de este genocidio se recrudecen las relaciones entre Haití y la República Dominicana y toman un rumbo incierto los vínculos de vecindad, provocando unas consecuencias que aún tienen vigencia.

Durante las tres décadas de dictadura trujillista y lamentablemente hasta nuestro tiempo, se ha insistido en estimular una cultura de odio entre ambos pueblos. A pesar de que Haití es uno de los socios comerciales más importantes de la República Dominicana, existen desafortunadamente sectores políticos y económicos que promueven el racismo, alegando siempre una supuesta invasión, anexión o fusión orquestada desde la sombra por ciertas potencias. Por otro lado, no faltan los medios de comunicación sensacionalistas que tratan de contagiar su indignación con esperpénticas posturas frente a una invasión más propia de la ficción que de la realidad, creando un discurso saturado de rancio ultranacionalismo.

Muchos años después de la matanza, un grupo de intelectuales de la diáspora dominicana en Estados Unidos, ha venido realizando en Dajabón (frontera domínico-haitiana), un evento llamado *Frontera de Luz*, que cada año, entre finales de septiembre y principios de octubre, conmemora el lamentable suceso histórico conocido como la Masacre de Perejil.

Frontera de Luz incluye a artistas, activistas, estudiantes, padres de familias, maestros y religiosos que se integran en las dos jornadas de trabajo comunitario que se desarrolla en las ciudades fronterizas de Dajabón y Ouanaminthe en memoria de las víctimas de una tragedia apenas recordada en la lista de los grandes genocidios del siglo XX. *La Frontera de Luz busca resucitar la historia olvidada del intercambio cultural, económico y la solidaridad de ambos pueblos fronterizos que la masacre y la campaña anti-haitiana gubernamental, ha intentado borrar.*[2]

Entre las personalidades destacadas que apoyan este proyecto y asisten a la conmemoración se encuentran la autora y activista, Julia Álvarez, y Edward Paulino, historiador y profesor universitario, junto a descendientes de haitianos y dominicanos de la diáspora, así como a activistas que se reúnen para denunciar las injusticias que todavía hoy sufren dominicanos de ascendencia haitiana.

La actividad se inicia con el trabajo comunitario en el que los voluntarios participan en proyectos de embellecimiento de parques y con exhibiciones artísticas. En la noche, se lleva a cabo una misa en memoria de las víctimas de la masacre dentro del ámbito del más importante acto de colaboración y solidaridad fronteriza. Para el segundo día, se continúan desarrollando los proyectos de embellecimiento en los parques de Dajabón y Ouanaminthe. Al mismo tiempo, se realiza una exhibición cultural interactiva; y en la noche, las comunidades de ambos lados de la frontera participan en una emotiva vigilia marchando con antorchas y velas encendidas, para confluir justo en el río que divide los dos países en lo que se conoce como "Frontera de Luces".

Cynthia Carrión, una de las organizadoras de esta actividad, manifiesta que "estos eventos no solo tienen el objetivo de recordar a las víctimas de la masacre, sino también de alumbrar las injusticias actualmente en curso, sufridas por los descendientes de haitianos en la República Dominicana".

Haciendo un poco de historia sobre las relaciones entre las naciones que comparten la misma isla, cabría recordar que en su política expansionista y hegemónica, los Estados Unidos de Norteamérica invadieron Haití en 1915 y la República Dominicana en 1916 y —para rentabilizar su operación comercial— recurrieron a la explotación de los ingenios azucareros dominicanos, trabajados fundamentalmente con mano de obra haitiana, con la finalidad de abastecer a la vieja Europa que, enzarzada en la Primera Guerra Mundial, había dejado de producir remolacha azucarera. Mucha de esa mano de obra se asentó en territorio dominicano y sus descendientes nacidos y criados en República Dominicana fueron reconocidos como dominicanos.

Pero en 2007, el Estado dominicano, a través de la Junta Central Electoral (JCE), inició la negación de cédulas de identidad y actas de nacimiento. Documentos esenciales para estudiar, trabajar, cotizar en la seguridad social o solicitar un pasaporte.

A partir del 2011, un grupo de dominicanos descendientes de haitianos se organizó en un movimiento llamado Reconoci.do para exigirle al Estado la restitución de su derecho a la nacionalidad.

En septiembre del 2013, el Tribunal Constitucional (TC) dominicano, emitía la Sentencia 168-13 en la que perdían la nacionalidad todos los nacidos de padres con estatus migratorio en "tránsito" entre 1929 y 2007, dejando en un limbo legal a más de 250,000 personas que veían cómo, de un día para otro, perdían su nacionalidad convirtiéndose en apátridas.

La decisión del TC generó una generalizada indignación internacional, al tiempo que provocaba una división en la opinión pública nacional, tanto en la prensa con opiniones encontradas a favor y en contra, así como a través de pronunciamientos en personalidades que desde diferentes ámbitos hacían lo propio.

El escritor y ganador del premio Nobel, Mario Vargas Llosa, publicó en ese tiempo el artículo "Los Parias del Caribe," en el periódico español *El País*, en alusión a dicha sentencia, aplaudido por los sectores progresistas y demonizado por los ultranacionalistas.

En la República Dominicana se creó una alianza de "defensores de la patria" que apoyaban a ultranza la Sentencia 168-13, como la Red Nacional por la Defensa de la Soberanía, quienes abogaban por la expulsión del país de los afectados; sin embargo, en sentido contrario se crearon otros en apoyo a los perjudicados, como el Comité de Solidaridad con Desnacionalizados dirigidos por intelectuales y artistas criollos.

Luego de la presión nacional e internacional, el presidente Danilo Medina se vio obligado a buscar una salida legislativa para atender la demanda de los dominicanos de ascendencia haitiana. En julio del 2014 entró en vigencia la Ley 169-14 que en teoría era devolver los documentos a los desnacionalizados por la Sentencia 168-13, decisión que si bien se inició, no se cumplió en su totalidad.

Para crear un buen ambiente de colaboración entre ambos pueblos, habría que comenzar por cambiar la cultura inculcada de que Haití representa el atraso, y cambiar, además, el discurso del periodismo radical que fomenta abiertamente el racismo. Por fortuna y en contraposición, cada vez se siente más el peso de comunicadores progresistas comprometidos con la justicia y la causa social.

Las relaciones mejorarán cuando se entienda que ya no corren buenos tiempos para rancios ultranacionalismos. Es necesario conocer la historia de ambos pueblos, sus realidades, sus costumbres, sus culturas, su arte; en suma, las ricas identidades de dos pueblos hermanos que comparten la misma isla.

Y esperemos que debacles como la masacre de 1937 y la desnacionalización de sus descendientes en el 2013 no vuelvan a escribirse en la historia con la pluma del racismo.

Notas

1. Deisy asistió a Frontera de Luces en 2017. Vea su reportaje aquí: https://youtu.be/oDiIKwB6Yps
2. Esta cita es de la página de web de Frontera de Luces: www.borederoflights.org

Border-Crossing in Theatre
2016 "Border Story Fest"

Nehanda Loiseau Julot

> Borders have different forms. Borders have different contours. Borders as places of limit. Borders as places of protection. In an aspirational sense, borders as what is the limit of what you can aspire for or what you can achieve and what that means? . . . Borders as love. Whom can you and can you not love? Whom is your heart able to contain . . . Borders define our interactions and everything that we do.[1]

From 2011–14, the John Hope Franklin Humanities Institute at Duke University (FHI) embarked on its first border-centered "humanities lab."[2] The Borderwork(s) Lab followed the Haiti Lab, which was FHI's first lab project tied to the humanities, and both were the spirits that galvanized a theatre festival aptly titled, "Border Story Fest: the Dominican Republic and Haiti." The curtains rose at Duke University on March 29, 2016, with the final bow on April 8, and the theatre festival provided ample space for pre-existing works to engage in conversations with each other. Also noteworthy are the moments that preceded any spotlight on the festival stage:

- Professor Edward Paulino (CUNY John Jay College of Criminal Justice) had recently written *Eddie's Perejil*, a one-man show describing his ultimate escape from New York City's Lower East Side via the Dominican Republic circa the 1980s.
- Professor Jaybird O'berski (Duke University) wanted to stage *Toussaint*, a play about colonial Haiti and Toussaint Louverture, written by Lorraine Hansberry, the first African-American woman to have her play performed on Broadway.[3] The play takes place just before the Haitian Revolution begins. Warring sides, thus borders, are starting to form, even in the confines of one couple's bedroom.
- Professor Évelyne Trouillot (Université d'Etat d'Haïti) would be in town for the "Telling Our Stories of Home" conference at the University of North Carolina at Chapel Hill,[4] where I was directing an excerpt of her play, *Le Bleu de l'île* (*The Blue of the Island*).[5] The entire story is set under a tarp covering a truck that transports twelve Haitians to the Dominican Republic. Her play would be one topic on the festival panel.

Monologues about the border of Haiti and the Dominican Republic and the 1937 Massacre[6] were performed twice during Border Story Fest. But they had their debut in New York City in 2012 to support Border of Lights during their inaugural year.[7] Giving a face, a name, and a living, breathing body to the Massacre meant infusing a network of playwrights with testimonies *from* and *about* the border[8], creating characters that were scarred yet somehow healed, and soliciting an audience who somehow saw in what transpired on stage a fragment of themselves.

Yet, why emphasize borders while trying to transcend them?

If "borders have different forms," as Nyuol Lueth Tong shared at the John Hope Franklin Humanities Borderwork(s) Lab, then borders could very well be personified as people, and if so, then borders exist in their stories. Consequently, theatre as a medium for stories could itself exist as a border. How, then, would actors and an audience sharing a dimly lit space together acknowledge, confront, cross, turn back from and/or move borders? Or have them disappear completely? These thoughts were integrated directly into the rehearsal process for Border Story Fest. On day one of rehearsals, a first-time actor entered the theatre fiercely ready to perform but immediately questioned how she would transition from the life she just lived outside the theatre doors to her character's. With each rehearsal, the goal was to never separate them from each other. If borders exist profusely within us and overtly displayed their scars in each Border Story Fest script, then the aim would be to invert that process with the actors and audience.

Before the monologue *Grand Connection*, written by Kathleen Gonzales, audience members were asked to join actress, Keizra Mecklai, on stage as "participants" in her group therapy session. Their responsiveness or unresponsiveness to her monologue propelled her next line, movement, or moment of stillness. By the time Sheila Dévis walked onstage as eighty-year-old "Amarilis" in the final monologue of the festival written by Martha Patterson, the audience/actor border had thoroughly been crossed and re-crossed. At one point, audience members responded aloud to a question posed hypothetically by the actress during her monologue. Likewise, just before "Amarilis" sat down in her easy chair, a baby cried in the dark. She searched for the owner of those tears in the audience, waved and smiled as if to soothe and calm both that child and herself before she began her story.

Following the first performance of monologues was Professor Paulino's one-man show, *Eddie's Perejil*, starring Paulino who was directed by Samantha Galarza (Rutgers University '11). The following day, artivist Ms. Galarza and Professors Paulino and Trouillot participated in a panel hosted by the Forum for Scholars and Publics at Duke University. The conversation started with a reflection on the performances from the previous evening still fresh on our minds. Also, center stage was the panel's (and audience's) assessment of border relations between Haiti and the Dominican Republic as they presently stand, along with questions concerning how one could advocate for the citizenship rights of Dominicans of Haitian descent currently living in the Dominican Republic.

Some of the panel's answers carried with them open-ended conclusions:

The border is not yet finished telling its story.
There is still work to be done.

As if to demonstrate these collective musings through theatre, the last Border Story Fest performance was the play excerpt, *Toussaint*. Through the direction of Professor O'berski, the audience caught a glimpse of the first (and only) act of the play that Lorraine Hansberry never finished before her death at age thirty-four.[9] When it was time for the bow, monologue performers joined the *Toussaint* cast on stage, unifying what could have been regarded as two separate shows to confirm the lessons learned: theatre-made borders should be crossed, and work not yet complete still merits a grand applause.

Notes

1. Nyuol Lueth Tong (Duke University '10) spoke on borders and their many representations during his involvement with the John Hope Franklin Humanities Institute's Borderwork(s) Lab.

2. Per the FHI website: "The core commitment of the Humanities Labs is to engage undergraduates in advanced research alongside faculty and graduate student mentors and collaborators. Each Lab is organized around a central theme and a constellation of research projects that bring together faculty and students from across the humanities and other disciplines. Lab participants work in physical spaces at the FHI that are designed to foster formal collaboration as well as informal exchange."

3. Lorraine Hansberry's play, *A Raisin in the Sun* had its Broadway premiere in 1959.

4. "Telling Our Stories of Home" was a NEH grant sponsored conference that took place at UNC Chapel Hill March 31–April 8, 2016. Lead organizers were UNC Professors Kathy Perkins (Africa/African Diaspora Theatre) and Tanya Shields (Women's & Gender Studies). Female artists and academics from countries throughout the African diaspora were invited to tell their stories in their chosen form of expression. A thank you to Dasha Chapman (Postdoctoral Associate, Duke University, African and African American Studies) for spreading the word about this conference.

5. Students from Professor Kathy Perkins's Women in Theatre from the African Diaspora and the African Diaspora at UNC (Spring 2016) served as actors in the reading. Those students were Raikija Allen, Anthony Cacchione, Victoria Collins, Lynn-Indora Edmond, Ashlei Heffernan, Garrett Ivey, Joseph Riley and Chinelo Umerah.

6. Known by many names (the Parsley Massacre, El Corte or Kout kouto-a), this genocide spanned the course of three days (October 2–4, 1937). Ordered by the infamous Dominican dictator Rafael Leónidas Trujillo, an estimated 20,000 Haitians and Dominicans of Haitian descent were killed along the Dominican-Haitian border.

7. Border of Lights (borderoflights.org), also known as Frontera de Luz in Spanish or Fwontyè Limyè in Haitian Creole, is a movement and three-day event on the Dominican-Haitian border each October that seeks to commemorate, collaborate, and continue the legacy of hope and justice that defines the two countries sharing the island of Hispaniola: Haiti and the Dominican Republic. The significance of the event scheduled during the first week of October each year marks the date of the Parsley Massacre (October 2-4, 1937).

8. "An Evening of Monologues in Remembrance of the Haitian Massacre" was a fundraiser for Border of Lights's first trip to the border. (Producers: Cynthia Carrión, Nehanda Loiseau Julot, and Professor Edward Paulino; Writers: France-Luce Benson, Magaly Colimon, Kathleen Gonzales, Shareen Knight, Patrick Mombrun, Rebecca Osborne, Martha Patterson, Edward Paulino, and Christine Suero; Actors: Paule Aboite, Tammi Cubilette, Juliette Jeffers, Antonio Lyons, Francis Mateo, Angela Polite, and Christine Suero; and Director: Patrice Johnson). Months prior to the event, a call for monologues about the Massacre included personal stories and testimonies as research material that might inform the writing of those who would submit pieces. Testimonies of massacre survivors came from Professors Lauren

Derby's and Richard Turits's article, "Temwayaj Kout Kouto, 1937." Personal narratives were written by Raymond Joseph, Former Haitian Ambassador to the US; Ana Maria Belique, activist for Border of Lights and Reconoci (reconoci.do); and other Border of Lights advocates.

9. This unfinished play was dated May 1958 and Hansberry had conceived it as "A Musical Drama in 7 Scene."

Una autobiografía fronteriza

Nancy Betances

Nací, el día 10 de octubre en una fría mañana del año 1967 en un hermoso pueblo situado en la frontera norte con Haití llamado Loma de Cabrera, pueblo cargado de historia. Donde dominicanos y haitianos se dieron las manos para derrocar la gran potencia invasora de España, logrando salir triunfante y demostrando que en la unión está la fuerza.

Los primeros años de mi infancia fueron muy felices, rodeado de mi familia, de amigos disfrutando de bellos paisajes, refrescando en verano el sofocante calor con baños en las cristalinas aguas del Río Masacre. Empezaba a descubrir el mundo que me rodeaba. Escuchaba historia y anécdotas vividas de hechos que marcaron la historia reciente, donde parte de esa historia, mi abuelo era protagonista.

Este hecho marco mi adolescencia y la tornó, para mí, complicada. Me convirtió en una persona extremadamente reservada, en aquella época me era difícil hacer amistades. También tuve algunos problemas de autoestima. Asimismo me encerré en un mundo de lectura. Empecé con el teatro, la poesía y la literatura, escribiendo e interpretando, si bien, solo como hobby. Con ayuda de un sacerdote, llegué a los grupos juveniles primero en un barrio y después en los grupos de la iglesia.

Otro aspecto que me fue especialmente difícil en aquella época fue cuando decidí, después de terminar los estudios secundarios, entrar a la vida religiosa; para mi familia no era la mejor opción, pero entendí que tenía que ayudar y con esto tratar de borrar lo que escuché de mi abuelo.

Pero estando en ella, cruzaron por mi cabeza múltiples opciones—ya que venía de una comunidad donde se practicaba la espiritualidad ignaciana y estaba en todo su apogeo la teología de la liberación—pero no encajaban mis ideales ni mi opción de trabajo por el pobre.

Salí de la congregación y decidí estudiar Derecho para poder adquirir conocimiento para ayudar al más necesitado sin tener que cumplir normas desde un instituto ni orden religiosa—solo la orden de Dios.

En el año 1999, me casé. Fue una etapa dura, haciendo frente a situaciones complejas. El 15 de julio del 2002, me convertí en madre por primera, y única vez, de un hermoso niño llamado Jhoshua. Las cosas en el matrimonio no salieron como esperaba. Yo era muy autosuficiente y sociable; siempre estaba preparada para ayudar a los demás, acogía jóvenes del campo para que pudieran estudiar en la ciudad. Mi compañero no lo entendía y decidí poner fin a la relación y volver a mi pueblo.

Desde el 2011, estoy viviendo en la provincia de Dajabón donde vine a trabajar en Solidaridad Fronteriza en el Departamento de Sociedad Civil. Desde ese departamento, ayudé al Departamento de Derechos Humanos donde pude conocer el grupo Frontera de Luces, y de mano con el sacerdote jesuita, Regino Martínez, ayudamos a preparar la primera celebración de la conmemoración de la Masacre de 1937. Eso me marcó porque, por fin, pude quitar esa carga que sentía desde la adolescencia.

Sentí que mi corazón fue como ese cirio encendido que liberó y sacó desde adentro todo lo que tenía, se purificó una luz desde el interior, que quemó toda esa oscuridad que no me dejaba respirar. Frontera de Luces me conquistó y me liberó.

Sigo trabajando; ayudé en la apertura del Hogar de Cristo para niños de la calle junto con el sacerdote Mario Serrano. Vivo promoviendo el intercambio cultural y comercial con Haití, promoviendo la feria binacional de Frontera de Luces, y canalizando ayuda para dotar de pasaportes a los nacionales haitianos, ayudando a niños que no son reconocidos al ser inscritos y poder obtener sus actas de nacimientos. Coordino la red de protección de niñas, niños y adolescentes, así defendiendo los derechos humanos en la red fronteriza Jano Sike.

Sigo haciendo incidencia y tratando de ser la voz de los que no la tienen. Estoy en un momento de mi vida en la que mi trayectoria y activismo social aún deben continuar durante muchos años y seguir ayudando a sanar y curar heridas. Porque cuando se ayuda a un hermano se ayuda a Dios, nosotros somos su imagen y semejanza.

SECTION II

ARTISTIC ENDEAVORS

Postcard and Portrait Projects

Scherezade García and William Vazquez

1937
República Dominicana & Haiti

Cuéntame que te contaron...

Scherezade García,
artista visual y educadora,
en colaboración con
Edward Paulino, Ph.D.
Borders of Light
www.scherezade.net
www.bordersoflight.org

Imagen "Paisaje compartido", 2012 © Scherezade García

Bearing Witness to Genocide

The 1937 Haitian Massacre and Border of Lights[1]

Edward Paulino and Scherezade García

How does one bear witness to the legacy of genocide? To crimes against humanity perpetrated by and against people of African descent? And how do you bear witness when it is your ethnic group, the perpetrators, that carried out mass murder decades before you were born in your ancestral homeland?

Each of these questions is interconnected; however, for us, it took many years before they could be answered. The genocide in question is the 1937 Haitian Massacre. During late September and October 1937, the Dominican dictator Rafael Leonidas Trujillo ordered the killings of an estimated 15,000 Haitian men, women, and children in the Dominican Republic. This mass murder was concentrated throughout the Dominican-Haitian border but extended to many non-border Dominican cities and towns. The operation was conducted by the Dominican military and conscripted civilians and volunteers. The weapon of choice: the machete. The machete was used so to project a spontaneous uprising by Dominican peasants defending their livestock, rather than a government sponsored and methodical plan, and it was prepared at least a year in advance. Some of the victims were shot but most were macheted-to-death, not unlike Rwanda almost sixty years later. Many of the corpses were burned and buried in unmarked graves; the forensic evidence to remain forever hidden. To be black and Haitian in those several weeks in late 1937 must have been as if the gates of hell had been swung opened, unleashing its demons upon defenseless bodies.

At the time, Trujillo's denial of complicity in the pre-meditated mass murder was rebuffed confidentially in Henry R. Norweb's, who was then the United States Ambassador to Santo Domingo, cable to President Roosevelt: "apparently with the approval of President Trujillo, a systematic campaign of extermination was directed against all Haitian residents . . . the drive was conducted with ruthless efficiency by the National Police and Army." Here was a United States Ambassador, not unlike his counterpart, Ambassador Henry Morgenthau, who twenty years earlier sent diplomatic communiqués to Washington D.C. warning about what would become the Armenian Genocide. In the annals of twentieth century genocides, the 1937 Haitian Massacre does not often come to mind.

Traditionally, genocides tend to be seen as cataclysmic events with high casualty rates. Armenia, the Holocaust, Cambodia, and Rwanda are remembered on a much larger, more frequent scale and smaller massacres, like the 1937 Haitian Massacre, are generally not considered to form part of humanity's genocidal legacy.

We believe that the Massacre should be seen as part of a genocidal continuum that easily satisfies the remarkable, but limited, definition of the United Nations Convention on Genocide describing mass murder as a crime with "the intent to destroy in whole or in part a group of people" (Lemkin and Power 2005). Unlike other crimes against humanity in the twentieth century, and despite overwhelming evidence, no individuals were punished for the 1937 Haitian Massacre. Despite the long-standing evasion of ceremoniously and publicly remembering the Massacre as a crime linked irrefutably to Trujillo, Dominicans are, for the most part, taught about the history of the event in school and mainstream Dominican historians use "genocidio" to describe the Massacre (Moya Pons 2004).

For us in the diaspora, the need to remember our past is as old as our first steps in trying to understand and make sense of our migration from the Dominican Republic to the United States. Over time we have learned that global precedents exist enabling us to better commemorate our respective histories, particularly with respect to violence against people of the African diaspora. Examples of such attempts to pay tribute to violent events of the past include the Selma-to-Montgomery, Alabama National Historic Trail, Monuments to the Cimarron in Cuba and Haiti, Elmina Castle, and the Door of No Return on Gorée Island ("Word Heritage Center: Slave Routes"). Throughout the last four decades of the twentieth century, many major crimes similar to the 1937 Haitian Massacre have yet to be prosecuted. Regardless of the fact that the history of the Massacre was and still remains taught in Dominican schools, it is not accepted as an inheritance of a cultural and political history whose legacy is seen today in cases like the 168-13 ruling in the Dominican Republic that strips many Dominicans of Haitians descent of their Dominican citizenship—retroactively to 1929. Unlike Germans, for example, "who still seem to grapple almost eagerly with their own historic guilt and shame" in reflection of the Holocaust, Dominicans do not feel shame about the Massacre and there is a vocal minority that, in fact, praise the killings as a patriotic response by Trujillo in defending the nation from a "silent invasion." (Kimmelman 2008).

The idea to commemorate the anniversary of the 1937 Haitian Massacre began with the death of the Dominican-born activist of Haitian descent, Sonia Pierre. A tireless activist for the inclusion of Dominicans of Haitian descent in Dominican society, Pierre was recognized world-wide for her organization Movimiento de Mujeres Dominico-Haitianas (MUDHA). Pierre was the recipient of many awards for her commitment to equality including the prestigious 2006 Robert F. Kennedy Humanitarian award. Moreover, MUDHA is counted among several organizations that brought legal suits against the Dominican government. In 2005 the organization was instrumental in bringing the seminal case of Dilcia Yean and Violeta Bosico—both with mothers who were Dominican nationals and fathers who were Haitian migrant workers—to the Inter-American Court. The court ruled unanimously in their favor, thus condemning the Dominican government (for more on this case see Wooding).

It is in an unexpected way that the humanitarian Pierre's death sparked a grassroots movement that takes place every year on the island of Hispaniola, comprised mainly of Americans of Dominican descent and Dominicans of Haitian descent; it is a movement seeking to bear witness to the genocidal 1937 Haitian Massacre and its legacies of exclusion while strengthening historic cross-border solidarity between Haitians and Dominicans. Pierre's death prompted Silvio Torres-Saillant to introduce Edward Paulino to Dominican-American writer Julia Alvarez.

Starting in late December 2011, Alvarez initiated correspondence with Paulino explaining her idea of a "border of lights." This dream of literally lighting up the border, raising candles alongside the Massacre River that separates Haiti and the Dominican Republic, is a concept Alvarez first shared years earlier with Michele Wucker, author of "Why the Cocks Fight" (2000). Due to time constraints and various other commitments, initially the idea never got off the ground, however, further inspired by the Occupy Wall Street movement and the Arab Spring, Alvarez grew increasingly inspired and deemed 2011 the appropriate moment to support a "grass roots gathering of artists, musicians, poets, farmers, people from both sides of the border, both countries, and supports from abroad, to come together on the anniversary of the Massacre and posit a new relationship and model how troubled borders and countries can turn themselves around if the goodwill of the people is there" (Alvarez 2011).

From the start, the idea was ambitious. Yet slowly a group of individuals emerged who would cofound the Border of Lights, an organic grassroots social movement of memorialization and solidarity. The establishment of the group itself, formed in February of 2012, was organic—some members already worked on social justice issues such as Cynthia Carrión, National Youth Program Coordinator at Amnesty International, Edward Paulino, Ana Ozuna, and Megan Myers, in academia; Sady Díaz, Rana Dotson, and DeAndra Beard, who had met Alvarez on her book tour promoting her recent memoir A Wedding in Haiti (2012), and others. From the United States, the group was also joined by author Michel Wucker, artist Scherezade García, playwright Nehanda Loiseau, and webmaster Miguel Díaz. Haitian Dr. Lesly Manigat joined the group from the Dominican Republic. For several months, the group had profound and intense discussions on what activities would be appropriate and how to carry them out, the discussions taking the form of weekly 10 p.m. conference calls. By August of 2012, Loiseau organized a Night of Monologues at New York University, an event that began with a Call for Submissions, asking for monologues from around the country informed by the history of the 1937 Massacre.

The Night of Monologues represents the first time in the United States that the Massacre was commemorated in a public way. By early September 2012, Border of Lights, thanks to the power of the internet, had organized a Kickstarter campaign and raised over $5,000 from worldwide donors. These funds would contribute to equipment, food, and supplies purchases in the Dominican Republic and Haiti. In the Dominican Republic, the Border of Lights group was confronted with the issue of discovering how to engage local residents in conversations about the Massacre, especially as friends and local activists on the ground advised us that the historic event remained a sensitive issue, especially in places like the

Dominican border town of Dajabón where many Haitians and Dominicans of Haitian descent were massacred. It was the Dominican artist's, Scherezade Garcia's, idea to address the sensitive issue by means of a part-art-installation and part-ethnographic-research.

Inspired by conversations and mutual interest in the history of Hispaniola and, therefore, the history of political division on the entire planet, Scherezade envisioned the action of "storytelling" as a way to "collect" memories. The "collection" of memories and the "decoding" of these memories resulted in a remedy for healing. The action-installation was titled "Memory of Perejil / Memoria de perejil / Memwa pèsi." The public art project was designed to provoke memory with the intention of healing through the actions of telling and sharing.

The inspiration muse is poignant: despite that the killings took place over seventy-five years ago, the event remains tattooed in the skins of both nations. Through the idea of creating multiple "postcards" depicting the landscape of Dajabón, a border-city between the Dominican Republic and Haiti and, also, the geographic space where many of the killings in October of 1937 took place, Scherezade's intention was to create a powerful tool for the collection of individual memories, a "souvenir" of sorts. This was to be carried out by asking pedestrians at the central the central market park in Dajabón, as well as locals in which is the social hub of Ouanaminthe—the border equivalent of Dajabón on the Haitian side—a simple, trilingual, question: What do you know of the 1937 massacre? Que sabes tú del "corte" de 1937? Ki konnen sou kout a? What have you been told? Qué te contaron? Ki konte ou?

The postcard was displayed much like a double-sided mural: one side with images, one side with written testimony. It was hung as "drying laundry" around the gazebo of both central parks—an allegory of the "cleansing" of both nations and the unofficial nation in between la frontera. The image on the front of the postcard consisted of two identical faces, alluding to two sister nations, their histories intertwined. The faces are located in reference to the map of the island: one nation toward the east, the other toward the west. There is the landscape in the middle, a reminder of our political frontier. The faces on the postcard are in color. These "cinnamon" colored faces follow the artist's, García's, tradition of the "action-aesthetic" politics of inclusion. These "actions" pertain simply to the mixing of all the colors on a painting palette until they turn into "brown". The aesthetic, on the other hand, refers to the use of these brown figures as the muses of the artist's paintings; García exercises the aesthetic of inclusion as a consequence of the Caribbean and American experience.

The image or blank space on the back of the postcard, where one usually writes a little note to send to family and friends, is where the questions mentioned previously are displayed. Rather, the back side of these postcards have a prompt and a purpose. Since the question is based on an individual's memory and not recent experience, it opens the doors to internal sentiments, poetry, and stereotypes. Furthermore, the postcards allow people the opportunity to vent, to open their wounds, and also to reconcile with the pains of the past. In this way, through proactive exercise, individuals—or a community at large—is able to begin a collective awareness of historical responsibility, stemming from the understanding that these stories are valuable and allowing individuals to claim ownership of their memory and become agents of solution.

Perhaps the most moving part of the three-day event in 2012, was the Friday night candle-light vigil. After attending mass in Dajabón, where the Jesuit priest remembered the victims of the 1937 Massacre, Border of Lights organizers handed a flower and a candle to each congregant upon exiting the church. What followed was an informal procession of churchgoers and those in support of the mission of Border of Lights. The group, in the hundreds, walked in the dark—guided only by the small fleck of flame emitted by each candle—from the church to the bridge: the border that divides Haiti and the Dominican Republic. At the bridge, near the seventeen-foot-high pyramid marker, the Jesuit priest and active member of Solidaridad Fronteriza, Father Regino Martínez, led a brief prayer. The prayer was followed by songs and poems written by Julia Alvarez, Edwidge Danticat, and Chiqui Vicioso. Everyone held out their candles toward the Massacre River and, on the Dominican side, someone climbed down to the riverbank and placed, in the water, a paper boat with a candle in the middle. At the same time, Haitians on the other side of the river were doing the same thing, holding their lit candles to the sky, singing, praying, and remembering. Both sides engaged in what was, at times, an unintelligible, multilingual exchange: "Hello! . . . We are your brothers and sisters . . . We love you."

Many who were there that night confess that the sea of candles on both sides of the border was emotionally overwhelming. It marked the first time that the thousands of victims, who perished during the Massacre of October 1937, were remembered in such a public, transnational act of solidarity. One could not help but think about that balmy hot night, back in 1937, in which literally hundreds, thousands of people raced for their lives to cross the very river we were overlooking; the carnage; the sounds of men, women, and babies screaming out of fear and the unknown; the cries from survivors, maimed and bleeding, splashing and thrusting their bodies across the river; some, but certainly not all, arriving miraculously on Haitian territory. On the border of this very river in October of 2012, there was an eerie sense of the initial stages of closure, a closure allowing for the thousands of dead spirits, who wandered for decades throughout the Dominican-Haitian borderlands, to finally rest. At last, their lives—and deaths—would be acknowledged; their spirits responding as if to say: "Despite being poor and black, I too, existed!" They did not die in vain.

For those of us living and working in the diaspora, bearing witness to this crime against humanity is especially important, because it openly responds to the inability of successive Dominican governments to grapple with this dictatorial and genocidal legacy. We recognize and abhor the reality that the second and third generation Dominicans of Haitian descent are being excluded from the Dominican melting pot; that they are being denied a birth certificate and a cédula (national identification card), denied the right to vote, denied entrance to a university, denied the right to marry, and denied the chance to become an integral part of society, like many Americans of Dominican descent in the United States. We are the Dominicans of Haitian descent. In the Dominican Republic, they are the "Dreamers" longing to be recognized by their country—the only nation they have ever known. By commemorating the anniversary of the Massacre, Border of Lights works to foster solidarity between Dominicans and Haitians on the border, and beyond, and to show that historic relations between Dominicans and Haitians have been far more collaborative than adversarial. What it means to be Dominican in the twenty-first century should

Figure 1: Poster for the Evening of Monologues

be an inclusive national identity where young black Dominicans of Haitian descent can realistically aspire to comprise part of the Dominican nation—like three-time Dominican presidential candidate of Haitian descent, José Francisco Peña Gomez—and someday of becoming president of the Dominican Republic.

Note

1. This article was originally published in the *Afro Hispanic Review*, vol. 32, no. 2, 2013, pp. 111–18, ; it is re-published here with permission from the editor. The version published here is slightly modified for readability.

Works Cited

Alvarez, Julia. "Re: Border of Lights." Message to the author. 9 Dec. 2011. E-mail.
Kimmelman, Michael. "Germany's new 'textbook' on the Holocaust." *The New York Times*. 27 Feb. 2008.

Moya Pons, Frank. "Las ocho fronteras de Haití y la República Dominicana," in *La frontera: Prioridad en la agenda nacional del siglo XXI*, ed. Secretaría de Estado de las Fuerzas Armadas, Editora de las I Fuerzas Armadas Dominicanas, 2004.

Lemkin, Raphael and Samantha Power. "Axis Rule in Occupied Europe: Laws of Occupation, Analysis of Government, Proposals for Redress." *Lawbook Exchange*, 2005.

Wooding, Bridget. "Haitian Immigrants and Their Descendants Born in the Dominican Republic." *Oxford Research Encyclopedia of Latin American History.* https://doi.org/10.1093/acrefore/9780199 366439.013.474.

"World Heritage Center: Slave Routes." United Nations Educational, Scientific, and Cultural Organization.

Yo soy esa negra[1]

Rosa Iris Diendomi Álvarez

Yo soy esa negra nacida en cafetales, crecí entre cañaverales en aquellas comunidades donde aún hay presencia de mis raíces ancestrales, esa que es condenada al desprecio de cobardes que solo les han interesado explotarlos con coraje.

Yo soy esa negra que el batey ha parido, con trabajo y sacrificio avanzando en el dolor, luchando junto a los míos, esos miles que hoy los han llevado a un limbo, quitándoles la oportunidad de un nombre y apellido, y lo peor está que la nacionalidad es un limbo indefinido, y no por casualidad.

Yo soy esa negra que siempre escucharás denunciando tus abusos, aunque me quieras matar, siempre denunciaré el amargo que has causado al truncar nuestras vidas, arrancar nuestros derechos, nuestros sueños anhelados, estudiar, trabajar, aportar más al Estado, pero has preferido violar los derechos más sagrados de una parte de la población, por estigma y discriminación, durante décadas has ignorado las leyes y el debido proceso contra los hijos de haitianos.

Yo soy esa negra que has intentado silenciar tocando lo más sagrado que es el fruto de mi vientre, a ellos los defiendo con uñas y dientes sin importar cuanto me cueste. Solo quiero recordarle nada dura para siempre, hoy somos más unidos y conscientes del derecho que tenemos constitucionalmente. No siga jugando a confundir a la gente, sembrando odio y dolor, distrayendo la atención de los verdaderos problemas que tiene la nación, el alto costo de la vida, endeudamiento sin compasión, el dólar por las nubes, la salud empeorando, el desempleo cada vez peor, salarios de miserias, la inseguridad ciudada ya no es percepción, los negocios de aposentos que mantienen impunidad, y la corrupción, mientras unos implacables se hacen dueños de la administración, no hay régimen de consecuencias, eso llora ante Dios y los ojos de un pueblo que ya no aguanta ésta situación.

Condenan a los que denuncian, informan o defienden los intereses del pueblo, acosan al que eleva su voz o no se somete a lo que diga el "jefe".

Me uno a aquellas voces disidentes que les duele este pais y que, de verdad, ama a su gente.

Yo soy esa negra orgullosa del batey, cuya mayor riqueza es su gente buena, trabajadora, que luchar es lo que sabe hacer, seguiremos adelante venciendo el mal con el bien.

Nota

1. Escrito en octubre de 2019 con motivo del segundo aniversario de la autora fuera de la República Dominicana como asilada política.

El corte

Óscar Zazo

Sus ojos enrojecidos, ahora desorbitados dentro de aquel rostro que se desencajaba por momentos, percibían incrédulos el dantesco espectáculo que ya su olfato le venía previniendo desde hacía rato.

El reflejo del inclemente sol reverberaba en la inamovible llanura, los cirros sesgados en el cielo carecían de movimiento aparente, solo unos chivos bajo la sombra precaria de un cambrón, mordisqueaban con parsimonia algunas briznas de yerba seca.

La mirada del hombre se perdía en el horizonte sin prestarle atención al abrasador paisaje, absolutamente ajeno a lo que el destino le tenía reservado, fantaseaba con lo que habría tras lontananza y en las oportunidades que brindaba la vida para los que no se conformaran con aquella existencia miserable. Su determinación y sus músculos, razonaba, debían servir para algo más que cavar la tierra seca. Y solo la idea de ver crecer a su hijo en un mundo mejor le inducía a soñar.

"Piensas demasiado" le había dicho su joven esposa. "Piensas mucho y eso puede ser pecado" le repetía con frecuencia. Ella, por el contrario, agradecía a Dios cada día por permitirle vivir con su hijo y su hombre en la choza que este le construyera con sus propias manos.

Para ella la vida en aquella región fronteriza transcurría tranquila y ajena a las intrigas políticas que respecto a la línea divisoria tuvieran por ese entonces Vincent y Trujillo, presidentes respectivos de Haití y República Dominicana, ni a las decisiones trascendentes que el mandatario dominicano estaba a punto de tomar en aquel otoño de 1937.

En la zona se hablaba creole y español, y en ambas riberas del río Masacre se comerciaba con todo tipo de productos, dependiendo de la temporada, y al alcance de quien los pudiera pagar. Dominicanos y haitianos convivían con naturalidad y se compadraban con frecuencia apadrinando niños de ambos orígenes.

Una noche calurosa, después de sopesarlo bien, el hombre confesó a su compadre la idea de llegar hasta Cap Haitian o Puerto Plata y pedir trabajo en el primer barco que lo llevara lejos. Estaba seguro que ningún lugar podía ser tan pobre y miserable como aquel. A donde fuera, ahorraría lo suficiente para llevarse a su mujer y a su hijo y vivir con dignidad. El vecino, aun escéptico por tan incierta aventura, le prometió que, dado el caso, daría amparo a la comadre y al ahijado hasta su regreso.

Sin embargo, la joven madre no quiso ni oír hablar de tan alocada empresa. "Aquí vivimos en paz y siempre aparece algo que comer" argumentaba tratando de disuadirlo. Y cada día se afanaba para que cuando él llegara del campo encontrara todo el confort que era capaz de procurarle. Le ayudaba a bañarse echándole agua con el higüero y le servía la cena que preparaba temprano para que estuviera lista a su vuelta del trabajo.

Pasaban los días y él iba retrasando la partida, pero no por eso olvidaba su proyecto. Por encima de todo, conservaba la idea obstinada de salir de la miseria; la misma terca obsesión que debieron mantener sus antepasados por lograr la libertad. Él sabía que en cualquier momento tomaría la decisión y se iría sin avisar . . .

Aún no había amanecido cuando escuchó el trote de los caballos y las voces afuera. Era la guardia apremiándoles a salir para llevárselos al cuartel junto a varias decenas de hombres, mujeres, ancianos y niños que iban llegando en caravana, custodiados por todos los flancos y azuzados como si fueran cabezas de ganado. Los soldados que entraron a buscarlos no atendían a razones ni a preguntas, por lo que solo pudieron vestirse aprisa, tomar al bebé e incorporarse al grupo que llegaba.

De camino, los detenidos entrecruzaban murmullos preguntándose la causa de su detención, varios susurraron "perejil" como la palabra maldita culpable de su desgracia. Algunos especulaban con algún problema ocasionado por un grupo de vecinos, ya que se había oído hablar de heridos y muertos, pero a ellos, razonaban, les soltarían en cuanto comprobaran su inocencia. Otros más pesimistas hablaban de deportación. Aun así, todos sabían que la frontera era bastante permeable, más bien una línea simbólica que albergaba actividad comercial a uno y otro lado; empleadas domésticas trabajaban de día en territorio dominicano pero dormían en el haitiano, y multitud de niños, para ir a la escuela cruzaban la frontera y en la tarde regresaban a sus casas. De manera que si en verdad, a partir de entonces cambiaban las cosas, la nueva situación afectaría gravemente sus vidas. Mientras, la cuadrilla de uniformados en avanzada, arrestaba a cuantos haitianos encontraban a su paso, revisando casa por casa.

Con esas lucubraciones y otras por el estilo, avanzaba la columna cada vez más nutrida y cada quien, haciendo sus cábalas y conjeturas. Pero todos, todos, acusaban el doloroso trance de dejar atrás, casa, trabajo y amigos. Ojalá obedeciera solo a una coyuntura y luego volvieran las aguas a su cauce habitual, pensaban con escasa convicción . . .

En el transcurso del día se había ido abarrotando de detenidos la explanada del cuartel. El desconcierto y la incertidumbre eclipsaban en parte el hambre y la sed de la muchedumbre; sin embargo, nadie se quejaba y el grave silencio solo era roto por el llanto esporádico de algún niño.

El hombre y su mujer permanecían juntos dando como podían sombra a su bebé, a quien ella amamantaba cada cierto tiempo para calmarle la sed.

Ambos habían observado preocupados cómo durante las últimas horas, los soldados tomaban ron sin recato mientras iban y venían con una actividad poco usual.

A una orden del capitán, que retumbó en la explanada, se abrieron los portones traseros y la muchedumbre fue avanzando hacia la llanura. Los soldados y algunos civiles armados con aspecto facineroso, se apostaban a ambos lados de la marea negra que avanzaba con pesadez.

El movimiento fue acogido con cierto alivio por el gentío, que ya en el transcurso del día había ido asumiendo su deportación, y quien más y quien menos iba pensando en parientes o amigos a quienes recurrir del otro lado de la frontera, mientras se calmaba todo.

Ya fuera del cuartel, se sintió cómo se levantaba algo de brisa que formaba pequeños remolinos de polvo aliviando algo el calor sofocante de todo un día de hacinamiento entre cientos, tal vez miles de semejantes.

Ahora la gigantesca marea se desplazaba lenta pero inexorable hacia adelante. A esas alturas ya todos encajaban la adversidad y daban por hecha su expatriación; sin embargo, él observaba con suspicacia un comportamiento extraño en los guardias y custodios cada vez más embriagados y alterados esquivando miradas, incluso cuando sacaban a alguna joven de las filas para desaparecer tras los matorrales. En esas ocasiones los esposos se miraban en silencio, pensando que si ese era el precio por evitar la deportación... resultaba demasiado caro.

Aunque el centro de aquel caudal humano era más caluroso que las orillas, ellos lo prefirieron deliberadamente para evitar la proximidad e incluso el contacto visual con cualquier custodio. Aun así, ya casi de noche, un guardia se fijó en ella y la llamó desde lejos, pero la joven madre se limitó a cambiar de brazo a su bebé y a aferrarse a él con la mirada baja. Por fortuna, el militar desistió y siguió buscando entre el torrente humano.

Al rato, a él le pareció que llegaban a la cabeza de aquella gigantesca columna que se perdía tras una pendiente que ascendía ligeramente unos doscientos metros. Supusieron aliviados que detrás de aquél promontorio estarían los camiones, pero les extrañó no escuchar el lógico trasiego de sus motores al salir cargados de gente y al regresar vacíos para volver a cargar.

Aquel silencio pesado, solo alterado por el arrastrar de tantos pies descalzos sobre la tierra seca, comenzó a convertirse en un lúgubre presagio. Él supo que algo no andaba bien y trató de alzarse y saltar para ver en la semioscuridad del crepúsculo, pero todo lo que distinguía era el cambio de rasante que producía el desnivel de allí delante y la fila estrechándose en forma de embudo, impuesta por los soldados y custodios.

Ahora estaba seriamente preocupado: arrestados sin explicaciones, conducidos como ganado, todo el día sin beber ni comer, y ahora entrando casi de uno en uno sabría Dios dónde...

De pronto se maldijo por no haberse decidido antes a realizar su éxodo; puede que a esas alturas ya estuvieran los tres muy lejos de allí viviendo la vida digna que había soñado. Quiso enrostrárselo a su mujer, pero dadas las circunstancias prefirió omitirlo.

Ya estaban a pocos metros del desnivel cuando alcanzó a ver movimientos siniestros, casi mecánicos y respiraciones entrecortadas, acompañadas de reniegos procedentes de los guardias.

Después de unos metros, se le detuvo el corazón.

Sus ojos enrojecidos, ahora desorbitados dentro de aquel rostro que se desencajaba por momentos, percibían incrédulos el dantesco espectáculo que ya su olfato le venía previniendo desde hacía rato.

Sangre. Mucha sangre.

El guardia de la derecha, con el uniforme ya teñido de rojo, sujetaba al desdichado de turno y el de la izquierda, igualmente ensangrentado, le levantaba el brazo y le hundía la bayoneta entre la tercera y la cuarta costilla, al instante se le doblaban las rodillas y con un leve empujón caía a la fosa. Así, con gestos parecidos repetían la acción con aquellos pobres desgraciados que, como animales domésticos, llegaban sumisos al matadero.

Aun aprisionados como estaban, él se colocó con un movimiento crispado delante de su mujer. No fue valentía ni sentido de protección. Más bien lo contrario. Se adelantó para recibir su puñalada y cerrar los ojos mientras caía a la fosa antes de ver como hundían el cuchillo, primero en el cuerpecito de su bebé sin que este apenas se removiera antes de expirar y en el de su mujer, justo detrás del seno, antes de caer aferrando a su hijo al regazo aún después de muerta.

Morir Soñando[1]

Jasminne Mendez

"Like a parrot imitating spring,
we lie down screaming as rain punches through
and we come up green."
-Rita Dove

I had a dream once:

My machete hands slice open
calcified white green *caña*.

I milk my tongue into a glass
of homemade *morir soñando*. Watch it
roll into "r's" *colorado*, singing: *perejil, perejil.*

Lash my sun kissed lips with sugar
to sweeten this *café con leche* skin.
Paint my pupil with the pulp of a *banilejo* mango
and bathe in seawater sweat singing: perejil, perejil

Cave into the earth that surrounds me.
Fill my flesh with *fango*. Swallow
the sounds of the island and bloom
from the bones buried beneath. Wake up
wounded. Wake up singing: perejil, perejil.

**

Cutting cane for the general:

Stalks of severed limbs lay bare.
Sea foam spills from veins.

Machetes hack at wounded flesh.
Fill breath to the brim with salt.
Bathe the earth in *sangre*––

Set the field on fire.
Fire to harvest the cane.
Fire to flower the *flamboyán*
Fire the scent of parsley.

Fire the sound of blade
hitting bone hitting body––
Fire 'till it swallowed me
crimson––Fire 'till I die
while dreaming.[2]

Notes

1. First published by *Label me Latina/o* Special Issue: Afro-Latina/o Literature and Performance. Summer 2017, Volume VII.

2. Listen to Mendez reciting "Morir Soñando" here: http://www.jasminnemendez.com/projects

Fwontyè Limye yo, 2019

Komedi Mikal PGNE

Fotograf: Presuma Bulgary

Videos from this performance are accessible online. Visit https://youtu.be/vx3UkRJVaxE and https://youtu.be/TWmveTTEj0g.

Dajabón en acuarela

Laura Ramos

Negritud de las fronteras[1]

Ilses Toribio

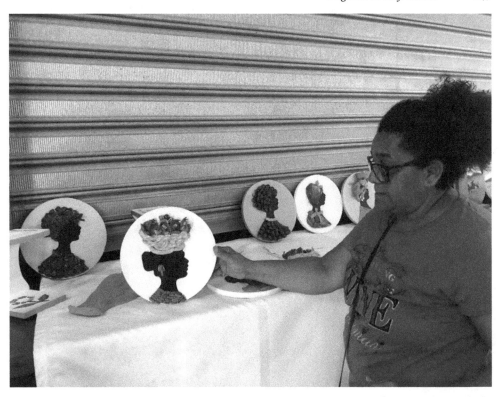

Nota

1. Escuche a Ilses hablando de esta serie en la sección IV, Voice Notes from la frontera. (Listen to Ilses talking about this series in Section IV: Voice Notes from la frontera online at acpress.amherst.edu).

In Dialogue with Pierre Michel Jean
Selected photographs from *L'oubli pour mensonge*
Pierre Michel Jean

What motivated you to tell this story (of the 1937 Massacre)?

J'ai réellement commencé à travailler sur la question du massacre de 1937 après juin 2015. Alors qu'avec mon collectif de journalistes d'Haïti, nous travaillions sur la crise migratoire à la frontière haïtienne sud-Est après la fin du PNRE (Plan National de Régularisation des Etrangers). Des milliers d'immigrés haïtiens illégaux vivants en République Dominicaine depuis des années sont retournés d'eux-mêmes en Haïti à la fin de ce programme au cours duquel ils n'avaient pas pu se régulariser. Cela m'avait étonné. Quand j'ai cherché à comprendre les raisons qui expliquaient ce phénomène. Quasiment toutes les personnes que j'ai interrogées m'ont dit avoir eu peur d'être victimes d'un autre massacre en République Dominicaine comme en 1937. En effet, le contexte tendu du PNRE a fait qu'une certaine parole s'était décomplexée et que certains Dominicains anti haïtiens avaient pu exprimer ouvertement leur aversion avec des référents de *perejil* en juin 2015. Ce qui m'a intéressé, à ce moment-là était: Pourquoi les Haïtiens avaient encore cet horizon-là 78 ans après le massacre? Mais aussi: Pourquoi certains Dominicains se sentaient en droit d'évoquer cet épisode sombre de l'histoire de l'île impunément? Je me suis dit à moi-même que quelque chose manquait dans la façon cette histoire est passée à la postérité. C'est en ce sens que j'ai entrepris mes recherches. Pour trouver des réponses à mes questions, mais aussi pour vulgariser le plus que possible l'atrocité que qu'a été ce chapitre noir de l'histoire de l'île Quisqueya.

Do you think this history is one more often told from the Dominican perspective or from the perspective of the diaspora?

Je pense que du côté Haïtien que les ouvrages et les recherches scientifiques sur ce chapitre de l'histoire de l'île manquent cruellement. Dans le cadre de mon travail, les auteurs et historiens haïtiens qui ont écrit des livres sur ce sujet ne sont pas nombreux. Le travail de Jean Price Mars, Suzy Castor, Lesly Francois Manigat sont éclairant. Des articles ici et là pour des revues scientifiques et spécialisées. Plusieurs romans, quoique cela soit des fictions écrit à partir des faits m'ont aidé à m'approprier des symboles et du ressentis des Haïtiens par rapport à ce drame. C'est le cas de l'œuvre d'Edwidge Danticat, de René

Philoctète, de Jacques Stephen Alexis et de Antony Lespes. Je n'ai pas connu pas tous les ouvrages dominicains se référant au massacre de 1937 en raison de la barrière de la langue, elles ne sont pas vendues en Haïti. Cependant parmi les ouvrages fournis sur la question j'ai trouvé celui de Bernado Vega (Trujillo et Haïti). Je n'ai pas fait un inventaire de toutes les publications dominicaines sur la question, mais de ce que j'ai remarqué, c'est que la diaspora dominicaine et haïtienne, aux Etats-Unis surtout. Est plus décomplexés à parler et à s'engager sur cette question. En témoigne les écrits et les positions d'Edwidge Danticat, d'Edward Paulino et Julia Alvarez. L'engagement des intellectuels locaux et contemporains sur cette question est attendu.

Why is it important for Haitians to tell their own story and to re-claim their own story?

Je crois qu'il est important pour les Haïtiens de s'approprier leur histoire, surtout par rapport ce drame. D'abord pour connaitre et faire connaitre mieux les faits afin qu'ils ne se reproduisent plus. Mais aussi parce que sur une histoire comme cela, les faits lorsqu'ils sont présentés par une entité extérieure sont souvent sujets à des doutes de manipulations. Je crois qu'il est toujours bien qu'une pléiade d'historiens et de chercheurs de tout horizon s'accaparent et travaillent sur une question telle que le massacre de 1937. La vérité se retrouvera toujours grandie.

What surprised you most while you were filming?

Mon travail sur la mémoire du massacre de 1937 est tant photographique que cinématographique. Dans le cadre de ce périple qui n'a pas encore terminé malheureuse j'ai été appelé à parler beaucoup de personnes rescapées, alors qu'ils étaient enfant du massacre. Ce qui me parait étonnant à chaque fois est la générosité avec laquelle elles me reçoivent et m'accordent du temps pour m'aider dans ma quête. Encore plus étonnant est que d'un site à un autre, même très loin, la mémoire de ces gens reste fidèle malgré leur grand âge. Leurs témoignages et récits concordent avec les livres d'histoires, comme si les gens ne vivaient que pour transmettre cette mémoire.

What images did you find to be the most moving?

Iralie Pierre, une femme rescapée qui avait 18 ans au moment du massacre, n'avait plus l'usage de la parole et moment du travail. J'ai interviewé son fils qui m'a raconté son histoire, elle n'écoutait pas loin et émettait des bruits certaines fois comme pour acquiescer. Malgré sa faiblesse dû à une maladie, visiblement Pakinston, elle a tenu à se lever pour la photo et sa petite fille lui a soutenu la tête comme si elle présentait à l'optique de ma caméra un vestige du passé. J'ai senti que c'était comme un cadeau, qu'ils m'avaient fait. Iralie est morte quelque mois après ma rencontre avec elle.

How do you describe the documentary? Do you think it is educational? Who/What groups of people do you feel most need to be educated about the Parsley Massacre?

Pour moi, le documentaire c'est avant tout une quête, une sorte d'ingénierie du réel vu par un auteur. Ce n'est pas forcément que je cherche à révéler quelque chose dans mes travaux.

Ce qui est important pour moi est de montrer ou d'expliquer l'envers des choses. Dans mon projet sur la mémoire du massacre de 1937 en photographie, il était important pour moi de donner un visage au massacre par l'entremise des rescapés, de leur vie et de comment l'état Haïti avait géré cet évènement. "Perejil" n'est pas étudié à l'école, donc c'est un projet qui visait avant toute chose à faire connaitre cette histoire. Oui, un documentaire a une portée pédagogique, mais c'est loin d'être que cela. L'esthétique compte pour beaucoup aussi. C'est vrai qu'on a tendance à l'oublier, mais un photographe et cinéaste de documentaire c'est aussi un artiste.

Where did most of the filming take place?

Dans le cadre d'une résidence de recherche j'ai pu faire un premier travail sur "Perejil". La restitution avait été bien accueillie pour le quatre-vingtième de la commémoration du massacre à Port-au-Prince. Cette première étape consistait à donner la parole aux rescapés et à mettre en perspective ce massacre avec les faits d'aujourd'hui. Un livret et une production vidéo de 6 minutes restituent cette première partie du travail. Présentement, je travaille en photographie sur un livre qui traitera plus de la migration haïtienne en République dominicaine, seulement un chapitre traitera de la mémoire de Perejil. En cinéma, je travaille sur un documentaire qui a comme sujet principal l'héritage du massacre. C'est-à-dire comment "Perejil" entrave aujourd'hui encore les relations haitiano-dominicaines. Ce travail sera un documentaire de 70 minutes que j'ai commencé à tourner à Port-au-Prince, un peu à Ouanaminthe et plus tard dans plusieurs villes dominicaines.

How did you locate some of the survivors with whom you spoke in the documentary?

Trouver les survivants n'a pas été facile. Avant mon travail, dans les villes frontalières je rencontrais des gens qui me racontaient avoir connu ou rencontré tel ou tel rescapé par le passé, mais qui était à présent décédé. C'est dans l'ouvrage de Jean Price Mars, Les relations haïtiens-dominicaines Tome II, que j'ai entendu parler des colonies agricoles pour la première fois. En effet, à la fin du chapitre où il traite du massacre de 1937 et l'indemnisation, il cite : *"Trois centres de colonies agricoles, destinées à retenir les paysans de la région frontalière sur le sol haïtien, l'un au morne des Commissaires, un autre à Dosmond et le troisième à Biliguy, sur le plateau Central, entre Maïssade et Saint Michel de l'Attalaye."* Il se révélera par la suite qu'il existe plus colonies que celles relatées par l'auteur, deux autres plus informelles existent l'une à Grand Bassin et l'autre au cœur de la Forêt des pins. Effectivement, il m'a fallu du temps pour les trouver puisque les lieux avaient certaines fois changer de noms. Je rappelle juste que le livre de Jean Price Mars date de 1953. Certaines fois, j'ai dû me rendre sur place et enquêter dans les villes voisines avant de trouver les emplacements de ces colonies. Des familles issues de la lignée des rescapés vivent encore sur ces terres, parfois je rencontrais par chance un rescapé ici et là, âgé et qui était petit au moment des faits. Certains ont encore de la mémoire, d'autres n'ont connu le massacre qu'au travers les histoires racontées par les parents. La plus âgée au moment de Perejil que j'ai rencontré avait 18 ans au moment des faits.

Figure 1: Mapou, Ferrier, 2015.

Figure 2: Des marchandes et travailleurs de Ouanaminthe (Haïti) obliges de franchir en toute hate la Rivière Massacre par la voie officieuse pour le marché binational de Dajabón (République dominicaine).

Figure 3: La problématique de la frontière haïtiano-dominicaine était au Coeur de nombreux conflits entre les deux pays avant l'accord bilateral définitif sur le tracé de la frontière en 1935, soit deux années avant le massacre "Perejil." Ce dernier, pour de nombreux partisans de Trujillo, borreau des Haïtiens, était une façon drastique d'établir une delimitation ethnique entre les deux pays après en avoir établi la frontière politique.

Derrière les masques/Detrás de las máscaras

Jacmel, Haiti – Haití

Polibio Díaz

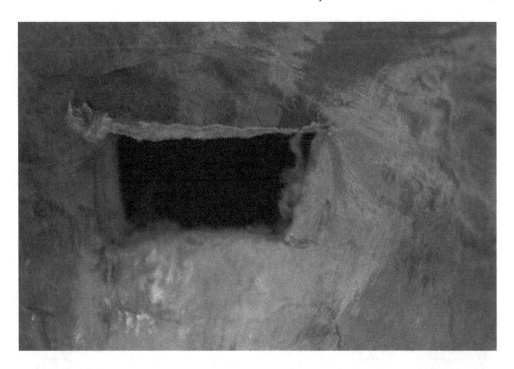

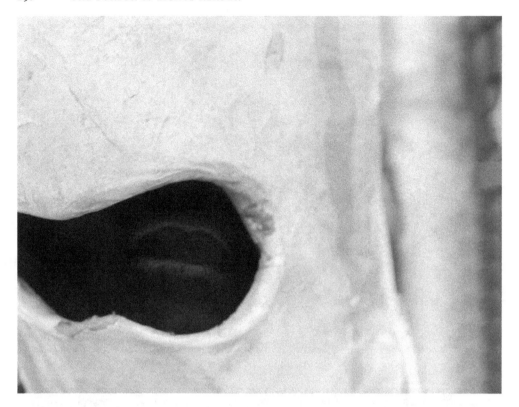

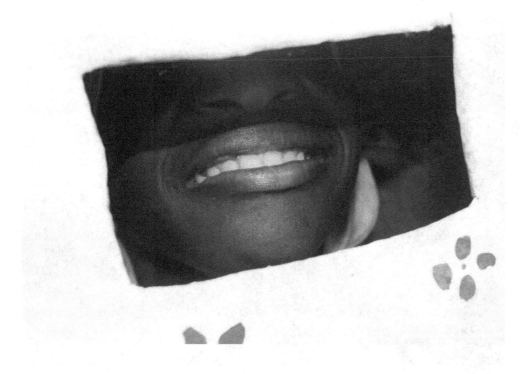

Border of Lights

Julia Alvarez

In 1937, a little-known massacre occurred on the border between Haiti and the Dominican Republic. Beginning in early October and ongoing for several weeks, the Dominican dictator, Rafael Leonidas Trujillo, ordered the slaughter of any Haitian caught on the Dominican side of the border, a border only recently redrawn and invisible to all but those privy to maps.

Historians differ on the number of casualties—from a "conservative" estimate of 6,000 to a possible 20,000, or more. Since the dead cannot speak and those thrown in the sea leave no trace behind, it's impossible to verify an exact count. Some historians cite this discrepancy as a reason to discredit the massacre altogether. Others insist it was not murder, but an act of self-defense. After all, in 1822, Haitian troops had occupied the Dominican Republic. Who was to say they wouldn't try again in 1937, or any subsequent year? During election season, it was especially convenient to have an enemy on whom to blame the problems of the current administration.

The massacre is popularly known as "the parsley massacre" from the purported use of the plant's name to determine who would die. An impromptu test was devised to distinguish between dark-skinned Dominicans and Haitians, who claimed to be Dominican, in order to avoid getting killed. The would-be victim would be asked to identify a sprig of *perejil*. A Haitian Kreyòl speaker would not trill the *r* as a Spanish-speaker would, so if the word was mispronounced, the man, woman, or child would be decapitated with a machete, stabbed with a bayonet, or bludgeoned to death. Trujillo's soldiers had been ordered not to use ammunition, so that the killings could not be traced back to his military. To this day, the Dominican Republic has yet to openly address or adequately redress this crime against humanity.

As a Dominican, I am ashamed of my country's refusal to acknowledge this disgraceful chapter in our history. For those who argue that the past is past, we need look no further than the September 2013 ruling (#168/13) by the Tribunal Constitucional, the highest court in the land, retroactively revoking the citizenship of an estimated 300,000 Dominicans of Haitian descent, rendering them stateless and legally nonexistent. As Padre Regino, an activist Jesuit priest working on the border, commented, "We eliminated them with knives in 1937; now we do it cleanly with laws."

Those of us who have spoken up have received threats and denunciations on a number of social platforms as traitors. This vehement defense of a violent crime is painfully ironic given that we are the country that gave the world the glorious example of the Mirabal sisters, whose murder by Trujillo's caliés brought down the dictatorship. In 1999, the United Nations declared November 25, the day of their murder, International Day for the Elimination of Violence against Women. We, Dominicans, should feel especially compelled to uphold their high standards in defending the rights of those who are victims of violence and discrimination.

In 2012, a group of Dominicans and Haitians of the Diaspora in solidarity with citizens from both countries and other advocates formed a movement called Border of Lights. That October, the seventy-fifth anniversary, we gathered to commemorate the massacre and initiate a series of collaborative community programs between the border towns of Dajabón and Ouanaminthe. The following year, soon after the ruling was passed, the authorities would not permit us to mass at the border for a vigil. In response, we instituted a "virtual" vigil whereby supporters around the world could post "a light" and a message of support. The participation proved even larger than if we had restricted ourselves to boots on the ground. Since then, we have continued to conduct annual Border of Lights gatherings, a core group participating with community members and organizations on the border, others joining in from afar through online participation and donations to fund the movement's collaborative programs and projects.

One of these projects took place the first year of our gathering. We wanted to assess what stories the townspeople on the border had been told about 1937. Since the massacre is rarely studied in history classes, it was no surprise that few townspeople had even heard of it. I myself only learned of the massacre in the USA in my twenties when I read Albert C. Hicks's chilling book on the dictatorship, *Blood in the Streets*; later I would encounter Rita Dove's poem, "Parsley," in an anthology. Some townspeople knew of the massacre and believed the regime's propaganda about a Haitian invasion. We posted the testimonials on postcards hung on clotheslines in the town center for all to read. A town meeting followed with locals and historians sharing stories and listening to discussions and lectures about the two countries and our intertwined histories. Border of Lights had facilitated a conversation which continues to this day.

In keeping with the postcard project, I wrote the poem, "1937: What Did They Tell You?" based on a story my tía Estela told me late in her life. In 1937, she had been living close to the border on a farm, which was overrun by the guardia. She was able to save a few Haitians by hiding them under a pile of laundry. One of her neighbors hid a Haitian infant in a wooden case with the statue of a saint which hung on the wall. That baby, José Francisco Peña Gómez, would grow up to run for president of the Dominican Republic in the early 1990s, in elections marred by fraud, racist and xenophobic attacks. *A vote for Peña Gómez is a vote to unite us with Haiti*, ran one of the slogans. Some of his supporters showed up to vote only to discover their names had vanished from the voting rolls. The past is not past but continues to this day. As the historian, Eduardo Galeano, once noted, "History never says goodbye. History says: 'see you later.'"

There is a tradition in Latin America of the testimonio, whereby those who have been the victims of violence bear witness to what has happened. The triumph of any oppressive system is complete if it results in silencing those who can speak about the atrocities that it has committed.

"Dar a luz," we say in Spanish. When a child is born, a mother brings him or her out to the light. The speaker in the poem, born on the night of the massacre, takes that phrase to heart, breaking the silence, bringing her testimony to light.

1937: WHAT DID THEY TELL YOU?
¿QUÉ TE CONTARON?
KI KONTE OU?

We lived in a small town on a border
we could not see, marked by a river
where women washed clothes, while
their children splashed in the shallows,
their laughter in Kreyòl or Spanish—
impossible to tell one from the other.
No one knew why the river was called
El Masacre—as nothing was written down.
We knew only what they told us.

They told us 1937 was a good year
for crops: sugarcane, mahogany, campeche
Germans bought for their dyes.
There was money to marry a sweetheart,
buy shoes for the children, silk stockings
for a querida, and for the wife a gold chain
with a medal of la Virgencita
to make her smile like a bride again.
Abuela helped a new generation of mothers
giving birth. It rained almost daily,
a downpour, afterwards the air smelled
of romero, oregano, cilantro, perejil.

They told us el Jefe would visit
in October, an honor for our town
far from the splendors of the capital.
For weeks, they prepared: laid down
hay on the streets to muffle the noise
of wheel carts. Beauties avoided
the sun, posed before mirrors,
trying out their new gowns,
draping mantillas over combs.
Who would his eye fall on?

At the welcome reception, el Jefe
asked about the border. *Todo bien,*
claimed those with Haitians cutting
cane in their fields, mining
salt on their coastal plains.
Others complained, *Ay, Jefe,*
los Haitianos are stealing our cattle,
raping our women, converting Christian
souls to their Vodou religion.
El Jefe's face darkened.
We must solve this problem
before Africa invades us from the west,
before we become so much like them,
no one will be able to tell
a Dominican from a Haitian.

That night was a quiet night, the stars
like sparks from cooking fires, the smell
of leña in fogones, the víveres boiling in pots,
the sizzle of queso frito and huevos frying.
It was Sunday, feast day of San Cipriano,
Santa Cándida, San Maximiliano—
mártires, the priest called them,
a word they did not know.
But before the night was over,
they would know thousands of them.

It was dark when they heard the howling
like the cries of the condemned
roaming the earth for souls
to pull down to hell with them.
They told us they banked their fires,
hurried the children indoors, clapped closed
the shutters, knelt and prayed in the dark.
My mother's legs parted as she labored
to bring me to the light. No one dared
go to the well for water after the buckets
they had filled for my birth were used up.

There was a knock on the door.
They told me they all fell silent.
Abuela stuffed the corner of a sheet
in my mother's mouth to muffle

her screams. *Silencio, silencio. No one home!*
But the knocking refused to believe them:
¡Abran! ¡Abran! a familiar voice shouted.
It was our neighbor Jacksaint, his skin
hanging from his arms like a shirt
he was taking off, a man who'd been to hell
and back. A martyr without an altar.

They told me they pulled him inside
and barred the door, just as my mother
brought me to the light. I wailed,
trying out my new lungs. I was wailing
when the guardia pounded at our door
¡Abran! ¡En el nombre de la patria!
Abuela gestured to Jacksaint to hide
under the bloody sheets piled
in the corner. I was wailing
when the guardia burst in, thrusting
their bayonets before them, as if to open
a birth canal for the dead to pass through . . .
—words failed them as they told us.

The guardia held up a sprig of green.
Name this! An odd command from men
with bayonets coated with blood,
machetes flecked with flesh, a question
a mother or grandmother might ask
a young girl learning the names of herbs
in the garden. *Perejil*, Abuela cried out,
along with my tías gathered to help
my mother bring me to the light.
¡Perejil! ¡Perejil! A chorus of cries,
rounding their vowels, trilling
their Spanish r's to save their lives.

They told me the guardia were satisfied,
but as they turned to go, a young recruit
spotted the bloody heap of linens on the floor
and stepped forward, bayonet drawn.
Abuela leapt up, shouting:
Don't you dare ruin my linens, Pepito!
You owe me more respect than that.
I helped your mother bring you to the light.

They told me that boy shrunk like the leaves
of the moriviví when touched; he took
his cap in his hands. *Con su permiso, madrina,*
he bowed, backing his way out of our hut.
They told me I wailed all night.
My mother's breasts could not fill me,
her caresses still me, her cooing voice
reassure me. They told me Jacksaint
was saved but he never spoke again.
They followed his example: keeping
their own counsel to save their lives.

They told me if anyone asked what
what I'd been told about 1937,
I should say it was a good year
for crops—sugarcane, mahogany, campeche
Germans bought for their dyes—
but for a scarcity of parsley,
not a sprig to be found in our gardens
to flavor the sancochos for navidad.
They told me never to tell what they told me;
they warned me what would happen:
I, too, would be sent to hell, come back
with ribbons of skin on my arms,
instead of satin ones in my hair.

But 1937 was the year I was born,
the year my mother brought me to the light,
not to the darkness of silence and lies,
which is why I am telling you
what they told me, bringing this story
to the light. Take it and tell it.
Do not let the dead die twice.

"For Petronila, the Weaver" and "Petronila"

Rhina P. Espaillat

FOR PETRONILA, THE WEAVER

Petronila, here on my family tree
I've found your name on a blurred, wavering line
that nonetheless proclaims your unity
with my forebear, who made you one of mine.
How many twists of fate had there to be
for us to intertwine!

Before the altar with Spain's migrant son,
you took his name, now mine. But was he true?
Did he honor, in you, that sad man who,
crossing the sea in chains—of many, one—
bequeathed your skin its color—and mine too—
of honeyed cinnamon?

And did your husband, with his love's coin, pay
for blood drawn with the lash, the hideous debt
owed to the unpaid labor of those yet
unrecompensed? Though we know it was they
harvested wealth for masters that none may
forgive, much less forget.

Your name, Petronila, on this page
conjures the various threads Fate gave you—doom
and blessings—to work with, on the loom
your flesh became. With what a blend of rage
and love—and pain love labored to assuage—
you wove us in your womb!

PETRONILA

Petronila, en el árbol familiar
de mi ascendencia, he dado con tu nombre,
en un borroso renglón que quiere aunar
tu vida con la vida de aquel hombre—
¿Cuántos *tátaros* son, si he de contar?—
que te llevó al altar.

Aquel hijo de España, enamorado,
te entregó mi apellido. ¿Te fué fiel?
¿Supo honrar en tu carne al desdichado
bis—o tátaro—abuelo que, secuestrado
en África, en trabas, nos legó esta piel
entre canela y miel?

¿Quiso, con la moneda de su amor,
pagar la horrenda deuda incalculable
debida a los que, a fuerza de labor
obligado, y trato abominable,
crearon en mi tierra gran valor
y culpa imperdonable?

Nombrada entre los míos en esta fila,
no hay seña que indica si sufriste,
pero tu origen abarca asunto triste.
Con tan ásperas fibras no se hila
vida de seda. Pero en tu vientre urdiste
mi pueblo, Petronila.

La matanza de haitianos, Movimiento 1

Juan Colón

En el 2010 fui llamado por la fundación del Señor Luis Mojica para componer la música de un ensayo literario sobre la "Matanza del Perejil" llevada a cabo por el dictador Rafael Leónidas Trujillo Molina.

Fue de gran significado para mí, desde joven había sentido mucha curiosidad histórica sobre ese evento que sucedió en el 1937. Traté de escuchar a las Cuatro Estaciones del compositor Antonio Vivaldi, para tomar la idea de llevar al pentagrama los paisajes, donde la emoción, la musicalidad, y las orquestaciones iban acorde a los diferentes estados de nuestra madre naturaleza.

Pensé durante una semana como podría aportar la alegría y, luego, entrar a la tristeza, al dolor, a la melancolía del abandono, a la depresión dentro de la familia, y como usar nuestros ritmos combinados con los ritmos haitianos y lograr un solo sentir, un solo dolor, un solo gemido, una sola expresión. Eso era un gran reto para mí, ya que solo tenía un tiempo máximo de treinta minutos, y dentro de ese lapso, tenia que dejar en el pentagrama todo un acontecimiento que estremecería al mundo.

Tristemente fue una matanza por abuso de poder, ya que nuestra población es, en un gran porcentaje, negra también. Creo que fue mi mayor desafío como músico. Al final me sentí satisfecho por haber logrado la aprobación de excepcionales músicos que tocaron dicha obra, un trabajo que me hizo crecer como ser humano y ver con mas profundidad el dolor humano y lo que es mas doloroso, la impotencia para lograr vivir una vida con dignidad.

Eschuche los comentarios de Colón sobre sus motivos por haber escrito La matanza de haitianos *y ver la partitura musical en la versión acceso abierto de* The Border of Lights Reader *a* http://www.acpress.amherst.edu.

Escuche la composición musical de Juan Colón titulada: La Matanza de Haitianos, Movimiento 1 *aquí:* http://www.acpress.amherst.edu

"Son para un negro que no está solo" and "Son for a negro who is not alone"

Osiris Mosquea

SON PARA UN NEGRO QUE NO ESTÁ SOLO

> *Hermano, yo recuerdo*
> *esa huella común que nos abraza*
> *y te amo sobre el muro de tu sangre.*
> Antonio Preciado

Cuando el sol esconde sus alas
y la luna se acuesta sobre el rio
el Masacre se pasa a pie.

Cuando el trapiche calla
el negro se tiende sobre el lino duro del bagazo por colchón
se estremece de ternura al lado de su negra
en la pleamar del amor
arropado con sábanas de estrellas
dibujando su cuerpo con la acuarela de sus dedos
el Masacre se pasa a pie.

Tras los conjuros de amor
el negro se olvida del trapiche
besa la noche toda suya
grande, grande, inmensa
nace de un pellizco la ilusión
se vacía el pecho, todo de un suspiro
pero el Masacre se pasa a pie.

El rio viene cantando, negra canción, negra
El negro canta, grita, gime, canta:
``Hay mi negra pancha vamos a bailar``
``Morena, la rumba tiene soltura pa tu cadera``

A lo lejos se oyen los acordes de un bolero
el botón de luz de la luciérnaga se deshace en el cañaveral
por la hendidura de la noche
se cuela el canto del gallo
el sol se desliza lento, lento sobre el río
cuando el Masacre, se pasa a pie.

SON FOR A NEGRO WHO IS NOT ALONE

> *Brother, I remember*
> *That common trace that embraces us both*
> *And I love you over the wall of your blood.*
>   Antonio Preciado

When the wings of the sun are hidden
and the moon lies on the river
the Massacre[1] can be crossed on foot

When the sugar mill goes silent
the negro lies on the crushed sugarcane pulp as a bed
and with tenderness lies by his lover's side
and in love's high tide
and under the sheet of the gazing stars
drawing his body with the watercolor of their fingers
they cross the Masacre on foot!

After the spells of love
the negro forgets the sugar mill
and kisses the night all his,
large, large and immense,
and from a pinch, an illusion is born
the chest empties out with a sigh
however, the Masacre is crossed on foot!

The river comes down singing, black song,
el negro sings, cries, moans, sings:
"Ay Mi Negra Pancha vamo'a bailar
Morena, la rumba tiene soltura pa'tu cadera"

In the distance the lyrics of a bolero can be heard
while in the sugarcane fields, a button of light vanishes from the fireflies
through the crevice of the night
the rooster's song sneaks along
and the sun disappears slowly, very slowly above the river
when you are crossing the Masacre on foot.

Note

1. The Masacre is the river that divides the island of the Hispaniola into two different countries, Haiti to the West and the Dominican Republic to the East.

For the Love of Lina
A Ten-Minute Play
Magaly Colimon

For the Love of Lina, Copyright 2012.

Playwright notes: While the names of the characters are real, the events in this play, to the best of my knowledge, are purely fictional.

CHARACTERS

Lina Lovaton Pittaluga – 19-year-old. Upper-class debutante. Future mistress of Rafael Leonidas Trujillo. Elegant, young, lithe, tall, regal, and beautiful. She is the only daughter of a very powerful attorney in the capital and a member of the old aristocracy of Santo Domingo. With the assistance of Trujillo's influence as ruler, she was ("the elegant female mascot") named the reigning Queen of the 1937 Carnival in Dominican Republic.

Rafael Leonidas Trujillo – 48 years old. Former Commander of the National Army, he is in the seventh year of his rule over the Dominican Republic. He is of humble origins. Trujillo joined the military when he was 18 and spent his entire adult life forming an alliance to service his professional and personal goals.

He is currently married to his third wife, Marie Martinez de Trujillo. Trujillo has been waging a long campaign to win over Lina's affections.

INT. SITTING ROOM - DOMINICAN REPUBLIC - OCTOBER 3, 1937

Lina Lovaton Pittaluga, 19-year-old, paces back and forth wringing her hands.

She is a beautiful, fair-skinned Dominican woman, wearing a long white tulle gown, and her hair is pinned up in a stylish chignon.

There is a knock at her door.

Lina sits down slowly and arranges her gown around her ankles with great care.

There is another knock at the door.

She slowly looks up. Her face is a fixed in an expression that is absolutely cold and disdainful.

LINA
    Enter.

Enter: Rafael Leonidas Trujillo, 48-years-old, male, medium height. He has grey hair at his temples, and a stature formed by years of military service. He has thick dark eyebrows and a moustache slightly reminiscent of Hitler's.

Rafael slowly closes the door behind him and stands at the door, staring at Lina.

Lina's chin comes up a notch as she stares him down.

RAFAEL
    Mi amor.

LINA
    (quietly)
    Where are they?

RAFAEL
    Lina, my queen, this is how you greet me?

Lina silently watches as Rafael approaches her.

RAFAEL (CONT'D)
    You don't apologize for upsetting me?

LINA
    Hah! Everything upsets you. Like I care.

RAFAEL
    You should not talk to me like that, *mi amor*.

LINA
    I will talk to you anyway I choose. Where is my doorman? My cook? My maids? Where is my dresser? Do you have any idea how difficult it is to dress oneself or style one's own hair?

RAFAEL

This difficulty will pass my love.

LINA

Rafael Leonidas Trujillo! Where are they?!

RAFAEL

Lina . . .

LINA

First you sent Esteban to Haiti and you get him killed.

RAFAEL

Yes, your little "Haitian-African-want-to-be Dominicano" suitor got caught spying in his parents' motherland. Is it my fault he could not do his job well?

LINA

You are such an egomaniacal animal.

RAFAEL

I like the animal part, mi amor, but the ego . . . What is that?

LINA

You want to stake your claim to everything. Our capital, Santo Domingo - is now Ciudad Trujillo. The highest peak in our country, Pico Duarte, you renamed Pico Trujillo. Your birthplace, San Cristobal - changed to Trujillo.
Now me - you want me to be known as "La Puta de Trujillo."

RAFAEL

I would kill anyone who called you *puta*.

LINA

Kill. Kill. Kill. Is that all you know how to do? You wish to kill my birthday party too?

RAFAEL

Well, not exactly—

LINA

Your wife, Maria Martinez de Trujillo, tells everyone that I am your new puta. You know I am still a virgin.

RAFAEL

She is just a little emotional right now.

LINA

Quiet! I have been planning this masquerade ball for two months and now - no cook, no doorman . . . no servants at all?! Has your wife stolen them all? Did you take them all away because I didn't invite you and your ugly wife to my party? Everybody knows she hates me because you are madly in love with me - something you haven't allowed to be a secret since Carnival this year.

Silence.

LINA (CONT'D)

Speak!

RAFAEL

But dear one, you told me to be quiet.

Beat.

LINA

You take everything literally.
Why is that?
(*Beat*) Where are my servants, Rafael Leonidas Trujillo?

RAFAEL

I got rid of them.

LINA

You had no right to. This is my house, not yours. I want them back.

RAFAEL

You told me to get rid of them

LINA

I did no such thing.

RAFAEL

Yes, you did.

LINA

No, I didn't.

RAFAEL

Yes, you did.

LINA

Stop that! You

RAFAEL

—did.

Beat.

LINA

(quietly)
How could I do something that stupid?
When did I say that?

RAFAEL

Yesterday, you told me that you love beautiful young Haitian brown-skinned men
and that you would never have anything to do with me as long as there was a
single Haitian man, woman or child in our country.

Beat.

LINA

Ah! Those were just words. You didn't take them seriously.

RAFAEL

Maybe. Maybe not.

LINA

Yesterday, at the dance held in honor *of you* . . . your speech . . . You said 3000
Haitianos were dead in Banica . . .

Silence.

RAFAEL

And that more will follow.

LINA

Thousands of Haitians who've lived here for years and worked for our families all
their lives . . . dead?

Trujillo shrugs and nods.

LINA (CONT'D)
　　You did this all because of me?

Trujillo smiles and shrugs. Silence.

Lina is torn between being frightened and aroused by this information.

LINA (CONT'D)
　　Mi amor. That is so . . . romantic.

Rafael rushes to her side and falls to his knees.

RAFAEL
　　I would do anything to win your love, mi amor.

LINA
　　Anything but divorce Maria.

RAFAEL
　　That is complicated, but yes . . . anything but that.

She kisses him.

LINA
　　Mi amor, you are such a . . .

Rafael smiles.

RAFAEL
　　What?

Lina struggles to contain her desire to laugh and/or cry.

LINA
　　So . . . my household staff . . . ? Dead?!

Rafael nods.

LINA (CONT'D)
　　All the men, women, and children!?!

RAFAEL
　　As many smelly, immigrant, dirty brown Haitian people as my men could find.

LINA

Your mama is a brown-skinned Dominicana. You are killing brown-skinned Dominicans as well?

RAFAEL

No sweetling. Just the Haitians.

LINA

How can you tell the difference?

RAFAEL

The Haitians can't pass the perejil test.

LINA

The perejil test?
What? Do they hate parsley?

RAFAEL

They can't trill the "r," mi amor. Stop worrying. You just reschedule your party for next week. I will make sure you have a new staff by then.

Rafael starts to lift the hem of Lina's dress.

Lina stops him.

RAFAEL (CONT'D)

You told me you would be mine if —

LINA

No. I will not reschedule. Get me new cooks today.

They stare each other down.

Rafael concedes.

RAFAEL

Very well, mi amor. I will send word for my troops to stop the purge. I am sure a few cooks and maids are still alive.

Rafael tries to life her skirt again. Lina stands.

LINA

I need an experienced doorman, dresser, hairstylist, and a butler.

RAFAEL

    I will do my best.

Rafael takes her hand, but she pulls her hand from his grasp, and walks away from Rafael.

LINA

    If you get me what I need for my party tonight, I will allow you to be my first and only lover. *Por todo tu vida.*

Rafael jumps to his feet and rushes over to Lina. He falls to his knees at her feet and kisses her hands.

RAFAEL

    Mi amor. Amor de mi vida. I will not fail you.

Lina pats him on his head.

LINA

    My beast—my birthday party is scheduled to start in exactly nine hours. Not a second later. The clock is ticking.

Rafael roars like a tiger and licks her palm, and quickly stands and runs out.

As Lina considers what she has learned.

LIGHT FADES TO BLACK

END OF PLAY

Nadia Jean-Marie

A monologue written for the Remembrance of the Haitian Massacre

Rebecca Osborne

CAST OF CHARACTERS

NADIA JEAN-MARIE - A Haitian woman with a Haitian Creole accent

SETTING

Place: The riverbank on the border between Haiti and the Dominican Republic

Time: October 1937; A day of the Haitian Massacre

NADIA JEAN-MARIE, presents herself as a child. She joyfully dances and sings the children's folk song, Ti Zwazo Koté Ou Pralé. in Haitian Creole. After the song, she continues the scene as a child. She recalls a memory from her young childhood.

NADIA JEAN-MARIE

> They call me Nadia—but my mother named me Jean-Marie. When mother would go to the river to wash clothes, I would play nearby.
> It was a day very much like today. The children begin a game of hide-n-seek. I'm a bit too young to play, so my dear older cousin Laurette, whom I worship, takes my hand and leads me behind some nearby brush. She ducks down and then so do I. My excitement over the hiding place and the game begins to build and I open my mouth to share my joy. Quickly, Laurette's finger press, ever so gently, against my lips. She does the same to her own lips and I hear a soft sssshh sound. She smiles. I smile. We are both quiet.

Nadia softly whisper-sings the childhood song again as she remembers the moment with her friend.

My anticipation grows as the game is ready to begin. I hear my mother chatting with my auntie. I stand to peak out and see her deep mahogany skin glowing in the sun. Her gauzy blouse and full skirt dance in the breeze. And her laugh! Oh! My feeling at that moment is beyond description. It is all I could hope for every child.

Then a loud commotion. There across the river. Men are shouting. They run toward us. They waive big, crooked sticks in the air. The sticks glimmer as none I've ever seen.

They race toward the women who begin to scream. Laurette grabs me by my shirt; I cannot move. The awful men grab my auntie. They drag her toward the water's edge. She falls into the river and struggles to stand. They force her forward. Just as quickly, they round up the remaining women. Children are crying. Women are screaming. Men are shouting. I cannot move. A sudden jerk on my shirt. Laurette, motions for me to get down. I see terror in her eyes.

"Name this," demands my auntie's captor. Auntie's Creole accent is clear and distinct as she responds, "Parsley."

(Pause. Nadia Jean-Marie transitions into the present. She is now an adult.)

What followed was a scream like nothing I could even try to explain. It continued till the sun began to set. The men left as suddenly as they had appeared. Where Laurette found the strength to act, I know not. She pulled me by the hand, and we peeked out. The slaughtered bodies of our mothers lay in the bloody river. Laurette's father found us that evening. Once a proud protector of his family, now he kneeled in the river, holding my auntie's body. He wailed.

(reflective pause)

Soon after, he began to call me Nadia. I would be a young woman before I would ask,

"Uncle, why do you call me Nadia?" "It means hope," he explained. "And hope makes one live."

Nadia repeats a portion of her song multiple times. She begins in a mournful state. With each subsequent singing she reflects greater healing until she has fully embraced the Haitian parable, "Hope makes one live" The final time she repeats the song she is a grown woman, strong and wise. All of the singing is in Haitian Creole.

Note to Director: The Haitian Massacre is referred to as the "Parsley Massacre" because Dominican soldiers carried parsley to aid in identifying Haitians. When soldiers suspected a person to be Haitian, a sprig of parsley would be displayed, and the person would be told to pronounce the word for it. For native speakers of Haitian Creole, the word, "parsley" was difficult to pronounce and, thereby, revealed their Haitian identity.

It is estimated that between 6,000 and 20,000 Haitians were killed in the Dominican Republic upon the orders of the Dominican dictator Rafael Trujillo. Bodies were often dumped in the Massacre River.

NADIA JEAN-MARIE was first performed in August 2012 at the historic Judson Memorial's Bailout Theatre in NYC. It was produced by CAFE (Caribbean Association for Females in Entertainment). Paule Aboite played the role of Nadia Jean-Marie.

Requests for permission to use this play should be directed to the author, Rebecca Osborne, at rebecca.osborne@sbcglobal.net.

SECTION III

INTERVIEWS

Padre Regino Martínez Bretón y el nuevo sujeto fronterizo

Megan Jeanette Myers and Edward Paulino

Los eventos de Frontera de Luces, en ambos lados de la frontera, se dan durante el primer fin de semana de octubre. La mayoría del programa toma lugar en el lado este del Río Masacre porque—incluso cuando la planificación comienza varios meses antes—el Ejército Nacional, estacionado al lado dajabonero de la aduana dominicana, no da permiso para el cruce en una manera puntual. Desde el 2012, Frontera de Luces ha trabajado con tres coroneles distintos—encargados del Departamento Dajabón del Ejército Nacional—y esa vuelta constante en cuanto al personal, además de los reglamentos vacilantes y las medidas de seguridad ampliadas, ha dificultado el hecho de obtener permiso oficial para el cruce de grupos con Frontera de Luces. Durante el primer año de Frontera de Luces en 2012, había un grupo de más de 40 voluntarios para llevar a cabo una limpieza del parque central en Ouanaminthe. La mañana programada para el cruce, de todos modos, el permiso de la guardia nacional no parecía ser posible (a pesar del hecho de que Frontera de Luces había coordinado el cruce con anticipación, enviando la información del pasaporte de todos los que iban a cruzar, etc.). El pronóstico desolador cambió por completo cuando el Padre Regino Martínez llegó a la frontera ese día. Con casi dos metros de estatura, es fácil divisar a Martínez. Con su voz profunda y resonante, la presencia de Martínez no pasa desapercibida. Su carácter imana autoridad y compasión a la vez y cuando él habla, todos escuchan. Así, cuando Martínez se acercó al edificio de Dirección General de Aduanas en Dajabón en su vieja motocicleta, con la llamativa funda del asiento multicolor, habló brevemente con el entonces coronel y el grupo entero obtuvo el permiso para cruzar de inmediato. Cruzamos la frontera con Martínez de guía. Julia Alvarez andaba con el grupo ese día y ha comentado que, ese momento, fue como si Martínez fuera Moisés partiendo el Mar Rojo. El Padre Martínez lleva una vida humilde; él se ve a sí mismo como un sirviente de Dios quien ha aceptado, como la misión de su vida, servir a la gente de la frontera norteña, tanto a haitianos como a dominicanos, sin dar preferencia a la raza o la nacionalidad de ninguno. Su humildad y gentileza no frenan su pasión ni su deseo por servir. Estos valores que caracterizan al Padre resuenan en la entrevista siguiente, grabada en la parroquia jesuita en Dajabón, Nuestra Señora del Rosario, en 2018.[1]

Regino Martínez (RM): Soy nativo del Licey al Medio en el Cibao central. Tengo trabajando aquí en la frontera del Norte 44 años. Yo vine aquí con 30 años acabado de ordenarme sacerdote y ya llevo 44, así que tengo 74 años.

Edward Paulino (EP): ¿Y cómo usted llega a conocer e integrarse con Frontera de Luces? Y para comenzar, ¿Cómo usted llegó a pasar tantos años en la frontera?

RM: Yo llego trabajando aquí en la frontera; primero llegué a Loma de Cabrera en el año 1974. En el año 1986, yo vengo a trabajar aquí en Dajabón. Vengo a trabajar como obrero. ¿Por qué? Porque yo, estando en Loma de Cabrera, después de 10 años trabajando allí, noto que la gente se acerca a mí a buscar cosas, a buscar servicio . . . que si una receta, que si un techo para la casa, que si quiere ir de viaje, personas enfermas . . . la gente viene aquí a buscar cosas, no a buscar un contenido de la evangelización. Esta estructura parroquial me ayuda para yo vivir mi sacerdocio de ser obrero, y Dios me ayuda para yo vivir y hacer lo suyo. Yo fui a vivir con una familia donde la gente no pueda buscar cosas, con una familia pobre. No fui a vivir con el sueldo de mis superiores de ser un obispo. Yo fui a vivir con una familia campesina. Porque la mayoría de la gente de la parroquia donde yo vivía en Loma de Cabrera vivía del cultivo de la tierra, de agricultura. Yo vivía lo que la gente vivía y por la noche, me enseñaba lo que yo quería comunicarle. Preparando a la gente para los sacramentos: bautismo, confirmación, matrimonio, y para las celebraciones de la eucaristía, la comunión. Entonces así es, así duré los años.

EP: ¿Qué pasa cuando usted llega a Dajabón? ¿Nos puede hablar de su trabajo con Solidaridad Fronteriza?

RM: Después del paso de los años, eso fue en el año 1986, el superior me dice "Queremos que tú vengas a trabajar a Dajabón." Entonces yo digo, si yo voy a trabajar a Dajabón tiene que ser en las mismas condiciones en que yo estoy aquí [en Loma de Cabrera]. Porque yo no llego al mundo del empobrecido de turista, yo llego como uno más de ellos. Cuando vine aquí a Dajabón, entonces busqué un trabajo de un obrero porque la familia en donde yo vivía trabajaba con unos ingenieros limpiando canales de riego. Entonces yo me puse a hacer el mismo trabajo por el día y por las noches, venía a las misas y a las actividades religiosas en los diferentes sectores de la ciudad en los diferentes barrios. Y los fines de semana visitaba las comunidades campesinas, y así me fui desarrollando.

En este proceso también hay una lucha por la tierra que comienza en el año 1989. Yo me uno a los campesinos con esa lucha con la tierra del estado en manos de terratenientes particulares. El campesino organizado reclama esas tierras para poder trabajar y yo lo acompaño en ese reclamo. Y allí duramos 11 meses. En esos 11 meses, la tierra quedaba en la misma frontera con Haití y entonces, nosotros comenzamos a relacionarnos con los haitianos, de campesino a campesino. Y allí comienza una nueva etapa de trabajo binacional con las relaciones con los campesinos. A los 11 meses, el gobierno nos entrega la tierra sembrada de arroz a los campesinos. Tres mil carreras, unas noventa hectáreas, más o menos, lo entrega como un proyecto agrario sembrado de arroz. Entonces yo me retiro de allí pero quedo con las relaciones con los campesinos dominicanos y los campesinos haitianos. Estas relaciones, de campesino a campesino, son las que hacen que surja Solidaridad Fronteriza aquí en Dajabón y Solitaritè Fwontyè en Ouanaminthe, en Haití. Tenemos dos instituciones que acompañan a los campesinos en un proceso de desarrollo económico en que la misma gente participa.

A partir de esas instituciones que se fundan en 1997, llevábamos una serie de años, cuando llega allí Cynthia [Carrión] y llega Eddie [Edward Paulino] y me encuentran a mí, en la oficina de Solidaridad Fronteriza, y me proponen a mí—y eso fue hace siete años en el 2011—celebrar, no, [sino para] recordar la memoria de la matanza que hubo aquí de dominicanos y de haitianos en 1937. La matanza que comienza para Trujillo de limpiar de negros en la frontera. Era una cosa grande para mí hacer este recuerdo porque aquí, la gente no habla de eso hasta esa época que yo tenía acá. En el 2012—y yo llegué en el 1974—ya tenía 30 años en la frontera y nunca habíamos hablado de eso, de la matanza, porque eso era un misterio. Sin embargo, la propuesta de Cynthia y de Eddie nos lleva a develar un misterio que nosotros teníamos escondido. Entonces nosotros comenzamos a hablar de esa situación. Para esa memoria vinieron Frontera de Luces e hicimos actividades aquí en Dajabón e hicimos actividades en Haití, en Ouanaminthe. Y eso nos ayudó a descubrir que la culpa de esa matanza no la tenía el pueblo sino que la tenía Trujillo. Trujillo fue él que impuso un control anti-haitiano en la frontera. Y a partir de allí nosotros comenzamos a hablar de esta situación; como a liberarnos. Frontera de Luces nos ha llevado a liberar de algo que nosotros teníamos oprimido.

Megan Jeanette Myers (MJM): Entonces, ¿A partir de 2012, aquí en Dajabón y también en Ouanaminthe, comenzaban estas discusiones binacionales en cuanto al masacre?

RM: ¿Nos hemos liberado para qué? ¿Lo recordamos? Para que nunca más se repita eso. Porque eso es una anti-humanidad el querer no reconocer algo que uno lo adquiere en la vida. Porque nadie quiere nacer en un sitio pobre y roto, nadie quiere comportarse de una manera y nadie escoge sitio o lugar para nacer. El ser humano, el ser gente, el ser persona que puede vivir, pero nadie escoge ser de un lugar o de otro. Entonces allí viene la situación; el hecho de que haya pasado esa matanza porque eran negros. Nadie tiene culpa de ser negro. La injusticia que cometió Trujillo . . . yo no puedo cargar con eso. Yo no puedo callarla. ¡Hay que denunciarla! Porque si no se denuncia puede ser que vuelva a pasar de nuevo. Al recordar a esa masacre que hubo de 20,000 o 25,000 muertes en esa época para dominicanizar la frontera, entonces nosotros no podemos tener la culpa ni tampoco podemos tener eso tapado para que nos vuelva a pasar. Es una mala [situación] que nos cubrió a todos, a ellos como haitianos y a nosotros como dominicanos.

Entonces, en ese sentido, Frontera de Luces ha sido como la luz que nos ha iluminado sobre una situación, nos ha abierto los ojos para caer en cuenta que callando eso, puede volver a pasar. Denunciándolo y abriéndolo al mundo, se puede evitar.

MJM: Y como nosotros hemos dicho, la idea de Frontera de Luces—la idea principal, básica—es llevar luz a la frontera.

RM: Y en la medida que nos ha iluminado, se va viendo más claro y van apareciendo otras luces a partir de esto, porque es lo que uno descubre con la luz. Entonces uno entra a una habitación oscura y no ve nada. Usted entra a una habitación con una luz y vea algo que le puede ayudar para fortalecer esta luz. Entonces lo usa y se va viendo la luz, se va agradeciendo la luz. Lo que nos ilumina al comportamiento humano es lo que nosotros queremos mantener.

MJM: ¿Y cómo ha sido mantenido? Como usted nos ha dicho y otros lo han dicho así también: después de 2013 y la sentencia, no están usando machete para castigar a los dominicanos de ascendencia haitiana, sino que usan las leyes, la palabra jurídica.

RM: En las élites dominicanas, permanece ese rechazo y ellos lo quieren inducir a la población. Trujillo indujo ese rechazo al haitiano, al negro haitiano, matándolo y quitándole la vida. [Los mataron] con palo y con cuchillo, no con armas de fuego, para decir que eran los mismos campesinos porque les robaban las vacas y les robaban las propiedades a los dominicanos de esa zona.

Ahora, para mantener esa división y ese rechazo, el tribunal constitucional dominicano mata también a los hijos de esos haitianos que están aquí y que son dominicanos ya, porque han nacido en tierra dominicana. No son de sangre dominicana sino que han nacido en tierra dominicana. Entonces en la nueva constitución, la reforma constitucional de 2010, esa constitución dice que para eliminar el derecho al suelo—a *jus solis*—que solamente son dominicanos los hijos de sangre, no porque hayan nacido aquí. Extranjeros que sean nacidos aquí no son dominicanos. Los extranjeros que nazcan a partir de 2010 para ser dominicanos tienen que ser legalizados, regularizados. Deben tener autorización del gobierno y tienen que estar cumpliendo con las leyes dominicanas para ser dominicanos. Entonces, ¿qué pasa? Como hay muchos nacionales dominicanos que tienen raíces negras y haitianas, para poder quitarles la nacionalidad dominicana que ya habían adquirida por el *jus solis* - ahora solamente se hace, a partir de 2010, por el *jus sanguinis*.

¿Cómo se elimina el *jus solis* de los dominicanos de ascendencia haitiana antes de 2010, dándole valor retroactivo a la sentencia de 2013? Aquí en 2013, hay una sentencia que le quita la nacionalidad dominicana a los nacionales dominicanos de ascendencia haitiana, diciendo que son irregulares, y como la constitución de 2010 dice que solamente son dominicanos los hijos de extranjeros regularizados, y como ellos no están regularizados, entonces le dan valor retroactivo a la constitución de 2010. Y allí se comete la muerte, el genocidio de miles de dominicanos quienes en actualidad no tienen acta de nacimiento, no tienen acta de carnet de identidad ni pasaportes. No pueden trabajar. No pueden estudiar. No pueden viajar. Son prácticamente muertos porque no tienen una identidad ni haitiana ni dominicana. Esta es la injusticia que se ha cometido a partir de la reforma constitucional de 2010. De la misma constitución de 2010, dice que los que tenían nacionalidad dominicana quedan, que es a partir de 2010 los que nazcan irregularmente. Pero, ¿qué pasa? El tribunal superior constitucional dice que no es solamente para el futuro, también sirve para el pasado. Los que han nacido desde 1929 hasta ahora, tampoco son dominicanos, aunque la misma constitución anterior de 1960 reconocía la nacionalidad dominicana a esos extranjeros que habían nacido aquí, porque ellos ya tenían hasta 30, 40, 50 años viviendo en el país. Hay generaciones—tres generaciones por lo menos hay—de nacionales dominicanos de ascendencia haitiana. A eso, a todos esos lo barrieron.

MJM: Entonces, ustedes en Centro Montalvo [anteriormente Solidaridad Fronteriza], ¿Qué han hecho para apoyar a los dominicanos de ascendencia haitiana en esta lucha para la nacionalidad dominicana?

RM: Bueno, son dominicanos. El extranjero que quiere venir aquí, para ser dominicano tiene que regularizarse, pero eso es a partir de 2010. Nosotros quienes han conocido su nacionalidad, hay que reconocerla, hay que respetarla. No podemos actuar arbitrariamente por una ley constitucional para una conveniencia para las élites, y eso es otro problema. Es que se benefician las élites y los gobiernos al mantener la irregularidad. Es muy largo el beneficio que da, si se mantiene de la disponibilidad de mano de obra barata, al no ser "gente" porque no tiene reconocimiento legal oficial ni en Haití ni en la República Dominicana. El patrón es que el que los emplea y puede hacer lo que le dé la gana, chuparle la sangre si quiere también, pagándole mal el trabajo, tratándolo mal, no reconociendo sus derechos con las prestaciones sociales, en los servicios sociales de salud, de medicina, de vivienda … y por eso los inmigrantes irregulares en la República Dominicana que son haitianos, viven en unas condiciones infrahumanas. Y se mantienen esas condiciones porque no son reconocidas legalmente como personas.

Nosotros estamos tratando de luchar—Centro Montalvo, Frontera de Luces, y las personas que tienen sentido de humanidad—luchando por el reconocimiento de los derechos de esas personas.

MJM: Desde el momento que usted llegó a la frontera, parece que siempre ha existido esa misma lucha.

RM: ¿Y por qué ha existido siempre esa misma lucha aquí en la frontera? Porque en los años de vida republicana que lleva Haití, que son 214 años, y la vida republicana dominicana, de 170 años … ¿en este tiempo qué ha pasado? Los gobiernos no se han interesado en hacer un marco jurídico fronterizo, no han hecho una leyes que regulen las relaciones entre los dominicanos y haitianos. Si no que lo que regula hasta ahora, en este momento, las relaciones domínico-haitianas es la represión, la corrupción, y el beneficio individual. Cada jefe que llegue a la frontera busca un beneficio y permite el tráfico de migrantes, el tráfico de drogas, y el tráfico de mercancía. Porque los beneficios que reciben las autoridades por ese tráfico irregular corrupto y violento es mucho más que su sueldo. El gobierno dominicano y el gobierno haitiano permite la corrupción en la frontera, porque eso es un regalo que se le da a las autoridades militares y a las autoridades oficiales, como un fruto y como un resultado, de haber apoyado en la campaña electoral al partido que está en el poder. Es decir, que, al venir a la frontera, es un premio para que se beneficien de la corrupción, de la impunidad, y del tráfico de las actividades corruptas que se hacen, y por eso se mantiene.

¿Quiénes más se benefician en ese sentido de la irregularidad de la frontera? Son las autoridades y son los militares. Por eso se mantiene. Yo llevo 44 años viviendo en la frontera y lo que se hacía hace 44 años, en 1974, se sigue haciendo en 2018.

MJM: Entonces, ¿cómo buscamos una solución frente a esa corrupción fronteriza?

RM: ¿Cuál es la solución? Según yo entiendo, es iniciar un proceso de organización, tanto de las comunidades haitianas como en las comunidades dominicanas, porque la organización nos puede dar lo que yo no aprendí en la escuela. Y nos puede dar la fuerza que yo no tengo a nivel individual. Y así los hemos hecho. Hemos defendido los derechos de las personas con la fuerza de la organización. La gente unida y organizada busca lo que le conviene, y lo que una sola persona no puede hacer.

MJM: Y que sea una organización binacional . . .

RM: Claro. Por eso nos hemos acuñado en este trabajo de relaciones domínico-haitianas; hemos acuñado la palabra binacional. ¿Por qué? Porque "binacional" es una concepción que considera a la otra persona, de otra nación, como sujeto. El concepto transnacional considera a la otra persona como objeto. Le pasa por arriba a todo el mundo y no convive con el oficio personal: "trans". El "bi" es de tú a tú. Nosotros queremos impulsar unas relaciones, no de frente ni de espalda, ni "trans"—pasándose por arriba a uno—porque entendemos que la otra persona en este sentido es un objeto—sino con una relación *binacional*, de dos personas—"bi"—tú y yo.

Tú haces lo que puedas, yo hago lo que pueda, cada uno en su lugar, lo fortalecemos los dos para que haya entonces un nuevo sujeto fronterizo. Este nuevo sujeto fronterizo se trata de "tú a tú" en dos situaciones diferentes. En dos culturas diferentes. En dos formas de comportarse diferente. Ellos como haitianos y nosotros como dominicanos; lindo complemento.

En las relaciones humanas, con sentido de humanidad y con sentido de fe, uno debe tener en cuenta el uno y el otro. Con sentido de solidaridad y con sentido de poder, viene la unión organizada.

EP: Y mi pregunta es, en cuanto a Frontera de Luces, ¿cómo veía la comunidad cuando comenzamos aquí hace 7 años? Sé que habían personas escépticas . . . trata de caminarnos por estos primeros años, cuando nosotros llegamos aquí. ¿Cómo ha cambiado?

RM: En primer lugar, Frontera de Luces era un parásito, una cosa rara que llegó aquí . . . ¿Por qué están recordando cosas que nosotros tapábamos y no queríamos recordar? Pero se aceptó, porque en el fondo, veíamos que era una cosa buena. Pero, al principio, las mismas autoridades decían: "¿esa gente, qué busca, los que vienen de otros países para acá?" Pero no sabían que son gente que han venido de aquí para allá. Y, como nosotros tenemos gente que viene de allá para acá, también tenemos gente que viene de aquí para allá. Los que han salido fuera de aquí, de la República Dominicana, conocen lo que pasa afuera del país. Y ellos vienen a enseñarnos lo que se aprende de allá cuando uno está fuera de su país. Cuando uno reciba en su país a una persona que venga de otro país, sepa entonces como tratarlo. Este aprendizaje, de lo que ha ido creando la presencia de Frontera de Luces, sabe enseñarnos cómo tratar al que llegue a nuestro país, sabiendo lo que ellos han pasado cuando salieron de este país, y como han querido ser recibidos en nuestro país, a dónde se pueda.

Nosotros somos, entonces, no así, conscientes de que somos un pueblo, un país de receptores de migrantes y de emisores de migrantes.—Esta situación hay que hacernos conscientes para poder iniciar un proceso de aceptación, de convivencia, de reconocer que lo determinante no es el color ni la condición económica de una persona, sino que el determinante son las relaciones . . . que es la gente, que es la persona . . . y que esa persona tiene derecho transnacional, así que está por encima de todas las naciones. Los derechos personales están por encima de todas las naciones y eso se ha reforzado con la presencia de Frontera de Luces.

EP: Ha habido gente que ha dicho que esa idea vino de afuera y que no es parte de la narrativa de lo que la gente aquí, de verdad, necesita. ¿Cómo le contesta a esa persona que dice que no fue algo atípico de aquí?

RM: Yo le respondiera de esta manera: si existe una riqueza en la humanidad—es precisamente la diversidad. Es que somos diferentes y nadie lo sabe todo y nadie lo conoce todo. Es decir, esa diversidad—en la medida que forme parte y en la medida que yo la integre desde mí [persona], y la coordine desde mí, nos enriquece. Fíjate tú, yo te voy a poner otro ejemplo. El año pasado, cuando ustedes vinieron, no solamente estaba presente en el lugar donde ambulamos la gente de la comunidad, también habían autoridades. Uds. han llegado a reunirse con las autoridades municipales. Al principio las autoridades municipales no estaban enterados de lo que era Frontera de Luces, y ya, aquí en Dajabón, no solamente las autoridades se han integrado en todo este proceso de defensa de los derechos y el reconocimiento—y es muy fuerte eso decirlo aquí—pero se han integrado para buscar un lugar para hacer un monumento, de que, en alguna manera es la memoria de la masacre del "corte", para hacer presente visiblemente, visualmente, un lugar donde se haga presente eso—para nunca volverlo hacer. ¿Te das cuenta? Eso ya se ha hablado con las autoridades principales. Lo que pasa es que no ha generado seguimiento. Ni se ha dado seguimiento por la parte de ustedes ni por parte nuestra. Porque las personas que estaban encargadas aquí para darle seguimiento a ese monumento ya [no están].

Sin embargo, el miércoles pasado, yo fui a Ounaminthe, a Dosmond, celebramos una eucaristía y allá hay un lugar donde se va a hacer un monumento a los caídos de 1937.[2] En el mismo sitio que vivieron los haitianos que salieron de aquí en Dosmond . . . ya la idea no está cuajando solamente aquí, sino que también se está teniendo presente en Haití para que nunca se repita más.

Notas

1. Esta entrevista tomó lugar el 6 de octubre, 2018.

2. Es notable que este memorial fue inaugurado en octubre de 2019, en el mismo sitio indicado por Martínez en esta entrevista en Dosmond.

Spreading Change and Sparking Light

A Conversation with Julia Alvarez and Bill Eichner

Megan Jeanette Myers

Dominican-American author and activist, Julia Alvarez, is well-known for her critically acclaimed novels *How the García Girls Lost Their Accents* (1991) and *In the Time of the Butterflies* (1994). More recently, a space other than New York's Dominican diaspora and the Dominican Republic during the Trujillo Era has captured her attention. Alvarez's focus on the Haitian-Dominican border reflects clearly not only in her recent memoir, *A Wedding in Haiti* (2011) and her *New York Times* essay, "Along the Seam of Hispaniola," but also in her actions and her activista platform as an award-winning Latina author. As the small group of Border of Lights cofounders refers to her, Alvarez is the madrina of the Border of Lights movement, and Bill Eichner, her husband, is the padrino. The interview to follow, recorded at Alvarez's and Eichner's home in Vermont, features the voices of both BOL padrinos as they reflect on the last seven years of BOL events. Moreover, they trace the earliest spark of the idea to bring "light" to the Haitian-Dominican border and discuss how the idea has evolved over the years. A humorous moment in our lively conversation is Julia's reference to the hundredth monkey effect, which we later discovered is a hypothetical phenomenon that attempts to explain how behaviors or ideas spread quickly in large groups. The coconut mentioned in our interview below, is, in fact, a sweet potato in the original research from the 1950s. This same research study, conducted in Japan, was later questioned and challenged. Coconuts or sweet potatoes aside, what is important about the reference is the underlying idea that cultural change can spread; that a new idea can take hold in a community once someone—or a group of people—shines a light on it.

Megan Jeanette Myers (MJM): I want to start by saying how important both of your roles in Border of Lights (BOL) have been over the years—and not only for Julia in the role of the BOL madrina, but Bill, too, as our padrino. It's important to foreground how central you both have been since BOL began in 2012. Bill is sometimes behind the scenes taking photographs or lending a helping hand as our trusted chofer; he really has worn so many hats! So, Bill, I want to start with you since you've been there from the beginning, but less in the public eye. Can you outline your history with BOL?

Figure 1: Julia holds up a light at the Border of Lights
vigil at the border, with CESFRONT guards behind her.

Bill Eichner (BE): I was involved in the initial conversations with Julia at the Malcolm X Center talking to Cynthia Carrión when she was at Amnesty International. I remember seeing this young woman's eyes light up when Julia mentioned the idea for BOL, and I remember Cynthia saying, "I think this is something we should do." I'll always remember how she was so excited and inspired. Of course, I always loved going [to the border] and once we had made our foray into Haiti, I became much more aware and politicized. That happened to me for the first time when I spent a year in East Jerusalem when I was thirty-one. Our two trips to Haiti, in 2009 and right after the earthquake in 2010, really changed me, too. Being able to step up in a small way for Border of Lights was natural.

MJM: So, it was an easy decision. Let's talk about the first meeting of BOL in 2012 and long before that, the very beginnings of BOL. I have these letters between Julia and Michele from 1999 and 2001 in front of me. What can you say about the first spark of bringing light and luz to the border?

Julia Alvarez (JA): Soon after the publication of Michele Wucker's *Why the Cocks Fight* in 1999, we invited her to give a talk at Middlebury College where I was teaching. I already knew about the Massacre from reading *Blood in the Streets*, where Albert Hicks describes the Haitian Massacre in grisly detail. It was the first time I realized what the dictatorship had done, not just to Dominicans. I literally could not sleep for weeks. I also learned about the Massacre in Robert Crassweller's book about Trujillo [*Trujillo: The Life and Times of a Caribbean Dictator*] as well as in Rita Dove's poem "Parsley." But it wasn't until I read Michele's book that I realized the particulars of what had happened and the whole history behind it. Michele's book was what really mapped it out for me. I began to wonder why we, Dominicans, hadn't addressed and redressed the situation? I thought, "It's not going to go away until we do." After Michele came to Middlebury, we stayed in touch, and met some months later in New York City to talk about starting something to create awareness, to begin to address the past. We hoped we could get some event in place for the sixty-fifth anniversary.

MJM: But 2012 was when BOL started, for the seventy-fifth anniversary of the Massacre. As you mentioned before, Cynthia [Carrión] was instrumental in pulling everyone in. That's how I joined the initial planning group of cofounders in early 2012. How did you and Michele come up with this metaphor of light? Was the initial vision one of bringing light and recognition to the history of the Massacre in the sense that it has been relatively forgotten in historical annals and that there were no physical memorials at the time, etc.? How does this metaphor work for you?

JA: To tell you the truth, I think we were having coffee and getting energized—the way we do when we talk—and it was sort of like, "I even have a name for it! How about Border of Lights?" Instead of focusing on the Massacre River and all of the associations with blood, why not reframe the whole idea of the border? Start a new paradigm for the place where two countries and communities meet? We quickly turned global and imagined other "borders" of light; the Haitian-Dominican border would just be one of the many such borders. Instead of a border of blood and division, we, the people, would create a border of light. We had found a name, but the idea itself didn't really take traction until Cynthia's eyes lit up.

BE: It's one thing to talk about it and another thing for someone or a group of people to really commit to doing the work.

JA: It took Cynthia saying, "It's going to happen," and the words were made flesh! What's interesting is that Cynthia did not grow up in the DR, she's a diaspora kid. But that's the wonderful thing that happens. The diaspora goes back to our origin homelands with these new ideas. Silvio [Torres-Saillant] was an earlier supporter, as well; he hasn't been on the ground for BOL, but he knew about Eddie Paulino and connected us to him. Then Sady [Díaz] got involved, and the sisters Rana Dotson and DeAndra Beard. Then you added a whole group of people in New York with the monologue night, and others from the Dominican diaspora in New York City, like Scherezade [García].

MJM: We also counted on the support of others from the very beginning that maybe weren't doing the planning but contributed to BOL in other ways. Edwidge Danticat and Junot Díaz, for example, have donated books for our fundraisers. BOL did begin as a project with diasporic roots, but always with the goal of connecting with organizations and non-profits on the ground that they were already doing really important human rights and advocacy work like Reconoci.do and MUDHA.

JA: And we really lucked out when we got to Dajabón and met the Jesuits who had been at the border for decades living in bateyes, walking the talk. Padre Regino had been doing the work for years. This is another thing that the diaspora can do: give visibility and voice to what is already there but needs solidarity and support. A further example of this happened in 2013. The law denationalizing Dominicans of Haitian descent had just been passed, and the guardia set up barricades and wouldn't let us gather at the border. So, we leapt over that barrier and started an online vigil, which made BOL more global. The virtual vigil helped the BOL movement spread. This is something I've loved about BOL—it's not about a leader, it's about broadcasting the seeds. Maybe Michele and I had this first thought, but it wouldn't have gone anywhere if it hadn't been picked up by Cynthia, by Eddie, by you, by others—a communal and horizontal organizational model. Over the years, the communities on both sides of the border have taken ownership of BOL. That's critical. Otherwise we end up with what I call "moral colonization." Even if it's well meaning, we continue the cycle of "we are the ones with solutions, answers." It perpetuates a debilitating paradigm. No! These ideas are there already. We come to support and listen and see and carry the stories back. This is why this reader is so important!

MJM: Right. It's a conversation, a collaboration.

JA: Think about Nancy [Betances], the granddaughter of one of the guards who had participated in the killings. Nancy took part in a BOL community panel meeting in 2012, alongside a young Haitian girl. Both were politicized because of the experience and became part of the movement. It is so important that BOL be a grassroots movement. It isn't one big leader or corporate organization. It's us. We, the people, following that wonderful Toni Morrison idea of "the function of freedom is to free someone else."

BE: And hopefully some of that will continue when we step back.

MJM: You were both there [at the border] from 2012 to 2017, those first five years. Beyond the community becoming involved and taking more initiative in the planning, what do you think has changed? Or, if you remember one moment, what stands out for you?

BE: The last year we were there, more meetings and community lectures took place. That was great, because that was community building.

JA: Nothing will be as powerful as that first year when we massed at the border. A small group set out with our little lights and all of a sudden, more and more people were joining us. They were stepping out of their houses, coming out of *barras* and *colmados*. Who knew why? Maybe they thought it was a party! Who cares? Then, we looked across the Massacre River, and lo and behold, we saw lights on the opposite side and heard our Haitian neighbors and collaborators calling out to us, and we were calling back to them. Call and response. I knew some healing spirit was afoot. But there were other little moments, too, like Nancy and that young Haitian girl getting involved, Padre Regino on his motorcycle, zipping here and there, trying to get us permits, dealing with the guardia . . .

BE: And the *misa* every year.

MJM: And the first plaque, the only physical memorial to the Massacre, erected in 2017 for the eightieth anniversary. I think that's another moment that sticks out. Plus, the fact that since 2019, there is now a memorial in Dosmond, Haiti, as a result of Border of Lights collaborations and fundraising assistance. Do you think BOL will evolve beyond what it has been in the last seven years? Do you still see this as a global vision?

JA: I think it's happening. Change happens but not always at the speed we want it to. And of course, we want it to happen during our watch. Bill and I are both getting older and not always able to participate at the border. But we can see that the movement is growing and going places that we could not have imagined. The plaque. This anthology. Our imaginations didn't go that far or we didn't believe it could happen. I think the important thing now is to get the young people involved, the new generations of Dominicans and Haitians. I don't mean just the people in Dajabón and Ouanaminthe, but also young people in other cities and areas of both countries, who might be open to new ways of dealing and healing our histories and of collaborating. We need to get these young people who are going to be the leaders and movers and shakers of this next generation on board. This would be key. The older generation, sometimes I have no hope for them. Sometimes there is this defensiveness and way of protecting their entrenched points of view, "their" history.

MJM: At its core, Border of Lights is about this, about a process of concientizarse. I describe it to people it in this way: it's not about just memorializing the Massacre, but about honoring and bringing light and recognition to this long history of cross-border solidarity and binational community that exists today and existed long before 2012.

JA: Yes, collaboration was already there! That other story about the border doesn't often get the attention and doesn't get into the dialogue. My hope is that we can get young people who are going to be making the policies and creating the border politics going forward . . . get them involved in Border of Lights, open up their eyes and imaginations.

But something I have to keep reminding myself is that we get to leave after the annual BOL commemoration is over. The activists who live and work there, they're under siege every day. It's easy for us to be impatient or take risks that really don't end up being that risky. I always remember how Ana Hernández, a wonderful Dominican writer based in the D.R., received death threats after writing a piece about protecting Haitians in the DR. Sometimes we forget that we are here, and we have the luxury . . .

BE: The luxury of coming home.

JA: We're not going to get ostracized. We're not going to lose our jobs. We're not going to get death threats or become actual targets.

MJM: There are groups that push for other voices to be heard in the Dominican Republic and who push back against racial and ethnic discrimination, many of which BOL has collaborated with and supported since 2012. For us, it's about allotting a bigger platform to these groups . . .

BE: BOL is also important for DREAM kids and Mariposa DR Foundation kids, two educational non-profits that have travelled to the border from the beginning with student groups each October.

MJM: Yes! I think that is one of the most important things Border of Lights has done. We invite young groups of Dominicans and Dominicans of Haitian descent to the border. They have come from the very beginning and represent a really integral part of our programming. It's important just for these youth to know they, too, have a voice and that their outlook and their perspective can shape Haitian-Dominican relations.

JA: The people there feel *apoyados*, supported. They feel seen. That gives them *ánimo* for when everyone is gone. That is important.

BE: Even though it happens once a year, people come in for two days . . . it is a big thing in Dajabón and Ouanaminthe. It had never happened before. I'm thinking of the hotel . . .

MJM: Yes, Hotel Raydan. This is where most BOL organizers and volunteers stay. I think they still have a picture of Julia in their restaurant . . .

JA: And the media coverage over the years. It's so important. Otherwise communities feel isolated in the border region, unseen, unheard, unprotected.

BE: The border is not all trouble . . . Dajabón and Ouanaminthe work.

JA: They need each other.

BE: If you close the border there, and there is sometimes talk of that, it would be like closing the border in El Paso. My God. Their world would fall apart.

JA: Doña Carmen from Hotel Raydan will talk about her hotel business and she hypothetically asks, "Who is going to come and clean? Who is going to come and cook? I can't do it without them." She is not someone who I think is particularly politicized. But she knows the two countries need each other, not just to survive, but to thrive.

MJM: It's just what she lives.

JA: But those are the people we have to convince. Those are most of the people in the world; the people who first think, "Well, how is this going to affect me?"

MJM: I want to bring up your article in the *New York Times*, "Along the Seam of Hispaniola," when you talk about your border trip. Why, for both of you, has the border captured—and kept—your interest? And a *Wedding in Haiti*, too. Why do you feel that pull toward the Haitian-Dominican border? What stories do you think are left to tell? Are they yours to tell? Will you return to the border in your own work?

JA: I am from a country that shares an island with another country—we're like conjoined twins! How can I not be interested in our only neighbor? We share such similar histories, topographies, stories. As for what stories are left to me to tell. I never know. I think stories come to my door and knock and knock. It's hard work, three, four, in some cases a decade of work getting them told. So, I resist! The stories that keep knocking and won't leave my doorstep, no matter how long or hard I ignore them, I know those are the stories for me to tell. I suppose that is what distinguishes what are "mine" to tell from the others. As for ownership—I don't think we own stories. You take even one story like that of the Mirabal sisters in the Dominican Republic. There are so many stories about them, canciones, plays, dances, movies. The stories continue, and we tap into them, but they continue to be told by others. Jean Rhys advised young writers: "Feed the sea, feed the sea. The little rivers dry up, but the sea continues."

My more personal connection with Haiti came from meeting Piti and the other Haitians who were working in farms around the property that we bought, where we started a coffee cooperative and little school, Alta Gracia. When we got there, Piti and Francois and Pablo and several others asked if they could work for us. And one thing led to another and ten years after our first meeting we were crossing the border to attend Piti's wedding in Haiti, as we had promised!

BE: Yeah. I think it was our experience of crossing the border and being in Haiti and realizing how difficult it was both times.

JA: Our eyes were opened by those friendships, which led us to want to explore Haiti further.

BE: Right, once our eyes were open to Haiti, then it seemed only natural to go there. What is this border really? It's hidden. Other than Ouanaminthe and Pedernales, there are all these miles and miles . . . there are about a dozen border towns where there is commerce. In our travels of the border we just skirted them, we didn't stop and see them. It drew us to want to see more of our neighbor country and to understand what the border means to those who live there.

JA: To me Haiti became a personal thing through friendship with Piti and others, like Pablo. Getting to know that Haitian community in Alta Gracia and learning about them, and their situation, the lives that they were living.

MJM: For you both, this draw to the border began off-border. This is what is so interesting about it. For me, too, my pull to the border and interest in the region began in off-border spaces simply because the Dominican-Haitian dynamic is everywhere. It goes so beyond borderlands and Ouanaminthe and Dajabón.

BE: Our first encounter on the farm was way, way back. When we first met Piti we didn't know much about Haiti—just facts—abstract knowledge and, of course, Dominican hearsay.

JA: The first time we met the whole group we were visiting Los Dajaos [the neighboring community of Alta Gracia]. It was the weekend, and we drove by a group of young Haitians, teenagers really—they all looked like they were fourteen or fifteen, playing these guitars they had made with olive oil cans and singing. Like young people around the world on a Saturday night, they were relaxing and playing music. I remember feeling, "What are these kids doing so far from home?" We stopped and befriended them. Next trip, and next trip, we sought them out. It became personal connection. From there came all these other connections.

BE: It went from that first musical encounter to having these same boys move into the sótano of a casita we built there. They needed a place to stay. They were safe and secure there, and the place was rent-free. And we got to know them.

JA: From talking with my family in Santiago, I learned that we had a paternal great uncle, I think it was, who was based in Monte Cristi, and he actually had a Haitian family across the border. His Dominican wife lived in Santiago, but this great uncle had negocios in Ouanaminthe and spent a lot of time there. He had a second family there, a Haitian mistress and one daughter that we know of. The elderly aunt who told me this story would always say to me about this mistress, "Era haitiana, pero una haitiana educada." A racist "compliment," to be sure. I've often thought about that story when we've gone to the border, about how my family also has Haitian relatives, connections of blood, comadres, compadres.

   Trujillo's program of "dominicanization of the border" initiated and also exacerbated this dialogue of antagonism of them and us.

MJM: Right; that's when the narrative of anti-Haitianism is really crystalized and becomes a state-supported national narrative. Trujillo gives a platform for anti-Haitianism as we know it today. And, sadly, the people who are threatening Ana Hernández and others, those voices today—maybe because of the internet, maybe because of the 2013 *sentencia*—are resonating stronger.

JA: We see that here with Trump. But he's voicing, bringing to light, an antagonism that was already there below the surface. And maybe that's a good thing in that we flush out and face the monster that otherwise stays hidden, the issues never addressed.

MJM: Yes; and a lot of the articles that reference la sentencia, for example, end by connecting the conversation to contemporary politics in the U.S. and link the Tribunal Court ruling to the situation of the DREAMERS or the Trump Era.

   Let's talk about the 2017 plaque, the first and only physical memorial to the Massacre in the Dominican Republic.

JA: Nationally, has it gotten any attention? It might be the first plaque that recognizes what happened.

MJM: I don't think it's gotten a lot of national attention. But, I wonder, what types of memorials speak most to a community. What really resonates in terms of a memorialization? Literature, also a memorialization, can be a space for community and local memory or memories. Do you view your own work, like *In the Time of the Butterflies*, as a way to memorialize counter-histories and counter-narratives in the Dominican Republic?

JA: I've been taken to task sometimes because the novel did not address the massacre and the Mirabal sisters were alive then. "Why didn't you say more about the Haitian Massacre?" It's important to remember that I was writing from the point of view of particular characters. None of my research into their lives yielded an awareness or a response to what happened. I can't colonize my characters and just plant sensibilities in their heads that were not there—especially in the case of historical characters. It would have been me manipulating the story in order to make my point rather than understand my characters, their personalities, motivations, thoughts. For me, that book was an effort to understand the toll that the dictatorship took on females. Just like *García Girls*. I had read so many immigrant stories from the male point of view, but I was curious about immigration from the female point of view. What was it like for women in the dictatorship, where they were prey to the rapacious appetites of Trujillo and his cronies? Women at that time were kept out of the public sphere. But the Mirabal sisters crossed that line, and it cost them their lives. I wanted to involve their story in the history. But I couldn't insert what wasn't there. You could say that they must have known about it [the Massacre]. Manolo Tavárez was from Monte Cristi, after all; he had to have known what had happened.

BE: They [the women] had enough on their plates. Not to mention that the country was in virtual lockdown, a dictatorship with censorship and control of all media—so not all information got out in a timely way. Travel even from one region of the country to another was controlled. And your book did bring things to people's attention, all kinds of people who had never even heard of Trujillo.

A *Wedding in Haiti* also introduces people to Haiti, even though it doesn't involve the Massacre. But it does allude and reference it.

JA: And so many people have never heard about the Massacre. People know about the Holocaust, but so many don't know about this episode that happened right here in the Americas. And still, we haven't come to terms with what has happened.

But now with the internet, the story can spread. It's another way to memorialize and pay tribute. You know, if you go on Gloria Anzaldúa's website, you can light a candle for her. Her friends have created this website memorial for her. This anthology will also be a way for readers to learn about the massacre and become involved.

MJM: We've been talking about some of these less-told stories, like the story of the dictatorship from the perspective of the Mirabal sisters. We know that a lot of the stories less told in the Dominican Republic are also those of Dominicans of Haitian descent. Take Jhonny Rivas, for example. His story, and others, make me reflect on how Border of Light's mission and vision has changed since 2013 and la sentencia. I always quote Ana María Belique from Reconoci.do who shared in a 2017 meeting on statelessness in the Dominican Republic in Santiago, following BOL, "*No nos estamos matando con machetes, nos estamos matando con las leyes.*"

JA: Padre Regino has said it, too. "*Antes los mataban con machetes, ahora los matan limpiamente con leyes.*"

MJM: Why are stories like Jhonny's so important to tell? When you visited him in jail, what was that like?

BE: We went to visit him in prison in the south side of Monte Cristi. That was an experience. I've been inside prisons in the U.S. and it's terrible, but it was like nothing I'd ever seen.

JA: The guards let us in, after a very thorough search—for instance, I could take in my notebook but no writing utensil. A female guard wanted me to squat naked above a mirror so she could see in my private parts. I said, *Come on, soy una viejita, por favor.* She nodded and made a sign to keep quiet, so the head guard outside the little frisking room wouldn't take her to task. Then, the guards led Bill and me to a door, unlocked it, and it clicked shut behind us. Inside, we were met by a crowd of prisoners, milling around, shirtless, sizing us up. A whole different world. A whole hierarchy and pecking order: There were prisoners who were in charge, the head honchos. You could buy most anything, space on the floor to spread out a mat to sleep, cigarettes, who knows what else?

BE: It's like you're walking into a community. If you walk into a prison here, you might see inmates, but it's all controlled. They're not just left to their own devices. We felt safe, but . . .

JA: One of the guys in charge led us down a long dark passageway. It was like a tunnel into hell. Mats on the floor, prisoners lining the walls. Finally, we got to Jhonny's "room," a cubby hole in the wall that he had paid good money for.

BE: Inside that hole, there were a couple of bunks, so he was better off than others because he had his own bed space. He also had a contraband cell phone that he kept under his pillow. Sometimes, depending on weather, I guess, he could get a signal if he went to a certain area of his bunk. So, we could call him from Vermont.

JA: We found out about Jhonny from someone who worked for CEFASA, an organization involved in the first Border of Lights. Jhonny was a labor organizer of Haitian workers on the Dominican side of the border. As you can imagine, certain factions wanted to get rid of him. So, they pinned these false charges of murder on him. He was condemned for five years, I think it was. Anyhow, Bill and I got involved personally—because you hear a story like his, and you want to do something. When you're a storyteller, you've got the microphone. What do you use it for? To get the story out. I wrote a short piece for *Orion*. Someone from the *Village Voice* wrote an article as well. Amnesty International got involved.

BE: It was a somewhat typical Dominican bureaucratic and legal response to a Haitian who has no money or power. There were all these trials that were supposed to take place, but nothing ever happened.

JA: Then a Dominican mother-and-daughter lawyer team from Santiago, working pro-bono, got him out.

BE: All of this experience, to me, brought back what I experienced in 1975 in the West Bank in East Jerusalem. The same thing over again. The injustice. That's forty years ago. But I have hope for the Haitian border.

MJM: As we talked about Border of Lights, it did change its mission after 2013, to more directly face these injustices and we connected with important organizations on the ground like Reconoci.do, MUDHA, Yspaniola, and others. Supporting these organizations has been one of the most important things that Border of Lights has done, working to connect the diaspora to these non-profits and organizations on the island.

BE: Border of Lights has given them more of a voice, another platform.

MJM: Julia, when people read *A Wedding in Haiti* or "Along the Seam of Hispaniola" they—Dominican-Americans or otherwise—sometimes ask you: "what can we do?" What do you tell them? How do you respond to someone who wants to take action?

JA: It's a question for all of us, who are lucky enough to live lives of relative ease and privilege. With that luckiness come responsibilities. We're back to Toni Morrison's mandate: "the function of freedom is to free someone else." Bill and I, as we become older, ask ourselves this often: what's the best use of our time and resources? How do we help? But with any of us who want to be involved, if we want to be sustainable, we have to do it from our own passions and capabilities—that's the fuel. How can you connect with the issues? I often send people your email, Eddie's email, Cynthia's email . . . and I say, please contact these people to become part of the Border of Lights group email; it's interconnected and an open group. Now we have the technology to find each other and to become that Margaret Mead group—a small group of people who are really passionate and connected and *can* begin to change the world. What's the story? The 101st monkey? The 100th monkey?

MJM: [Laughter] I don't know anything about the 101st monkey.

BE: [Laughter] You've lost me there.

JA: It's another way of saying "the tipping point." The story I heard was that some monkeys on a certain island started washing their coconuts before cracking them open, or perhaps it was washing their sweet potatoes? Other monkeys joined in and soon there were a hundred monkeys. When the 101st monkey joined in, then all the monkeys on the island and surrounding islands began washing their coconuts. It might be an Aesop fable, Monkey See, Monkey Do. In the internet, we talk about something "going viral." The idea is that a behavior or an idea can spread rapidly after enough members of a group acknowledge it; the fact that you hit a critical mass and then the change happens.

BE: I do think that over the years of Border of Lights and spreading the word—and the internet helps—having people aware who would have no awareness otherwise . . .

JA: I am thinking of the Civil Rights movement, too. It began with a small community, a congregation, and it spread and became an international movement.

MJM: You know the mural that Grupo Azueï did, in 2016, on the street corner next to the central park in Dajabón, that reads "*No más + acre*"? That mural was later vandalized with buckets of hot black oil. There is a video of an ultra-nationalist group defacing the mural. But you can hear voices of resistance in the background. You hear these voices in the video, these visceral community responses that are standing up and saying "no." And afterwards, the community themselves cleaned up the oil and restored the mural. That response says more than the vandalism in the first place. Community members—after BOL supporters and organizers were gone— carried on the work and the mission.

JA: That's very moving. Thank you for that story.

BE: Getting people to speak out against racism here, I think, has an effect everywhere.

JA: It's hard for those voices to be heard and feel heard. We talked earlier about what Border of Lights does: it lets those voices know "we hear you, we join you." And we can spread that voice further.

"An Invitation to Further Explore"

Talking Borders and Borders of Lights with Edwidge Danticat

Megan Jeanette Myers

> *I remember hearing about the 1937 massacre quite a bit when I was a girl in Haiti. Nothing in great detail, but a phrase here and there, from one of my relatives.*
> *Ou kwè yo tiye l tankou yo te tiye lòt yo nan 1937? Do you think he was killed like the others were in 1937?*
>
> —EDWIDGE DANTICAT ("NATURE HAS NO MEMORY," BORDEROFLIGHTS.ORG)

Edwidge Danticat's *The Farming of Bones* (1998) confirms the Haitian American author's interest in telling—and re-telling—the history of the 1937 Haitian Massacre. In the conversation with Danticat to follow, she shares that. long before paintings and novels portrayed the massacre, Haitians commemorated and remembered the massacre orally. Eventually, this oral remembrance shifted onto the canvas and the page. *The Farming of Bones*, for which Danticat was awarded the American Book Award for fiction in 1999, offers readers another way to remember and honor the lives lost. An act of fictional testimony from multiple perspectives, the novel invites readers to experience the Dominican-Haitian borderlands in 1937 from various viewpoints, including that of the young Haitian-born Amabelle Désir. Danticat returns to the border in other fictional and non-fiction works—including in her most recent publication of short stories, *Everything Inside* (2019), —and she also constantly revisits themes of (im)migration, (national) identity, and ancestral bonds in her numerous publications, including award-winning novels *The Dew Breaker* (2004) and *Brother, I'm Dying* (2007). The interview with Danticat included here in the *Border of Lights Reader*, addresses more than the physical Haitian-Dominican border and the history of Border of Lights, but also touches on the importance of collaboration, the 2013 Dominican Tribunal Court sentence, and Port-au-Prince as a testimonial city. Danticat has supported Border of Lights's mission from the start, evidenced by her participation in the annual virtual vigil, donation of signed books for fundraisers, and monetary donations to Border of Lights's fundraising campaigns. As BOL wrote in an October 1, 2014 post on Facebook,

Figure 1: Oct. 8, 2016, Border of Lights virtual vigil, shared photo via BOL Facebook.

just days before the third meeting in Dajabón, Dominican Republic and Ouanaminthe, Haiti: "From the very beginning, [Danticat] has understood the vision of BOL and uses the art of storytelling not only to tell our narrative but to improve relations between the Dominican Republic, Haiti and the diaspora."

MJM: I wanted to start, Edwidge, by foregrounding how you have supported Border of Lights from the onset in 2012. Among other things, you have donated signed books for our fundraisers and shared photos and answered questions during our annual virtual vigil. We wanted to begin by thanking you for your support over the years.

I want to jump in by talking about something you referenced a few years ago in a conversation with Myriam J.A. Chancy.[1] In the interview, you mention a "living memory" in reference to the fact that there were no physical memorials to the 1937 Massacre that paid tribute to the lives lost. Beyond discussing living memories, you refer to literature as a "chain of memory." Could you expand a little bit on this idea?

ED: As I wrote in my essay on the Border of Lights website, orality is at the center of how things come to life for me. The flow of Haitian workers to the Dominican Republic has always inspired these stories, oral stories.[2] I had relatives of my own who went to work in the cane fields and when they didn't come back, different stories emerged to explain what might have happened to them. Some of them, when they did come back, they came back un-done. Just worn out. Some eventually died after. Most of them would say they were ashamed to come back sooner. I mentioned this idea of a chain of memory, because it's more than one or two memories. It has a long, lasting, living, even inherited, component. The memories live inside a body until they are given voice. For every important event, the human body becomes a monument. When things are silenced, or when we haven't heard of something, we might say to ourselves "How come nobody talks about this?" Then maybe, I should paint, talk, write, or sing about this, or however the story wants to come out and be memorialized.

I first thought of writing *The Farming of Bones* when I came across a painting by Ernst Prophète. That painting ended up being on the cover of *The Farming of Bones*. The novel was a first attempt at memorializing or even visualizing the event. The painting had some version of these lines written in, on the canvas itself, in French: "My grandmother told me that the Massacre River ran with blood." It was an invitation to further explore something. It was like when you find an amulet and you think, "I need to find out more about that." For me, once that started, I was looking for ways to commemorate. There are ways that we do this in private, the way that people might keep a lock of hair. Before Border of Lights, that was the only way that this event was remembered—in this very private way. There are private rituals based on people's religious beliefs, based on family, and based on personal history or connection to the event. There were no public rituals that I know of. It wasn't until I found this panting that I thought, "This is the way that this person remembered." But it was because it came from a family line. I think that, just as the canvas for Prophète was a place of memory, the pages, too, are, for me, a place of memory. A novel inevitably allows us a way to fill in gaps and flesh out lives. I see the writing as an act of remembrance, of putting flesh on old bones. Just seeing the painting, which is now in my house since it was given as a gift to me, I felt like it had expanded the possibility of what could be said about such a massive event. I thought: "We can do this on canvas. We can do this with words." Just as people have been doing it with oral history, but this was another way of remembering, of mourning.

MJM: I like the idea of thinking about it as more than a memory and focusing on the living components. I think some of the other fictional recreations of the 1937 Massacre in particular, sometimes tend to be one-sided in that they solely place blame on Trujillo, or they approach the massacre primarily from the perspective of male figures, or they don't lend themselves equally to both Haitian and Dominican voices. For me, *The Farming of Bones* breaks with this observation because it gives voice to a young Haitian female, Amabelle. But I also think that it breaks from the trend by also shining light on the nuances of the event and holding various parties accountable. Can you speak to the importance of not only using literature as a memorial and creating a canvas for memorialization with words, but also to the importance of sharing these un-told and multitudinous stories of the massacre?

ED: Thank you for saying that. I was trying very hard to have some nuance, because these types of stories are never simple, or even singular stories. There are, of course, the perpetrators, and then, people who the violence is acted upon. Instinctively in that act there are many actors. There are people who, when I was writing the book, were very cooperative and overtime, they have completely revised their views of the massacre, even in terms of whether it happened at all or how many people have died. Some have gone as far as to say, "If that many people died, where are the bones?" It's a polyphony, not just in terms of how many people have said different things, but also in terms of how many people have changed their minds about which side they're on, as the years have gone by. The Haitian elders who

I interviewed before writing the book would often say things like, "That night the water was kissing the bridge." And that would have been a natural event we would have heard about if the water was that high. The bridge might have been lower, but it didn't seem like it was geographically possible. But in their imagination, the river had swollen because the world they knew had completely lost its scale. This is why for Prophète's grandmother, the massacre river ran with blood.

To others, with time, the event had diminished, as if the bloody water had retreated. It always seemed to me that because so many people experienced these events differently, that you would have to be able to tell it in different voices. I always wanted the book to be testimonial, an act of documentation. There were these documents in Ouanaminthe, these swollen papers in a dark room I visited, which were supposed to hold many narratives that time had physically yellowed and erased, papers that were so crumbly and dusty, you could tell they were going to evaporate. But there were these priests who had collected testimonials. There was also an American journalist, Albert Hicks, who had accessed some of the testimonials for an article for *Collier* magazine that ended up in the book *Blood in the Streets*. But you could tell that so much of this stuff was going away with the people who died.

It was important in the book to have different types of beliefs about what had happened, whether it could have happened . . . Even with people from different classes who are Haitian. That night, everyone wasn't experiencing the massacre in the same way. For me, it was important to excavate different perspectives in order to get a full picture of that moment. There was also a kind of frontier feeling to the time. You had Gulf and Western with their commercial sugar interests on the island and then, you had the nationalistic feeling around the world, the fascism in Europe around the same time. There was a lot happening both on our island and in the world in general, and I felt like it was important to show what the environment was like at that time, along with what was happening locally.

MJM: You mentioned some historians and others who helped you with research when you were beginning to write *The Farming of Bones*. In particular, in the acknowledgements, you thank Jacques Stephen Alexis for his work, referring to *Compère General Soleil* (1955, *General Sun, My Brother*). You also thank Julia Alvarez and refer to directions that she had given you at one point. How important was it for some of these earlier literary representations of the event, for you, in your own writing? How important was the collaboration, from both Haitians, Dominicans, and others, that went into writing the novel?

ED: These encouragements were absolutely important. Initially, a historian was so helpful with things even in terms of flora and fauna. Even people I spoke with, geographically, who said there were earthquakes then, sharing that if you were talking about the mountains, people there would have experienced some tremors. People read the book now and think, "Oh my gosh, there were earthquakes in Haiti then." Even things like that in terms of guidance, it was so important. I felt like when I was beginning it was a kind of collaborative work. There were certain things I sort of needed to know about Dominican life. Especially from that period, there were some details that were so important, and it helped to have Dominican allies.

This brings me back to reading Julia's "By the Book" article in *The New York Times* this past weekend.[3] First I thought, "God, she is a good student." They send you that "By the Book" questionnaire and you don't have to answer every question, but I think she did, and she was so kind and inclusive toward Haiti. She always brings our side, the other side. I think that was also a model of what you are talking about. There is something that, when we are writing about both sides of the island—when we are talking about Haitians on that side or Dominicans on this side—that has to be collaborative in some ways. No matter how tense things get, one side really cannot fully exist without the other. Also, when you're writing about the past from the present, book research can only go so far. Especially since a lot of the Trujillo-related research—aside from Bernard Diederich's fabulous book, *Trujillo, the Death of the Goat*, a lot of the stuff written about Trujillo was so curated to make Trujillo look good.[4] It was important to have other cultural details from people with lived experiences, or people with an objective point of view, who had at least lived during that regime.

MJM: Definitely. And just ten or twenty years ago, there were not nearly as many collaborative studies that approach Hispaniola as a whole, focused on a trans-border and transnational approach—sometimes framed as "Transnational Hispaniola" studies—that we have today.[5]

ED: No, there were not. And what did exist made it seem as though we had always been at war.

MJM: Expanding beyond *The Farming of Bones*, how important is the idea or the obligation—or even the human capacity—to memorialize? Do you feel this is an idea, including in your children's literature, to which you keep returning?

ED: I think my obsession with memorializing has a lot to do with my being plucked from my original home, Haiti, at a young age to join my parents in the United States. Of course, I wasn't plucked as drastically as some of my forebears, who were exiles and had been persecuted during the Duvalier/Trujillo dictatorships, but when you have to leave home at an early age and not of your own choosing, you realize that you have little control over what home is. Some of that feeling guides a lot of my work. We don't always choose where we call home. Those of us who are crossing borders are not the ones drawing borders. When you leave the place, you considered your home, you have to create a new life with what you bring with you. For me, everything became an act of collection and re-collection. I was trying to recreate myself by trying to merge my old memories with the new memories I was making. I would write down things that I didn't want to forget. This feeling gets more amplified when you have children because you feel like, "I want them to have these memories too, the ones I am trying to hold on to, the ones I am trying not to forget. I want them to have these anchors as their own." You want them to know that this is who they are, and this is who they come from—good or bad.

MJM: I want to talk a little more about these literary portrayals of the massacre—and in your work, I'm referring not only to *The Farming of Bones*, but also your story in *Krik? Krak!* titled "1937"—and about border narratives that portray violence at and along the Haitian-Dominican borderline. What is the common tie for these creative works that return to instances of border violence, even beyond the 1937 Massacre? Why do we have this recurring theme of the border as a violent space?

ED: The books on the massacre, or border life that have had the most impact for me, are of course, Jacques Stephen Alexis's *Compère, General Soleil*, which was translated by Carrol Coates as *General Sun, My Brother*, and René Philoctète's *Au Pays des Terres Mélées*, which was translated by Linda Coverdage as *Massacre River*. I think we have this recurring theme of the border as a violent space because borders are often violent places, be it overt or less visible violence. Look at the US southern border. Even the most seemingly peaceful borders have armed guards. So, by nature, borders are like scars or wounds. Our particular border though, has shifted a lot, and not always by us. It was shifted by the US core of engineers, in the twenties, during the US occupation of the entire island, and it kept moving with their interests. It's been a border—as Michele Wucker writes in her book—that some days you could wake up in another country if the border had moved. Sometimes you have the sensation that the border marker was a rock that they could decide to move. All that made for increased hostilities.

When you have a shifting border, people resent suddenly not being in the country they thought they were. And then they are resistant to suddenly having more of these "other" neighbors. René Philoctète's novel, *Massacre River* presents us with a less brutal border, as does Louis Phillipe Dalembert's *L'Autre Face de la Mer*. Those books show us—Alexis does too—with another story, which you also see, when you go to the border. Even in difficult times, you still have some harmony on the border, and a whole group of people who inhabit this middle space. It's important we remember this exists. But when you go to the border, even at a very difficult time when they were deporting people and dumping them at the other side, you could be at the border at someone's house and they would say "Your drink is warm. Let me go to get ice at the neighbors." And the neighbor is across the border. And that person is able to walk past the guard, get the ice, and come back in less than half an hour. There are children who are able to go to school and come back. I think that is also worth remembering. There is another border space. It's not all violent.

MJM: I'm glad you signaled this other, non-violent border. To go back to Border of Lights, that is one of the movement's main objectives. Beyond paying homage and tribute to the lives lost in the 1937 Massacre, it is also about honoring the solidarity that exists in border towns. Oftentimes, those who have not been to the border or experienced it for themselves, never see this border because they aren't able to read about it or see it portrayed in the media this way. I think this kinship is often not represented as such. Since 2012, Border of Lights has worked to highlight this openness.

ED: And Border of Lights has done a wonderful job at it. In the actual space, on the ground itself, there still is, thankfully, a kind of openness between people who live on the border. Even linguistically, this openness exists, and I think it's important that Border of Lights honors it. It's frankly important that we all honor it, because that truth also exists.

MJM: Building on this idea of borders and migration, you mentioned the space of the border after the 2013 sentence in the Dominican Republic. Reflecting on this ruling and your public response—calling for political pressure and being a part of rallies and travel boycotts, for example, at the press conference with Junot Díaz in 2015, just before the Dominican Republic started to deport at higher frequencies—can you talk a little about your role as author-activist?

ED: I am always surrounded by activists—I live in Little Haiti after all—so I know what constant activism looks like. I always feel that to call myself an activist reduces what people on the ground do, all the time, day in and day out, people like Ana María Belique and so many others, like the late Sonia Pierre, for example. Now those women are activists. For my part, I've always seen my role as supporting people who are actively working on the ground, and to let them lead. Sometimes when you speak to people on the ground, they say that there are a lot of things they can't call for, because of where they are and because of other work they are doing. So, I follow their guidance. The *sentencia* was a canary of mines, and not just for Haitian-Dominicans. So much of what happened there is also being called for, here in the United States, in this violent anti-immigration era of Trump. In relation to Haitian migration, the Bahamas also followed in the same vein as the D.R., soon after *la sentencia*. There were some echoes and ripple effects of similar actions in Turks and Caicos. We could tell that it was something that was going to snowball, and it has, and it continues to.

I felt like my role at that time, and still now, is to listen to what people were saying on the ground, people I knew. Not everyone had the same approach and some people felt and stated that we should have kept our mouth shut, but I was talking to Haitian activists I knew and trusted and groups they had been working with here in the US for years. It goes back to the type of collaboration you were talking about—that we could do it together from both sides. You had young college students who were part of Quisqueya clubs, both Haitian and Dominican-Americans who were speaking out together against this. That was extremely moving. Whether it was me and Junot or Julia, the sort of work that we did together was a lot more powerful than what we could have done individually. If you do it just from the Haitian side, it would have seemed like more complaining, but the fact that it was collaborative, and that it was voices from both sides speaking together, even though it wasn't a Border of Lights project, it was a kind of Border of Lights.

MJM: Right, totally. And I think you're also being conscious of this complex interplay and the fact that there can sometimes be conflicts between Dominicans on the island and the Dominican diaspora or Haitians on the island and the Haitian diaspora. But, as you've shown, there are also ways that the diaspora can work as a unique collaborative space.

ED: I am thinking, for example, about all the work done: France Francois, the Founder & CEO of In Cultured Co⁶, an organization that is working to, as she writes, "decolonize Hispaniola" and "sow the seeds of peace, conflict resolution, reconciliation, collaboration, healing and dialog in young black and Latinx leaders in order to move from a divided past towards a shared future." We need more spaces like that, more conversations that address the common needs and problems of the entire island, as well as the things we joyfully share. France is facilitating some powerful conversations between young Dominicans and Haitians; the solidarity is very powerful.

MJM: I recently read the edited collection *La Vil: Life and Death in Port-au-Prince* and I found it very impactful. It's part of the Voice of Witness series, and I wanted to end by commenting on this frequent or repeated characterization of Haitians, in Port-au-Prince and in the country at-large, as resilient. In your foreword to *La Vil*, you mention Port-au-Prince as a city of survivors, but you also call it—and this definition really spoke to me—a "testimonial city." I wanted to end by thinking about how space can embody testimony. What does this idea mean to you?

ED: To start by bringing it back to the border, when I first went there, I went with such expectations of that being quickly visible to me as a testimonial space. I thought I would see and identify signs of history everywhere, especially along the river I had been reading about. And when I went, it was at a point of the dry season and there was just a thread of water. What I thought was, "nature has no memory." It behooves us if we want to remember certain things to mark them on the earth. Port-au-Prince is a city that does that on its own, it's a city of scars, especially after the earthquake. You have three million people in a city where you are supposed to have at most 300,000 people, so it's a city that people have stamped their existence on. That's what I mean by testimonial city. You turn around and there is a story everywhere. The border space is more of a nature space. You have to speak to the people, and ask "Who is buried here? What happens here?" In Port-au-Prince, it's such a big collage. You have that feeling when you go to the cemetery. I go and I try to find my grandfather's burial place, and I find that strangers are buried there with him—if indeed you have strangers in death. The people who run the cemetery have rented out the family mausoleum and have piled bones on top of bones—blending the bones of people I've known and the bones of people I've never met. It's that kind of city. It's a city filled with all kinds of stories. There are so many stories that many are buried and are struggling to emerge. And others are right there, in your face, and hard to avoid. Even the walls are speaking to you in Port-au-Prince, with words as well as images on banners, on tap taps. There are things drawn and written in there. The graffiti artist, Jerry Rocembert, drew some incredible images after the earthquake. He kept reminding us that "*Ayiti Pa p Peri.*" Haiti will not perish. His work, like the tap tap, was part of that living memory and part of that testimonial space. You don't have to go far to find memorial spaces. There are living stories everywhere.

Notes

1. Chancy, Myriam J.A. "Violence, Nation, and Memory: Danticat's *The Farming of Bones.*" In *Edwidge Danticat: A Reader's Guide,* edited by Martin Munro, 130-46. U of Virginia P, 2010.

2. See Danticat's essay on the Border of Lights webpage here: https://www.borderoflights.org/edwidge-danticat

3. Alvarez, Julia. "Julia Alvarez: By the Book." *The New York Times.* 11 April 2019. https://www.nytimes.com/2019/04/11/books/review/by-the-book-julia-alvarez.html

4. Diederich, Bernard. *Trujillo: The Death of the Goat.* Vintage/Erbury, 1978.

5. See, for example, Mayes, April J. and Kiran C. Jayaram, Eds. *Transnational Hispaniola: New Directions in Haitian and Dominican Studies.* U of Florida P, 2018.

6. http://inculturedco.org/

SECTION IV

VOICE NOTES FROM LA FRONTERA

The open access version of *The Border Lights Reader* includes audio recorded voice notes, featuring:

1. Radio Marién, Border of Lights on "A primera hora" show, October 3, 2019
2. Doña Carmen Rodríguez de Paulino, Owner of Hotel Raydan in Dajabón, Dominican Republic
3. Polibio Díaz, Dominican photographer
4. Nancy Betances, resident of Dajabón
5. Ilses Toribio, Dajabón artist discussing her "Rostro" series
6. Carlos Alomia Kollegger, Centro Montalvo

Visit https://doi.org/10.3998/mpub.12278109 or http://www.acpress.amherst.edu to access *The Border of Lights Reader* online.

Trilingual Contributor Biographies

To access the contributor biographies in Spanish, English, and Kreyòl, please see: https://lib.dr.iastate.edu/language pubs/227

Amanda Alcántara is a writer and journalist. She is the author of *Chula* (2019). Her work has been featured in the anthology *Latinas: Struggles & Protests in 21st Century USA*, the poetry anthology *LatiNext*, and several media publications including NPR's *Latino USA* and *Remezcla*; *The Washington Post's* The Lily; *Acento*; *The San Francisco Chronicle*; and others. Amanda has a BA in Journalism from Rutgers University and a master's degree in Latin American and Caribbean Studies from New York University. She also is co-founder and previous editor of *La Galería Magazine*. A map of the world turned upside down hangs on her wall.

Carlos Alomia Kollegger is a Peruvian Jesuit. He was educated at the Colegio de la Inmaculada- Jesuitas, in Lima, Peru. He completed his studies in Humanities and Philosophy at the Universidad Antonio Ruiz de Montoya in Lima, Perú. He has collaborated with various volunteer projects, pastoral, and social programs in indigenous communities and marginalized urban neighborhoods in Peru. For two years, he worked at the Centro Montalvo, the social center of the Society of Jesuits in the Dominican Republic, as project coordinator of the Hogar de Cristo project, and assisting migrants and vulnerable populations in Dajabón, Dominican Republic and Lakay Jezi, Ouanaminthe, Haiti. Currently, he is preparing for theological studies in Rome.

Julia Alvarez is an author of numerous works including *How the García Girls Lost Their Accents* (Algonquin Books, 2010); *In the Time of the Butterflies* (Algonquin Books, 2010); *A Wedding in Haiti* (Algonquin Books, 2013); *Afterlife* (Algonquin Books, 2020) a novel; and *Already a Butterfly: A Meditation Story* (Henry Holt & Co., 2020) for young readers. **Bill Eichner** is a doctor and farmer. For over forty years, Bill practiced ophthalmology in Vermont, India, East Jerusalem, as well as in several countries in South America and the Caribbean, including the Dominican Republic. Julia recently retired as a writer-in-residence at Middlebury College. Together they founded Alta Gracia, an organic coffee cooperative and literacy project in Julia's native Dominican Republic, which they ran for a decade (1998–2008). Along with others, they collaborated in founding Border of Lights in

2012. They are honorary chairs of Mariposa DR Foundation, and Bill is one of the founders of the Middlebury community garden, which supplies fresh produce to the local homeless shelter.

Azueï is a project that was born in 2015 to create a culture of peace between Haiti and the Dominican Republic through art. In 2019, the Azueï band recorded their first album to be released in 2020, plans that were postponed due to the pandemic. They are currently working on a virtual launch and continue to participate in activities to foster creativity beyond the crisis. For more information, see their Facebook page: https://www.facebook.com/artistazuei/.

DeAndra Beard is the CEO and founder of Beyond Borders. Beyond Borders has been recently featured in local and national media, including *The New York Times* and *HLN* (live television). Her early entrepreneurial efforts helped subsidize her undergraduate degree. She is a former Spanish K-12 certified classroom teacher, now turned award-winning business owner, who holds a BA in Education and Spanish with Reading Specialist and Teachers of English to Speakers of Other Languages (TESOL) endorsements from Bethune Cookman University. She is passionate about working to create common ground and connect with the world through the study of language and culture. In 2016, to further expand the mission of creating common ground, she opened a multicultural bookstore, Beyond Barcodes Bookstore, and Bind Café, an internationally focused cafe. Since opening this community space, she has facilitated difficult conversations about racism, discrimination and racial reconciliation in a community that was only beginning to openly acknowledge the necessity of such conversations. Her business model and experiences have opened opportunities to lead workshops, provide professional development, and share her story in various venues. DeAndra's passion and focus on sustainable community development led to a mayoral appointment to the Greater Kokomo Economic Development Alliance (GKEDA). Along with this prestigious appointment, in the first two years as a business owner, she was awarded the EDGE Award for successful emerging business presented by the Lieutenant Governor & the 40 Under 40 Award presented by the Young Professionals of Howard County. The same passion she has for the local community extends to the island of Hispaniola. In 2007, she and her sister co-founded the Organization of Dominican Haitian Cooperation (OCDH) in the northern region of the Dominican Republic. The mission of OCDH is to empower the most marginalized communities of Dominicans of Haitian descent. Through the work with OCDH, they connected with and helped found Border of Lights, a collective working at the border of the Dominican Republic and Haiti to increase solidarity between the two countries. DeAndra is a co-founder of Impact Hub Port-au-Prince, and a fellow at the Institute for International Public Policy (IIPP).

Nancy Betances was born in 1967 in Loma de Cabrera, Dominican Republic. Since 2011, she has been living in Dajabón and working with aspects of border solidarity with the Department of Civil Society. Since its opening—guided by Father Mario Serrano—she also has worked with the Hogar de Cristo for homeless children in Dajabón.

Jésula Blanc is the daughter of a tailor and a merchant who struggled to ensure their daughter's education. She carried out her university studies at the University of Jean Price Mars in Ouanaminthe, Haiti, where she obtained a bachelor's degree in law. She is part of the Fort Liberté Bar. Jésula also studied at the Universidad Quisqueya (UNIQ) in Port-au-Prince in the field of Interpretation and Languages but has yet to finish those studies, albeit being multilingual. She taught Spanish in the American English and Spanish School (ENSPANAC), the Wonderful Institute, and the Sunshine Institute. Currently, Jésula is the coordinator of the local Coopération Internationale Sud (CISS). She is recognized internationally for her commitment in the struggle for human rights; more specifically, the rights of women. Jésula created and currently coordinates the Plataforma de Género del Noreste (PGNE) that is formed of two community organizations: six community network organizations and fifty-eight grassroots community organizations. Jésula is now the mother of three kids. As a feminist, activist, defender of human rights, and trainer, Jésula constantly travels to various countries to promote women's demands and advocates for gender equality and equity for a world free of gender violence. She is one of the pioneers for the petition of the memorial to remember the Haitian victims of the 1937 Massacre. This memorial has already been built in Dosmond (Ouanaminthe) and every year, the commemorative activities are carried out October 2–4.

Regino Martínez Bretón was born on January 6, 1944 in the Dominican Republic. He is the fifth child of his family from the union of Juan José Martínez Fernández and Amada del Carmen Bretón Trinidad. After his primary studies, he entered the Pontifical Seminary Santo Thomas Aquinas for priestly formation. In 1965, he entered the Society of Jesus as a novitiate and in 1967, he received a degree in philosophy from the PUCMM. In 1969, Martínez became a teacher at the I.P.L in San Cristobal, Dominican Republic. By 1971 he was part of the theology faculty in Granada, Spain, receiving his priestly ordination in 1974. He then began his first priestly ministry in Loma de Cabrera and the Restauración Parish in the Dominican Republic. Later, in 1976, Martínez earned a Social Pastoral Diploma at the CELAM in Medellín, Colombia and in 1977, he returned to the Dominican Republic. He became a Peasant Priest by Option in 1987 in El Maguito, Loma de Cabrera, and in 1988, he was the Parish Priest of Dajabón. In that same year, Martínez became part of Resistencia Pacífica with Victoria Campesina and in 1992, he occupied the Dajabón City Council to recover the community land that had been illegally sold by municipal authorities under the Popular Housing Plan. In 1997, Martínez joined the Solidaridad Fronteriza and in 2004, he was a member of the Asomilin Foundation: Migrant Workers Associations of the Northwest Line. Martínez joined the parish of San Lorenzo, Guayubin in 2012, and in 2015 he returned to Dajabón for a new Pastoral Plan; the plan has formed a vital component and link with the Frontera de Luces Dajabón and the nearby communities of the northwest and Ouanaminthe.

Matías Bosch Carcuro was born in Havana, Cuba in November 1977. He is currently the Director of the Department of Social Sciences at la Universidad APEC in the Dominican Republic. He has lived in Chile and the Dominican Republic where he has worked in research and teaching, public debates, and civic education for almost twenty years. His primary and secondary studies were in Cuba and Chile, where he also earned an undergraduate degree in Science and Environmental Arts, a master's in Social Sciences and Politics, and a master's in Management and Public Policy. Since his youth, he has been involved in social and political activism as a student-leader and as an activist and researcher on environment, migration, human and social rights, labor and wealth, sovereignty and Latin American integration, feminism, overcoming racism, historical memory, and democracy.

Presuma Bulgary is 25 years old. He was born in Bois-de-Laurence, Haiti. He grew up in Ouanaminthe, Haiti, and lives with his mother and father who are merchants/farmers. He completed his primary studies at College Vision Nouvelle during the years 2000–2007. His secondary studies were at Lycée Capois La Mort/College Oswald Durand 2007–2017. He is still not in university. He takes photographs and is an operator in "Mise en Onde" on the radio.

Cynthia Carrión had led community engagement efforts for non-profit and for-profit organizations locally and internationally for over two decades. Currently she is the Director of Community Development for School in the Square, an innovative education charter in Washington Heights, New York. Cynthia served as the Deputy Director at the Northern Manhattan Coalition for Immigrant Rights, committed to expanding access to legal immigration services, participating in policy making, and community organizing from 2014–2018. Prior to NMCIR, Cynthia launched a national youth leadership series, mobilizing and training hundreds of youths behind human rights-centered programming as the National Youth Programs Coordinator at Amnesty International USA. On the international stage, she elevated the role of human rights education, facilitating a side event at the UN High Level Meeting on Youth, and served as the Youth Producing Change Coordinator for Human Rights Watch, working with youth activists from across the globe advocating for human rights issues. In addition, she was the Partnerships and Programs Manager for The Urban Assembly, a network of over twenty public schools in New York City, ensuring that over 10,000 students had access to quality enrichment opportunities. Cynthia also served as the Director of Youth Channel, the youth-serving division of Manhattan Neighborhood Network (MNN), teaching youth storytelling and producing short documentaries. Since 2012, with author Julia Alvarez, Cynthia has co-organized Border of Lights, a yearly volunteer initiative along the Dominican-Haitian border, working towards restorative justice from the 1937 Haitian Massacre. Cynthia received her BA from Hunter College with a dual major in Media Studies and Latin American and Caribbean Studies and holds an MA in International Relations from City College.

Raj Chetty is associate professor of English at St. John's University, specializing in Caribbean literature across English, Spanish, and French languages. He is at work on two projects. The first, *"On Refusal and Recognition": Disparate Blackness in Dominican Literary and Expressive Cultures*, focuses on black recognition, principally as theorized by Frantz Fanon, to study the articulations between Dominican literary and expressive arts in the post-Trujillo period and conceptualizations of black and African diaspora. The second is a study of the performance and theatrical legacies of C. L. R. James's plays about the Haitian Revolution (*Toussaint Louverture*, 1936, and *The Black Jacobins*, 1967). With Amaury Rodríguez, he is the coeditor of a special issue of *The Black Scholar* on "Dominican Black Studies" (2015), and his work has appeared in *Small Axe*, *Callaloo*, *Anthurium*, *Palimpsest: A Journal on Women, Gender, and the Black International*, *Meridional: Revista Chilena de Estudios Latinoamericanos*, and *Afro-Hispanic Review*.

Magaly Colimon is a first-generation Haitian American actress, playwright, director, and producer. She writes new works from a viewpoint heavily influenced by the stories her family members shared about the complexities and wonders of Haitian culture and history. She is the Artistic Director/Founder of Conch Shell Productions. The company's mission is to develop and produce and workshop new works by Caribbean-American playwrights and other artists of Caribbean descent who share her passion for innovative storytelling that inspires social change. Magaly received a BA from Columbia University, an MBA from Binghamton University, and an MFA in Acting from Yale School of Drama. Her credits include: **Producer** (AH-HA MOMENTS Play Festival; BN4REAL (https://www.youtube.com/user/BNFOURREAL); YES MADAME; HER STORY (https://www.youtube.com/watch?v=uaMiycnC6F8); The Hunting Season; Hear Her Call Caribbean-American Women's Theater Festival, #Bluelightseries (https://conchshellproductions.com/), RESET Series (https://conchshellproductions.com/reset-tc)); **Writer** (Awards: Princess Grace Semi-Finalist (Destination Ooh Aah Yummy), O'Neill NPC Finalist (Silent Truth, https://www.youtube.com/watch?v=KFLL0yxwOw4); The Hunting Season, https://www.youtube.com/watch?v=zh8GhywaR20); and **Co-Founder** Cafe "Ki Gan P'oun Geri' Fundraiser, SFC Women's Film Festival (https://www.youtube.com/watch?v=m3hTbZeq8BQ).

Juan Colón is a Dominican-born-and-based musician, composer, and arranger in Santo Domingo. He attended the National Conservatory of Music in Santo Domingo and studied under a variety of teachers such as Susan Barna, Flutist for the Detroit Philharmonic, and jazz composition and arrangement under Frank Foster. He is the only composer/arranger to compose a score inspired by the memory of the 1937 Haitian Massacre.

Edwidge Danticat is the author of several books, including *Breath, Eyes, Memory* (Vintage, 1998); *Krik? Krak!* (Soho Press, 2015); *The Farming of Bones* (Soho Press, 2013); *Claire of the Sea Light* (Vintage, 2014); as well as *The Art of Death* (Graywolf, 2017), a National Books Critics Circle finalist. She is also the editor of *The Butterfly's Way: Voices from the Haitian Dyaspora in the United States* (Soho Press, 2001), *The Beacon Best of 2000* (Beacon Press, 2000), *Haiti Noir*, and *Haiti Noir 2* (Akashic Books, 2010; 2019). She has written seven books for young adults and children: *Anacaona Golden Flower* (Cayena Press, 2019), *Behind the Mountains* (Orchard Books, 2002), *Eight Days* (Orchard Books, 2015), *The Last Mapou* (One Moor Book, 2013), *Mama's Nightingale* (Dial Books, 2015), *Untwine* (Scholastic, 2017), and *My Mommy Medicine* (Roaring Book Press, 2019); a travel narrative, *After* *the Dance: A Walk Through Carnival in Jacmel* (Vintage, 2015); and a collection of essays, *Create Dangerously* (Vintage, 2011). She is a 2009 MacArthur Fellow, a 2018 Ford Foundation Art of Change fellow, a 2020 United States Artist Fellow, and a 2020 winner of the Vilceck Prize. Her most recent book, *Everything Inside: Stories* (Vintage, 2020), is a winner of the Bocas Fiction Prize, The Story Prize, and the National Books Critics Circle Fiction Prize.

Catherine DeLaura has led the DREAM Project in the Dominican Republic since 2009. DREAM focuses on early childhood education, high-quality primary education, and holistic youth development. Catherine was assistant principal and principal of School of the Future (SOF) in New York City from 2002–2007. SOF is a Coalition of Essential Schools Mentor School located in New York City. Her administration experience also includes founding an interdisciplinary arts program at Taft High School in the South Bronx and earning an MBA from Columbia Business School. Previously, she taught ESL and history in New York City public schools for over ten years, and started her lifelong passion for education and creating a culture of reading as a Peace Corps Volunteer in Micronesia.

Lauren Derby is an Associate Professor of Latin American History at UCLA. Her research has treated dictatorship and everyday life, the long durée social history of the Haitian and Dominican border, and how notions of race, national identity and witchcraft have been articulated in popular media such as rumor, food and animals. Her publications include the prize-winning *The Dictator's Seduction: Politics and the Popular Imagination in the Era of Trujillo* (Duke University Press, 2019), the coedited *Activating the Past: History and Memory in the Black Atlantic World* and *The Dominican Republic Reader* (Cambridge Scholars Publishing, 2010), and *Terreurs de frontière: le massacre des Haïtiens en République dominicaine en 1937*, with Richard Turits and Watson Denis, forthcoming from Centre Challenges, Port-au-Prince.

Polibio Díaz lives and works in Santo Domingo. He studied photojournalism at Texas A&M University, graduating with a degree in Civil Engineering. He is a multidisciplinary visual artist, and he works in series through photography, video, installation, and performance—the latter almost always done in numerous pieces where large audiences participate in public spaces, addressing issues on migratory flows, ecology, vernacular, and colonial architecture, and appropriating and reversing the canonical tradition of landscape and portraiture in order to land in "the Dominican" today. In all his work, Polibio accentuates the social and racial inequality of his country within the Dominican mulatto poetics. He has participated in the Biennials of Havana, Venice, and the Caribbean, as well as in Infinite Island: Contemporary Caribbean Art, at the Brooklyn Museum; First ACP Cultural Festival, Museum of Modern Art of Santo Domingo (MAM); and in Kreyòl Factory in the Grande Halle de la Villette in Paris. His photos were included in *100 Years of Photography, 1899-1999: A Personal Vision of the 20th Century* at the Discovery Museum in Bridgeport, CT. Polibio's photographs are part of the permanent collection at UNESCO, in the Museum of Modern Art (Paris), in Centro León (Dominican Republic), and in private collections.

Rosa Iris Diendomi Álvarez is a lawyer, defender, and human rights activist currently pursuing a master's in Human Rights and International Humanitarian Law at the American University, specialized in training on statelessness research. She is also an essayist and poet. She is of Haitian descent and was born in Moca, Dominican Republic. Since 2001, she began promoting and defending rights in San Pedro de Macorís, together with the Pastoral de la Movilidad Humana creating a network of human rights in twenty-six communities (*bateyes*), a space that allowed her to learn first-hand the situation of extreme vulnerability and violation of rights experienced by Haitian migrants and their descendants. In 2007–2010, she coordinated the Higuamo Region Social Policy Roundtable, made up of thirty-four organizations. She is a founding member of the Reconocí.do Movement, performing different functions and coordinating in 2014–2016. Diendomi was a candidate for Congress in 2016 for district #2 of San Pedro de Macorís. She is the protagonist of the documentary "Our Lives in Transit" ("*Vidas en Trànsito*") and "Stateless" ("*Apatridas*").

Rana Dotson is an entrepreneurial promoter of social and economic inclusion. She is a fourth-generation daughter of Black Church pioneers. Rana has worked for over twenty-six years in human rights, public policy, and economic and international development. She is a senior international affairs officer at the Bureau of International Labor Affairs (ILAB), the US Department of Labor's international arm, working to fight labor exploitation around the world. Her most recent project, *COGICgarden*, is an initiative promoting economic and food security in partnership with the Black Church Food Security Network. She is a co-founder and lead organizer for Border of Lights. Rana holds an MPP from the Maryland School of Public Policy and a BA in Political Science from Tuskegee University. She is a fellow with the International Career Advancement Program (ICAP), and the National Security Education Program (NSEP) David L. Boren Graduate Fellowship. She lives in the D.C. metropolitan area with her family.

Rita Dove, recipient of the 1987 Pulitzer Prize in poetry for *Thomas and Beulah*, was the US Poet Laureate from 1993 to 1995. Author of numerous books—most recently, *Sonata Mulattica* and *Collected Poems 1974–2004* (W.W. Norton & Company, 2016)—she also edited *The Penguin Anthology of Twentieth-Century American Poetry* (Penguin Books, 2013). Her drama, *The Darker Face of the Earth*, premiered at the Oregon Shakespeare Festival in 1996 and was produced at the Kennedy Center in Washington, D.C., and the Royal National Theatre in London, among other venues. In 1998, the Boston Symphony Orchestra debuted her song cycle "Seven for Luck," with music by John Williams, under the composer's baton. Her many honors include the 2019 Wallace Stevens Award, the 2011 National Medal of Arts from President Obama, the 1996 National Humanities Medal from President Clinton, and twenty-eight honorary doctorates, among them from Yale and Harvard. Rita Dove is the Henry Hoyns Professor of Creative Writing at the University of Virginia.

DREAM was informally founded in 1995 by residents of Cabarete, Dominican Republic, who saw great need in the community. It was clear the country was woefully underinvesting in its schools. DREAM began its journey with a combination of international volunteers, construction of additional classrooms, libraries, and sanitary facilities at local schools. Realizing a lot more could be done by having its own facilities and organizing as a registered non-profit, DREAM was formally established in 2002 in both the US and Dominican Republic to create high quality educational programming. Since then, DREAM has grown to work with non-profits and governmental agencies like USAID, the Peace Corps, Open Society Foundation, the Dominican Ministry of Education, and companies like Banco Popular Dominicano, Federal Express, JetBlue, and Major League Baseball. DREAM's programs focus on literacy, early childhood education, youth leadership, the Bachata Academy music program, and we now work with more than 8,000 children and youths through seventeen programs in twenty-seven different communities.

Rhina P. Espaillat is a Dominican-born bilingual poet, essayist, short story writer, translator, and former English teacher in New York City's public high schools. She has published twelve books and five chapbooks, has earned numerous national and international awards, and is a founding member of the Fresh Meadows Poets of NYC and the Powow River Poets of Newburyport, Massachusetts, where she now lives. Her most recent poetry collections are *And After All* (Able Muse Press, 2019) and *The Field* (David Robert Books, 2019).

Maria Cristina Fumagalli is Professor of Literature at the University of Essex, UK. She is the author of *On the Edge: Writing the Border between Haiti and the Dominican Republic* (Liverpool University Press, 2015; 2018), the first cultural and literary history of the region; *Caribbean Perspectives on Modernity: Returning Medusa's Gaze* (University of Virginia Press, 2009), *The Flight of the Vernacular: Seamus Heaney, Derek Walcott and the Impress of Dante* (Brill, 2001); and "'When Dialogue is No Longer Possible, What Still Exists Is the Mystery of Hope': Migration and Citizenship in the Dominican Republic in Film, Theatre and Performance" in *Border Transgression and Reconfiguration of Caribbean Spaces* edited by Myriam Moïse and Fred Réno (Palgrave, 2020). She is the editor of *Special Issue on Hispaniola After the Earthquake*, BLAR (2013); and coeditor of *The Cross-Dressed Caribbean: Writing, Politics, Sexualities* (Virginia University Press, 2013) as well as *Surveying the American Tropics: A Literary Geography from New York to Rio* (Liverpool University Press, 2013). Maria Cristina is *Investigadora Asociada* of OBMICA (*Observatory Caribbean Migrants*), Dominican Republic.

Saudi García is an Anthropology PhD student at New York University, a facilitator for the peace and reconciliation organization In Cultured Company, a writer, and documentary filmmaker. Saudi uses her skills as a bilingual, bicultural scholar, facilitator, artist, and organizer to create equity, peace, and resource access for Afro-diasporic people in the United States, Latin America, and the Caribbean. She is a medical anthropologist and political ecologist who produces high quality, policy-oriented research to advance racial and social equity. Her dissertation project examines the production of knowledge about, and the enactment of, grassroots interventions against contamination from gold mining on the island of Hispaniola. Saudi is a proud working-class, queer, feminist immigrant, and alumnae of the Leadership Enterprise for a Diverse America, Brown University, the Mellon Mays Foundation Research Fellowship, and the Institute for the Recruitment of Teachers.

Scherezade García is an interdisciplinary visual artist born in Santo Domingo, Dominican Republic, and based in Brooklyn, New York. Through her practice of drawing, painting, installation, sculpture, animated videos, and public interventions, she creates contemporary allegories of history, colonization, and politics. Garcia's work frequently evokes memories of faraway home and the hopes and dreams that accompany planting roots in a new land. By tackling the collective memory as well as the ancestral memory in her public intervention and studio base practice, Garcia presents a quasi-mythical portrait of migration and cultural colonization. Scherezade's work is included in the permanent collection of The Smithsonian Museum of American Art, Washington, D.C.; El Museo del Barrio in New York City; The Housatonic Museum of Art in Connecticut; and El Museo de Arte Moderno in Santo Domingo.

García is a member of the Advisory Committee of No Longer Empty, Arts Connection, and is a board member of CAA. She is currently represented by Praxis Art Gallery in New York City and is a faculty member at the Parsons New School for Design.

Juan Carlos González Díaz is a sociologist, writer, and documentarian, and is also a researcher and social activist. He is a graduate of the Andrés Bello Catholic University in Venezuela, with degrees in Narrative Journalism, Conflict Communication, and Peacebuilding, as well as a master's degree in Documentary Film from the Autonomous University of Barcelona in Spain. He won various narrative competitions and was selected for audiovisual exhibitions in countries in Europe and Latin America. He is the producer and director of the documentaries *Voces de Mindanao* (2010); *El Microcrédito en Iberoamérica, Honduras and El Salvador (chapters)* (2011); and *Hasta la Raíz* (2017), selected for documentary film festivals in eight countries. His professional work has led him to work with non-governmental organizations in five countries on three continents, generating and supporting strategic communication and political advocacy processes. He believes in the stories that confront power and give voice to people on the margins.

Kiran C. Jayaram is an Assistant Professor in Anthropology at the University of South Florida. His research focuses on the topics of the politics of knowledge, political economy, and mobility in the Caribbean. His publications include two coedited volumes (*Keywords of Mobility*, 2016; *Transnational Hispaniola*, 2018) as well as articles in *Critique of Anthropology*, *Radical History Review*, *Caribbean Quarterly*, and the *International Journal of Educational Development*. He is co-founder of the Transnational Hispaniola Collective, former co-Chair of the Haiti-Dominican Republic Section of LASA, and former board member of the Society for Latin American and Caribbean Anthropology. He is currently working on a volume that examines anthropological knowledge production of Haiti and the Dominican Republic.

Pierre Michel **Jean** lives and works in Port-au-Prince as a freelance photojournalist. He is a member and contributor of the Haitian journalist collective (K2D) and their magazine *Fotopaklè*. He collaborates with the local press *Le Nouvelliste* and executes contracts for numerous European and North American newspapers. Jean made his first feature-length documentary in 2016, *Les Guérisseurs de l'ombre*, and finished his first feature film in the summer of 2020. He won the young journalism prize for 2018 for his work on the LGBTQ in Haiti. In August 2011, he graduated from Haiti Reporters, a program to train Haitian professionals in Multimedia. Pierre Michel Jean has exhibited his photos in multiple collective exhibitions and also, in a solo exhibition. His work focuses on migration, the memory and legacy of the parsley massacre, voodoo culture, and the Port-au-Prince urbanization.

Jake Kheel is a sustainability innovator, thought leader, and award-winning documentary filmmaker. For fifteen years he has confronted social and environmental challenges in the tourism industry as Vice President of Grupo Puntacana Foundation in the Dominican Republic. The foundation has received international awards from the World Tourism and Travel Council, *Condé Nast Traveler*, *Travel & Leisure*, and *National Geographic Traveler* for its programs. His upcoming book, *Waking the Sleeping Giant: Unlocking the Hidden Power of Business to Save Our Planet*, uses his experience in Punta Cana to demonstrate how companies can drive breakthroughs in sustainability. Jake is also the President of the National Association of Businesses for Environmental Protection (ECORED) in the Dominican Republic, an association of nearly 100 prominent companies committed to sustainability. Jake directed and produced the award-winning documentary *Death by a Thousand Cuts*, which explores Dominican-Haitian deforestation and escalating human conflict on the border. The film was acquired by Participant Media and Univision and screened at three dozen international film festivals.

Nehanda Loiseau Julot is a financial advisor and theatre artist. Her theatre work has taken many turns: performing, playwriting and, of course, producing more than one iteration of the Border of Lights monologues. After traveling and living in several US states and the UK, she now resides in the Chicago area with her husband and daughter. She is Founder and CEO of Wealth I Am LLC, a company that uses the art of storytelling to teach financial empowerment. She looks forward to hearing your story. Visit Wealth I Am at the following links: wealthiam.net; facebook.com/wealthiam.net/; instagram.com/wealthiam2020/

Sophie Maríñez is a 2021-2022 Mellon/ACLS Fellow and a Distinguished Teaching Award recipient at Borough of Manhattan Community College (CUNY), where she is a Professor of French and Spanish. She is also a former Faculty Fellow at the Center for Place, Culture, and Politics of the Graduate Center, and a CUNY William P. Kelly Research Fellow. At BMCC, she has served as a Faculty Leadership Fellow and as the advisor of its major in Modern Languages. She holds a PhD in French from The Graduate Center, is an awardee of the National Endowment for the Humanities (NEH), and currently serves in the Executive Council's Committee on Community Colleges of the Modern Languages

Association (MLA). Dr. Maríñez is the author of *Mademoiselle de Montpensier: Writings, Chateaux, and Female Self-Construction in Early Modern France* (Brill, 2017). She has authored several articles and essays on Haitian-Dominican relations, and coedited, with Daniel Huttinot, *Jacques Viau Renaud: J'essaie de vous parler de ma patrie* (2018). She has also published poetry in *The Caribbean Quarterly, The Caribbean Writer, Small Axe Salon,* and *The Cincinnati Romance Review,* and translated into French poems by Julia Alvarez, Jacques Viau Renaud, and Frank Baez. Prior to her position at CUNY, she was a visiting assistant professor of French at Vassar College.

April J. Mayes is an Associate Professor of History at Pomona College and author of the monograph *The Mulatto Republic: Class, Race, and Dominican National Identity* (University Press of Florida), winner of the Isis Duarte Prize from the Haiti-DR Section of the Latin American Studies Association. She coedited, along with Kiran Jayaram, *Transnational Hispaniola: New Directions in Haitian and Dominican Studies* (University of Florida Press) and, with Ginetta Candelario (Smith College) and Elizabeth Manley (Xavier University), the two-volume collection, *Cien años de feminismos dominicanos, 1861–1961* (Archivo General de la Nación, Santo Domingo, Dominican Republic). She is currently working on a study about Haitian migration to the US–Mexico border.

Jasminne Mendez is a poet, educator, and award-winning author. Mendez has had poetry and essays published by or forthcoming in *The Acentos Review, Crab Creek Review, Kenyon Review, Gulf Coast, The Rumpus,* and others. She is the author of two poetry/prose collections, *Island of Dreams* (Floricanto Press, 2013), which won an International Latino Book Award, and *Night-Blooming Jasmin(n)e: Personal Essays and Poetry* (Arte Publico Press, 2018). She is a 2017 Canto Mundo Fellow and an MFA candidate in the creative writing program at the Rainier Writer's Workshop at Pacific Lutheran University. You can find more info about her and her work at www.jasminnemendez.com.

Osiris Mosquea was born in San Francisco de Macorís, Dominican Republic. She received her degree in accounting from the University Autónoma in Santo Domingo. She has an MA in Spanish Language and Literature form The City College of New York and she also studied short stories and twentieth-century Spanish art in the University of Rioja in Spain. Mosquea is a poet, storyteller, founder of the Trazarte Huellas Creativas in New York, and coeditor of the magazine *Trazos.* Her work has been published in journals, newspapers, and anthologies in the United States and other parts of the world. Mosquea's publications include: *Una mujer: todas las mujeres* (miCielo ediciones, 2015 (poetry)); *Viandante en Nueva York* (Artepoetíca Press, 2013 (poetry)); *Raga del Tiempo* (Argos, 2009 (poetry)); *De segunda mano* (Books&Smith, 2018, (narrative)); and *Desde la soledad de los puertos* (Proyecto Editorial La Chifurnia (Colección Hypatya), 2019).

Megan Jeanette Myers is an Associate Professor of Spanish at Iowa State University. In 2019, Myers published *Mapping Hispaniola: Third Space in Dominican and Haitian Literature* with the University of Virginia Press. *Mapping Hispaniola* considers the ways

Dominicans, Haitians and their US diasporas have imagined the physical and metaphorical border(s) that divide the island of Hispaniola. She has recently published on Caribbean and Latinx literature in journals including *Hispania, Chiricú, Confluencia,* and *Caribe*. Further, Myers has an active research agenda in the field of the Scholarship of Teaching and Learning (SoTL) and was a 2018–2019 Iowa Campus Compact Engaged Research Fellow. She co-directs a Global Seminar titled "Education and Environmental Sustainability in the Dominican Republic: Learning Through Community Engagement" and is a co-founder of Border of Lights.

Rebecca Osborne is a playwright. Staged throughout the United States, her dramatic writings feature strong female characters. Political and social topics, as well as myths in different cultures, shape her work. Osborne enjoys creating one-act versions of her full-length plays for performance by high school and college students. She holds a BFA and MA in Theatre and earned her PhD from The University of Texas at Austin. Rebecca makes her home in Austin.

Ana Ozuna earned a PhD in 2009 from the University at Buffalo in Spanish Literature. Her dissertation examined the maroon figure in Caribbean literature and concomitantly explored the theoretical discourses related to slavery in the New World. Ozuna's current research and publications examine the African presence in the Caribbean and the history of resistance and rebellion in the Americas. Her article titled "Rebellion and Anti-colonial Struggle in Hispaniola: From Indigenous Agitators to African Rebels" examines the sustained rebellious activity of indigenous and Black rebels from the inception of Spanish colonization up to the end of the eighteenth century. Over the last fifteen years, Ozuna has taught at Syracuse University, University at Buffalo, and Indian River State College. She currently serves as Assistant Professor and Black Studies Coordinator at Eugenio María de Hostos Community College in New York, teaching courses in Black Studies and Caribbean Studies.

Edward Paulino, PhD is an Associate Professor in the Department of Global History at CUNY's John Jay College where he teaches History of Genocide, among several other courses. He is a co-founder of Border of Lights. Since 2014, he wrote and has performed his one-person show entitled "Eddie's Perejil." Paulino is the author of the 2016 book *Dividing Hispaniola: The Dominican Republic's Border Campaign Against Haiti, 1930–1961*. In 2018, he wrote the script for the Ted Ed animation video series "Ugly History: The 1937 Haitian Massacre," which has garnered more than one million views. Between 2015 and 2018, he was a Public Scholar for the New York State Council for the Humanities. Paulino is also a board member for the non-profit The Coalition for Immigrant Freedom.

Guillermo José Perdomo Montalvo (of Radio Marién) has a degree in Economics from the Pontificia Universidad Católica Madre y Maestro in Santiago, Dominican Republic. He has two degrees in planning, the first from the International Institute of Social Studies (1977), and the second in Regional Planning from Universidad de Los Andes (1978). He has a master's in Development Studies from the International Institute of Social Studies

(1980). Perdomo entered the Compañía de Jesús in 1980 and studied Philosophy in Santo Domingo, Dominican Republic, and Theology in Belo Horizonte, Brazil. He was ordained in 1990 in Barrio Los Guandules, Santo Domingo, where he served until 1996. In 1997, Perdomo was transferred to the northern border of the Dominican Republic, where he served as priest until 2003 in Loma de Cabrera and Restauración. Since August 15, 2003 he has served as the director of Radio Marién, "The Educator of the Border."

John Presimé is a community organizer and social entrepreneur, empowering local youth and marginalized populations in the Dominican Republic through information and communication technologies, as well as through sustainable online resources with affordable and reliable access to the internet provided by his Social Entrepreneurship Easy Connect. He is a local expert on cross-border migration, conflict, and statelessness in the Dominican Republic and Haiti. Presimé's expertise lies in social media, community development, and humanitarian assistance programs. He has played a key role in the largest to-date emergency food distribution effort supporting refugees in the new displacement camps on the Dominican-Haitian border. Presimé is also involved with Young Leaders of the Americas Initiative (YLAI) Alumni, a program run by the US Department of State, attracting 250 of the brightest young entrepreneurs from Latin America and the Caribbean. He is currently a student in Computer Science at the Universidad Tecnológica de Santiago and a local youth leader. Multi-lingual in French, Kreyol, Spanish, and English, Presimé also forms part of local and international media and non-government organization networks.

Daniel Ramos (Mario Alterio Ramos) is a painter and sculptor. He was born and still lives in Dajabón. In 2012, Ramos painted the mural for Frontera de Luces, currently installed on the exterior wall of the Parroquia Nuestra Señora del Rosario in Dajabón.

Laura Ramos was born in Santo Domingo, Dominican Republic in 1979. Raised in Dajabón, she became involved in artistic and educational activities at a very young age, influenced by her uncle, the painter and sculptor Daniel Ramos. She studied advertising with a minor in illustration at the Universidad Autónoma in Santo Domingo, where she is currently preparing her master's thesis in visual arts. She has worked in graphic design, silk screen-printing, typographic design, drawing, and painting, and is an educator and organizer in promotional art activities for fairs and artistic exhibitions.

Jhonny Rivas (birth name: Jackson Lorrain), was born in 1973 in the small Haitian community Baine, Foulon. Rivas has spent more than 15 years advocating for migrant workers in the northeastern border region of the Dominican Republic. He works with the organization Asomilin (Solidarity Associations of migrant workers on the northeast border). Rivas spent 12 years working with Solidaridad Fronteriza (Border Solidarity), the organization once directed by Father Regino Martínez. He currently works as a promotor of AVSI and continues to coordinate Asomilin. Rivas has lived for over 20 years at Ranchadero Guayubín with his wife and three children, where they have their home and a small office.

Amaury Rodríguez is a translator and independent researcher. His current project focuses on the international impact of the 1965 US military occupation of the Dominican Republic. With Raj Chetty, he is coeditor of "Dominican Black Studies" (Routledge, 2015), a special issue of *The Black Scholar* journal, and his work has appeared in *NACLA*, *Tripwire*, *Jacobin*, *Memorias: Revista Digital de Historia y Arqueología desde el Caribe*, InTranslation, ESENDOM, Marxists Internet Archive, and *Plenamar*.

Doña Carmen Rodríguez de Paulino is the owner of both the Hotel Raydan, where BOL volunteers and members have stayed during BOL events since 2012, and the Farmacia Raydan (pharmacy).

Tony Savino is a photojournalist and documentary photographer who has been working on the island of Hispaniola since 1987. His photographs of Haiti and the Dominican Republic have appeared in many publications including *Time*, *Newsweek*, *The New York Times Magazine*, and *Paris Match*. His project *The Face of Neocolonialism* has been exhibited in New York and Santiago de Cuba; it is focused on sugar workers and the communities (called *bateyes*) in which they live, and their struggle for labor and human rights as Haitian nationals and Dominicans of Haitian descent. Savino also co-founded *Black Lives Matter in the Dominican Republic*, an organization that mobilizes New Yorkers in opposing racist immigration policies in the Dominican Republic.

Ilses Mercedes Toribio was born in 1964 in Dajabón, Dominican Republic. Since she was a child she has been interested in art, but could never study it in Dajabón because there was no—and still there is not—an art school. In 2004, Toribio began workshops, among other activities, in brush-stroke painting, crafts, and costume jewelry at the Yaque school. The same year, she took private art classes with a Peruvian artist in the public gardens in Santiago. By December 2010, Toribio held her first art exhibition, and she has been involved in offering courses at Infotep. Currently, she is working on crafts in her own workshop which reporters such as Marino Zapete, Altagracia Salazar, Edith Febles, and Altagracia Ceballos (Univisión television), have broadcast for the general public.

Deisy Toussaint is a Dominican journalist and writer. She has degrees from the Universidad Autónoma of Santo Domingo and a master's in Digital Journalism from the Universidad de Nebrija in Madrid. Her stories have been published in the anthologies and journals *El Fondo del Iceberg*, *Mujer en pocas palabras*, *Sospecha colectiva*, *auteurs dominicains du XXIe siècle*, *Revista Digital MiNatura* (Spain), *Trazos* (US), *Afro-Hispanic Review* (US), *Voces del Caribe* (US), and in the digital French collection *Lectures de République Dominicaine*, among others. Her articles have appeared in Dominican newspapers *Hoy Digital* and *Acento*, plus her international news reports on *TeleSur TV*.

Silvio Torres-Saillant is Professor of English and Dean's Professor of the Humanities at Syracuse University. At Syracuse, he has headed the Latino-Latin American Studies Program and served as William P. Tolley Distinguished Teaching Professor in the Humanities. His books include *Caribbean Poetics* (1997; 2nd ed. 2013), *El tigueraje intelectual* (2002; 2nd ed. 2011), *Introduction to Dominican Blackness* (1999; 2nd ed. 2010), *An Intellectual History of the Caribbean* (2006), *Diasporic Disquisitions: Dominicanists, Transnationalism, and the Community* (2000), and *El retorno de las yolas: Ensayos sobre diáspora, democracia y dominicanidad* (1999; 2nd ed. 2019). He co-authored, with Ramona Hernandez, *The Dominican-Americans* (1998) and *The Once and Future Muse: The Poetry and Poetics of Rhina P. Espaillat* (2018). With Nancy Kang, he coedited volumes in Caribbean, Dominican, and Latina/o Studies. A frequent lecturer at home and abroad, Torres-Saillant inaugurated the Birmingham Modern Languages Lecture Series at the University of Birmingham, UK, in 2012; delivered the 2013 Annual Walter Rodney Memorial Lecture at the University of Warwick in Coventry, UK; and gave the keynote opening address for the 58th Casa de las Américas Literary Prize, in 2017 in Havana, Cuba.

Richard Lee Turits is Associate Professor of History, African Studies, and Latin American Studies at the College of William & Mary. He is the author of *Freedom Roots: Histories from the Caribbean* (University of North Carolina Press, 2019), written with Laurent Dubois, and *Foundations of Despotism: Peasants, the Trujillo Regime, and Modernity in Dominican History* (Stanford University Press, 2003). The latter received the John Edwin Fagg Prize of the American Historical Association and the Bolton-Johnson Prize of the Conference on Latin American History, and was also named a Choice Outstanding Academic Title. Turits is also the author of the prize-winning "A World Destroyed, A Nation Imposed: The 1937 Haitian Massacre in the Dominican Republic," *Hispanic American Historical Review* 82, no. 3 (Aug. 2002). Forthcoming soon is his book of essays and oral histories in French, co-authored with Lauren Derby and edited with a preface by Watson Denis, related to the 1937 Massacre in the Dominican Republic and to Haitian-Dominican history: *Terreurs de frontières: le massacre des Haïtiens en République Dominicaine en 1937* (Centre Challenges, 2020).

William Vazquez is a humanitarian/commercial photographer based in New York. His work has taken him around the world, from the corporate boardrooms of Fortune 500 companies, to disaster areas and war zones. His artistic philosophy is to capture the beauty and the best of humanity for all to see. "Finding something ugly in ugly places is easy, finding something beautiful in an ugly place is magical." Growing up in multicultural New York City gave William the foundation to feel comfortable in any setting and get the shot, whether he speaks the language of his subjects or not. William graduated from Parsons School of Design and apprenticed with some of the legends in photography.

Chiqui **Vicioso** was born in Santo Domingo in 1948. She is a a poet, essayist, and playwright with a BA in Sociology and Latin American History from the City University of New York (Brooklyn College), a master's in Education from Columbia University, and a degree in Cultural Administration from the Fundação Getúlio Vargas in Rio de Janeiro. She has written the following collections of poetry: *Viaje desde el agua* (1981); *Un extraño ulular traía el viento* (1985); *Intern/A/miento* (1992); and *Eva/Sion/Es* (2007). She has also written essay collections, including *Algo que decir: ensayos sobre literatura femenina* (1983, 1992), the first work of feminist literary criticism in the Dominican Republic; *Julia de Burgos la Nuestra* (1983 and 1990); *Salome Ureña de Henriquez: A cien años de un magis-*

terio (1997); and *Hostos y su visión de la mujer* (1998), among many others. Vicioso's plays include: *Wish-ky Sour* (the first play written by a woman to receive the Premio Nacional de Teatro, 1996); *Salome U: Cartas a una Ausencia* (2001, Casandra Prize); *La Carretera* (based on Juan Bosch's story "La Mujer"); *Desvelo*, a dialogue between Salomé Ureña and Emily Dickinson; *Magdalena*, danza teatro; *Perrerias*; and *Andrea Evangelina*, based on the life of the first female Dominican doctor. Since 1986, Vicioso has published a national column in *Listin Diario* and *El Nacional*, as well as a monthly essay in the cultural supplement *Areíto*. Between 1981 and 1983, she worked with the cultural supplements *Aquí* and *Cantidad Hechizada*, which she both created and directed.

Bridget Wooding is the Director of OBMICA (*Observatory Caribbean Migrants*, http://obmica.org/), a think tank carrying out applied research on migration, based in Santo Domingo, Dominican Republic. She is the author of the article "Haitian Migrants and their Descendants born in the Dominican Republic" (ORE 2018, https://oxfordre.com/latinamericanhistory/view/10.1093/acrefore/9780199366439.001.0001/acrefore-9780199366439-e-474), and co-author of the book *Fanm Nan Fwontye, Fanm Toupatou: Making visible the violence against migrant, in-transit, and displaced women on the Dominican-Haitian border* (2012). In 2018–2019, Wooding was the principal researcher in a pioneer study on the Dominican-Haitian border which examines the situation of unaccompanied children and adolescents on the move between Haiti and the Dominican Republic. She is the author of the chapter "The seeds of anger: contemporary issues in forced migration across the Dominican-Haitian border" in *Border Transgression and Reconfiguration of Caribbean Spaces* (2020).

Évelyne Trouillot was born and lives in Port-au-Prince. Novelist, romanticist, playwright, and poet, she has published four collections of stories. Trouillot also has published two collections of poetry in French, *Sans parapluie de retour* and *Par la fissure de mes mots*, and two collections in Kreyòl, *Plidetwal* and *Yon kòd gita* (2020). Her first novel, *Rosalie l'infame* (Dapper, 2003) received the prize for French novels from Soroptimista in Grenoble, and she later wrote six other novels. *La Mémoire aux abois* (Hoëbecke, 2010) received the Carbet Prize for the Caribbean and the World in December of the same year. *Désirée Congo* was published in 2020 by Ediciones Cidihca. Her first play, *Le Bleu de l'île*, awarded by Etc Caraibe and The Association Beaumarchais, was inspired by the tragic incident in which a group of Haitians crossing the Dominican-Haitian border in June of 2020 were assassinated by Dominican guards.

Óscar M. Zazo Martín was awarded a degree, with honors, in Pedagogy with a minor in Language; a master's in Applied History and Education; and earned a PhD in Caribbean History from the Pontificia Universidad Católica Madre y Maestra (PUCMM) in the Dominican Republic. He lives in Sosúa, Puerto Plata, Dominican Republic and is a founding member of the group "Jueves Literarios de Sosúa." His stories have won awards in contests such as Alianza Cibaeña, Radio Santa María, Sociedad Renovación, and Casa de Teatro. He is the co-author of *Operación Azabache*, and author of the historical novel *Bue-*

naventura: Paseo por la memoria de un guerrillero español, the adolescent novel *La aventura de Diego y Roko,* the story "Mateo 71," and the thesis "Asentamiento de los judíos en Sosúa." Zazo is also the author of two collections of stories: *El regalo y otros cuentos* and *Destiempo y otros cuentos.* He is the producer and director of cultural television programs TV Talento and Palabras al Viento. He is a professor of Social Studies and Spanish Language at the International School of Sosúa, an adventure excursion guide, and an expert in martial arts.

Acknowledgments

The initial idea for this project first took shape among a group of Border of Lights organizers and volunteers at a hotel bar in Santiago, Dominican Republic in 2015, (the third Border of Lights gathering). We had just wrapped up a successful day-long meeting and educational forum with local leaders and as we reflected on the breadth of individuals who supported, attended, and believed in the Border of Lights' mission, we asked ourselves how *all* of these individuals' voices could be included in an anthology. We knew then that what we imagined was not your typical academic anthology. Fast forward to the annual Modern Language Association convention in 2018 when Megan connected with Beth Bouloukos, Amherst College Press Editor, and we had an answer to our initial query. With an open-access, digital platform we would be able to not only share color photos, artwork, and audio files, but to share them widely and freely. Key to our vision of centering the voices and experiences of border residents, both Dominican and Haitian, was also placing the final product back into these same communities. We are grateful to Beth and the team at Amherst College Press for championing an open-access model that fits our project so well. Thanks also to Amanda Karby at the University of Michigan Library for ushering the project through the final stages. Further, we want to thank Michael Pfeifer and Adam Jones for their careful readings of our introduction, and Cynthia Carrión for her constant support of the project and for being the backbone of the BOL planning process throughout the years. Both Cynthia and Scherezade García spoke on a panel alongside us both, Megan Myers and Eddie Paulino, at the 2018 Dominican Studies Association (DSA) conference when our plans for this Reader began to crystalize. Rosa Diendomi Álvarez joined us on a virtual DSA panel in 2020. Like Cynthia, Julia Alvarez is yet another backbone of Border of Lights—*la madrina*—as well as Michele Wucker and Bill Eichner; we are encouraged by your unending support. We also owe a heartfelt thank you to American Jewish World Services (AJWS) for supporting Border of Lights and for allowing us to consider how this project fits into the BOL vision and strategic planning. Gracias/mèsi/thank you to John Presimé, too, for his help translating the contributor biographies.

Individually, we also both need to thank our families for their continued support. From Megan: Two of my three children were born in early/mid-October and the year of their births mark the only two Border of Lights gatherings that I have ever missed—37 weeks pregnant for one and 39 weeks pregnant for the other. I also weaned both of my oldest daughters, Marcela and Holly Dolores, from breastfeeding the week before BOL during the years following their births before leaving them for the first time to attend BOL. In more ways than one, BOL has become another "baby" of sorts—a gathering and a movement that I feel privileged to have had a role in nourishing, watching grow, and now cheering it on as it goes in new directions and expands in different ways. I am also grateful for and thankful to my partner, Peaches, for his unwavering support; we were thrilled to welcome a baby boy, Del Ronald, when this project was in its final stages. From Eddie: Bearing witness to the 1937 Haitian Massacre meant leaving my family every single year as a volunteer since 2012 for several days to visit Haiti and the Dominican Republic. Since the beginning, my incredible partner and friend, Zaire Dinzey, has been my biggest intellectual and emotional supporter and throughout the years, has participated in online vigils with our kids Lelolai and Caribe, who during our inaugural year, were five and one year of age respectively.

Finally, together we offer our heartfelt thanks to the contributors to this multidimensional volume. Your support, expertise, and creativity resonate in the essays, articles, narrative, art, interviews, and more that fill the pages of *The Border of Lights Reader*. Our hope is that the diverse experiences and perspectives included in this project spark connections and offer a multidisciplinary, anthologized form of bearing witness for readers in the Dominican Republic, Haiti, the US diaspora, the Americas, and beyond. Thank you, mèsi, and gracias to the people of Dajabón and Ouanaminthe, the Dominican and Haitian border residents—the real protagonists—who taught us that, despite constant divisive state policies, historic and local solidarity also defines the Haitian-Dominican border.

CPSIA information can be obtained
at www.ICGtesting.com
Printed in the USA
LVHW062031010921
696710LV00005B/55

9 781943 208265